America, Scandinavia, and the Cold War, 1945–1949

America, Scandinavia, and the Cold War 1945-1949

Geir Lundestad

Columbia University Press

New York   1980

Library of Congress Cataloging in Publication Data

Lundestad, Geir, 1945–
  America, Scandinavia, and the Cold War 1945–1949.

  Includes bibliographical references and index.
  1. Scandinavia—Foreign relations—United States.
2. United States—Foreign relations—Scandinavia.
3. United States—Foreign relations—1945–1953.
I. Title.
DL59.U6L86   327.73048   80-13994
ISBN 0-231-04974-9

Columbia University Press
New York   Guildford, Surrey

Acknowledgments

THIS STUDY HAS been made possible by the generous support of many individuals and institutions. On the financial side, always so important, the following have contributed toward meeting the expenses of my several trips to the United States: the Norwegian Research Council for Science and the Humanities, the Nordic Cooperation Committee for International Politics, the University of Tromsø, the United States Educational Foundation in Norway, and Nansenfondet.

In my search through libraries and archives in several countries many have assisted me beyond the call of duty. I would like to thank the staffs of the Tromsø University Library, and the Library of the Nobel Institute in Oslo. I also appreciate the kind assistance given me by Kathie Nicastro of the National Archives, Fredrick Aandahl of the Office of the Historian in the State Department, Arnold Dadian of the Office of Public Affairs in the State Department, and Erik-Wilhelm Norman of the Norwegian Foreign Office.

Friends and colleagues have taken of their valuable time to read parts of previous drafts and have thereby improved the quality of this book. Its remaining shortcomings can only be blamed on the author who did not listen even more to their advice. On the Norwegian side Knut Einar

Eriksen and Olav Riste have been helpful. In Sweden Göran Rystad has encouraged me with his interest in my work. In the United States I take particular pleasure in acknowledging the assistance of the Charles Warren Center at Harvard University under its director, Donald Fleming. This study would not have been whatever it is without the Charles Warren Center, within whose precincts I had the fortune of spending the academic year 1978–79. Ernest May and the participants in his cold war seminar in the fall of 1978 provided a stimulating background for my work.

My appreciation certainly goes to those who have labored long hours in typing various drafts of this study. At the University of Tromsø the entire staff of the Social Science Institute has at one time or another done more for me than they would probably like to be reminded of. At the Charles Warren Center Cindy Draine and Sally Sweet have given me more of their time than I could reasonably expect.

At Columbia University Press I want to thank Bernard Gronert and Joan McQuary for their kind assistance. Dolly Stade helped me with my many footnotes and did a most important job in improving the language of my manuscript.

As always, above all I want to thank my wife Aase and our two sons, Erik and Helge, for their support and patience at almost all times.

Contents

America, Scandinavia, and the Cold War, 1945–1949

Introduction

THE AMERICAN POLICY TOWARD Scandinavia in the period from 1945 to 1949 has not received the attention it deserves. Very little in the way of scholarly analysis has been published on this topic. In this chapter I will first present a brief historiographic sketch of what has after all been written about American-Scandinavian relations during the time of transition from World War II to the cold war, and after delineating that sorry state of affairs, I will formulate the problems this study will address.

America and Scandinavia: A Review of the Literature

The term "Scandinavia" will here refer to the three countries Norway, Sweden, and Denmark. The Norwegian islands of Spitsbergen will be included because of their proximity to the Scandinavian mainland. Greenland, despite its distance from Denmark, will be dealt with to some extent since it is impossible to study American-Danish relations without bringing in Greenland.

Those on the American side who have taken an interest in Scandinavian affairs have generally seen the region in very broad terms. An example of this is Franklin D. Scott's

Scandinavia, which takes up the history, politics, and culture of these countries.[1] Not only does Scott deal with Norway, Sweden, and Denmark, all in a long-term perspective, but he also includes Finland and Iceland. The book contains little on American attitudes and policies toward Scandinavia in 1945–49.

An impressive study in many ways is Barbara G. Haskel's *The Scandinavian Option.*[2] Among other things, it deals in some detail with the negotiations for a Scandinavian defense pact in 1948–49. But again, this is a study of Scandinavia by an American, not of American relations with Scandinavia.

On the Scandinavian side, several excellent books and articles have been written on the position of the Scandinavian countries in international politics in the early postwar period. Most of these have dealt primarily with Norway. Both Magne Skodvin's *Norden eller Nato? Utenriksdepartementet og alliansespørsmålet 1947–1949* and Knut Einar Eriksen's *DNA og NATO: Striden om norsk NATO-medlemskap innen regjeringspartiet 1948–49* concentrate on the world as seen from Oslo.[3] This is particularly true for Eriksen's book. Skodvin goes somewhat more deeply into American policies. In general he sees the United States as taking little, if any, interest in Scandinavian affairs until the summer of 1948—when the State Department slowly came around to formulating a policy, Washington's attitude was based on the desire to have Norway participate in the Atlantic alliance which was in the process of development. Skodvin does not examine the American attitude in any detail. Neither does he make any serious attempt to explain the U.S. policy toward Norway.[4]

Another study which deals briefly with America's policies toward Scandinavia is Nils Morten Udgaard's *Great Power Politics and Norwegian Foreign Policy: A Study of Norway's Foreign Relations November 1940–February 1948.* From a perspective similar to Skodvin's, Udgaard apparently concludes that the United States had very little interest in Norway after World War II. Great Britain and the Soviet Union are therefore of much greater interest to him. One interesting aspect of Udgaard's study is the extent to which he sees Washington's interest in Norway, small as it was, as determined by a strongly developing military concern about the polar strategy. According to Udgaard, this strategy was of importance even during the war.[5]

Most of the discussion on Scandinavia in international politics in the 1945 to 1949 period has centered on Norway. One reason for this is that most of the studies have been written by Norwegians. The Swede who has dealt most extensively with the role of Scandinavia in the early cold war period is political scientist Krister Wahlbäck. However, his perspective is also that of looking at the Great Powers from Scandinavia, in this case from Stockholm. As a result, Wahlbäck is quite brief in his comments on the American attitude in his *Norden och Blockuppdelningen 1948–49*. In general he too sees the United States as taking little interest in Scandinavia until the summer of 1948. In this he follows the Norwegians who have written on this topic. Yet, somewhat unlike the Norwegians, Wahlbäck tries to reconstruct the advantages which later made the United States want to include Norway and Denmark in the NATO alliance. These advantages are seen as primarily of a military nature, related to the resources and bases which the Scandinavian countries could offer in wartime.[6]

Valuable books have been published on various aspects of Danish foreign policy. These deal so briefly with the role of the United States that they will not be included in this brief historiographic sketch.[7] One or two of them will be referred to in other contexts instead.

None of the studies mentioned concentrates on Washington's policies toward Scandinavia. In addition, it should be pointed out that they were generally written before most of the American material now available for the 1945 to 1949 period was opened for researchers.

A basic concern of this study will be what the policy toward Scandinavia may reveal about overall U.S. policies. If we look at how historians dealing more generally with American foreign policy in the early cold war years have treated the question of American-Scandinavian relations, it does not take long to give an answer. American cold war historians have hardly paid any attention to this topic. Most of these historians only mention the Scandinavian countries in matter-of-fact contexts. What is usually brought out is that Norway, Denmark, and Sweden all participated in the Marshall Plan, while only Norway and Denmark came to join NATO. A few works are a bit more inclusive, but no study on American foreign policy in this period analyzes American-Scandinavian relations in any detail. In fact, quite a few of the works on cold war history do not mention the Scandinavian countries at all.[8]

Questions To Be Discussed

When so little attention has been paid to American policies toward this region, one might ask why there is a need for a long book on this subject. My answer is twofold. Least important, even if Scandinavia was not an area of major significance for the United States, the United States was of considerable importance to Scandinavia. In these years Washington gradually came to influence Scandinavian foreign policy more than did any other capital. To a great extent it became the task of the Scandinavians to react to initiatives which were either predominantly American in origin, such as the Marshall Plan, or which could not have been brought forth without American participation, such as NATO.

More important, it is my opinion that this study of Washington's policies may be of interest not only from a Scandinavian point of view, but also from an American. An understanding of policies toward Scandinavia may add significantly to our understanding of American foreign policy in general in this important and controversial period. There are several hotly debated questions concerning America's foreign relations in the 1945–49 period. I feel that a study of U.S. policies toward Scandinavia may bring valuable insight and some possible answers. This book will focus upon these questions.

The first question is one which lies under much of the

discussion between so-called revisionist and traditionalist historians: To what extent was the foreign policy of the United States firmly set in an anti-Soviet perspective at the time World War II ended? Or, to ask the same question from a slightly different angle: To what extent was the foreign policy of the United States created as new situations arose, only becoming a coherent policy in 1947 with the introduction of the Truman Doctrine and the Marshall Plan? I will go into these questions in general, but in particular I will explore what American policies toward Scandinavia may reveal about the answers that have already been given by prominent historians.

The second question this study will deal with is: What was the American reaction to the so-called bridge-building policies of the Scandinavians? These policies were not meant to place the Scandinavian countries halfway between East and West, but represented an attempt to maintain close relations with all the Great Powers, including the Soviet Union. The continued Swedish policy of neutrality could be said to represent a special version of bridge building. How did Washington react to this attitude of giving less than all-out support to the West?

Third, what was the American attitude to left-of-center governments? Again, this is a question which has provoked much debate among historians. No one, however, has made any attempt to find out what the American attitude to Scandinavian social democrats would mean to their generalizations. Both Norway and Sweden had social democratic governments in the 1945 to 1949 period, while Denmark was led by social democrats from 1947 to 1950.

The fourth question has to do with the Marshall Plan and its effects in the countries that chose to participate in the Plan. To what extent did the United States, through the Marshall Plan, have an opportunity to influence the foreign and domestic policies of the participating countries? And, even more important, to what extent did Washington actually use the opportunities it had?

And fifth, what were U.S. intentions in relation to the creation of the North Atlantic Treaty Organization? I will try to answer to some degree the question of what induced the United States to step up its economic and political engagements in Europe to such an extent as to include even formal military commitments in time of peace. But basically I will examine the question of the role Washington policy makers saw for the Scandinavian countries in the planned military alliance. In this context, what means did the United States use to influence the foreign policy choices of the Scandinavian countries?

It is a main purpose of this book to relate the discussion about Scandinavia to U.S. policies in other parts of Europe. This is done in order to place my own findings in some perspective and to avoid falling into the trap of making too much of an area which undoubtedly has not received the attention it deserves, but still was hardly at the very center of attention in Washington. Occasionally areas even outside Europe will be brought into the discussion.

I will try to place my own findings in some perspective in one other way as well. In dealing with the five major problems of this study, I aim at giving a sufficiently broad description of the general state of research so that my own view can be defined within the scholarly debate on the origins of the cold war. I hope that in this way the book may shed some new light on problems in areas where generalizations have been frequent and caution often lacking.

1

American Historians and American Foreign Policy 1945–1947

THE FOCUS in this chapter is on the European, even the global, side of Washington's foreign policies in the years from 1945 to 1947. Then, in the following chapter I will examine how Washington's attitudes and actions toward the Scandinavian countries in particular can be related to this overall picture.

Schools of Thought: How Many Are There?

With considerable justice it could be argued that there are as many schools of thought among American historians dealing with the origins of the cold war as there are American historians. Almost any one of them will differ from what has been written by others on at least one significant point. Therefore, it can be asked whether nuances are given their due weight when historians are put into a small number of categories for the sake of comparison.

The fundamental dividing line is usually seen to be between traditionalist or orthodox historians on the one hand and revisionists on the other.[1] Undoubtedly significant differences exist not only between those two groups, but also within the two. This is particularly true on the revisionist side. Nevertheless, I will frequently use the terms traditionalist and revisionist historians. This is done because I feel that, despite significant differences, basic similarities can still be found within each group.

It is impossible, however, to adhere consistently to any rigid division into only two groups. First, I will often distinguish between those who definitely fall on one of the two sides and those who must be seen as less clear-cut representatives of their school of thought. Second, in the last years a school has developed which cannot easily be fitted into either category. Its representatives may lean to one of the two sides. What seems to characterize this group, however, is the extent to which these historians have been influenced by revisionist writings, but still break with revisionist interpretations on basic points. This new wave will be called post-revisionism.

To establish categories we need criteria according to which a selection can be made. I have previously argued that the three most meaningful criteria in establishing a historiographic picture on the origins of the cold war are the following: whether a historian places greater blame on the Soviet Union or on the United States for initiating the cold war; what the historian in question sees as the main motive powers of American foreign policy; and the degree of foreign policy activity the historian attributes to the United States, particularly in Europe in the years from 1945 to 1947.[2] In this chapter I will deal only with the third criterion.

It is impossible to deal with all historians or political scientists who have written on the origins of the cold war. I will focus on those who have written particularly influential articles or books on the transition period from World War II to the cold war.

On the traditionalist side I would mention Herbert Feis,[3] Arthur M. Schlesinger, Jr., Martin F. Herz, Gaddis

Smith, and Joseph M. Jones.[4] Others who write in the traditionalist spirit, although somewhat less decidedly so, are Robert Divine and William McNeill.[5] It could be argued that even Louis Halle,[6] despite his apparent impartiality and distance to the events he is writing about, should be placed in this category.

In the middle 1960s a strong reaction developed against the traditionalist position. A wave of revisionism took to the offensive in scholarly debates on the origins of the cold war. There had of course been revisionist writers before, like William Appleman Williams and D. F. Fleming,[7] just as traditionalist writings continued into the sixties and seventies. There was, however, a marked shift in predominance. Representative of the new group were such historians as Gabriel Kolko, Lloyd Gardner, Walter LaFeber, Gar Alperovitz, and David Horowitz.[8]

In the last years the historiographic picture has become more complicated. Some established traditionalists have undoubtedly become influenced by revisionist writings. One example may be found in parts of the biography of Dean Acheson written by Gaddis Smith.[9] At the same time, however, traditionalist ranks have been swelled by new historians. Such new names, they too holding views somewhat different in emphasis, are Lisle A. Rose, Lynn Etheridge Davis, and, most strongly antirevisionist of these, Robert James Maddox.[10]

New names also have been added on the revisionist side. One important figure in recent revisionist literature is Barton Bernstein. Although some of Bernstein's writings are definitely revisionist in spirit, it could be argued that others should be placed in the new category of postrevisionism.[11] Another important development is that both Alperovitz and Horowitz have in later writings placed less emphasis on the atomic bomb and ideology as driving forces of American diplomacy and more on the economic factors stressed by other revisionists. This has tended to make the revisionist group slightly more homogeneous than before.[12]

It seems that most recently the initiative in the cold war debate has been with the new wave of postrevisionism. Yet this school is so diverse that it is often difficult to separate these writers from what might be called moderate revisionism and moderate traditionalism.

I would mention John Lewis Gaddis as the most typical exponent of postrevisionism.[13] Other representatives of this school are George C. Herring, Jr., Martin J. Sherwin, and Daniel Yergin.[14] I would also include here my own book *The American Non-Policy Towards Eastern Europe 1943–1947*. As the foremost examples of those who take a postrevisionist stance very close to moderate revisionism I would mention Stephen E. Ambrose and Diane Shaver Clemens.[15] With Richard M. Freeland and Thomas G. Paterson[16] it is more difficult to decide whether they should be placed with the revisionists or with the postrevisionists. I would argue that they belong in the former group. In this complicated picture there are some, John Gimbel, for example, who could not with justice be easily fitted into any of these categories.[17]

Most of the so-called postrevisionists pay little attention, at least explicitly, to the question of responsibility for the cold war. The subject of interaction among the Great Powers, which of course is never entirely absent from any traditionalist or revisionist study, is prominent in most works of this new group.

As to the question of motive forces of American foreign policy, the new wave undoubtedly places more emphasis on economic considerations than have traditionalists. Postrevisionists do not, however, concentrate so exclusively on this aspect as have most revisionists. Generally, they see various political, strategic, and economic considerations as all exerting their influence, the weight of each decided by the circumstances of the special case in point.

The Years 1945–1947: Change or Continuity?

Traditionalists are generally of the opinion that the United States played a passive role in the cold war until the introduction of the Truman Doctrine and the Marshall Plan. Most of them definitely see Washington as making little if any use of its military and economic strength to influence Soviet actions in the early period of the cold war. They apply this interpretation to the atomic bomb, which they see as little more than an instrument in the war against Japan; to lend-lease, which was terminated due to the attitude in Congress with regard to postwar rehabilitation; and to ground forces, which the U.S. rapidly demobilized while the Soviet Union maintained most of its forces.

The most clear-cut examples of the underlining of this passive role for the United States are found in Jones and in Halle. In his *The Fifteen Weeks: An Inside Account of the Genesis of the Marshall Plan,* Jones states that the Truman Doctrine and the Marshall Plan ". . . laid the basis for a complete conversion of American foreign policy and of the attitude of the American people toward the world."[18] Similarly, in *The Cold War as History* Halle asserts that the United States was ". . . without a workable foreign policy until the spring of 1947." In the spring of 1947 came the Truman Doctrine, which Halle sees as ". . . the commitment of the United States to active responsibility for freedom and justice throughout the world."[19] Herbert Feis entitles the chapters on the Truman Doctrine and the Marshall Plan in his *From Trust to Terror* respectively "The Communist Thrust Confronted" and "To Salvage Western Europe."[20]

The moderate traditionalist position may be found in the works of William McNeill. Even he emphasizes that it took considerable time after the war for the United States to overcome its aloofness to the affairs of Europe and its "honest broker" attitude in dealings with Britain and Russia.[21] On the other hand McNeill clearly implies that most of the pieces in a coherent American foreign policy had fallen into place well before the spring of 1947. If a turning point exists in his presentation, this would be July 1946, when Congress passed the loan to Britain: "The decision to support Britain marked a real turning-point in American policy. The idea of post-war withdrawal from Europe soon faded away after July 1946; American leadership of free Europe against Russia and her satellites came rapidly to the fore as a substitute of American policy."[22]

Despite their many differences, revisionists all agree that it is certainly a myth to describe American foreign policy as largely passive until the formulation of the Truman Doctrine and the Marshall Plan. Most revisionists conclude that at least the major assumptions upon which Washington would base its actions existed no later than the summer of 1945.

As usual, the extreme revisionist version is found with Gabriel and Joyce Kolko. In a typical passage, they state that "There was nothing new in containment and insulation, for they had been explicit parts of the anti-revolutionary policy of the United States and the West since 1918, and at no point since then, much less since 1943, did Washington doubt that it was a fixed policy to thwart the Left wherever it might do so."[23] From such a perspective no reason exists to see the spring of 1947 as of any particular importance. The Truman Doctrine and the Marshall Plan followed logically from actions and premises of the past.

Other revisionists do not go as far as the Kolkos. Fleming and Alperovitz see the transition from Roosevelt to Truman as the turning point. In his *Atomic Diplomacy: Hiroshima and Potsdam,* Alperovitz thus writes that "It is now evident that, far from following his predecessor's policy of cooperation, shortly after taking office Truman launched a powerful foreign policy initiative aimed at reducing or eliminating Soviet influence from Europe."[24]

An even more moderate version is presented by Lloyd Gardner and Walter LaFeber. They both certainly play down the Truman Doctrine and the Marshall Plan as turning points and argue that the preconditions for action had been set well before the spring of 1947. The assumptions on which American policies rested were the depression of the thirties, World War II, and a near half-century of distrust of Soviet Communism. In Gardner's phrase, the world view of the American political leadership was based on "their nightmare-like memories of the depression, their newfound economic power, and the reality of a profound challenge seemingly centered in the Soviet Union."[25] The fact that the preconditions for action had been set does not, however, mean that the action itself had unfolded. Both Gardner and LaFeber, therefore, see this period as more of a developing process than Kolko and Alperovitz do.

Revisionists all agree that the United States used various levers to further its foreign policy objectives. While there is fairly general agreement on the way in which economic instruments were brought to bear on the Soviet Union by the Truman administration, all possible nuances can be found in revisionist views on the role the atomic bomb played in American diplomacy at the end of World War II.[26]

How do postrevisionists deal with the problem of the degree of activity shown by the United States in the 1945 to 1947 period? A rough conclusion is that again they adopt some kind of middle position between revisionists and traditionalists, although this position may vary considerably in its details from historian to historian.

With John Lewis Gaddis it is difficult to find any single one decisive point, be it the Truman Doctrine or the transition from Roosevelt to Truman. The emphasis on gradual change found both with moderate traditionalists and moderate revisionists is even more pronounced with Gaddis. If he were to single out a turning point, it would probably be February-March, 1946. This, again, would seem to place him somewhere between McNeill on the one side and Gardner-LaFeber on the other. In his *The United States and the Origins of the Cold War 1941–1947*, Gaddis states that "The period of late February and early March, 1946, marked a decisive turning point in American policy toward the Soviet Union. Prior to this time, Washington officials had frequently resisted Russian demands, but not on a consistent basis."[27] This consistency was apparently there after February-March.

The aspect which probably best exemplifies the middle position of postrevisionists is that of the various levers at the disposal of the United States. Unlike traditionalists, the new group of historians pays considerable attention to these levers. That does not mean that they accept revisionist interpretations. The picture to emerge is that considerations other than anti-Soviet attitudes had a great deal to do with actions that revisionists have interpreted almost exclusively in this anti-Soviet light.

This perspective is best illustrated in the works of Herring and Sherwin. Herring agrees that a growing hostility toward Soviet policies played a part in the cuts in lend-lease to the Soviet Union in May and August 1945 but unlike revisionists he does not stop at this point. Instead Herring brings in the domestic situation in the United States. In particular he stresses the role of Congress, which also, for reasons other than anticommunism, had long insisted on very restrictive policies in using lend-lease for postwar rehabilitation purposes.[28]

Similarly, Sherwin agrees that reasons related to a growing opposition to Soviet policies influenced Washington's decision to use the atomic bomb against Japan. There were other factors as well, however. The administration had to justify to Congress and the public that enormous amounts had been spent on such a project. This could be accomplished by using the bomb in the war. Some officials even hoped that the bomb would make people understand that no more wars should be fought. Yet, Sherwin still insists that the most important reason behind the decision to drop the bomb was to end the war against Japan as soon as possible.[29]

Some Revisionist Points

After this brief presentation of some prominent American historians, I will comment on their views. This will be done in the form of an analysis of my own of American policies in this period.

I feel it is necessary for purposes of discussion to split up American policies. In some respects the policies of the Truman administration had been determined long before the spring of 1947. In others even the Truman Doctrine and the Marshall Plan would not set Washington's policies firmly in an anti-Soviet light. In short, the discussion about turning points in American foreign policy easily becomes misleading.[30] A meaningful conclusion will depend on what field one is dealing with—economic, political, or military. It may also depend on the geographic area in question.

In this light I will first examine those parts of Washington's policies which would seem to support the revisionist view that the containment policies of the Truman Doctrine and the Marshall Plan originated well before the spring of 1947 and at least to some extent were in existence as early as the end of World War II. This does not necessarily mean that I fully accept the revisionist interpretation even where unanimity might exist within this group of historians. I only think that revisionists have generally appreciated these parts of U.S. policies better than have traditionalists.

A most controversial point concerns Washington's handling of the atomic bomb. Gar Alperovitz's view is that the United States used the bomb against Japan because ". . . a combat demonstration was needed to convince the Russians to accept the American plan for a stable peace. And the crucial point of this effort was the need to force agreement on the main questions in dispute: the American proposals for Central and Eastern Europe."[31] This argument has met with more and more opposition in the last years from traditionalists as well as from other revisionists. It is my opinion, too, that in this form the argument should be rejected.

This conclusion does not mean that the atomic bomb had little or no influence on the American policy toward the Soviet Union, as traditionalists seem to think. Even if it did not change American objectives as such, I think it should be argued that the bomb made some policy makers pursue their objectives with greater determination than they had earlier. This was particularly noticeable in the period from the Potsdam Conference through the Council of Foreign Ministers meeting in London. Alperovitz is undoubtedly wrong in viewing nonrecognition of the Axis satellites in the Balkans as an outcome of Washington's possession of the new weapon. Nevertheless, it may well be that the bomb was one of the factors that invigorated this policy, as, for example, in the crisis over the Rumanian government in August-September 1945.[32]

The bombs over Japan did not fall in a political vacuum.

The new weapon was seen as reinforcing the American diplomatic and military position, also in relation to the Soviet Union. There are numerous indications that Secretary of State Byrnes, Secretary of War Stimson, and other policy makers welcomed the additional political strength which the new weapon bestowed upon the United States.[33] It is another matter that it was impossible for Washington to exploit the atomic bomb openly to temper Soviet policies in Eastern Europe or elsewhere.

With Sherwin's studies there has been a change of interest from the alleged break in policies during the transition from Roosevelt to Truman, which was so crucial to Alperovitz, to the fact that not even Roosevelt wanted to share the secret of the atomic bomb with the Soviet Union. Roosevelt too was aware of the way in which the new weapon might strengthen the position of the United States.[34] In this context it should be noted that Roosevelt evidently wanted to see if not even economic support in the form of a large loan could in some way be used to temper the foreign policy behavior of the Soviet Union.[35]

Aside from the diplomatic consequences of American possession of the atomic bomb, the weapon also had military implications in the cold war. Although it would still take some years before the Truman administration broke with a general mobilization strategy in its defense planning,[36] the bomb was immediately seen as having important effects as a deterrent. On August 22, 1945, President Truman told General de Gaulle that "the bomb will give pause to countries which might be tempted to commit aggressions."[37] In November 1948 Secretary of State Marshall told Norwegian Foreign Minister Lange that ". . . in my judgment the main deterrent to Soviet aggression has been the possession by the United States of the atomic bomb."[38]

I think it is evident that traditionalists have generally paid too little attention to the ways in which the atomic bomb influenced America's policies toward the Soviet Union. It is an even easier task to demonstrate that revisionists are also in great part right in emphasizing that considerable skepticism and hostility existed toward the Soviet Union as early as 1944–45. This attitude had certainly arisen long before 1947. Skepticism toward Soviet intentions had flourished before the war, but the common struggle against Germany had in part created a new impression of the Soviet ally. In 1943–44, when it became evident that the war would be won, political problems could no longer be postponed. Old fears of the Soviet Union were reawakened.

Those who first expressed such feelings were often found in the State Department among officials who knew the Soviet Union well. In his study *Shattered Peace: The Origins of the Cold War and the National Security State,* Daniel Yergin has dealt with what he calls "the Riga axioms." Although he undoubtedly exaggerates the ideological implacability of their views, Yergin at least shows that an ingrained distrust of the Soviet Union filled many of the members of the Foreign Service who had served in Moscow or in the Baltic States before they were absorbed by the Soviets. Some of these, George F. Kennan, Charles Bohlen, Loy Henderson, Arthur Bliss Lane, and Elbridge Durbrow, for example, were to hold prominent positions during and after the war.[39]

After the Tehran Conference fast-rising Soviet expert Charles Bohlen summed up Moscow's goals in Europe by stating that the result of their realization was ". . . that the Soviet Union would be the only important military and political force on the continent of Europe. The rest of Europe would be reduced to military and political impotence."[40] Similar analyses were soon made by the embassy in Moscow, by Ambassador Harriman and Chargé Kennan. While Harriman had earlier voiced considerable optimism about the possibilities for Soviet-American cooperation, Soviet policies in 1944 toward Bulgaria, Rumania, and, in particular, Poland, reactivated latent fears of Soviet expansion.[41] The Soviet response to the uprising in Warsaw in the late summer and fall of 1944 had a crucial influence on evaluations of Soviet intentions. From then on Harriman and Kennan issued numerous warnings.[42] Secretary of State Cordell Hull and many others in the State Department were influenced by their cables. As a result, similar analyses were made in Washington long before Kennan's famous Long Telegram to the State Department in February 1946.[43]

Secretary of the Navy James Forrestal represented another focal point of skepticism and hostility toward Soviet intentions. Although even Forrestal had evinced some optimism during the war about Soviet-American relations in the future, his attitude changed in about mid-1944. He then became most emphatic about the danger of Soviet communism.[44]

There are indications that President Roosevelt himself, in the last weeks before his death, modified his belief in the possibility of cooperating with the Soviet Union.[45] After Truman's accession to power, the influence of the State Department increased. The new President had to rely much more than did Roosevelt on the foreign policy professionals. The meeting between the new President and Soviet Foreign Minister Molotov in late April, as well as the internal preparations for that meeting, revealed that fairly broad agreement now existed among Truman and his advisers on the need for a firm attitude toward the Soviet Union. Henry Stimson and General Marshall were definitely in the minority when they cautioned against the sharpened policy of the administration.[46]

Although evaluations of Soviet intentions might temporarily become somewhat more positive again, the post-Yalta period had broken the administration's confidence in the Soviets. Hopkins' talks with Stalin in May-June and the Potsdam Conference could not bring back what had been lost.

Even if by the spring of 1945 a majority of the foreign policy leadership was convinced that the Soviet Union would not tolerate independent governments in its neighboring states, that does not exclude the possibility that appraisals of Soviet intentions would become still more pessimistic in 1946 and 1947. Washington then came to fear that areas more crucial than Eastern Europe would be threatened by Soviet-Communist expansion.

Furthermore, voices of moderation could be heard in prominent places. Although James F. Byrnes could certainly act in accordance with the prevailing attitude, as was evidenced at the London Conference of the Council of Foreign Ministers in September-October 1945, the new Secretary of State gradually came to believe that concessions had to be made to the Soviet Union. This was necessary if agreement was to be secured on the peace treaties for the Axis satellites. The reaction Byrnes met with from Truman, Admiral Leahy, other presidential advisers, and Congressional leaders like Vandenberg and Connally modified his attitude considerably. This was best illustrated by their reaction to the concessions Byrnes made in the December 1945 meeting in Moscow with his Soviet and British counterparts.[47]

Other voices of moderation belonged to Secretary of Commerce Henry Wallace, foreign policy adviser Joseph Davies, some of the military leaders and, to some extent, even Secretary of War Stimson. Stimson, the most influential of these, came to modify his attitude even before he left government service in September 1945. In the fall of 1945 most of the military leaders had also come to make analyses quite similar to those worked out in the State Department months earlier. Davies was gradually excluded from his informal advisory position on Soviet-American relations. Henry Wallace was becoming more and more of an outsider within the Truman administration. His resignation in the fall of 1946 only illustrated his loss of influence in a most explicit way.[48]

John Lewis Gaddis has argued that revisionists have neglected the influence of Congress and public opinion in creating a policy of getting firm with the Soviets.[49] I think this point can easily be exaggerated. Negative evaluations of Soviet intentions developed earlier and more strongly in the executive branch than in Congress and with the public. This is confirmed by a study of Gallup polls and by several minor incidents which took place in 1945–46. As late as August 1945, 54 percent of the public thought that the Soviet Union could be trusted to cooperate with the United States. That was only one percent less than the wartime high, immediately after the Yalta Conference.[50]

The State Department's negative evaluation of the Soviet Union came as a shock to informed reporters when Har-

riman confronted the press with it during the UN Conference in San Francisco in the spring of 1945.[51] Almost a year
later, when former Prime Minister Churchill delivered his
"Iron Curtain" speech in March 1946, the negative reaction
the speech met with in parts of the press and among the
public made the administration try to create the impression
that it did not share the views of Churchill to the degree it
actually did.[52] I think it can be argued that to a large extent
it was only after the already established friction between the
United States and the Soviet Union came to public attention
that opinion decisively swung around to the pessimistic appraisals which the administration had already been making
for some time.[53] But, then, once public opinion had been
awakened to the Soviet danger it had a tendency to over-
react.

The Truman administration also faced considerable
problems in maneuvering foreign assistance appropriations
or loans through Congress. To help break opposition, leading
officials came to present the Soviet threat in more dramatic
terms than those used internally. This tendency could first
be noticed in the spring of 1946 when the loan to Britain met
with much resistance in Congress. The best illustration of
the executive trying to frighten Congress and the public into
supporting assistance to noncommunist countries is found in
the administration's handling of the Truman Doctrine in
February–March 1947.

A good example of hostility toward Moscow and countries dominated by it is found in the lending policies of the
United States. In some ways the Marshall Plan represented
a continuation of policies that had already been pursued for
some time. First, the focus on the needs of Western Europe,
which was evident in the Marshall Plan, was certainly nothing new in 1947. An examination of the amounts granted by
the United States from July 1945 through June 1947 reveals
the priority which Western Europe had been given even before the Marshall Plan. During this period countries which
later came to participate in the Marshall Plan received loans
and property credits totaling $7.4 billion. The Eastern Euro-
peans got $546 million. This included $106 million for Fin-

land and $242 million for the Soviet Union to finance so-called pipeline deliveries from lend-lease.[54]

Second, the Marshall Plan represented no increase in U.S. assistance to Western Europe, although the organization of and, to a lesser extent, the motivation behind, this aid changed significantly. In the period from April 1948 to July 1952 the United States gave the Marshall Plan countries approximately $14 billion. Washington actually granted more than $10 billion from the time the war ended in Europe to mid-1947. Even if we leave out the explicitly humanitarian part, Western Europe received more on a yearly average in 1945–1947 than it did through the Marshall Plan.

The discrepancy between aid to Eastern and Western Europe had been increasing from 1945 onward, thereby showing the growing influence of cold war considerations on American aid policies. In August-September 1946 the State Department had already become thoroughly disappointed at the policies of most Eastern European countries. Now the list of unacceptable countries was extended to include even Czechoslovakia. Although the Department realized that there was little evidence of direct Soviet interference in Czechoslovak affairs, Washington was only more infuriated by Prague on its own acting in harmony with Moscow's wishes.[55]

The result was that in August-September 1946 Byrnes initiated a reconsideration of aid policies to the whole of Europe. At the end of September the Secretary of State presented the following analysis:

> . . . the situation has so hardened that the time has now come, I am convinced, in the light of attitude of the Soviet Government and the neighboring states which it dominates in varying degrees, when the implementation of our general policies requires the closest coordination. In a word, we must help our friends in every way and refrain from assisting those who either through helplessness or for other reasons are opposing the principles for which we stand.[56]

Czechoslovakia was the first country on the enemy side to which the new principles were applied.

This period also represented a stepping up of commitments to the other side, the friends of America. This was best illustrated by Washington's attitude to Greece and Turkey. In September-October the British and the Americans agreed that Britain was to take care of the military needs of these countries, and Washington was to handle their nonmilitary needs. At the end of October the State Department interpreted this to mean that if the United Kingdom required arms for this purpose which were not in its possession, the arms should be furnished to Britain by the United States. Washington for its part was to send arms to Iran direct.[57] This change of policy did not affect just the State Department. President Truman and the War and Navy departments also favored strong American commitments in the Eastern Mediterranean in the fall of 1946.[58]

The organization of U.S. assistance to Western Europe would be basically changed with the Marshall Plan, a fact which would be of great importance in American-Scandinavian relations. Despite this, in a Great Power context the plan represented to a considerable extent a public proclamation of policies which had already been in existence for some time. This element of continuity is probably the major reason why there was little discussion within the executive branch about the need to initiate these programs. The Truman administration, unlike many members of Congress and a large part of the public, did not have to be convinced of their soundness.

It has often been noted that despite a proclaimed aversion to the idea of spheres of influence, the United States developed arrangements with other countries which came very close to being exactly that. The best example, which revisionists always make much of, is of course that of Washington's policies in Latin America.[59]

Latin America was not the only area where the United States held a sphere-of-influence-like position. In December 1945 British Foreign Secretary Ernest Bevin complained that the United States was extending the Monroe Doctrine to the Pacific.[60] Bevin's reference to the Pacific concerned the policies pursued by Washington with respect to Japan and the Japanese Mandated Islands. After a protracted squabble between the State, War and Navy departments, the islands were formally placed under UN trusteeship. This was done in such a way, however, that those most strategically important were actually ruled by the United States. The military leadership insisted on such an arrangement.[61]

Truman and the State Department were also quite determined not to let the Soviet Union in on the affairs of Japan. Not only the Soviets were to complain about the role assigned to them. The British did the same, as Bevin's comment illustrates. Although Washington had to give the other Allies some formal say in Japanese affairs, this could not hide realities. As the White House itself stated in September, 1945, ". . . in the event of any differences among them [the Allies], the policies of the United States will govern."[62] The Soviet Union and the British would only be heard to the extent that they agreed with American policies. (Even the State Department soon felt it did not have much say in Japanese affairs—General MacArthur was determined to rule Japan himself. But that is another matter.)[63]

The relationship with the Philippines was another example of American hegemony. Despite the United States leading other colonial powers in granting independence to the islands in 1946, Washington still exercised basic control over the military-political affairs of the new country. The United States maintained military bases, and the islands were so closely tied to the U.S. economy that Washington's preferential trade relations broke with America's own guidelines for international trade.[64]

The United States wanted to obtain bases in many other countries as well. In November 1945 the Joint Chiefs of Staff presented a long list of required bases, in addition to bases in occupied areas. Nine of these were considered essential to the United States. The State Department objected that the presentation of such a list would lead to a deterioration in relations not only with the Soviet Union, but possibly also with Britain. The JCS agreed to reduce the numbers. On the list of so-called essential areas six remained. Those six, however, were found in the most different parts of the world—

illustrating the extent to which the United States now considered itself a power with global interests. The three of most outstanding importance were Greenland, Iceland, and the Azores. The other three on the essential list were Casablanca, the Galapagos, and Panama.[65] The desire for such a far-flung net of bases was not at this time primarily related to cold war considerations. Yet these were undoubtedly part of the general picture. As the threat from the Soviet Union came to be seen as growing, such considerations became of increasing importance.

In Europe, as in other liberated areas, American policy makers had tried to distinguish rather sharply between military areas of responsibility and political spheres of influence. The former was an established part of U.S. policies, the latter was not. The State Department considered the civil affairs agreements as being principally of a military nature, but agreed that they "obviously have a political flavor."[66] This political flavor was most pronounced in the armistices concluded with Italy, on the one hand, and with Rumania, Bulgaria, Hungary, and in some measure even Finland, on the other. In the Eastern European armistices Washington tried to protect its interests in the postmilitary period, while agreeing to a Soviet lead during the military phase.[67]

It was no easy matter to change from one occupational system to another once the war ended. It was to be expected that the United States was more concerned about increasing its role in the countries where it had little influence than in improving the position of the Soviet Union. In Italy, formal agreements gave the United States and Britain a leading role. While trying to increase its role in the Eastern Europe Axis satellites, the United States did not want to strengthen Soviet influence in Italy. The system of Western control therefore continued virtually unchanged in Italy after the surrender of Germany.[68]

In addition to Italy, Germany was the other major country in Western Europe where the United States took on strong commitments. Contrary to original U.S. intentions, Washington soon subsidized the German economy to make it viable in the face of destruction caused by the war and various forms of reparations. In the political field the United States became more and more concerned with limiting communist influence in its own and in the other Western zones. In the military field Byrnes's famous speech in Stuttgart in September 1946 made it clear that, despite rapid demobilization, American forces would remain part of the army of occupation as long as there was one.[69]

The American aversion to political spheres of influence was soon modified in Western Europe in important respects, not only in practice, but even in theory. As early as July 1945, the State Department, in evaluating an earlier paper from the Joint Chiefs of Staff, still presented the principles against such spheres. At the same time, however, the Department noted that "In view of the actual Eastern European sphere and the Western Hemisphere bloc (Act of Chapultepec) we are hardly in a position to frown upon the establishment of measures designed to strengthen the security of nations in other areas of the world." The measures in question were British ones to strengthen Western Europe against Soviet influence.

Even at this early stage the Department recognized that the much-heralded United Nations Organization would not be effective in preventing conflicts among the Great Powers. The Department also pointed out that the British had always been "our first line of defense and . . . any threat to their security would most likely cause armed intervention on our part."[70] So, in the end the opposition to a British sphere of influence in Western Europe was much modified. Although it is noteworthy that Washington did not see itself as leading a Western European bloc, in some important respects the British contributed to the realization of American foreign policy objectives as well. In addition, London was becoming heavily dependent upon support from Washington in performing its foreign policy tasks.

In particular through its participation in the occupation of Germany, Italy, and Austria and through its policies of economic assistance to Western Europe as a whole, the United States had taken on strong economic, political, and military commitments in Europe in 1945–46. Depending on the definitions used, most of Western Europe could, in foreign policy terms, be described as a Western sphere of interest. This of course does not imply that the means of control used by the United States and Britain in the West were the same as those of the Soviet Union in Eastern Europe.

Some Traditionalist Points

The points which I have so far examined may to a considerable extent be said to support a revisionist interpretation of the years 1945 through 1947. Although revisionists have often been too sweeping in their conclusions, the arguments dealt with on the preceding pages lie closer to the average revisionist position than to a traditionalist one. However, there are many points which I feel have not been given due consideration by revisionists. These points have either been entirely overlooked or, more likely, not been given the emphasis they deserve. Again, the arguments which I will now present are not used by all traditionalists or by no revisionists. What is important is that they generally fit in best with what traditionalists have written.

The American policy toward China should be viewed in this perspective. It is true that the United States gave support to Chiang Kai-shek in the Chinese civil war. Washington ordered the Japanese to surrender only to Chiang's troops, U.S. planes were provided to bring his troops out to reestablish control over the Chinese countryside, American forces protected railroads and harbors, and, finally, Washington made it fairly evident that it would continue to support Chiang even if no coalition government was established with Mao's Communists.[71]

Compared, however, to what the United States did in Europe to combat communism and compared to a revisionist viewpoint of a dominant U.S. aggressively bent on securing its capitalist interests all over the world, the surprising thing is not the extent of the assistance given, but its limitations. There was little serious talk of intervening in China with American armed forces; those which were left after the war were on the whole rapidly withdrawn. The U.S. did give considerable financial and military aid to Chiang, but this was done halfheartedly. The Nationalists got far less than they desired and, on occasion, assistance was suspended to put some pressure on Chiang to modify his policies.[72]

There were several reasons for this reticence on the part of Washington. Dissatisfaction with Chiang's internal policies contributed to America's reluctance to increase it support. Also, American policy makers came to consider the task of stopping communism in China as beyond the means of the United States. Yet, this decision also represented a question of emphasis, of which areas were to receive the most attention from the Truman administration. The United States adhered to a Europe First policy. In Europe nothing seemed to be beyond Washington's means. It should also be noted that while the administration undoubtedly held the initiative in shaping policies in Europe, the roles of Congress and the GOP were somewhat larger in questions concerning China. But even the Republicans did not propose that the U.S. intervene with large-scale military forces to support Chiang.[73]

Extreme revisionist Gabriel Kolko is certainly aware of the limitations in the China policy of the United States. The same is the case with other revisionists. Yet, somehow, this does not always lead to modification of their statements to the effect that the United States, by far the strongest power in the world, was intent on doing all in its power to combat communism.[74]

Despite the rhetoric of the Truman Doctrine and the generalizations of most revisionists, the United States clearly did not do all in its power to stop communist advances. The Truman Doctrine did not apply to China. Neither did it apply to some other parts of Asia which only a few years later came to represent crisis areas in the cold war. American assistance to the French in Vietnam was long quite limited and based more on the importance France held for the situation in Western Europe than on a desire to fight communism on the Asian mainland. Similarly, the day after the proclamation of the Truman Doctrine, Syngman Rhee sent a letter to President Truman asking for the application of its principles to Korea. The letter was not answered. Instead the administration was soon to withdraw its troops from Korea.[75]

The Truman Doctrine did not even apply to all of Europe. At the very time Truman proclaimed his doctrine, the Nagy government in Budapest, which had resulted from free elections in the fall of 1945, was under strong pressure from the Soviet Union. As in China, however, and as Under Secretary of State Dean Acheson explained to the Senate Foreign Relations Committee ". . . what we can do in Hungary, what we should do, the whole circumstances of that case are very different from that [Greece and Turkey] we have before us."[76] With quite limited support from the United States, the Nagy government would soon fall. Washington in turn did little more than to voice new protests.[77]

Despite the enormous strength of the United States, Washington had to admit that not all parts of the world were of equally great significance to American interests. This showed not only in Hungary in 1947, but in policies toward the whole of Eastern Europe in the first years after the war.[78] Eastern Europe was an area of less than essential interest to the United States. This explains why policy makers never seriously thought of using their strongest levers, such as the atomic bomb and ground forces, to challenge the Soviet position in Eastern Europe. It also serves to explain why these policy makers on several occasions acted in ways that actually strengthened Soviet supremacy in the region.

There are many examples of the United States having acted in such ways. In part because Washington did not want Moscow to enter into civil affairs agreements with Western European countries, it refrained from concluding such agreements with the Allied states in Eastern Europe. Similarly, the American insistence on virtually excluding the Soviet Union from Italian affairs led to the U.S. being given very little influence in the occupations of Bulgaria, Hungary, and, in particular, Rumania.

Such practices continued after the war as well. For instance, the need to maintain exclusive control over Japan is one factor which explains the American consent to the one-sided agreements on Rumania-Bulgaria in December 1945. These agreements recognized communist control over the local governments. Concessions also had to be made to the Soviet Union in the peace treaties for the Eastern European Axis satellites in order to obtain similar concessions in the treaty for Italy. Finally, the fact that the rehabilitation of Western Europe through the Marshall Plan was seen by many prominent policy makers in Washington as only leading to a further tightening of Soviet control in Eastern Europe, did not deter these policy makers from concentrating on the needs of Western Europe. Eastern Europe constantly had to be "sacrificed" to protect more substantial American interests.

The elements of restraint in America's policies toward parts of Asia as well as toward Eastern Europe lasted well beyond 1947. In both areas there could be little doubt about the direction in which Washington's attitude was developing. In China it changed from establishing a coalition government with substantial communist representation to more definite, if still limited, support of Chiang Kai-shek. In Eastern Europe the United States tried harder and harder to strengthen its role while at the same time limiting Soviet influence in crucial Western Europe. And yet, Washington did not meet with any more success than it had before.

Some areas simply were of greater importance than others to American interests. In addition, definite limitations existed on the resources of the United States. These resources were enormous, much greater than those of any other country. Yet policy makers could not commit too large a part of these resources to combat Soviet Communism. Restraints of a domestic as well as of a foreign policy nature entered the picture. What was to be spent had to be concentrated on Western Europe.

We have already seen that a majority of the makers of American foreign policy developed an early skepticism of Soviet intentions. They hoped that the atomic bomb would give pause to any aggressive moves on the part of the Soviet leadership. Washington exploited its economic resources to aid its friends and punish its enemies. Nevertheless, America's commitment to the protection of its interests and its opposition to Soviet expansion have been exaggerated by revisionists.

Some examples from the military field will further illustrate the limitations of America's policies in the early cold war period. Revisionists, unlike most traditionalists, hardly dwell on the significance of the rapid demobilization of U.S. armed forces after the war. Policy makers from Truman down complained that the program followed was not demobilization, but disintegration of the forces, and that this disintegration was undermining the diplomatic position of the United States. By the summer of 1946 the Army had been reduced from 8 million men to 1.5 million. In the Navy the corresponding figures were 3.5 and 0.7 million. Only about a third of those remaining actually belonged to functioning units as opposed to units simply being processed for discharge.[79]

Little could be done about this, however. Delay in bringing the boys home was regarded as political suicide. George Marshall gave a telling description of the dilemma a Secretary of State was in when faced with demands for giving the Kremlin "hell": "At that time [March 1947] my facilities for giving them hell . . . was exactly 1 and ⅓ divisions over the entire United States. That [to give them hell] is quite a proposition when you deal with somebody with over 260 and you have 1⅓rd."[80] It is another matter that demobilization of the Soviet Union forces was underestimated in Washington.[81]

The size of the defense budget also revealed limitations which American policy makers had to cope with. It is, of course, true that budgets in the first postwar years were considerably higher than they had been in the interwar period. Nevertheless, if we take into account the new role the U.S. played and its responsibilities in occupied territories, the remarkable thing is how small these budgets were. In the 1945–50 period defense expenditures in the U.S. were probably smaller than in the Soviet Union. On the whole they constituted no more than one-third of what they became after the introduction of NSC-68 and the outbreak of the Korean War. John Lewis Gaddis is therefore right when he argues that the turning point in this respect was not the Truman Doctrine, but the outbreak of the Korean War.[82]

The two, later three armed services tried to play up such foreign dangers as best suited their budget needs. They could not increase the total budget, however. Truman and his economic advisers were quite determined that the United States would not "spend itself to death" to meet the Soviet danger. In a most curious way, the limit was somehow calculated to be 15 billion dollars. Both Democrats and especially Republicans paid more attention to demands for lower taxes than for higher defense budgets. The great majority of the business community was far more interested in keeping taxes down than in trying to exploit the defense budget. The National Association of Manufacturers and the Chamber of Commerce argued not for bigger budgets, but for smaller ones.

The influence of the military-industrial complex is therefore easily exaggerated, at least for the years before 1950. The Air Force was able to increase its allotments considerably due to the feeling within the administration and particularly in Congress that it could provide maximum security at small cost. Despite this, even this branch did not reach its cherished goal of seventy groups before the Korean War. What success the Air Force had, it obtained largely at the expense of the Army and the Navy. With the forces of budgetary restraint from March 1949 having a strong ally in Secretary of Defense Louis Johnson, the Navy even lost its long-planned super carrier. That led to the resignation of the Secretary of the Navy and the so-called "admirals' revolt." The Army met with even less success than the Navy in protecting its share of the defense budget.[83]

As to the influence of the economic interests of the United States, it is again my opinion that its strength may easily be exaggerated and that most revisionists have done so. I shall not dispute that economic considerations have played a significant part in the foreign policies of the United States. It is evident from numerous internal policy memoranda that they did so on many occasions. Traditionalists have undoubtedly paid too little attention to this dimension in American policies.[84]

What is lost in revisionist presentations, however, is the fact that the United States is one of the countries in the world which is least dependent on foreign trade. True, the foreign trade of the U.S. is enormous in absolute figures. But the importance of trade is often measured better in proportion to the size of the economy as a whole. According to such a rod of measurement, as late as 1965 the United States tied for 101st place with Poland on a list of 114 countries based on foreign trade as a percentage of the Gross National Product. In the years from 1945 to 1950 the foreign trade of the United States, again measured as a percentage of GNP, was rather lower than it has been in most periods of this century. The same is true for the foreign investments of American firms.[85] For quite a few years after the war direct U.S. investment in Western Europe was less than the European capital invested in the United States.[86]

A main objection to the writings of American historians, revisionist as well as traditionalist, is that they concentrate too much on the policies of the United States. The fact that so little source material is available on the Soviet side is an important explanation for this deficiency. Nevertheless, more could be done, especially in the way of comparing U.S. policies to those of the Western European countries. Revisionists generally see the United States as thrusting itself into the affairs of other countries. There are, of course, many examples of this, in recent as well as in earlier years. But as a general perspective on American policies after World War II, in particular in relation to Western Europe, I would consider an opposite view closer to reality. Instead of the United States trying to pull Western Europe in the direction Washington desired, I would emphasize the extent to which Western Europeans tried to influence the Americans in the direction of taking greater, not lesser, interest in their affairs.

Britain offers the best example of this preoccupation with involving the Americans more intimately in the affairs of Europe. The Attlee government wanted both more financial assistance and a stronger U.S. military presence in Europe. Bevin's way of handling the British withdrawal from Greece as well as Britain's occupational policies in Germany and its response to the Marshall Plan were aimed at increasing the American commitment to Europe. The same was the case in the negotiations leading up to the North Atlantic Treaty. As a matter of fact, both in the Marshall Plan and in the NATO discussions the United States tried to limit the role it was to play and instead make the Europeans carry more of the load. This could be done by encouraging European integration. Fears of communism and of Soviet intentions were definitely not limited to the leaders of capitalist America. Most social democrats and nonsocialists in Western Europe had similar fears. And many of them worried that the United States would not do enough to strengthen their respective countries against the Soviet-Communist danger.[87]

To conclude, it is very difficult to strike the right balance between the degree to which the foreign policy of the United States was established in an anti-Soviet perspective already at the end of World War II, and the extent to which it only gradually developed in this direction in response to short-term situations. A traditionalist view which states that basically the United States had no such policy until the introduction of the Truman Doctrine and the Marshall Plan is, in my opinion, incorrect in several ways. Washington had a decidedly negative view of Soviet intentions long before these measures were launched. The United States also tried to use various instruments at its disposal to stem or reverse the process of Soviet-Communist expansion. Well before 1947 American policy makers had established unilateral control in some of the areas that were of basic concern to them. Latin America, the Pacific, and Japan were such areas. In Europe the United States had at least by the fall of 1946 developed a comprehensive policy of aiding its friends and punishing its enemies. That entailed large-scale assistance to Western Europe, and nothing to the Eastern part.

Revisionists are right in emphasizing that even in 1945–46 the United States was ready to oppose moves which would strengthen the Soviet position. That was certainly nothing new in 1947. But the anticommunist mold of U.S. policies has been exaggerated by most revisionists. The Truman administration was ready to do far more to "save" Western Europe than it was to stop the disintegration of Chiang's control in China. Other areas were of even less importance to the United States. In Eastern Europe the United States entered into numerous arrangements which actually served to strengthen Soviet domination over the region.

The atomic bomb served to support the American position vis-à-vis the Soviet Union. The new weapon could not, however, be used very actively to further Washington's diplomatic objectives. The bomb was not the only lever at Washington's disposal that was severely circumscribed as an instrument of diplomatic maneuvering. Neither could American ground forces be used for such purposes to any great extent. Political repercussions in America and in Western Europe would have been serious had this been attempted. In addition, the military forces of the United States were disintegrating at such a speed that those who reflected on using ground troops for diplomatic purposes soon had few troops left to exploit. Only America's vast economic resources remained. These could be used and were used to further Washington's political and economic objectives. Economic levers were easy to apply, but their effect was limited. American aid policies could not prevent the rapid expansion of communist influence in China and in Eastern Europe.

The consistency with which the United States opposed the Soviet Union is exaggerated by revisionists. As a result, they generally underestimate the extent to which U.S. policies changed as a reflection of changed surroundings. It is not sufficient to demonstrate that policy makers held negative opinions about Soviet intentions as early as the end of the war. Many had feared the Soviets even before the war. There is a significant step between making a negative appraisal and taking up world-wide commitments of an economic and military nature to combat the threat which only in part is inherent in such an appraisal. One does not automatically lead to the other. Neither is there anything automatic in economic commitments leading to military ones.

In some respects the pieces had fallen into place as early as 1945. In others it took considerably longer. Events in 1946–47 created a more consistent pattern in Washington's actions. The expansionist side of America's policies was further strengthened. But many limitations of this expansion were still there, easy to see, even after the Truman Doctrine and the Marshall Plan.

2

American Policies Toward Scandinavia 1945–1947

AFTER WORLD WAR II the United States became ready to take on ever-widening commitments in various parts of the world. Economic assistance was granted, military support extended, political prestige invested. America's interest in as well as its influence on the affairs of other countries expanded. It should be emphasized that this is as seen in a peacetime context and not as compared to the temporary explosion in commitments, interests, and influence which took place during the war.

This widening of commitments, interests, and influence is what is meant by the term expansion. Expansion could be witnessed on many different levels, political, economic, and military. At the same time, as we have already seen and will note again and again, definite limitations existed on this expansion. These limitations were seldom absolute in the sense that they represented the opposite of expansion. Policies were generally flowing in the direction of expansion, not contraction. Instead, the limitations were relative in the sense that the United States was holding back from playing an even more dominant and anti-Soviet role than it actually was. Such limitations will almost always exist, yet to point them out will tell something about the nature of U.S. policies. Limitations were strong in 1945, weaker four years later, but even then they represented an important part of Washington's actions and attitudes.

To the extent we can generalize, revisionists stress the expansionist side, and pay little attention to the limitations on Washington's actions throughout this period. Traditionalists, although they agree that the United States was taking on new commitments, especially in Western Europe, emphasize the hesitancy with which policy makers embarked upon such a course. Expansion is a term they generally reserve for actions of the Soviet Union, a term not applicable to the actions of the United States. Yet revisionists argue, and I think with considerable justice, that the expansion of the United States was more comprehensive than that of the Soviet Union, although the forms of expansion were clearly different in each case.

Traditionalists and revisionists also disagree on what lay behind the commitments taken on by the Truman administration. Traditionalists create the impression that U.S. policies primarily reflected a response to Soviet aggressiveness.[1] Revisionists instead see Washington's actions as stemming from various internal pressures in America itself. In the phrase of moderate revisionist Walter LaFeber, "American actions abroad did not respond primarily to the pressures of other nations, but to political, social, and economic forces at home."[2]

What can an examination of attitudes toward Scandinavia reveal about these theories on the nature of U.S. policies? Do American policies in this area fit in best with the expansionist side or are the limitations more characteristic?

American Interest in Scandinavia

The focus of this study will be on the Soviet-American confrontation and America's actions and attitudes toward Scandinavia from this point of view. Therefore, I shall not take up the high-level treatment that Scandinavia received in connection with the struggle against Germany. For instance, in the volume of the memoirs of President Truman dealing with the year 1945, Norway is referred to primarily in relation to Allied fears that the Germans would try to hold out there after they had capitulated elsewhere. Developments in Sweden and Denmark are also seen mostly in the light of the war against Germany.[3]

During the war Norway and Denmark were seen as a British-American area of military responsibility. Naturally military authorities paid attention to Soviet plans in the area, but this did not necessarily mean that American military leaders opposed any Soviet presence in these two countries. Generally, anything that would hasten the end of the war was seen as beneficial to the Allied and, thereby, also to the American cause.[4]

In the summer of 1944, as a result of the flow of military events and Norwegian interest in the working out of an Allied policy for Norwegian territory, British authorities took the initiative in formulating some guidelines concerning an Allied military presence in Norway. In August the American members on the Combined Chiefs of Staff agreed to a British proposal which stated that

> Although it is to our advantage for the Russians to harass a German withdrawal as we have insufficient forces to do this ourselves, our long term requirement is to ensure that they should not permanently occupy Norwegian territory in view of potential threat to North Atlantic trade routes, Iceland and the northern approaches to the North Sea. Our purpose must be therefore to avoid any clash with the Russians in Norway and yet to safeguard our long term interests.[5]

This spelled out the military analysis in fairly general terms. On the one hand, it was in the Allied interest to make the Germans withdraw as soon as possible and to preserve a good working relationship with the Russians. On the other, it was obvious that Norway was of considerable strategic interest to Britain, and even to the United States. After the fight against Germany, the Soviet Union was seen as a potential threat. In August 1944 there was no need to spell out in detail how the military would solve any conflict between these two elements. Perhaps no conflict would arise.

The quotation from the Combined Chiefs of Staff illustrated a feeling of uncertainty about Soviet intentions in the area. This feeling is brought out more strongly in a few other sources from late 1944 and early 1945. Within the State Department Assistant Secretary of State Adolf Berle was one of those who worried early and strongly about Soviet intentions. In late September he presented a pessimistic analysis of Soviet objectives for the Department's Policy Committee. Berle stated that he thought the Soviet leaders would want to have governments "acting in substantial compliance" with the Soviet Union in at least Poland, Rumania, Bulgaria, Czechoslovakia, and Hungary. This was not much different from what many other officials were predicting. He went on, however, to argue that similar attitudes would probably prevail in Moscow toward Yugoslavia, Austria, and Greece. Finland was threatened and "possibly also . . . Norway and Denmark although the degree of influence in both places will be far less than in the other countries mentioned."[6]

Berle's analysis was made before the Red Army moved into Eastern Finnmark—the northeastern part of Norway— in October 1944.[7] The State Department of course not only supported the liberation of any occupied territory, but at least officially it also played down the danger of the Soviet Union exploiting its military position for political purposes. This happened in the Norwegian case as well. In late October even Berle tried to calm worries expressed by Norwegian Ambassador Morgenstierne that the Soviets would find some pretext to seize Norwegian ports. He told the ambassador "to pull himself together and . . . not to be worried about false rumors." The Assistant Secretary emphasized that he did not believe the Soviet Union had "the slightest designs on Norwegian territory."[8]

At the nexus between the military and the political leadership in Washington stood Secretary of the Navy Forrestal. After he became preoccupied with the question of Soviet intentions in 1944, he started to read widely about communism and the Soviet Union. He also had several studies made about the postwar role of the Soviet Union.

One of these gives a good impression of how those most skeptical of Soviet intentions viewed the position of the Scandinavian countries. The study was finished on February 7, 1945, and obviously made a significant impression on the Secretary of the Navy since he decided to include it in full in his diary, despite its great length.

In this study Western Europe was seen as an area where the Western Powers would have greater interest than Russia and where they would also be able to exercise greater influence. The Soviet influence was in turn seen as larger than that of the United States and Britain in Eastern Europe.

There was one exception to this generally optimistic picture as to the Soviet role in crucial Western Europe. That was the northern part of Norway. The group around Forrestal evidently feared that the status of Norway and, in particular, that of its northern part would be different from the rest of Western Europe and in fact come to resemble that of the Eastern European countries. The study noted that the Russians had given no indication of aggressive intentions in northern Norway. Nevertheless, ". . . the acquisition of a common frontier with that country [Norway] in the Far North and the proximity of Norwegian territory to Murmansk, Russia's only ice-free port opening directly on the high seas, give Norway a very special place in Russian eyes." The conclusion was that while it was likely that the Russians would recognize the primacy of British influence in most of Norway, "it appears quite possible that the Russians will seek a pact with Norway which will provide for joint Norwegian-Soviet defense of northern Norway against any third power."

Between Western and Eastern Europe the study placed a gray zone, Central Europe. In practice Central Europe meant Germany, Austria, Yugoslavia, and Sweden-Denmark. Since the Soviet Union was seen as likely to have a controlling influence in Finland, this would also give Moscow the opportunity to exercise greater influence in Sweden and Denmark than it had done before the war. On the other hand, the tendency of the two countries to look toward the West made it probable "that they will fall in the category of those small states where the influence of Russia on the one side and that of Britain and America on the other are roughly equal." [9]

On February 20 Under Secretary of State Joseph Grew told Secretary of War Stimson and Under Secretary of the Navy Bard that the Russians were attempting to extend their influence rather far to the West. The immediate background for his conclusion was found in Soviet communications to Denmark, although it is far from clear what exactly worried him in these. [10] Thus, Sweden, Denmark and, probably even more, the northern part of Norway were seen by some as areas where the influence of the Soviet Union would be greater than in the rest of Western Europe.

The fact that a few important policy makers in the State and Navy departments expressed early skepticism and even fear of Soviet intentions in Scandinavia did not mean that they, let alone Washington, were ready to take any significant action to limit Soviet influence in the area. Washington did little to strengthen the position of the Western Allies in response to the Soviet advance into Norway.

The most relevant project in this context was a Norwegian proposal to send a Norwegian military expedition to northern Norway. At the time this plan was considered the British had already rejected a Norwegian request for an Allied invasion of Norway in the region of Bodø with a view to cutting off the German retreat. Despite the British probably being somewhat more worried than the Americans about Soviet influence in northern Norway, there were simply no forces available. [11]

The State Department took no great interest in the Norwegian project. In a military matter like this the Joint Chiefs of Staff had to bear prime responsibility on the American side, although there were political aspects about which the Secretary of State felt he could express himself. Yet, even in that respect the department did not voice any strong opinion. Secretary of State Stettinius only told U.S. Ambassador Winant in London that the Norwegian plans had "political aspects which from that point of view we would not disapprove." It is doubtful that the unspecified political considerations were related to the Soviet position in northern Norway. They probably had more to do with U.S. relations with the Norwegians. The Division of European Affairs within the department thus worried that a refusal to send in Norwegian forces would weaken the position of the Norwegian government in London. However, the division also noted that such a weakening would strengthen the communists in their criticism of the Norwegian government as allegedly following a policy of passive resistance.[12]

The State Department maintained a low profile in a matter in which it had little influence anyway. The British and American military did not reject the Norwegian proposal out of hand—they were not opposed to the Norwegians using resources not under British operational command. In practice, however, this amounted to a refusal, since the plan was based primarily on forces under such command. When Norwegian Crown Prince Olav submitted a new plan meant only to ensure minimum control and supervision of relief in the liberated area, both the Joint Chiefs and the Combined Chiefs agreed to it on April 24. Their agreement had little importance, as the German forces capitulated on May 8. From the military point of view the important question was how to beat the Germans as rapidly as possible, not how to limit Soviet influence in northern Norway which could certainly be seen as one aspect of the Norwegian proposal.[13]

The feeling on the part of American military leaders that it was their job to ensure the quickest possible defeat of Germany, and not to establish a political edge in future dealings with the Soviet Union, was also illustrated by their refusal to back Churchill's plans for thrusts toward prestige objectives like Berlin and Prague. The State Department, after some hesitation, supported the proposal to reach for Prague. President Truman favored the prime responsibility of the local commander, especially when General Eisenhower had the support of the Joint Chiefs. Roosevelt had reached the same conclusion in the case of Berlin. This meant that no effort would be made to beat the Red Army to these two capitals.[14]

The military leadership was not immune to political considerations. This showed most clearly where less conflict existed between what was militarily sound and what was politically preferable than had been the case over Berlin-Prague. The liberation of Denmark was to prove this point. Then the Western Allies were apparently influenced by political considerations related to the Soviet Union. Eisenhower told President Truman that when he pushed on toward Lübeck as rapidly as he did, one of the main considerations was his fear that "the Russians might arrive in the Danish peninsula before we could fight our way across the Elbe."[15]

With the exception of Bornholm, all of Denmark was in the end liberated by the Western Allies. The liberation of Bornholm illustrated some of the same limitations in U.S.-British policies as could be seen in northern Norway. Since the island was situated east of the East-West line of division in Germany, it was seen as being of special importance to the Soviet Union. When Eisenhower on May 8 finally made a move to fill the military vacuum there and asked the Soviets whether this would conflict with their plans, they simply replied that the island was being taken over by the Red Army.[16]

During the war the influence of the State Department was quite limited in most Scandinavian questions. In military matters only the Joint Chiefs of Staff could speak with authority. In addition, Scandinavia was clearly regarded as being of more interest to Britain than to the United States. The American military would follow the lead of their British counterparts while the State Department would quite often follow the Foreign Office. Scandinavia was a part of Western Europe where Britain's strategic, political, and economic interests were considerably greater than those of the United States.

As a matter of fact, Washington generally assumed that Britain would play a more important role than the United States in the whole of Western Europe. This was clearly noted by the State Department before the Potsdam Conference in an important briefing paper on the question of a

Western European bloc. Despite its general opposition to spheres of influence, the Department would not go directly against a British lead in Western Europe.[17]

With the withdrawal of American forces from Western Europe, it was foreseen that Washington's influence would be significantly reduced. While the United States would undoubtedly continue to exercise influence in occupied countries such as Germany, Austria and Italy, its role in Allied countries would be much smaller. For despite all Allied forces in the West being subordinated to Eisenhower's Supreme Headquarters Allied Expeditionary Force (SHAEF), and despite American participation in the planning for Denmark's and Norway's liberation, the British were the senior partners. British officers held most of the important positions in the planning process and the greater part of the forces used in Norway and Denmark were British.[18] These facts delineated the early postwar roles of Washington and London in Scandinavia.

The Truman administration therefore played a minor role in matters concerning Scandinavia in the transition from war to peace. Nevertheless, although there are few indications of an active American interest in Scandinavian affairs, this part of Western Europe was not entirely neglected. In the first months after his sudden inauguration President Truman received daily information bulletins from the State Department. These bulletins give a good picture of what the department considered important at this time.

The few items related to Scandinavia brought to Truman's attention, with the exception of those about the German surrender, concerned Soviet moves in the area. On May 11 the President was informed that Soviet troops had landed on the Danish island of Bornholm two days earlier. The bulletin went on to state that the British Foreign Office believed the situation was worth watching. There was no explicit appraisal from the State Department itself. A week later the President received new reports about the Soviet troops on Bornholm. The Soviets were increasing their forces and fears had been expressed that the Red Army might remain on the island for political purposes.[19] Again, there was no explicit evaluation of the situation from the State Department.

The other area brought to the President's attention was the northern part of Norway. On June 7 Truman was informed that Russian officers had arrived in Tromsø, a main city in northern Norway and outside the area liberated by the Red Army. Since SHAEF had not been notified, the Western Allied command had decided to restrict the movement of the officers in question.[20]

It was obviously feared that the arrival of the officers represented a move to strengthen the Soviet position in northern Norway. As a result British General Andrew Thorne, who was in charge of the Allied forces in Norway, decided to show a more active interest in that part of Norway. Naval ships and even some British troops were dispatched to Narvik and Tromsø.

The dispatch of British troops represented an important modification of the policy of SHAEF that only Norwegian forces were to be used in northern Norway. In great part this had been decided to avoid any conflict with the Soviet Union. An active Western policy might only stimulate Soviet interest in the North. Moscow had nothing against Norwegian forces being used in this sensitive area, but had given indications that it was unfavorably disposed to a British-American presence. Two civil affairs officers who had gone into Finnmark with the Norwegian forces had been forced to return due to alleged difficulties in obtaining a permit to work in the Soviet operational zone.[21]

The Soviet Union also made a rather weak effort to obtain a voice in the Allied military government in Norway. In mid-June a Soviet colonel reported to the Allied headquarters in Oslo indicating that he was the forerunner of a group that wanted to be attached to the military command in Norway. Eisenhower instructed his representatives that no official relationship was to be established with the Soviet colonel and that his movements were to be restricted to the Oslo area. The Soviet General Staff did not press this matter at all and U.S.-British requests for information led to the response that the matter was being investigated. On the Western side only military authorities seem to have been involved. There is no indication that the Soviet feelers for a role in the occupation of Norway had any impact on evaluations within the State Department, if indeed they were known there at all.[22]

Washington continued to focus on the political implications of the Soviet presence in eastern Finnmark. The first comprehensive report on the situation in Norway worked out by the Northern European Division within the State Department dealt, among other matters, with the question of the Soviet forces. The Division alluded to fear and uneasiness felt by many Norwegians about Soviet intentions in the North. The May 1945 report then went on to state that "it is quite possible that as a minimum concession they [the Soviets] will request free port privileges at Kirkenes and the right to construct a railroad to Petsamo." From this perspective the Soviet announcement in September 1945 that the Red Army would withdraw without any quid pro quo and before the troops of the Western Allies had completed their withdrawal, was certainly welcomed by the embassy in Oslo as well as by the State Department in Washington.[23]

The Red Army took longer in withdrawing from Bornholm. While relations between the Soviet forces and Bornholm authorities remained cordial, the Danish government gradually became uneasy about the Soviet presence. The State Department made little attempt to influence the Danes in the direction of pushing for a Soviet withdrawal. Although it certainly wanted to be kept informed about Danish-Soviet negotiations, the department wanted even this to be accomplished in such a way that it would not be interpreted as U.S. intervention. Moscow insisted that the Soviet stay was only temporary and in March–April 1946 the Red Army withdrew from Bornholm.[24] No Soviet troops remained in Scandinavia.

After the Soviet withdrawal the War Department wanted to send American personnel to the island, apparently for the purpose of examining what the Red Army had been doing there. This was refused by the Danish government, which obviously feared that an American presence would only serve to increase the possibility of a Soviet return. In July 1946 Copenhagen's noncooperative attitude was even brought to Truman's attention when the War Department prepared a general report for the President on the Soviet attitude in those places where the U.S. Army was in direct contact with the Soviets.[25] Yet, this was not a sign of increased American interest in Scandinavia. Quite the contrary, with the Red Army out of the region, there was little need to pay attention to its affairs at all.

Washington and Scandinavian Bridge Building

After the defeat of the Germans, it became the policy of the Scandinavian countries to avoid alignments with political blocs and military alliances.[26] The word neutrality was avoided, particularly in Norway and Denmark, but in some ways the policies of the Scandinavians came to resemble just that.

This did not mean that the three countries had equally close relations with all the Great Powers. Norway and Denmark especially, but also Sweden, felt much closer to Britain and in part to the United States than to the Soviet Union. This showed in their economic and cultural contacts as well as in their voting behavior in forums such as the UN. In the case of Norway and Denmark there was considerable military cooperation with Britain. They received most of their military equipment from Britain and Norwegian and Danish officers were to a large extent trained by British personnel.

At the same time, it was important for the three countries to preserve a good relationship with the Soviet Union. The press was encouraged to avoid criticism of the Soviets. In some controversial cases at the UN the Norwegians, like the Swedes and the Danes, abstained. Attempts were made to strengthen economic and cultural contacts with the Soviet Union and Eastern Europe. As a result, relations between the Scandinavians and the Soviet Union were generally satisfactory, at least until the beginning of 1947.

The position of the Scandinavian countries may thus be

described as somewhat in the middle in the growing confrontation between East and West. All three states were definitely closer to the West than to the East, but they were not firmly committed to any Western side. Therefore, as an indication of Washington's attitude to various middle positions in the cold war, it might be interesting to examine the American reaction to these Scandinavian policies.

Neither revisionists nor traditionalists have dealt with the question of Washington's reaction to the so-called bridge-building policies of the Scandinavians. From their general perspective, it may be assumed that traditionalists would generally regard such policies as being in fairly good harmony with Washington's own attitude. Many traditionalists see the United States itself as a moderator of Soviet and British policies, standing closer to the British but still somewhere in the middle trying to protect world cooperation and national independence against the balance-of-power schemes of older and, presumably, more evil powers. Even a moderate traditionalist like McNeill writes of the Americans that "they felt no direct responsibility for European affairs except in Germany, and if their offer failed to satisfy the Powers most directly concerned, there was little an honest broker could do but retire gracefully." [27]

On the revisionist side the implication is that the United States would be skeptical or directly hostile to anything less than full support for its policies. From their perspective of the United States being firmly anti-Soviet at least from the end of the war, revisionists generally consider it a myth that the United States tried to mediate between the Soviet Union and Britain. [28]

With the Red Army out of Scandinavia, the affairs of the region were dealt with almost exclusively by the regional specialists in the State Department and by the personnel of the local American embassies. The number of such persons had increased greatly as compared to the prewar period. In 1944 six regional divisions had been created in the State Department under the Office of European Affairs. One of these was the Division of Northern European Affairs. From 1944 through 1947 this rather small division was led by a chief (Hugh S. Cumming, Jr.) and two assistant chiefs. After Cumming became second in command in the embassy in Stockholm in July 1947, Benjamin Hulley became the new chief, in November of that year.

In July 1939 the legation staffs in Copenhagen, Oslo, and Stockholm had numbered respectively ten, nine, and eleven officials. In October 1945 the corresponding figures were twelve, twenty, and thirty-six. Because the legation in Stockholm had grown so much during the war, it experienced a decline in numbers in the first years after the war. But by July 1949 the staff numbered thirty-eight officials. The growth in personnel in the embassies in Oslo and especially in Copenhagen was impressive even in the years 1945 through 1949. In July 1949 they totaled twenty-four each. (The legations in Stockholm and Copenhagen became embassies in 1947. The United States and Norway had exchanged ambassadors, as opposed to ministers, from 1942 on.) While the increase in personnel in Scandinavia from 1939 to 1945 was much greater than for the foreign service as a whole, that from 1945 to 1949 was rather smaller than the general increase.[29]

The growth in personnel did to some extent reflect a more ambitious policy on the part of the United States. Washington's role would certainly be different from what it had been before the war. However, the scale of U.S. ambitions in the Scandinavian region in the first postwar years may very easily be exaggerated.

The American attitude to the three northern countries in 1945–46 is most easily studied by comparing the Policy and Information Statements worked out by the State Department in August–September 1946. In the one on Norway, the Department noted that Norway had made intensive efforts to establish closer ties with the Soviet Union. "As a result, Norway possesses better relations with the Soviet Union than either of the other Scandinavian states." The Department in one context even stated that "Norway will probably continue to follow an ostensibly pro-Soviet line."[30]

Despite the emphasis on Norway trying to maintain close relations with the Soviet Union, Washington did not express any dislike of this policy. The State Department understood that beneath the surface of cordiality toward the Soviet Union the Norwegian government in many ways leaned toward the West. Norway's close relations with Britain were underscored, although an alleged reduction in the number of troops sent to participate in the policing of the British zone in Germany was felt to be the result of the Norwegian policy of always keeping "an eye toward the East."

At heart the Norwegians were regarded as leaning toward the West. This was well summed up in the Policy and Information Statement: "Norway has adopted a foreign policy which may be described as being pro-US and UK to the greatest extent it dares, pro-Soviet to the extent it must, and pro-UN to the greatest extent it can."[31] It was evident from this analysis that the regional specialists in the State Department not only had considerable understanding of the main features of the Norwegian policy, they also had some sympathy with it.

The State Department's analysis was in line with the view of the American embassy in Oslo. This was to be expected since the department had relied on the embassy for its information about Norway. On April 11, 1947, the embassy completed a long account of conditions in Norway in the last year. The general tone was the same as it had been in the Policy and Information Statement. To a considerable extent Ambassador Bay, who had taken over after Osborne in July 1946, identified himself with Norwegian policies. However, to make such an identification possible he somewhat exaggerated the Western and American orientation of the Norwegians. The ambassador noted that "Norway instinctively affiliates itself with the West but is determined not to offend the East." Norway's relations with the United States were described as following "their natural friendly course."[32] Since the policies of Norway were regarded as the closest to Moscow while still being acceptable to the U.S., it was to be expected that Washington had no basic disagreement with the policies of Denmark and Sweden.

This was indeed the case. Few problems existed between Denmark and the United States. The most important one concerned the status of Greenland, which will be discussed later. Another was Denmark's desire to get rid of its 200,000 German refugees. These disagreements could not prevent the regional specialists in the State Department from concluding that "relations between the United States and Denmark are basically sound." As in the case of Norway, it was pointed out that Denmark had particularly close relations with the British.[33]

Even with regard to Sweden it was stressed that "Sweden's natural orientation is toward the West, particularly toward the United Kingdom."[34] This affinity to Britain was seen to arise from a common democratic tradition, from both countries being ruled by social democrats, and from a substantial trade. The fact that the Soviet Union had absorbed the Baltic States and that Finland to a large extent fell inside the Soviet orbit had led the Swedes to make strong efforts to improve relations with the USSR. On the other hand, the Policy and Information Statement went on to point out that "This policy [toward Moscow] will not be blindly followed, however, for Sweden is cognizant of the danger of too intimate a relationship with the Soviet Union."[35]

In its relations with the various European countries, Washington put considerable emphasis on where a country naturally felt it belonged. If "the heart" of a government was felt to lie on the right side, American policy makers were ready to accept the fact that a country developed close relations with Moscow.[36] The Scandinavian countries had their hearts on the right side. Their proximity to the Soviet Union made their genial relationship with the Soviets understandable.

There can be little doubt that the United States accepted the basic features of the foreign policies of the Scandinavian countries. Yet an equally important part of the American attitude was the limited interest shown in this part of Western Europe. Scandinavian matters were left largely to the local American embassies and the regional specialists in the State Department. For example, the embassy in Oslo was never led to believe that there was any great interest in Washington in what was going on in Norway. The only exception, as we shall see, was in matters concerning Spitsbergen. Aside from that, the embassy in Oslo did not receive any instructions. from the State Department on foreign policy issues in the entire period from 1945 to early 1947. The situation was basically the same with regard to Sweden and, with the exception of the Greenland issue, Denmark.

The established practice of the British having the initiative in dealings with the Scandinavian countries continued in 1946, although the United States was gradually coming to play a somewhat larger role. In January 1946 London brought up with Washington the status of the entrances to the Baltic Sea. This was done in response to Molotov's interest in the topic at the Council of Foreign Ministers meeting in Moscow in December. The British evidently feared that the Soviets would try to change the present status of these entrances, of the Sound and the Belts. Such an attempt could be made from a position of some strength as long as the Red Army remained on Bornholm.

On February 6 the British reminded the State Department of the aide-mémoire they had sent Washington on January 14. The Americans replied on February 28. Byrnes saw little urgency in the question since he did not think the Red Army would withdraw from Bornholm even if the status of the Baltic entrances was resolved. Yet, he did show more sympathy for Soviet desires than did Bevin. Both wanted to maintain the right of free passage for all ships in time of war as well as peace, but Byrnes also favored the explicit neutralization of the Sound and the Belts.[37]

When the Foreign Office replied in June, the Russians had left Bornholm. The British did not want to include any reference to neutralization in a declaration and saw no objection to Swedish and Danish fortifications on their respective sides of the Sound. Further illustrating the British lead in this question, the State Department replied one month later that it was in general agreement with the position of the Foreign Office.[38]

Since the Soviets had left Bornholm and Moscow showed no inclination to bring the question up again, the matter lost its urgency. The United States and Britain did not want to bring it up on their own.

The American and British governments were both ready to extend military support to the three Scandinavian countries. But, again, the United States expected the British to take the lead in these matters. As Norway and Denmark had close relations with Britain in the military field, the State-War-Navy Coordinating Committee observed in a March 1946 study that although the United States wanted a strong Scandinavia "it is expected that these countries will receive outside support of military supplies from the United Kingdom." If, however, requests were received by the United States, these would be reviewed with sympathy. The committee stated that this would in particular be the case with requests for commercial and trainer-type aircraft. In addition, the Danes should be supplied with naval equipment for use in Greenland, "as it would aid our negotiations for rights in that area."[39]

It was no obvious matter that the United States would be ready to supply the Scandinavians with limited quantities of military equipment. The list of countries in Europe not eligible for such assistance was fairly long: Poland, Rumania, Bulgaria, Yugoslavia, Austria, Hungary, Albania, Spain, Finland, Switzerland, Germany, and generally also the Soviet Union and Czechoslovakia. Military aid would only be given to Portugal to the extent that such assistance might help in negotiations for U.S. base rights on the Azores. Considerable reluctance could be found even in the case of the Netherlands, because of Dutch policies in Indonesia.[40]

Although the quantities actually sold to the Scandinavians were small, these supplies might be seen as indicative of the generally friendly relations between the United States and the Scandinavian countries. To Norway the United States was willing to sell, among other things, various surplus naval ships. U.S. regulations stated that these generally be sold in a demilitarized state, even if the ships could easily be rearmed afterward. The State and War departments stuck to this rule, despite arguments on the

lower military-political level that "we consider in this connection Norway's close proximity to Russia and that we
might find it advisable to stretch a point here to keep the
Norwegian democracy friendly to us by equipping the Norwegians with American armed vessels."[41] It was another
matter that the Norwegian government was not always satisfied with the price offered by the United States and therefore acted slowly on American offers.[42]

Due to the protracted nature of the negotiations and the
many agencies involved on the American side, it is not easy
to determine exactly what quantities of supplies the three
countries received. The Danes were able to buy at least ten
motor torpedo boats of German origin which had been
awarded to the United States after the war. They also ac-
quired several trainer planes in addition to considerable
quantities of surplus ammunition.[43]

Apparently, Washington sold more military equipment
to Sweden than to Norway and Denmark. The most important transaction between the United States and Sweden concerned the sale of Mustang aircraft. In April 1945 the United
States had sold fifty of these planes to Sweden. In March
1946 the Swedes wanted to buy up to one hundred more. The
State Department had no objections from a political point of
view. In fact, Acting Director of the Office of European Affairs John D. Hickerson, who in the fall of 1947 would be
among the earliest and strongest critics of Scandinavian
foreign policy, argued that "in view of our extremely cordial
relations with Sweden, our interest in the continuance of the
Social Democratic type of government now existent there
because of its pacific influence in Europe, and the fact that
the planes would not be used for aggressive purposes . . . favorable consideration be given to their sale."[44]

One argument against the sale of the planes was that
Scandinavia was an area of special interest to Britain, so
London, and not Washington, should take care of military
deliveries. The Division of Northern European Affairs, however, noted that this argument should no longer have such
binding force in view of a newly discovered British interest
in selling military equipment to Latin America. This point,

which prevailed within the department, illustrated that the United States was certainly not always committed to following the British lead. In addition, the Swedes had requested these specific planes from the United States while they had asked for, and received, a large number of other planes from Britain.[45]

For a while it appeared that there would be no further sale of American aircraft. The reason was not dissatisfaction with Swedish policies, but the fact that such a sale would be contrary to Senate regulations on the disposal of surplus tactical aircraft. The State Department itself had earlier assured Congress that there would be no such sales except to a few specifically mentioned countries.[46]

Yet, after endless confusion the sale was completed. It was important for this decision that the American authorities in Europe who handled surplus property had in fact signed a contract with Sweden without consulting the State Department. If the sale was not completed, the Swedish government threatened to take legal action against the U.S., action which in all likelihood would be successful.[47] But, as we have seen, the State Department had also taken a strong political interest in the sale. It only felt that it could hardly proceed against the expressed attitude of the Senate. Even the War Department intervened in favor of the Swedes. In a letter of July 24 to the Secretary of State, Secretary of War Patterson argued that the sale "would tend to reaffirm the friendly attitude of this government toward the government of Sweden and would serve to continue the hitherto harmonious relations between the two countries." Probably equally important, the War Department felt that a refusal would jeopardize a joint mapping project of Sweden which the United States and Sweden were carrying out at this time.[48] For these reasons the sale of ninety Mustangs was completed. Not only that, the Swedes had also been able to buy one hundred surplus trainers from the United States. In part this sale had been completed to mollify the Swedish government after the initial refusal to sell the Mustangs.[49]

While the British could handle most military requests from Norway and Denmark, London's ability to take care of their financial needs was more limited. In that field Norway and Denmark had to turn to the United States and, even more, to Sweden. The Swedes were not only more self-sufficient in armaments, but their strong economic position also made it possible for them to furnish their Scandinavian friends with large and reasonable loans.[50] In the period from July 1, 1945, to December 31, 1947, Norway received $92 million, Denmark $30 million, and Sweden only $1 million from the United States. (These figures include loans and property credits as well as relief and other grants.)[51]

In chapter 1 we have seen how American lending policies came to be strongly influenced by political considerations related to the conflict with the Soviet Union long before the launching of the Marshall Plan. To some extent the loans to Scandinavia can be tied to this general picture. Just the fact that money was granted is of some importance. Not all countries in Eastern Europe received any assistance from the United States. It is also true that of the countries in Eastern Europe only Finland and the Soviet Union received more than did Norway.[52] (The assistance to the Soviet Union was in the form of pipeline deliveries from lend-lease. It would have harmed U.S. interests if these deliveries had been canceled. Finland was a special case, clearly different from other countries in Eastern Europe.) Norway thus received more than did, for instance, Poland and Czechoslovakia. And this was so despite the fact that the latter two countries were more interested in U.S. credits than were the Norwegians.

Nevertheless, the amounts granted to the Scandinavians were so small that too much should not be made of them. Once the political orientation of a country was basically acceptable from the American point of view, economic criteria were usually more important than political ones when Washington decided upon the exact amount to be extended.

Sweden's position was such that for long it did not need foreign assistance. The Danes were also somewhat reticent in pressing their needs in Washington. They apparently feared that they would lack dollar exchange to service U.S.

credits. This was in turn connected with the relatively poor prospects for substantial Danish exports to the United States. On one occasion Denmark did not accept a surplus property credit it was offered.[53]

Even the Norwegians, who got the most, held back in seeking financial assistance from the United States. As of December 31, 1947, a substantial part of a $50 million credit which had been granted by the Export-Import Bank in 1946 was still unused.[54] Although the terms of the credit were generally acceptable, there was one important exception. That was the shipping proviso.

In line with similar agreements with other countries, the United States insisted that goods bought under this credit be shipped on U.S. ships. This was most objectionable to the Norwegians, who themselves had one of the largest merchant fleets in the world. In fact, in 1946 the Communists and most of the nonsocialist members of the Storting (Parliament) voted against the loan, even after the government had agreed to a provision stating that the matter would be put before the Storting again before the government could draw on the credit.[55]

The State Department was opposed to the shipping clause. It was too obvious a break with the free trading principles the United States preached in most other respects. Under Secretary Clayton tried to intervene in favor of the Norwegians. Various domestic interests promoted through the Maritime Commission insisted, however, that the clause be maintained.[56] The State Department's attempt to have the shipping proviso removed from the loan was rejected. Yet, it is likely that the attitude of the State Department was of importance when Washington later decided that not all, but 50 percent of the goods had to be carried in American bottoms.

We can see from these examples that the United States was coming to play an increasingly stronger role in Scandinavia, especially in the field of economic assistance. But there can be no doubt that Britain was holding the lead in relations with the Scandinavian countries. All the three countries had a closer relationship with London than with Washington. However, to a great extent American-British objectives toward Scandinavia were similar in nature.

The most important common goal for the two Western Powers was the prevention of Soviet control over Scandinavia. As early as May 1945, Secretary of War Stimson had told Truman that it was vital for the United States to prevent certain countries "to be driven to revolution or communism." Stimson was most concerned about unrest caused by adverse economic conditions or even famine. The countries specifically mentioned by the Secretary were France, Luxembourg, Belgium, Holland, Denmark, Norway, and Italy.[57] (This list was probably not meant to be conclusive.)

Even if the threat of famine passed, the objective of preventing any strong Soviet influence remained. In 1946 some interesting analyses were made of the way in which the United States should combat Moscow's attempts to strengthen its position in the region. The most remarkable one was a top-secret memorandum from Ambassador Osborne in Oslo to Under Secretary Acheson dated January 25, 1946. Osborne's memorandum in some ways resembled Kennan's famous Long Telegram of February 22 and really dealt more with U.S. policies toward the Soviet Union than toward Norway and Scandinavia. The "ideological struggle now taking place in Norway" was going on in most other countries as well, and the ambassador's suggestions for winning this struggle were of a rather general nature. He proposed that Washington strengthen its information services considerably and also that it step up its gathering of intelligence both on the Soviet Union and on local communists. In both respects he considered Norway's position of importance.[58]

Acheson forwarded Osborne's recommendations to the intelligence community. Few changes seem to have resulted in 1946–47. (From 1948–49 the Embassy became more active, but in other directions than Osborne had primarily favored. CIA activities then focused on the planning of a stay-behind network in case of a Soviet invasion. Implementation of these plans was significantly stepped up from 1950–51.)[59]

It could perhaps be expected that analyses along Osborne's lines would lead to recommendations that efforts be made to have the Scandinavians modify their policies. This does not seem to have been the case. Osborne offered little criticism of Norway's attitude except that its defenses were much too weak. He considered Norway a firmly democratic country with strong leanings toward the West. His suggestions were primarily meant to counteract Soviet steps to move the Norwegians away from these leanings.[60]

A study prepared in the Northern European Division in July 1946 described the Soviet policy toward Scandinavia as

> designed to strengthen its relations with the countries in that area, to increase their economic dependence on the USSR and thereby make them less likely to oppose Soviet proposals in the United Nations, to weaken the influence of the Western Powers in Scandinavia, particularly that of the UK, and to prevent the establishment of a close political relationship among Norway, Denmark and Sweden which might lead to the creation of a northern bloc.

But again, despite these goals and despite minor Soviet successes in some fields, the division concluded that "the USSR is under no illusion as to its ability to wean Scandinavia away from the West."[61]

From these analyses it was evident that the United States wanted to prevent any significant increase in Soviet influence in Scandinavia. But as long as the danger of any such increase was seen as small, Washington did not make any serious attempt to modify the attitudes of the three countries. American-Scandinavian relations were on the whole regarded as satisfactory. In March 1946 the State-War-Navy Coordinating Committee pointed to the rather obvious fact that "United States policy favors a strong . . . Denmark, Norway and Sweden."[62] A year later, Secretary of State George Marshall emphasized in his report to the Cabinet on the meeting of the Foreign Ministers in Moscow that "We must be very careful to preserve our good relationships with the 'fringe' countries in Europe—Belgium, France, Denmark, Norway, Sweden, Holland, etc., because otherwise Communism can infiltrate into all of them."[63]

The fact that the United States basically accepted the foreign policies of the Scandinavian states did not mean that no criticism whatever was offered. The most important point of complaint in Swedish-American relations concerned the one billion kronor credit the Swedes granted the Soviet Union in 1946. Despite their general lack of interest in Scandinavia, both Joyce and Gabriel Kolko and Lloyd Gardner have in fact noted the American opposition to this credit. Gardner implies that it was connected with U.S. dissatisfaction with "Swedish neutralism in the early Cold War clashes between East and West."[64] But both the Kolkos and Gardner fail to place the American reaction to the credit within the larger picture of Swedish-American relations.

Although American objections came at a time when the United States itself had adopted a firm policy against granting a loan to Moscow, the reaction was apparently related primarily to Washington's fear that the credit would tend to freeze trade in a bilateral pattern based on political considerations as opposed to commercial ones. Opposition to such practices was a basic principle in American policies as expressed in the often emphasized Proposals for Expansion of World Trade and Employment of December 1945. The note to Sweden on the credit stated that Washington's comments did not refer to the extension of external credits by Sweden if the resulting sales were based on commercial considerations.[65]

Despite the obvious possibility that the reference to economic considerations was only a cover for East-West sentiments, it is a fact that Washington expressed its dislike in very mild terms. The note was weakly worded. Swedish politicians and officials who have written about the Soviet loan do not even mention the American attitude.[66] Furthermore, Washington's policy at this time on military and economic assistance to Sweden illustrates that its objections to the credit were not really indicative of the climate in American-Swedish relations in general.

Something needs to be said about those elements in the foreign policy of Norway that were not to the liking of Washington, despite the overall friendliness in American-Norwegian relations. The State Department was not satisfied with all sides of Norway's handling of the Soviet request for a stronger position on Spitsbergen. The active Norwegian policy against Franco's Spain was seen in the light of largely communist-inspired agitation. Neither of these questions caused any great stir, however. Washington maintained a low profile in the Spitsbergen matter, and with regard to Spain did not question the principle of opposition to Franco, but only the lengths to which the Norwegians carried their opposition. The United States had no ambassador in Spain at this time and President Truman in particular held strongly negative opinions about Franco.[67]

Important Republican Senator Vandenberg criticized Norwegian foreign policies on at least two occasions in 1946. With partial support from that other prominent Republican foreign policy spokesman, John Foster Dulles, he was against supporting Norwegian Foreign Minister Trygve Lie's candidacy for Secretary General of the United Nations. Vandenberg considered Norway too much influenced by the Soviet Union to allow a Norwegian to be entrusted with such a post. At the Paris Peace Conference in October 1946 Vandenberg again attacked Norway. Now he was not satisfied with the voting behavior of the Norwegian delegation.[68]

On the first of these occasions it is evident that the senator did not have the support of the State Department. After the candidacy of Lester Pearson of Canada had floundered, the United States came to support Lie as Secretary General.[69] In discussions within the American delegation at the UN, Charles Bohlen in particular argued against Vandenberg's impression that Norway could be considered as falling within the Soviet orbit. Neither did Bohlen, Special Assistant to the Secretary of State, share Vandenberg's fear that the Soviet Union could come to take direct action against Norway. Although I have not found any source which can throw light on the extent to which the State Department supported Vandenberg's criticism in October, it is a fact that the Norwegians were not voting as closely with the United States and Britain at the Paris Conference as did other Western European countries.[70]

It is not the purpose of this book to analyze British attitudes toward Scandinavia. It should be noted, however, that the British did not actively support Foreign Minister Lie either for the post as Secretary General or as Chairman of the First General Assembly. (The Soviet Union supported Lie on both occasions.) There may have been many reasons given for this, but it seems likely that some degree of dissatisfaction with Norway's foreign policy contributed to the British stand. On several occasions British embassy officials in Oslo complained about the hesitant nature of Norwegian foreign policy. The Gerhardsen government was seen as too afraid of Soviet reactions.[71] The British were also dissatisfied that the Norwegian armed forces were not cooperating even more closely with the British than they actually were.[72]

At least in the case of Norway, it therefore seems likely that the Americans held more positive attitudes toward its foreign policy than did the British. Although no studies have been made of British policies toward Denmark and Sweden, a similar situation may have prevailed with regard to those countries as well. For example, at this time British-Danish relations were disturbed both by problems in their mutual trade and by London's policies in Schleswig-Holstein.[73]

The United States was in this period willing to accept less than full support from the Scandinavians in the cold war. This would seem to fit in better with a traditionalist interpretation than with a revisionist one which would see the United States as hostile to countries trying to take up positions somewhere in the middle. The traditionalist case would appear to be strengthened by the British having been more critical than the Americans of at least Norwegian foreign policy.

In late August 1945 Ambassador Osborne had had a meeting with the Commanding General of the Norwegian Armed Forces, Otto Ruge. The general voiced his impression that Norway was in the "British zone." He also stated that he did not want Norway to become too dependent on the British and inquired about the attitude of the United States. Ambassador Osborne replied that he thought "the United States from one end to the other had been thoroughly shaken out of any remnants of isolationism; as much perhaps by the atomic bomb as by the war, and that we [the Americans] must take an intense interest in European affairs as a matter of our own self-preservation."[74]

To a considerable extent the ambassador was right in his analysis of the situation in the United States, particularly in relation to America's policies toward the major countries in Europe. However, American policy makers showed little interest in Scandinavia, on the periphery of Western Europe. They generally left the initiative there with the British. In Great Power terms Scandinavia, particularly Norway and Denmark, could well be considered a British sphere. (It is another matter that the British may have felt that the Scandinavians were not following London's lead closely enough.)

There was really little need for Washington to take a close interest in Scandinavia. Not only were the British following objectives which to a large extent were identical to those on the American side, but events in Scandinavia were also flowing in the right direction. The governments in power were seen as friendly toward the West. That fact should not be lost when we conclude that Washington took little exception to the bridge-building policies of the Scandinavian countries. Bridge building was no middle way between East and West. Scandinavia was definitely leaning toward the West. But there is a difference between leaning in this direction and going all out in support of the West. In this early period Washington was satisfied with leanings. The demands for loyalty would soon be stepped up, however.

Bases and the Polar Regions

One element in the policies of the United States which showed the extent to which Washington was ready to take on commitments in different parts of the world long before the Truman Doctrine and the Marshall Plan, was its desire to obtain a network of bases circling the globe. There were several reasons for this desire. Bases were of general importance to the United States as a Great Power which had to be prepared for any eventuality. They were also meant to facilitate communication between the homeland and the many parts of the world where U.S. forces were now found. The main task of these forces was the occupation of Axis countries, in particular Germany and Japan. Gradually, considerations related to the role of the Soviet Union came to represent an important factor in the presentation of U.S. base requirements.

Together with the Azores, Iceland and Greenland were regarded as essential for communications between America and Europe. Greenland and Iceland were of basic importance for the control of the North Atlantic and the approaches to the United States as well. In 1945 the significance of Greenland and Iceland was only to a very limited extent seen in the light of the so-called polar strategy.[75]

While the British were generally favorable to policies which meant a strengthening of the American presence in Europe, they were somewhat critical of U.S. endeavors to negotiate long-term base agreements with Iceland and, particularly, with Portugal. Bevin recognized that in the case of Iceland there was a "need to forestall the Russians." In the case of the Azores no such need was foreseen.[76] Perhaps more to the point, London was afraid that Portugal would continue to gravitate away from its historically close relationship with Britain.

Besides having interests of their own to protect, the British indicated that the American base requirements signified a lack of confidence in the United Nations. Not only that, Bevin argued that these bases "might encourage the Soviet Government to seek base rights in the Dardanelles, Eastern Europe generally and in Scandinavia."[77] Bevin feared that extensive American requests for bases in Western Europe could lead the Soviet Union to present similar claims even in Scandinavia. This line of reasoning could also be found within the State Department. There, however, it was not an argument against bases in such crucial areas as Greenland, Iceland, and the Azores. It was an argument against U.S. bases in Norway and Denmark.

Parts of the American military, in particular Air Force

circles, had taken an interest in bases in almost every European country. Their list of desirable areas not only included Greenland, Iceland, the Azores, and Britain, but also "Finland, Sweden, Holland, Belgium, Greece, Rumania, Yugoslavia, Hungary, Poland and Czechoslovakia." Recognizing that this was beyond the pale of the possible, the military concentrated on four countries on the European continent, France, Italy, Norway, and Denmark (in addition to occupied Germany and Austria). In Norway they wanted a base in the Stavanger area and in Denmark one on the Jutland peninsula. The desired bases were to accommodate one heavy bomber group (2,680 personnel), one service group (700 personnel), one fighter squadron (290 personnel), and, in Stavanger, one depot group (850 personnel).[78]

These bases were, again, related primarily to the responsibilities of the United States in enforcing the terms of surrender against Germany. Any anti-Soviet perspective was clearly of subsidiary interest at this time, the summer of 1945. This was evident from the readiness of the military not only to inform Moscow about the American requirements, but also to invite the Soviet Union and Britain to participate in the negotiations with the respective countries and even to accept similar rights for the Soviet and British Air Forces, if they so desired.[79]

At its meeting on June 2, 1945, the State-War-Navy Coordinating Committee approved the recommendations of the Air Force. The State Department was asked to undertake the necessary negotiations at the earliest time the Secretary of State considered favorable.[80]

However, the State Department leadership did not consider such negotiations at all advisable in the case of Norway and Denmark. At a meeting on June 26 with Secretaries Forrestal and Stimson, Acting Secretary of State Grew argued that while "he had no question as to the desirability of obtaining bases in France and Italy . . . there was real objection in attempting to acquire bases in Norway and Denmark." To request bases in these two countries would open the door for the Soviet Union to do the same. This the Soviets could do from a position of strength since they still

remained in eastern Finnmark and on Bornholm. The State
Department was therefore strongly against obtaining bases
in Scandinavia even for the period of occupation in Europe.[81]
At a meeting of the SWNCC on September 5, the Joint
Chiefs of Staff were asked to reconsider the necessity for
bases in Norway and Denmark in light of the comments of
the State Department.

Grew's arguments were supported by the embassy in
Norway, which evidently only came to know about the interest in bases from a visiting U.S. general. In addition, Ambassador Osborne felt that it was in no way certain that the
Norwegians would agree to American bases on their territory.[82] After further study, even the military in Germany,
which at first had supported the planned request, backed
down and argued that bases in Britain, France, and Italy
would suffice.[83]

After the reaction of the State Department, the embassy
in Norway, and the headquarters of the American forces in
Europe, there could not be much doubt about the outcome.
At the end of October the Joint Chiefs informed the State
Department that they had concluded that the bases in Norway and Denmark were not absolutely necessary for the U.S.
occupation forces. That settled the matter as far as those two
countries went. In the end the military did not even secure
such bases in France.[84]

Bevin and Grew had not specified where in Scandinavia
they thought the Soviets might press for base rights. However, after the withdrawal of the Red Army from Bornholm
and northern Norway, one particular place was in focus.
That was Spitsbergen. As a matter of fact, Spitsbergen was
the only place in Scandinavia where the Russians actually
pressed for such rights. In November 1944 Molotov had proposed to Lie that Bear Island be ceded to the Soviet Union
and that Spitsbergen become a Soviet-Norwegian con-
dominium with joint bases on the island.[85]

In the first two years after the liberation, no question
related to Norway was of greater interest to American policy
makers than the status of Spitsbergen. In January 1945
Crown Prince Olav had informed Roosevelt about the Soviet

proposals. Roosevelt in turn may have told Secretary of State Stettinius about them. If Stettinius was informed, he must have told few or no others in the department because when Ambassador Osborne was briefed by Lie in July and reported back to the department, his information came as a surprise to Washington.[86] At this time Roosevelt and Stettinius had been replaced by Truman and Byrnes.

Osborne's information and the possibility that the Soviet proposals might be brought up at the Potsdam Conference put pressure to formulate an American policy on the departments involved. The State, War, and Navy departments obviously preferred that the Norwegian government turn down the Soviet request. Washington desired that Norwegian sovereignty and the demilitarized status of Spitsbergen be preserved. The SWNCC also noted that according to the Spitsbergen Treaty of 1920 this was not a question which the Soviet Union and Norway could decide on their own. The other signatory powers, including the United States, had to agree to any change.[87]

So far the American attitude was what one would have expected. The Acting Chairman of the State-War-Navy Coordinating Committee, Hickerson, did point out, however, that "The interest of the Soviet Union in acquiring military bases in the Spitsbergen Archipelago is natural in view of the experiences gained in the war respecting the safeguarding of convoys to Murmansk."[88] This seemed to indicate that Washington did not intend to press its views very firmly, and in fact, Washington didn't. It was up to the military to decide on the strategic implications of concessions made in favor of the Soviets. The Joint Chiefs did not favor any firmer attitude than that which Hickerson represented.

The one who was willing to go furthest in meeting Soviet desires was the President's Chief of Staff, Admiral Leahy. At a Joint Chiefs of Staff meeting during the Potsdam Conference, he stated that "it was difficult for him to see that there were any military implications in the acquisition by Russia of bases in Bear Island and the Spitsbergen Archipelago." If the Soviets brought up the question, Leahy just wanted to inform the Russians that the United States intended to acquire bases in Iceland and Greenland. Two of the three members of a subcommittee of the Joint Chiefs favored a wording which simply declared that "The United States had no important military interest in the Spitsbergen Archipelago," and Secretary of State Byrnes had a similar attitude. Like Leahy and the JCS subcommittee, he was far more concerned about Iceland and Greenland than about Spitsbergen. He preferred that the Russian proposals be dealt with in the peace treaties, "but if the Russians brought the question up now our reply should include United States demands for bases [presumably on Iceland and Greenland]."[89]

In the end the American position was strengthened somewhat compared to what these comments might seem to indicate. Some of the military argued that the Soviet desires were not only unnecessary for Soviet security, but "contrary to long-range and overall security considerations from our point of view." In part this related to Spitsbergen's possible future importance as a staging point for commercial and military aviation flying arctic routes.[90] More important than this polar aspect, however, was a general feeling that "until the post-war situation and Soviet policy can be seen more clearly, we should, in so far as practicable, resist demands and policies which tend to improve Soviet position in Western Europe." Even those who felt Spitsbergen had little or no strategic importance could hardly agree to the Soviet Union and Norway disposing of this matter on their own. The State Department in particular had to be unfavorable to any such move which would be contrary to the Spitsbergen Treaty.[91]

Therefore, the State, War, and Navy departments agreed that in principle the United States should oppose the Soviet demands. Nevertheless, the readymade fallback position of the three departments made it obvious that Washington would not make much of this opposition:

> If it is not practicable to successfully oppose the Soviet proposals, then we should insist that the Soviets in return agree to the following:
> a. No objection to the United States obtaining exclusive base rights in Iceland.

b. Remove all Soviet troops from and renounce military control of Northern Norway.

c. Make no bids for Jan Mayen Island.

d. Agree that Norwegian coal and economic rights in Spitsbergen be preserved.[92]

The Americans would also insist on bases on Greenland. Since Greenland was seen as falling within the scope of the Monroe Doctrine, it was judged neither necessary nor desirable to obtain any Soviet consent to these bases.[93]

The obvious conclusion is that the United States was not interested in having a conflict with the Soviet Union over Spitsbergen. If the Soviets insisted on their desires, Washington was not unwilling to make a deal: American bases on Iceland and Greenland in exchange for Soviet bases on Spitsbergen. In addition the sovereignty of Norway proper had to be safeguarded. For a while the State Department evidently feared that it would have to make a choice between Soviet bases on Spitsbergen and on the Norwegian mainland.[94]

This came to be the position in 1945–46. The Norwegian Foreign Office also interpreted the American policy along these lines. The United States did not come to sharpen Norwegian opposition to the Soviet proposals. In April 1945 the Norwegians had gone quite far in meeting Russian desires. But no agreement had been concluded and Moscow seemed to be in no hurry.[95]

In 1946 few new developments took place relating to the Spitsbergen question. The State Department did, however, indicate to the Norwegians in slightly more explicit terms than before that the Soviet Union and Norway could not on their own change the Spitsbergen Treaty. Washington was also putting more emphasis on being informed about what was actually going on in this matter between Oslo and Moscow.[96]

If the United States had to make a choice between bases on Iceland and Greenland and the prevention of Soviet bases on Spitsbergen, the result was not in question. Priority had to be given to crucial Iceland and Greenland. In that respect the American policy toward Spitsbergen came to resemble the attitude toward Eastern Europe. In order to protect its interests in a crucial region—Western Europe—Washington had to make concessions in a region of subsidiary importance —Eastern Europe.

There was never any question of abandoning the base requirements on Iceland and Greenland. An agreement, which was not very satisfactory to Washington, was finally worked out with Iceland in October 1946. U.S. troops were to leave the island and Icelandic authorities were to control the Keflavik base. The Americans were only permitted to keep some 600 specialists at the base for the purpose of servicing airplanes en route to bases in Germany. Even these rights were temporary, for a minimum of six-and-one-half years.[97]

With regard to Greenland no definite date had been set for the United States to give up its wartime bases. Washington was therefore able to proceed at a leisurely pace in this case. Nor were the Danes in any great hurry, making few moves to get the Americans out of Greenland. What moves they made seemed largely determined by domestic considerations and by attempts to secure advantages in Danish-German questions.[98]

The best solution from Washington's point of view was simply to buy Greenland from Denmark, but this was out of the question for the Danish government. As a minimum the United States insisted upon an agreement which would give it long-term rights to construct and maintain military facilities in several parts of Greenland.[99]

Talks between Byrnes and Foreign Minister Rasmussen in December 1946 produced no results. The fact that the State Department was still concerned about the connection between Greenland and Spitsbergen was illustrated in the Secretary's instructions to Ambassador Marvel in Copenhagen on January 2, 1947. Byrnes told the ambassador to suggest to the Danes that they might wish to defer taking any steps "until after Soviet-Norwegian negotiations re Spitsbergen materialize or at least until the possibility of such negotiations become public."[100] The Russians were not to be given any excuse to resurrect the Spitsbergen question. But if they did, then Washington would like to bring up Greenland.

Another way in which the State Department tried to strengthen its influence in the Spitsbergen question related to the Jan Mayen Island. During the war the United States had obtained the right to operate a direction finder on the island. In January 1945, the Norwegians proposed that the Americans withdraw as soon as the war was over, in accordance with the original agreement. In March the State and Navy departments responded that they would comply with the Norwegian request.[101] But when the State Department became aware of the Russian desires with regard to Spitsbergen, the attitude changed. Instead of withdrawing, the Americans sent new personnel to Jan Mayen. The reason was obvious. On the proposal of John Hickerson, the State-War-Navy Coordinating Committee had decided that "pending settlement of the question of proposed Soviet bases in the North Atlantic, no steps be taken to withdraw United States Navy personnel presently attached to the radio-sonde station on Jan Mayen Island."[102]

The Norwegians pointed out that such tactics would be counterproductive and only increase chances of the Soviet Union adopting a firm line in the Spitsbergen matter. The Norwegian government therefore formally proposed that negotiations be started on the withdrawal of the American forces. The Norwegian aide-mémoire to the State Department was even shown to the British and the Russians before an answer had been received from Washington.

The State Department was much irritated by the Norwegians having transmitted to third parties information that dealt with what was seen as a purely Norwegian-American question.[103] As to the realities of the matter, the State Department and the military did agree to withdraw the personnel. The Joint Chiefs pointed out that there was "no military reason for the continuance of a United States military force on the island."[104] The State Department was probably convinced that the Norwegians were right about the effects of a continued presence on Jan Mayen. In February 1946 the Americans left the island.

If the Americans kept a low profile in the Spitsbergen question, the British did the same. Their military concluded that Soviet military activity on Spitsbergen would not have any influence on the security of Britain. This did not preclude the Foreign Office's being opposed to the Soviet desires on political grounds. But like Washington, London long left the initiative entirely with Oslo in this matter.[105]

After the Spitsbergen question had been restudied by the State Department and the military in January–February 1947, the United States seemed ready to adopt a slightly firmer position. A division into spheres of influence with the United States getting Iceland and Greenland and the Soviet Union Spitsbergen was now seen as less desirable than it had been in 1945–46. Stronger emphasis was put on Washington obtaining the much-wanted rights on Greenland while at the same time opposing Soviet demands. In contrast to their vague analyses of 1945, the Joint Chiefs of Staff in early 1947 pointed out that a Soviet military presence on Spitsbergen "would have an offensive potential against the United States." It was emphasized, however, that this potential was not "sufficient . . . to justify military action by the United States to prevent a measure of Soviet control." Just the fact that military action was seen as a possibility at all underlined that the situation had changed.

Yet, the JCS did not feel sure that concessions could be avoided. Bothersome at it might be, the connection still existed between Soviet and American bases in the North Atlantic. The military also felt that whatever was agreed upon, the Soviet Union could undertake some militarization of the islands under the guise of commercial exploitation. Therefore, the JCS prepared a fallback position. They concluded that in the event it became necessary for the United States to accept a change in the status of Spitsbergen, "either a joint Norwegian-Soviet regional defense arrangement under the United Nations, or demilitarization under the United Nations would be acceptable from a military standpoint." If the Soviets obtained bases on Spitsbergen, then American bases on Iceland and Greenland became ever more important.[106]

When Secretary of the Navy Forrestal and Secretary of War Patterson transmitted the views of the Joint Chiefs to the State Department, they used the occasion to reinforce the position of the military considerably. In their letter of February 4 nothing was stated about the relationship between Iceland-Greenland and Spitsbergen or about Soviet possibilities for clandestine activities. Instead, in rather strong language Forrestal and Patterson recommended that "the United States oppose any Soviet gains which could be interpreted in this country or abroad as appeasement of the USSR."[107] There was little doubt that recognition of Soviet military rights on Spitsbergen would be seen by the two as such an act of appeasement.

The State Department, more than Forrestal and Patterson and more than the military, had to keep in mind the close connection between American rights on Iceland and Greenland and Soviet rights on Spitsbergen. It would be the job of the diplomats to explain the American position to Moscow, just as it would be their job to handle contacts with Denmark, Norway, and Iceland. Nonetheless, the main points in Marshall's answer of February 18 to Forrestal and Patterson were simply slightly changed versions of arguments used by the Joint Chiefs, but without their overall military analysis. The letter dealt not only with the connection between American bases and similar rights for the Soviets, but Marshall also stated that maintenance of the status quo "would not preclude clandestine Soviet military activity in Spitsbergen under the guise of development of the extensive Soviet coal mine properties in the Islands."[108] The State Department still preferred a low profile. American rights on Iceland and Greenland counted most, particularly since the Soviets would have considerable opportunity to do what they wanted on Spitsbergen anyway.

The conflict between the State Department on the one hand and the War and Navy departments, only in part supported by the JCS, on the other, soon disappeared. The reason was that the Norwegian Storting made it clear that Norway would be opposed to any change in the demilitarized status of the archipelago.

Washington's attitude was not of any great importance to this shoring up of the Norwegian position. The government in Oslo was of course aware of the fact that Washington, just like London, preferred that no changes be made in the 1920 treaty. To a certain extent the government even appears to have hoped that the United States would oppose any Soviet proposals which it might feel forced to accept itself. On the other hand, the stiffening which could be noticed in the United States in 1947 took place mostly after the Norwegian government, still unknown to Washington, had already decided to adopt a firmer course. And, until the very last, fears existed within the Norwegian government that the United States and the Soviet Union would agree on an Iceland-Greenland-Spitsbergen deal over the head of Oslo.[109]

The stiffening on the American side occurred primarily within the defense departments and the military. In 1945 their position had been, if anything, more detached than that of the State Department. Forrestal's concentration on the Soviet threat is well known. This probably best explains his strong opposition to making any concessions. In 1945 he had not really been involved in this issue. In addition, however, changes were taking place in the strategic thinking of the military. The polar regions were slowly becoming more and more important to the United States. Udgaard maintains that the polar strategy was of great importance to Washington even in 1944–45. Danish political scientist Niels Amstrup argues that this aspect did not come into prominence as far as Greenland-Iceland-Spitsbergen were concerned before the early 1950s.[110]

My position would be between these two extremes. Few indications exist that the polar strategy was of much importance in 1944–45. There are many more in 1947, even if it is definitely true that the importance of the Arctic regions was seen primarily in the light of their strategic potential in the future. We have seen that only in 1947 did the JCS clearly point out that Soviet bases on the Spitsbergen Archipelago had an offensive potential against the United States. Spitsbergen would be about 500 miles closer to New York than any other military base.

The JCS estimated that the 500 miles might make

flights from Spitsbergen to the United States feasible five to ten years earlier than if Soviet planes were required to operate from bases on Soviet soil. An attack across the Arctic would also be much more difficult to detect than one across the Atlantic. As the JCS emphasized, "In these days of atomic explosives the above factors deserve full consideration." In a report from September 1947 the Central Intelligence Agency agreed that the Spitsbergen Archipelago and Jan Mayen Island both had considerable strategic importance. The importance of Spitsbergen was the greater, but Jan Mayen might afford an excellent location for a radio communication or weather station.[111]

It was becoming increasingly popular, especially in Air Force circles, to argue that an attack on the United States would come by way of the north polar basin. This route would be the shortest from the major industrial centers of the Soviet Union to the heartland of the United States. Even if the distance from Moscow to New York was shorter by the conventional approach than across the Arctic, as an attack route the former was well guarded and the element of surprise would be small. Air Force generals like wartime heroes "Hap" Arnold and Jimmy Doolittle and Strategic Air Command chief George Kenney took an active interest in this new strategy. So did Admiral Richard Byrd, an important Navy figure.[112]

It would still take some years before the new generation of bombers could fly such distances round trip with bombing loads, and it was thought that long-range guided missiles would take another ten to fifteen years to develop. Severe technical and climactic difficulties also existed in operating in the Arctic.[113] Therefore, the new strategy did not yet have a decisive impact on American base requirements on Greenland. The desired bases were all concentrated in the south, instead of in the north as would have been logical if the polar strategy had dominated.[114] The Spitsbergen situation was different, however. Even if the Soviets could make little use of bases there in the first few years, it was only a question of time before they would take on great importance. The

United States could still wait before altering its base requirements on Greenland, but if a Soviet advance on Spitsbergen was to be stopped, it had to be done immediately.

From 1947 on the United States paid more attention to what was going on on Spitsbergen. On numerous occasions the State Department received reports from various American officials that the Soviet Union was carrying out military activities on the islands. One report expressed suspicion that Spitsbergen was "teeming with Russian activity veiled even to the Norwegians."[115] Such rumors all turned out to be false. They indicated, however, the closer interest the United States was beginning to take in the affairs of the archipelago.

After the Norwegian Storting had rejected the Soviet proposal for joint Soviet-Norwegian bases on Spitsbergen, the Norwegians felt that their refusal could be used to some economic advantage. In March 1947 Arne Skaug, Director of the Bureau of Statistics and economic adviser to the government, was in Washington to argue for greater support from the United States. He was most interested in assistance to rehabilitate the Norwegian merchant marine (the procurement of steel for the construction of Norwegian ships in Sweden). To buttress his case, Skaug asked if ". . . the Department was pleased with the action of the Norwegian Storting in rejecting the Russian demand for bases on Spitsbergen." Mr. Lacy, working with economic questions, replied that he could not answer for the department but that he personally thought the rejection "admirable."[116]

The State Department gave "the strongest support" to Skaug's request. Again, the Department, as in the case of the shipping clause of the Export-Import Bank loan, met with the opposition of other agencies. The Office of Temporary Controls even argued that it was illegal to give the Norwegians the assistance they wanted. The State Department also supported a request for some surplus tankers. But the number of ships transferred to Norway seems to have diminished after American shipping interests intervened and received the support of some important senators.[117]

Introduction of the Marshall Plan

Despite the limitations on Washington's policies there could be no doubt about the direction in which policy makers were moving. Their interest in Scandinavia was increasing, and their opposition to gains for the Soviets was growing stronger. Although the Marshall Plan represented an increase in American involvement in Scandinavia, it should not be seen as constituting a fundamental break in policies. On the one hand, Washington's concern about Scandinavia had started growing before June 1947. On the other, Marshall's speech was to lead to few immediate changes in the attitude toward Scandinavia.

With a rising interest in the affairs of Scandinavia, a tendency toward increased criticism of the policies of the local governments could be noticed. This had been at least implied in the position of the defense departments in the Spitsbergen question. Those who had been somewhat critical of Scandinavian foreign policy continued their opposition. This was illustrated by some critical comments made by John Foster Dulles in a conversation with Marshall on February 24, 1947. The Republican foreign policy spokesman pointed out that the "economy of Central Europe, including Scandinavia, was being integrated into, and drained into, that of the Soviet Union, and that if this tendency extended into Western Europe, western civilization and personal freedom, as we had known it, would be impossible." [118]

Remarks critical of Scandinavian policies had also been heard in 1946. What was new was that such criticism was no longer largely confined to people outside the State Department. Although the embassies in Scandinavia were still showing a generally sympathetic attitude, they were beginning to make more negative comments than before. The clearest example of this was conveyed in a May 28 report from the legation in Stockholm. After a Swedish poll had shown a surprising number of Swedes in favor of the Truman Doctrine, a representative of the legation had complained to

Foreign Minister Undén about the official attitude. The American stated that he "could not understand why other democratic countries [meaning Sweden] did not show more solidarity with our desire to have democratic governments in eastern European countries."[119]

The appraisal of Scandinavia among the State Department leadership, to the extent that it cared about the region at all, was still favorable, however. This was evident from the recommendation made by Secretary of State Marshall, in his report to the cabinet after the Council of Foreign Ministers meeting in Moscow in March-April 1947, that the United States had to be careful to preserve its "good relationships with the fringe countries in Europe." In this context he particularly mentioned Belgium, Holland, France, and the three Scandinavian countries.[120] Since it was quite unusual for the Secretary to deal with these countries, simply the fact that Marshall served notice to the cabinet about Scandinavia could be seen as indicating a rising interest in the affairs of the area.

The visit of strong naval units to Norway and Sweden in June-July was another indication of that interest. The unit that visited Norway consisted of two large battleships and some other vessels under the command of Admiral Conolly, chief of U.S. naval units in Europe. Included in the group that visited Sweden were two carriers. The British as well showed their interest in Scandinavia and Norway by sending strong units to Norwegian ports as far north as Tromsø.[121]

Naval visits represented an important element in U.S. foreign policy. The rising interest in the eastern Mediterranean which had led to the Truman Doctrine had been marked by the gradual deployment of the U.S. Navy in these waters. In fact, Secretary of the Navy Forrestal had given considerable thought to this aspect. In July 1946 he had stated his view in his usual forthright manner:

. . . The American policy will be to have units of the American Navy sail in any waters in any part of the globe. I am anxious to get this established as a common practice so that the movements of our ships *anywhere* will not be a matter of excitement or speculation.[122]

John Gimbel repeatedly emphasizes in his book *The Origins of the Marshall Plan* that there was no "plan" in June 1947.[123] It is true that the extent of the planning that went before the Secretary's speech at Harvard on June 5 may easily be exaggerated. No firm decisions had been reached on exactly what countries were to be involved, what would be the size of the assistance given, and how this money would be distributed.

But some things had been decided. It was agreed that something should be done to alleviate the economic situation in Europe and primarily in Western Europe. Leading policy makers concurred that this effort should not be in the form of piecemeal solutions, but in the nature of one comprehensive program. The sum of money involved would be considerable, although no set figure had been agreed upon.[124]

The role of Scandinavia in the considerations leading to the Marshall Plan is of primary interest here. Three basic studies had been made in Washington at the time the Secretary delivered his famous speech. These three were the preliminary report of a subcommittee of the State-War-Navy Coordinating Committee dated April 21; the memorandums by the Director of the Policy Planning Staff, George F. Kennan, dated May 16 and May 23; and a memo by the Under Secretary for Economic Affairs, William Clayton, probably written on May 27.

None of these studies directed attention to Scandinavia. This is not surprising, since they dealt with the situation in Western Europe as a whole. (The Eastern part was hardly mentioned at all.) The introductory statement in Kennan's May 16 memo was typical in that respect: "The most important and urgent element in foreign policy planning is the question of restoration of hope and confidence in Western Europe and the early rehabilitation of the economies of that area." To the extent that any emphasis on particular countries could be noticed, this was on the major powers in Western Europe. The memos by Kennan and Clayton contained no analysis of the situation in any of the smaller countries.[125]

Scandinavia was of course a part of Western Europe and

had long been seen as such by the State Department and other makers of foreign policy in Washington. A note of uncertainty, however, could be detected. In March, in the discussions of the ad hoc committee of the State-War-Navy Coordinating Committee which led to the preliminary report of April 21, the committee members grappled with the problem of what was meant by "Europe." The Army and Navy members of the Committee interpreted the term "to include Great Britain but not Iceland, which it is assumed is omitted along with the Scandinavian countries."[126]

Nothing is stated about the reasons for this startling omission on the part of the War and Navy departments. It could not have much to do with their estimates of the strategic importance of the countries involved, because on that point Iceland at least would score very high. But the omission did reflect the uncertainty and confusion which existed as to the exact size and scope of the assistance to be undertaken.

Although Kennan and Clayton did not deal explicitly with the geographical definition of Europe, it was fairly evident that there would be a place for Scandinavia in their programs. Even in the SWNCC deliberations the State Department prevailed over any wish in the Army and Navy not to include Scandinavia in Western Europe. Scandinavia was incorporated in the April 21 report. Yet considerable uncertainty remained as to exactly what areas were to be covered. Despite the emphasis on Western Europe, even Iran, Korea, and the Philippines were mentioned as possible aid recipients.[127] No areas outside Europe were referred to in the Kennan and Clayton memos. (It should be noted that those associated with the SWNCC study were not among the top policy makers in their departments. It is unlikely that Forrestal and Patterson would have taken the initial position of their subordinates with regard to the role of Scandinavia.)

In its April 21 report the ad hoc committee of the SWNCC discussed an export program for critical commodities. One such commodity was coal. (As a matter of fact, Kennan proposed that the short-term program of assistance be called a "Coal for Europe" program.) The committee declared that the United States should continue its coal exports to

Europe at the maximum rate. One major reason for this was that "The major coal importing countries are France, Italy, Belgium, Denmark, the Netherlands, Sweden and Norway—all countries of special interest to the U.S." [128]

In another part of the report the committee included Norway on a list of countries where it was in the U.S. interest to initiate, or to be prepared to initiate, programs involving provision of military equipment and assistance. The other countries in Western Europe on the list were Italy, France, Austria, and Spain. [129] One reason for the inclusion of Norway was probably its position close to the Soviet Union. Its weak state of defense and its strategic importance to the United States and to Western Europe may also have counted.

The situation in Norway could not be seen as critical in any sense. Whether this was the reason or not, Norway was dropped from lists where the Joint Chiefs of Staff tried to set down priorities as to what countries to supply with assistance. [130] In fact, the JCS lists differed considerably from the SWNCC list. This too illustrated the uncertain nature of much of the planning going on in Washington at this time. Neither did Sweden figure on the JCS lists, while Denmark was included. Along with Italy, Belgium, the Netherlands, and Spain, Denmark was regarded as being of "more than ordinary importance to our national security for military or political reasons." The strategic importance of Denmark did not relate to the mainland, but to Greenland, "which, by reason of geographic position, is a major outpost for defense of North America." But, again, there was little urgency in the situation of Denmark-Greenland. [131] Relations with Denmark were satisfactory, the United States was able to maintain its wartime bases on Greenland, and there was no significant threat from either the Soviet Union or from internal communism in Denmark. It was also a fact that both Norway and Denmark were able to handle most of their military needs through Britain.

Even if the confusion and lack of planning in advance of Marshall's speech may easily be exaggerated, much was still undecided at the beginning of June. One who came to contribute greatly to the hammering out of an overall program was British Foreign Secretary Bevin. Under his lead the British and the French made no opening either for the Economic Commission for Europe (ECE) or for the Soviet Union in the reconstruction program. On July 4, after the Soviets had withdrawn from the British-French-Soviet meeting in Paris, Bevin and French Foreign Minister Bidault decided to invite all the countries of Europe, with the exception of the Soviet Union and Spain, to a new meeting in Paris. This meeting was to give further substance to Marshall's offer of assistance.[132]

We have seen that London had been somewhat disappointed with the Norwegians and probably also with the Danes. The Scandinavians had not been willing to cooperate with Britain and to stand up to the Soviet Union to the extent that the British had hoped. Since the Soviet Union could not take part and since Molotov had made some remarks which could be interpreted as a warning to Norway not to participate in the new Paris conference, Bevin actually doubted that Norway would join. His prediction for Sweden was slightly more optimistic: "Sweden might join although she was in a difficult position." The Foreign Secretary seems to have thought that the Danes would have few problems in accepting. The French too were somewhat uncertain about the intentions of the Scandinavians. But both London and Paris definitely wanted Scandinavia to take part.[133]

The situation was much the same in Washington as in London and Paris. While the State Department obviously wanted the Scandinavians to participate in the new Paris conference, it had no definite information as to whether their participation was likely or not. On July 9 Norwegian Ambassador Morgenstierne cabled the Foreign Office in Oslo that the American appraisal was that Finland would reject the offer, while Norway, Sweden, and Denmark would "probably" want to participate. If they did join, expectations within the State Department were that the Scandinavians would make it clear that they were not willing to take part in any political bloc directed against the Soviet Union. Ambassador

Bay in Oslo was also of the opinion that it was likely that Norway would choose to come in.[134]

No instructions were issued from Washington to the embassies in Scandinavia to try to influence the choices of the three countries. Bay, however, apparently on his own, decided that some prodding might be useful. At the end of June he told the Norwegian press that he knew that some of the leading members of the government were in favor of the ideas expressed by Marshall.[135] Although this was before formal invitations to the Paris meeting had been issued, the ambassador's comments have to be regarded as a personal effort to make the Norwegians associate themselves with the Marshall Plan.

The decision of the three countries to participate was certainly welcomed in Washington, London, and Paris. The reservations they attached to their affirmative answers counted less than the fact that they had decided to be represented in Paris. The Scandinavians wanted to make it clear that they would not take part in any Western bloc. To avoid this, they preferred that the reconstruction program be worked out through the ECE. If any new organization had to be established, they would favor a powerless one. Finally, the Scandinavians would try to avoid any repercussions both for their trade with the Soviet Union and Eastern Europe and for their highly controlled domestic economies.[136]

Washington had not yet made final decisions with regard to questions such as these. For instance, although many were hostile to using the ECE as the coordinating body of the program, the United States did not in June insist on excluding that organization. Bevin was more emphatic than Marshall on this point. Even Bevin, however, was satisfied in mid-July by the three northern states having decided to join, and by their having put "the best people to work" on the problems related to the reconstruction of Western Europe.[137]

Washington considered itself as having had satisfactory relations with Scandinavia in the entire 1945 to 1947 period. Despite policy makers being on the alert to prevent any expansion of Soviet influence, this clearly did not apply in equal measure to all parts. On the edges of the region, in relation to Spitsbergen, the Truman administration had in 1945–46 flirted with the possibility of making a deal with the Soviet Union in which Moscow would obtain bases on Spitsbergen in return for American bases on Iceland-Greenland.

Although some persons in Washington wanted to strengthen the Western orientation of the Scandinavian countries, most did not take strong exception to their bridge-building policies. There was still room for those who did not want to go all out in support of the West.

In considerable measure due to the satisfactory nature of American-Scandinavian relations, the State Department had seen little need to take an active interest in the affairs of Sweden, Norway, and Denmark. If contacts between Washington and the Scandinavian capitals were not intimate in the first two years after the war, on the whole they were friendly.

3

Neutrality Rejected

WITH AMERICAN POLICY MAKERS taking a stronger interest in the affairs of Western Europe, there was a concomitant increase in concern with the affairs of Scandinavia. It could also be argued that Scandinavia was becoming a more important part of Western Europe than it had been. The Soviet expansion in Eastern Europe brought into focus those areas which bordered on the Soviet Union, but were still independent. We have already seen that the polar strategy somewhat increased the importance of Norway, and of Denmark through its possession of Greenland. Scandinavia was strategically important in several other ways as well. With its long coastline toward the Atlantic, Norway was of significance for communications between the United States and Western Europe, and Sweden and Denmark held the key to passage through the Baltic Straits.

Nevertheless, in 1947 such strategic considerations were not yet of crucial interest. They were to come fully to the fore only a year later. The United States concentrated not on a potential military confrontation with the Soviet Union, but on the political struggle. With the powers of Britain declining and with the United States increasingly coming to the

front as the leader of the West, American relations with
Scandinavia were to change.. Washington increased its demands for loyalty. Policy makers came to insist that the
Scandinavians agree to "stand up and let themselves be
counted" in the struggle with Soviet Communism. It was no
longer enough to be generally friendly to the Western cause.
The United States now began urging the Europeans to organize their resources in such a way that they were able both
to combat communism more effectively and to diminish their
need for economic assistance from the United States. These
developments were soon to cause difficulties in American-
Scandinavian relations.

The United States and a Scandinavian Bloc

The fall of 1947 represented a period of transition in
U.S.-Scandinavian relations. On the one hand, State Department officials and other important policy makers still
showed a rather limited interest in Scandinavia. Positive
evaluations of the prevailing foreign policy in the region
could still be found. On the other hand, there was no doubt
that Washington was taking a greater interest in the affairs
of the region, and with this came increasing dissatisfaction
with Scandinavian bridge-building policies.

The lack of compelling interest in Scandinavian affairs
could be seen in Washington's deliberations over what attitude to take to the question of a Scandinavian military bloc.
This topic was, again, brought up on the initiative of the British. In October 1947 their Joint Planning Staff of the Chiefs
of Staff had recommended that the U.K. encourage the greatest possible measure of coordination in matters of defense between Norway, Sweden, and Denmark.[1] Although the military hoped that such an arrangement could be tied to a wider
Western European bloc, any degree of cooperation among the
Scandinavian powers was better than none. The three countries would be strengthened vis-à-vis the Soviet Union. This
would make it easier for the Scandinavians to stand up to
the Russians in time of peace and they would not so easily

fall prey to Soviet aggression in case of war. The strategic importance of the region was seen as great. The Planning Staff in fact stated that "We regard the integrity of Scandinavia in the event of war with Russia as almost as important as the integrity of France, Holland and Belgium."[2] The British military maintained contacts with their Scandinavian counterparts, apparently in particular on the Danish side, to examine the possibilities for a Scandinavian arrangement, preferably one with close ties to London.[3]

The British Foreign Office was skeptical. This skepticism was based more on the feasibility than on the desirability of such plans. With the Soviet Union opposed to joint Scandinavian arrangements, it was seen as unlikely that the Scandinavians would decide in favor of military cooperation. Moscow's opposition would be particularly strong if close ties were established with Britain. If such ties were not established, then London's interest would diminish.[4]

How did Washington react to these plans? In examining the American attitude, we should keep in mind the fact that when the question of a Western military alliance came up in 1948, most policy makers would be strongly opposed to plans for Scandinavian cooperation unless these were closely linked to a wider Western European arrangement.

In the fall of 1947 the attitude was different. When the British military brought up the question of Scandinavian cooperation with their U.S. counterparts, the latter asked the State Department for its foreign policy reactions.[5] The conclusion of the Department, as stated in a letter of October 30 from the Director of the Office of European Affairs, John Hickerson, to Admiral Woolridge, was that "the advantages and disadvantages of an effort to create such a bloc under present circumstances appear to us to be fairly well balanced and we therefore would wish neither to encourage nor discourage its formation." As to another topic brought up by the British, the manufacture of arms under U.K. license, the department only declared that "We see no objection to the manufacture of arms in Scandinavia under British license."[6]

These comments indicated that the question of Scandinavian military cooperation did not arouse great interest

within the State Department. Scandinavia was still a peripheral part of Western Europe. In addition, the department
quite clearly thought the formation of such a bloc unlikely.
No reason could be seen why Sweden "would be willing to
join with two such decrepit partners in a bloc which would
jeopardize Sweden's traditional and overriding policy of self-
sufficient neutrality."[7]

As to its desirability, the State Department seemed to be
somewhat against the creation of a Scandinavian bloc, despite the balanced wording in the letter from Hickerson.
True, reasons existed for supporting the scheme. These had
been presented by the British military. On the other hand,
there were arguments against it. Interestingly, one of these
would be discarded by many policy makers only half a year
later. The Division of Northern European Affairs argued primarily that the formation of such a bloc "would have disas-
trous results for Finland since the Soviets would unquestionably regard such a bloc as hostile and, therefore, take
steps to speed up the complete absorption of Finland as a
countermeasure."[8] When the Swedes were later to use this
argument against the participation of the Scandinavian
countries in a Western alliance, it had only little effect on
most American policy makers.

However, one argument presented by the Division of
Eastern European Affairs was to be heard again and again.
The Division declared that "if a bloc were successfully
formed with British and American support we might find it
difficult in time of war to get the Norwegians to provide us
with facilities or even to enter the war on our side unless the
entire bloc were in agreement." It was feared that the
country most frightened of the Soviet Union would block any
attempt to take action which the Russians might resent.[9]

The reaction of the State Department showed that no
clear policy had been worked out in Washington on so important a question as that of a Scandinavian military bloc. The
department did not really make its influence felt either way.
Hickerson stated that advantages and disadvantages seemed
to be well balanced. Although the internal discussion revealed that few arguments were given why the United

States should support such a bloc, those made against it were somewhat contradictory. If the United States pulled the Norwegians to the West, as was the obvious desire of the Eastern European Division, a strong Soviet reaction against Finland would follow, according to the reasoning of the Northern European Division. This discrepancy illustrated the many uncertainties in Washington's policy toward Scandinavia. In 1948 guidance would be imposed from above to avoid such contradictions.

Positive evaluations of the foreign policies of the Scandinavians could still be found. A long report on Norway worked out by the CIA in September 1947 was one example. The report revealed hardly any criticism at all of Norwegian foreign policy. On the contrary, in the part where the agency analyzed future trends, it stated that "there are no signs at present that Norway's present westward orientation will change." If Soviet demands were made on Norway—Spitsbergen was the main case in point—"Norway can be relied upon . . . to resist any Soviet westward expansion but will seek moral support for its actions in resisting Soviet demands."[10] This indicated little or no dissatisfaction with Norwegian policy, at least within the CIA or those parts of the agency which had written the report. It is true, though, that Norway's Western orientation was probably exaggerated.

Other parts of the policy-making establishment were coming to a different conclusion. This would bring the bridge-building policies of the Scandinavians under increasing pressure from the United States.

Organization of the Marshall Plan

At the beginning of July 1947, the United States had not yet formulated a clear policy as to how the Marshall Plan assistance was to be organized and as to what strings were to be attached to the money given. This would soon change. With Washington making up its mind, considerable strain would arise in Scandinavian-American relations.

In his Harvard speech Marshall had underlined that the role of the United States would consist of "friendly aid in the drafting of a European program and of later support of such a program so far as it may be practical for us to do so." He strongly emphasized that "it would be neither fitting nor efficacious for this Government to undertake to draw up unilaterally a program designed to place Europe on its feet economically. This is the business of the Europeans."[11] Thus, there was little doubt that Washington wanted to leave the initiative with the Europeans, with the United States being called in from time to time to give advice.

This attitude was contrary to what Under Secretary Clayton would have preferred. In his memo of late May, he had made it clear that he preferred a European economic federation on the order of the Benelux customs union. Such an ambitious goal would encounter resistance from several countries. Clayton's solution was obvious, *"The United States must run this show."* [Italics in original][12]

For a short time Washington stuck to its policy of doing no more than giving friendly aid in the drafting of a recovery program. Clayton was warned that he should not aim too high in his efforts to convince the Europeans that their economies could no longer be divided into small compartments. Under Secretary Lovett told him on July 10 that "we are in agreement with you on the point that a customs union is a desirable long-run objective but that to attempt to work it out now would bog Europe down in details and distract from the main effort." When Clayton, as the U.S. representative in Paris, continued to press for goals which the State Department regarded as unrealistic, Kennan was sent to the French capital to work out a common American policy. The department not only thought Clayton was working too hard for a customs union, it also felt he was paying excessive attention both to multilateral arrangements in general and to the fiscal stability of the various countries. In short, he was told to take more notice of the attitude of the Western Europeans.[13]

This criticism of Clayton did not mean that the State Department was in agreement with the Europeans. More and more the impression developed that the Europeans were concentrating too much on what the United States could do to speed up European recovery and too little on what they could do themselves. In the middle of August the State Department therefore came to modify its attitude of giving no more than friendly aid in the drafting of a recovery program. When this did not seem to help much, the American position stiffened further. On August 24 Acting Secretary Lovett cabled Marshall, who was away in South America, that "Progress so far is disappointing in that all that has come out so far is sixteen shopping lists which may be dressed up by some large-scale but very long-term projects such as Alpine power, etc." The shopping lists were becoming very expensive for the United States. Furthermore, even if Washington actually granted what Europe wanted, there was little assurance that this would do the job as a dollar deficit was still foreseen at the end of the four-year period. The remedy was to accomplish more in the way of reform of the European economies as a whole.[14]

The question of a customs union was not revived. Instead the Europeans would have to agree to other, somewhat smaller steps to facilitate the exchange of goods and services among themselves. A multilateral organization was to be established to review the progress achieved in the course of the four-year period in which the program would last. Measures would have to be taken to achieve monetary and financial stability. To the Americans these requirements represented the minimum if Western Europe were to create a workable economy independent of special, outside aid.[15]

Clayton in Paris and the American ambassadors in the various countries were to press for the adoption of policies along these lines. In case urgings would not suffice, the State Department went on to state that the "US believes . . . political consequences of rejection by US of any aid program immeasurably worse" than for the Europeans to accept what the Americans demanded.[16] Washington hinted that no assistance would in fact be extended unless a satisfactory program was worked out.

Most continental states had little difficulty in meeting

the American demands. Some of them wanted to go even further than the United States in pushing for European integration. That was especially the case with the Benelux
countries. The British were much more reluctant to adopt
such an approach. Gradually, however, they came to act as
mediators between the Americans and the least integration-
minded of the Europeans, the Scandinavians (particularly
Norway and Sweden), and in some respects Switzerland.[17]

The increasingly firm U.S. policy was much at odds with
the attitude of the Scandinavians. Their position was much
closer to that of the Russians in the Paris three-power meeting than to that now presented by Washington. Until early
September Sweden and Norway favored no common plan for
recovery, just a balance sheet of what the Europeans needed.
The necessary follow-up should be left to the European Economic Commission. On that commission the Soviet Union
and the Eastern European countries were represented. That
was no drawback for the Scandinavians. On the contrary,
such a setup would mean less of a break with bridge building than would joining a strong Western European organization working closely with the United States.[18]

It could come as no surprise that the Americans became
exasperated at the policies pursued by the Scandinavians.
On July 20 the ambassador in Paris, Jefferson Caffery, cabled the State Department about reactions to a proposal from
Belgium on the promotion of multilateral trading. The Benelux countries naturally supported this, while France and the
United Kingdom were not opposed. The ambassador went on
to state that "Doubt has been expressed whether Scandinavian countries, in view of their commercial ties with
east, will be prepared to go along on this project." The Scandinavians were seen as looking more to the East than the
others. Actually their trade with the Soviet Union and Eastern Europe was quite small, but Scandinavia's open attitude
toward Eastern Europe was based more on political than on
economic considerations.[19]

American representatives in Paris worried about the attitude of the Scandinavians toward Eastern Europe. Their
view that the reconstruction program ought to be little more

than a listing of what was required from the United States caused considerable irritation. Clayton and others also complained about the bilateral nature of Scandinavia's trade agreements.[20]

What tied all this together was the question of the organization to administer the program. At the end of August four of the five members of the executive committee of the conference had agreed on the need for a continuing organization for the period of the program. France, Italy, and the Netherlands had no problem with this. Even the British finally agreed. The one member opposed was Norway, the Scandinavian representative on the executive committee. This would create the first postwar crisis in relations between the United States and Norway and Sweden.

The fact that Norway and Sweden were still trying to work through the ECE must have contributed greatly to Kennan's harsh denunciation as expressed in his analysis of September 4: "particularly the Scandinavians are pathologically timorous about the Russians. Finding themselves somewhat unexpectedly in a gathering denounced by Molotov as politically wicked, they have the jumpy uncertainty of one who walks in pleasing but unaccustomed paths of sin."[21] Kennan was not among those who had pressed most actively for integrationary measures. Nonetheless, there could be no doubt about his strong dislike of the attitude of the Scandinavians.

The Director of the Policy Planning Staff, like many others, referred to Scandinavia as a unit. The similarities among the three countries can be exaggerated, however. The Danes were following a policy of less opposition to European integration than were the other two nations. This difference was probably due in part to Denmark's closer contact with the European continent and in part to Denmark's unfavorable balance of exchange at this time.[22]

In an analysis that Marshall presented to the U.S. ambassadors in London and Paris on September 8, the Secretary of State saw three forces in particular as working against the coordinated approach which Washington wanted for the recovery program. The first was disagreement over the role of

the Western zones of Germany. The Americans were insist-
ing on the full participation of the Western zones, to the dis-
may of many Europeans. The second was the determination
of the French that nothing be done which would interfere
with their Monnet Plan for the reconstruction of France. The
third was referred to as the "Scandinavian tendency to withdraw from full participation."[23]

In the end Swedes and Norwegians felt they had to modify their position. The possibility existed that they would not
receive any assistance if concessions were not made. On the
other hand, the British, who were under considerable pressure themselves, warned Washington that "Any effort to
press further would . . . so impair national sovereignty that
many countries would rebel, particularly since the Soviets
had already threatened some with withholding coal if they
proceeded." The State Department knew nothing about such
coal threats. Some days later Bevin specified that the Scandinavian countries were those in question.[24]

At a cabinet meeting on September 9 the Norwegian
government decided to give way on the U.S. demand for an
organization for European Economic Cooperation. Like Denmark, Norway was now willing to support a British compromise proposal. Sweden and Switzerland held out a few
days longer. In the end they too felt they had little choice if
they wanted to take part in the recovery program.[25]

"Stand Up and Be Counted": the Cold War in the UN

With the United States becoming more and more involved in the affairs of Western Europe and in the struggle
against Soviet-Communist influence, its attitude changed toward those who wanted to be less than fully committed to
one side in the cold war. This development was evident in
the worsening of relations between the United States and
Sweden and Norway over the organization of the Marshall
Plan. If the Americans were to step in with large-scale financial assistance, Washington felt that the least the Europeans
could do was to agree to establish such a relationship among

themselves that they would be able to stand on their own feet when the four-year recovery program would be over.

The Western European countries could show their commitment to the West in other ways as well. In the fall of 1947 a decisive point was to be willing to break with the Soviet Union. This was the foreign policy equivalent of breaking with the communists in domestic matters. With the United States publicly committing its resources in a worldwide struggle, it was only fitting and proper that those countries that were actually threatened be willing to do their part. In short, Western Europe had to stand up and be counted in the struggle against Soviet Communism.

The impression was rapidly spreading that the Scandinavians were doing far less than their share. True, the social democrats were willing to fight the local communist parties. But they were much more hesitant in their foreign policies.

The forum in which loyalty to the United States could most easily be registered was the United Nations. The Scandinavian countries usually voted with the West when differences arose between East and West. On particularly troublesome issues, they sometimes abstained. Yet, there had been a few occasions on which Norway, as an example, could be said to have followed a line somewhat closer to that of the Soviet Union than to that of the United States. In the discussions about the political reorganization of Germany, the Norwegian government preferred a rather centralized model considerably at a variance with the position of the United States. And, while strongly in favor of freedom of navigation on the Danube, in the Paris Peace Conference Norway was the only country outside Eastern Europe that voted against a French proposal on the organization of a new authority to regulate traffic on the river.[26]

With the exception of some complaints from Senator Vandenberg and a few others, this attitude had not caused any conflict with Washington in the first two years after the war. This was now to change. In an East-West context the main issues before the General Assembly of the UN in the fall of 1947 were the proposal for an interim committee, and developments in Greece and Korea. All were felt to be very important from the American point of view. On none of these issues did Washington feel it received full support from the Scandinavians.

With regard to the interim committee, the Scandinavians argued that this could be seen as a way of getting around the Soviet veto. Such an attempt would not only be resented by Moscow, but it would probably also be against the charter of the world organization. The Swedes were more strongly against the American proposal than were the other two countries. Nevertheless, after considerable doubt all three voted for a British compromise formula.[27]

The Scandinavian attitude with regard to Greece and Korea created even more of a stir on the American side. In the Greek matter the Scandinavians argued that the Western Powers were too preoccupied with the support the Greek guerillas received from the outside and cared too little about their native support and the nature of the Greek government. The northern states voted against a Soviet resolution, but they abstained on an American one. The only others that abstained were the Arabs, while the Eastern Europeans voted against the U.S. proposal. In the Korean case Sweden, Norway, and Denmark were joined only by Bolivia when they, again, abstained on an American proposal to create a national government on the basis of free elections. Their main argument was that Korea should be dealt with in the peace treaty for Japan, not in the UN.[28]

While the rest of Western Europe lined up with the West under United States leadership, the Scandinavians hesitated. This made a bad impression in Washington. Their behavior in the UN gave rise to quite negative comments in the State Department. The strongest reaction came from John Hickerson in a note of October 28 to the Division of Northern European Affairs:

> It seems to me that the Norwegians, like the Swedes, have tended to regard the General Assembly meeting as a contest between the US and the USSR in which they were privileged to occupy a seat as a spectator. In Greece we feel that we are

fighting the battle of small countries and their territorial and political independence and integrity. In other words, we have been fighting Norway's fight with no help whatever from Norway, not even an appreciative nod from her officials.[29]

In December George Kennan complained to the Norwegian ambassador about the Swedish attitude in the Greek matter. Kennan said he was "strongly disappointed" by the Swedes.[30]

Kennan focused on the Swedes while Hickerson was most concerned about the Norwegians. Too much should not be made of this difference. Kennan probably meant to give the Norwegians the message more indirectly, since little separated Swedes and Norwegians in the Greek matter. Hickerson's focusing on Norway was quite likely the result of Washington's having expected a somewhat more favorable attitude from the Norwegians than from the Swedes or even from the Danes. During the war only the Norwegians had belonged to the Allies, while the Swedes had remained neutral and the Danes had only slowly taken up resistance. The Norwegian government had cooperated intimately with the British. After the war both Norway and Denmark worked much more closely with Britain than did Sweden.

The point that Hickerson's criticism of Norway had more to do with expectations than with factual differences in the policies of Norway and Sweden is supported by a letter Hickerson sent to Assistant Secretary Armour on October 7. In that letter the Director of the Office of European Affairs in fact judged the situation in Norway to be more favorable to the United States than that in the other Scandinavian countries. This conclusion was based on the extent to which the three states were paying attention to Soviet foreign policy "propaganda."[31]

Despite this, Hickerson reflected on the possibility of doing something to correct the situation, primarily in Norway but also in the other two countries. His suggestion was a coordinated campaign to correct wrong impressions of the U.S. Of most concern seemed to be the idea that "whatever noble motives we may profess, we are in fact actuated by a spirit of imperialism." Hickerson's analysis was based on reports both from Americans in Norway and from the Norwegian ambassador in Washington, Morgenstierne. The Director of the Office of European Affairs was aware of the fact that Norwegian Social Democrats had succeeded in whittling down communist strength. "Where the Communists have their success is in throwing doubt on the United States as a world leader." He found indications of this in the way the Social Democratic press dealt with the United States, in the Norwegian attitude to the Marshall Plan and to Franco's Spain, and in the reaction to a speech by Marshall at the UN. In short, Norway "has sought consistently to avoid an open choosing of sides—East or West."[32]

The main part of the plan to correct any wrong impressions was to send prominent Americans to Norway and the other Scandinavian countries to lecture about the United States. This idea was accepted by Assistant Secretary Armour and by Under Secretary Lovett. Morgenstierne also supported the project. One reason for the ambassador's interest was his fear of what consequences the visit of Henry Wallace might have had. The former Vice President and Secretary of Commerce had paid brief visits to Norway, Sweden, and Denmark in April 1947.[33]

Nothing came of the planned campaign. Former Under Secretary Dean Acheson, present Under Secretary Robert Lovett, and Republican spokesman John Foster Dulles were all among those contacted about going to Norway on a publicity tour. Despite the interest of the State Department and of Ambassador Morgenstierne, none of these persons found time or showed any desire to go.[34] The fact that nothing came out of the publicity campaign probably indicated that the situation in Scandinavia, although serious, was not regarded as urgent.

The State Department's negative evaluation of developments in Norway coincided with shifts in the attitude of the embassy in Oslo. While no significant criticism of Norwegian foreign policy had been found in a survey report from Ambassador Bay dated April 11, the tone had definitely changed in the half-year report he dispatched on October 9. Now Bay addressed himself to the question of why "the Norwegian delegation to the last assembly of the United Nations sometimes surprised the American delegation by its pro-Soviet attitude on certain questions."[35]

The ambassador warned against pressing the Norwegians to align themselves firmly with the West. "I do feel, however, that it is incumbent upon Norway's Government and statesmen to insure that Norway maintains an independent position and declares itself consistently and forthrightly for the morals and principles for which this naturally westward-inclined country and people are known to stand."[36]

Thus, both Ambassador Bay and the State Department felt that Norway belonged to the West. The Americans did not insist on an all-out commitment. What was on their mind was primarily a recognition of the immorality of political neutrality. In the sharpening struggle between East and West—between good and evil, in Washington's analysis— each country had to make it clear where it belonged. The Scandinavians could only maintain close relations with the United States if they were willing to stand up for those principles of which Americans now considered themselves guardians.

The State Department could hope for improvements in Norwegian-American relations. Some Norwegians wanted to adopt policies more acceptable to the United States. There was no doubt in the Department where Ambassador Morgenstierne stood. The embassy in Oslo kept in close contact with the Secretary General of the Labor party, Haakon Lie. Not only was Lie himself pressing for a more "forthright" attitude, he also gave the embassy the impression that developments were moving in the right direction within the ruling Labor party.[37] In November Chargé Villard reported that Foreign Minister Lange himself was moving closer to the West. The embassy was most impressed by a speech the Foreign Minister had delivered in the Storting on October 30.[38]

Although the three Scandinavian countries were often dealt with as a unit, in the fall of 1947 the Danes seemed to enjoy better relations with the State Department than did

Sweden and Norway. This was indicated by the omission of Denmark in the denunciations by Kennan and Hickerson, despite the fact that Copenhagen had taken basically the same position as Sweden and Norway in the General Assembly. There was also a tone of relative satisfaction in the reports from the U.S. Embassy in the Danish capital, different from that which now prevailed in reports from Oslo and Stockholm.

I have already dealt with the possibility of varying expectations on the part of the United States. It was also a fact that on the question of the scope of the organization to handle Marshall Plan assistance, the Danes took a position more to the liking of the United States than did the Swedes and the Norwegians. Furthermore, the Danes themselves cultivated an image of being the most Western-oriented of the Scandinavians. In July 1947 the Danish ambassador to the United States, Kauffmann, had told Ambassador Marvel in Copenhagen that Denmark was much more inclined to the West than were the other two countries. He also volunteered—probably on his own authority—that if Denmark could receive some protection against the Soviet Union, it would be ready to move even further in the direction of the West. What Kauffmann had in mind was an assurance that "the Truman Doctrine would be extended so as to protect Denmark from any threatened aggression from Russia."[39]

A few days later Prime Minister Kristensen expressed himself in similar, although definitely vaguer, terms. According to Marvel, the Prime Minister indicated that he thought Danish-American relations would be strengthened in the future "but that all-out expression of this view by Denmark was retarded by caution of Norwegians and more particularly Swedes." On November 15 the new Prime Minister, Hans Hedtoft of the Social Democrats, told the ambassador that immediate announcement of a pro-Western policy was prevented by the present Danish antipathy toward Britain and, again, "the attitude of Norwegians and Swedes." Hedtoft even stated, with reference to the governments in Oslo and Stockholm, that "He hopes to persuade them into American viewpoint, but admits difficulties."[40] With the exception of their attitudes to the Marshall Plan organization, little evidence existed to support Copenhagen's view of Denmark as more pro-Western than Norway and Sweden.

One reason for the Danes presenting themselves in such a fashion was probably related to the question of American bases on Greenland. The Danish government recognized that the United States would insist on having bases on Greenland. By exaggerating their Western orientation and the hesitancy of Sweden and Norway, the Danes could hope to postpone the delicate negotiations for a new base treaty. This did not prevent Copenhagen from pointing out that concessions as to Greenland would be easier to make if Washington could help Denmark get rid of its many German refugees.[41]

Despite Washington's preference for either buying Greenland or obtaining an agreement for long-term base rights (99 years), the continuation of the status quo was an acceptable interim solution. Secretary of State Byrnes had told Foreign Minister Rasmussen in December 1946 that "we are willing to continue the status quo for a reasonable period while a definite solution is being sought by the two governments."[42]

The United States was firmly opposed to any attempt to eliminate the bases on Greenland. After the Danish Communists had introduced a resolution seeking the termination of the Greenland Defense Agreement, Secretary of State Marshall emphasized that the United States would be "profoundly shocked by passage Communist resolution and should Dan Govt acquiesce in passage we could not avoid conclusion such action carried implied charge US in some way failed to live up to its international obligations or obligation to Den." Washington was also strongly opposed to suggestions that the Greenland matter be brought up in the United Nations.[43]

The Danish government made the Communists withdraw the resolution by stating that it would try to bring about the termination of the bases. Little was actually done to accomplish this.[44] But as it was hardly possible to conclude a new agreement in this political climate, signs of impatience could be detected in Washington.[45] Yet, both the State Department and the military were prepared to live with the status quo at least until ongoing internal discussions on the contents of a new draft agreement had been completed.[46]

Since Sweden was seen as the least pro-Western of the Scandinavian countries, the question could be asked whether the appointment of H. Freeman Matthews as ambassador to that country represented an attempt to change Swedish attitudes. Matthews was a very prominent Foreign Service officer. From 1945 to 1947 he had served as Director of the Office of European Affairs. As such he was well acquainted with the highest levels of policy making in Washington.

His appointment was probably not part of a larger strategy. Nothing in the sources indicate such a connection. The explanation Matthews himself has given, which is supported by others, is simply that as a Foreign Service officer he could only spend four years at a time in Washington. In mid-1947 his time was up and few other embassies available.[47] There had in fact been a Foreign Service ruling that Matthews had to take up a post abroad before the end of August.[48] In addition, at the time he was appointed, on July 17, the relationship between the United States and Sweden was still satisfactory. Only later did differences over the Marshall Plan and at the UN General Assembly lead to a deterioration.

Nevertheless, the appointment of Matthews as ambassador to Sweden illustrated the growing importance of Sweden and Scandinavia in the East-West conflict. One other point should also be noted in connection with his appointment. With Matthews in Stockholm, it was likely that the embassy there would take on such importance that it would have consequences for American attitudes even toward the other two countries. Ambassadors Marvel in Copenhagen and Bay in Oslo did not have anything like the standing of Matthews within the State Department. They were both political appointments, but with little political leverage.[49]

The extent of Washington's dissatisfaction with Swedish policies was revealed a few months later in the American response to Stockholm's feelers for economic assistance in December 1947. Since a financial crisis was expected in Sweden in the first quarter of 1948, the Erlander government had decided to explore the possibility of obtaining a credit of approximately 75 million dollars from the United States.

American financial experts agreed with the Swedish analysis of the seriousness of that country's economic problems. The State Department recognized that if the Swedes applied formally to the Export-Import Bank, they would quite likely obtain assistance.[50] Yet the department decided to discourage the Swedes from seeking such assistance. In January 1948, the embassy in Stockholm was informed that Sweden would be advised not to seek a loan. The Swedish government followed this advice.

The attitude of the State Department stemmed from several factors. For one, it would be inopportune to grant assistance at a time when it was still not clear what effect the Marshall Plan would have on the Swedish economy. Also, the European Recovery Program had not yet made its way through Congress. But there could be little doubt that dissatisfaction with Sweden's policy of neutrality represented another factor behind Washington's negative attitude. Such considerations probably figured most prominently in the European Office and in the Northern European Division within the State Department.[51]

The opposition of the department to a loan should not be interpreted to mean that Washington was opposed to every form of assistance. Sweden would of course be eligible for support through the Marshall Plan. In addition, the administration advised Stockholm that it would not be opposed to attempts to alleviate the dollar shortage in other ways than through a loan. The State Department was prepared to give Sweden considerable freedom of action to restrict imports from the dollar area and possibly even to postpone dollar payments for current business transactions.[52]

Although differences existed in evaluations of the policies of the three Scandinavian countries, the tendency was to look upon them as one unit. This, as well as the fact that the State Department was not alone in regarding the three countries as among the most neutralist-minded in Western Europe, was illustrated by a study made by the Joint Strategic Plans Committee of the JCS, dated December 11, 1947. The committee was making an estimate of probable developments in the world political situation up to 1957. In Western Europe the military planners expected most countries to follow the lead of the United States and Britain. They saw only two exceptions: "Switzerland, because of its tradition, and Scandinavia, because of its vulnerability to Soviet force, will attempt to pursue a course of neutrality."[53]

New Demands for Loyalty

The direction of the changes taking place in U.S. policy after 1945 was abundantly clear—a stronger commitment to anticommunism and a rising interest in almost every part of the world. As we have seen, toward some areas and in some fields policies had been fitted into an anti-Soviet mold already in 1945 or soon thereafter. Toward other parts of the world and in other fields it took considerably longer before actions and attitudes were decisively shaped in such a pattern.

The fact that policies developed gradually can be shown in several ways. One way is to examine how Washington's definition of what constituted an "unacceptable" government changed. Similar changes took place in Moscow, with the Soviet leaders constantly stepping up their demands for loyalty. Since this is a study of American foreign policy, I will only study this process in any detail from the American side.[54]

From the very beginning, Washington expressed strong dislike of the Groza government in Rumania. That government came to power in March 1945, and was only recognized a year later as part of a wider understanding between the United States and the Soviet Union. In return for that recognition, the United States received satisfaction for higher priority interests, especially in Japan. But recognition did not change the strongly negative American appraisals of the Groza government. It received no financial assistance from the United States.

With regard to the governments in Poland and Bulgaria, no such firm dates can be set as to the time when they definitely fell out of favor in Washington. The Fatherland Front Government in Bulgaria was seen as somewhat preferable to the Groza regime in Rumania. Nevertheless, at the Potsdam Conference President Truman pointed out that in Bulgaria as in Rumania governmental reorganization was a necessary precondition for recognition. In the summer of 1945 it was quite evident that the government in Sofia was also unacceptable in Washington.

Poland was different from the two other governments in that the United States and Britain recognized the reorganized Lublin government as early as July 1945. American policy makers hoped that the presence in the government of peasant leader Mikolajczyk and some of his supporters, together with an active Western interest in the affairs of Poland, could prevent full communist domination. In late 1945 few hopes remained in Washington. Even if Poland received American financial assistance in the spring of 1946, this did not represent any acceptance of what was going on in that country. The most important reason for the granting of credits was Western Europe's need for Polish coal.

Gabriel Kolko suggests that in 1945 not even the Fierlinger government of Czechoslovakia was acceptable to American policy makers.[55] Traditionalists such as Feis and Schlesinger imply that Prague met with sympathy in Washington until the communist coup of February 1948.[56] My own study of U.S. policies toward Eastern Europe indicates, as already touched upon, that the government in Czechoslovakia ceased to be acceptable to dominant policy makers in September 1946. At that time financial assistance was abruptly stopped.[57]

From the fall of 1946 the bridge builders on the Eastern side, the Czechs, were out of favor. At that time the bridge builders on the Western side, the Scandinavians, still possessed satisfactory, even friendly, relations with Washington. Implications by Kolko and Gardner that this was not the case are not confirmed by the present study.[58]

One year later, however, the American attitude changed. With the United States coming to regard itself as the leader of the noncommunist world and the intensity of the Soviet-American struggle rising, Washington's demands for loyalty increased. In the fall of 1947 Sweden and Norway

were seen as stumbling blocks to the creation of a strong
Western European organization to make the Marshall Plan
assistance effective. The Scandinavians did not vote right in
the UN. In short, they were not willing to stand up and be
counted in the struggle against Soviet Communism. While
parts of the Republican foreign policy establishment had
long complained about the lack of firmness in Scandinavia's
relations with the Soviet Union, only in the fall of 1947 did
the State Department leadership begin to make similar complaints. Secretary Marshall, Under Secretaries Lovett and
Clayton, Director of the Policy Planning Staff Kennan, and
Director of the Office of European Affairs Hickerson all expressed opposition to elements of the policies of Scandinavia
in general, and of Sweden and Norway in particular. As we
have seen, the Danes fared somewhat better than did the
other two nations.

Washington did not apply the same restrictions to the
Scandinavians as had earlier been done to the Eastern Europeans. With Sweden, Norway, and Denmark in the Marshall
Plan, this was impossible. More important, even if dissatisfaction with at least Norway and Sweden was strong, the
State Department had little desire to put them in a group
with the Eastern Europeans. And yet, the department's attitude to Swedish feelers for economic assistance revealed that
Washington was beginning to consider even economic reprisals.

In the fall of 1947 little ground existed for those who
wanted to be less than fully committed to one side in the cold
war. The United States recognized that the Scandinavians
felt closer to the West than to the East. But that was no
longer sufficient. A moral-political break had to be made,
with the Soviet Union in foreign affairs and with the communists in domestic matters.

The policies of the Scandinavian countries had become
increasingly Western-oriented in 1947. Despite hesitation,
they did join the Marshall Plan and they did agree to expand
the scope of the OEEC. The trouble was that this was not
sufficient to keep up with the rising demands for loyalty in
Washington. On the other side, these modifications of bridge
building were certainly enough to make the Soviet Union in-

creasingly skeptical of their intentions.[59] Instead of having bridges to both East and West, the Scandinavians were in the process of having their bridges cut in both directions at the same time.

Bridge builders were falling out of favor. The reverse side of the same coin was that authoritarian regimes on the right were now seen in a more favorable light than had been the case at the end of the war. This development was best exemplified in relations with Greece and Turkey, and only to a lesser extent with Spain.[60] Obviously, none of these states was living up to the standards for democracy which Washington espoused. They compensated for that by their firm stand against the Soviet Union and against communism.

And yet, a few countries could still be found where Washington demanded less than a full commitment against the Soviet Union and local communism. Finland and Switzerland were the two examples of this.

With Switzerland's special kind of neutrality, its relatively unexposed geographic position, and its insignificant Communist party, it was perhaps not surprising that no serious attempt was made to force the Swiss into any stronger modification of their neutrality than that which resulted from their acceptance of the Marshall Plan and the OEEC. Under Secretary Lovett told President Truman in September 1947 that "Swiss-American relations are on a most friendly basis with no immediate prospect of their deterioration." Furthermore, as Lovett also told Truman, "The Swiss Government is probably the most stable, and certainly one of the most conservative in Europe, and Communist influence in politics and labor unions is of small significance."[61]

The background for Lovett's memo to the President was a letter Truman had received from "a fellow in whom I have considerable confidence." The letter had complained about Soviet Communist influence in Switzerland, thereby illustrating that even in the Swiss case there were some who felt that the demands of loyalty should be stepped up. Truman only sent the information on to the State Department without comment.[62]

More interesting than the American attitude toward

Switzerland was that toward Finland. The United States had recognized Finland as early as August 1945. Washington had also gone far in extending financial assistance to the former Axis satellite. The State Department recognized that both Soviet and communist influences were strong in Finland, but did not really take any strong exception to this state of affairs.

Finland was considered a special case. Having been at war with the Soviets, some degree of reconciliation was desirable. Washington also appreciated that its exposed geographic position had to lead to concessions to Soviet interests. At least equally important for America's acceptance of Finnish policies was the fact that, unlike for instance the Czechs, the Finns were regarded as "tough, dogged" in their spirit of independence.[63] Although they would adjust to Soviet desires, this would be done not from the conviction of the heart, but from the pragmatism of the head. The Finns could be relied upon to set definite limits on Soviet influence.

In a review dated July 1947 departing Director of the Office of European Affairs H. Freeman Matthews told the Secretary of State that the United States should continue to give encouragement to Finland in the form of financial assistance. At the same time Washington should refrain "from acts in Finland which might reasonably be regarded by the USSR as a challenge to its essential interests."[64] Illustrating continuity in America's policies, this analysis could be seen both as a description of past actions and as a guideline for the future.

Nevertheless, Finland and Switzerland represented the special cases. The rule was that Washington was coming to insist that a clear choice be made in favor of the West. Attempts to avoid such a decision would strain relations with the United States. And Matthews, who in mid-1947 showed such understanding of Finnish policies, was soon to argue that pressure be exerted on the Scandinavians to increase their Western orientation.

4

Socialism
and Scandinavian
Social Democrats

AT THE END of 1947 strains had developed in relations between the United States and Scandinavia, in particular Norway and Sweden. This strain apparently arose from dissatisfaction felt by important policy makers in Washington with the foreign policies of the two countries. Sweden and Norway had gradually become more oriented toward the West, but their shift of attitude had not been sufficient to keep up with the rising demands for loyalty in the State Department.

It could be argued that American policies toward the various parts of the world were determined not primarily by the foreign policy attitudes of the countries involved, but by their economic systems. According to this hypothesis, Washington's attitude would depend on the extent to which a country was willing to enter into close economic relations with the United States. Of particular interest in such countries would be the size of American imports, the export of basic materials which the United States did not have in sufficient quantities, and the climate for U.S. investments. Having this perspective in mind, the present chapter will analyze the American response to the policies of the Scandinavian social democrats.

Views of American Historians

Neither revisionists nor traditionalists deal with Washington's attitude to the economic policies of Scandinavia. To concentrate first on revisionists, while the Kolkos and Lloyd Gardner in their brief mention of the Swedish loan to the Soviet Union imply that Scandinavia's less than all-out commitment to the West met with a negative response, they write practically nothing about the U.S. attitude to the domestic policies of the region. To place my own findings in some perspective, I will therefore have to examine revisionist analyses of Washington's response to policies similar to those of the Scandinavians. The British Labour party is a natural choice in this respect since the policies followed by the Attlee government in Britain were in many ways quite similar to those of the Scandinavian social democrats.

Most revisionists agree that the basic motive in American foreign policy was the need to promote the interests of U.S. capitalism, despite differences in the degree of primacy attached to this factor as opposed to noneconomic factors. The most extreme position is found, as usual, with the Kolkos. To Gabriel and Joyce Kolko the driving force was "to restructure the world so that American business could trade, operate and profit without restriction everywhere."[1] From such a point of departure, the United States is seen as opposed not only to all obstacles for American exports, but to all measures in any way detrimental to U.S. investments abroad. Any hint of socialism would arouse profound distrust. In a rather sweeping statement, the Kolkos indicate that the United States was opposed to the British "economic program of social security, high taxes, and nationalization." Thus, even high taxes and social security met with opposition in Washington.[2]

On the other hand, the Kolkos are not consistent in seeing policy makers as firmly opposed to communists, socialists, moderate social democrats, and even progressive nonsocialists. For instance, despite the sweeping nature of the statement just quoted, the Kolkos are able to write about the British Labour party that "Suffused with anticommunism, such social democracy might indeed become a most natural, perhaps the most reliable, ally of the special brand of internationalism the United States was now offering the world." A similar judgment is made of the attitude toward the French Socialists, the SFIO.[3]

The fact that the United States came to cooperate fairly closely with the Attlee government presents a problem to other revisionists as well. Even a moderate such as Thomas G. Paterson emphasizes that the quest for raw materials, investments, and markets represented the main theme in American foreign policy in the early postwar period. At the same time he maintains that "the issue of socialism never seriously disrupted Anglo-American relations; American government and business leaders learned to accommodate themselves to the British system."[4]

Walter LaFeber and Lloyd Gardner are not so sweeping as the Kolkos in analyzing the motive forces of American foreign policy. But they both find the United States opposed to any domestic radicalism in Labour's policies. LaFeber states that the British "received severe warnings from Washington about further nationalization of industry." He also sees the United States as intent on removing restrictions on American trade with the Commonwealth. Gardner basically holds the same view. In his reconstruction of events, the Labour government represented a threat to American policy makers on three levels. The British Labour leaders might bring about a socialist economy in Britain itself, they might impose such an economy on the U.K. zone in Germany, and, finally, they might choose to close the sterling bloc.[5]

Traditionalists see a quite different picture. To them the promotion of economic interests is no basic concern in U.S. foreign policy. Instead they concentrate on legitimate security needs and on the promotion of self-determination. This group of historians, therefore, hardly pays any attention to the question of the Truman administration's reaction to the domestic policies of Britain or of other countries in Western Europe. As long as the country in question had a popularly elected government, Washington, in their opinion, did not take significant opposition to the economic policies pursued.

In connection with the loan to Britain, Herbert Feis just barely mentions that the Americans were interested in reducing tariffs and in ending restrictions on foreign exchange. Nothing is said about opposition to other aspects of Labour's policies. One is led to believe that no such opposition existed. Similarly, in his analysis of the situation in Germany, Feis notes in passing that the Soviets attacked the West for the decision not to nationalize the mines and industries of the Ruhr. He does not elaborate on what he, as opposed to the Soviets, thinks. Even William Hardy McNeill emphasizes Washington's insistence on democratic regimes, although he certainly acknowledges that the Americans generally desired freer trade among the countries of the world.[6]

Post-revisionist John Lewis Gaddis places more emphasis on economic factors than do most traditionalists. Nevertheless, in most cases he too finds the principles of self-determination more important than economic considerations. Even Gaddis sees little or no U.S. opposition to socialist or social democratic measures in Western Europe or elsewhere.[7]

The Truman Administration, Trade, and Socialism

There can be little doubt that the United States was generally working for a world with freer trade and, thereby, an environment suitable to American economic expansion. Attempts to promote free trade principles can be found in parts of the Atlantic Charter, in the famous Article 7 of the Master Lend-Lease Agreement with Britain, in the U.S. Proposals for Expansion of World Trade and Employment, in the founding of the World Bank and the International Monetary Fund, in certain clauses in the loans to Britain and several other countries, and in the interest taken in the establishment of an International Trade Organization.

American policy makers argued that while the promotion of freer trade ought to be the concern of all nations, it was up to each country to decide for itself on questions such as the balance between the public and private sector. Thus, the Proposals for Expansion of World Trade and Employment of 1945–46 contained special sections which were meant to make it easier for state-controlled countries such as the Soviet Union to participate in the freer trading world that Washington wanted to establish.[8]

The separation between international free trade and national economic control was difficult, if not impossible, to maintain in practice. Invariably, controlled economies would have problems in adjusting to the American plans for closer international economic relations. Just to accept the principle that commercial considerations alone were to regulate the setting of prices for all companies, whether state-owned or private, would be contrary to the desires of many socialist countries.

It can come as no surprise that politicians and officials in Washington generally considered the American economic system a model which other nations would do well to emulate. Private enterprise had made the United States the most prosperous country in the world. Other states would benefit more from learning from the United States than from strengthening the government-controlled sector of their economies.[9]

The loan agreements with Britain of December 1945 and with France of May 1946 both contained several clauses which were meant to promote freer trade. The British had to agree to make the pound convertible with the dollar and in principle to remove restrictions that discriminated against imports from the United States. The French accepted somewhat different clauses which had some of the same effect, to promote trade with the rest of the world and to discourage the setting up of regional trading blocs. They also had to promise to return trade between the United States and France to private channels.[10]

While the United States undoubtedly pressed for the promotion of freer trade among nations, a more interesting question is the extent to which Washington tried to influence more domestic sectors. What was the American position on socialization, governmental regulations, and welfare economies? Again, before dealing with the Scandinavian countries, I will go briefly into the attitude to countries in Western Europe considered more important.

Considerably less was done with regard to domestic matters than with regard to foreign trade. In private conversations prominent members of the Truman administration expressed strong dislike of some of the policies pursued by the British Labour government. Secretary of Commerce Harriman, Secretary of the Navy Forrestal, and atomic energy adviser Baruch often did so.[11] (They were only three of the many businessmen who occupied important posts. Others were Robert Lovett, William Clayton, Edward Stettinius, Robert Patterson, and Ambassadors Steinhardt, Douglas, Griffis, Bruce, and Gardner.[12]) Sometimes the British were informed about the dislike most officials of the Truman administration felt for socialization.[13] More important, however, than such more-or-less private views would be the extent to which Washington more directly tried to influence the domestic policies of other countries.

Walter LaFeber quotes the answer Clayton, American negotiator of the loan to Britain, gave when he was pressed by Baruch to do something to stop socialization: "We loaded the British loan negotiations with all the conditions that the traffic would bear."[14] From the perspective of interference in domestic affairs, what immediately follows—and that part is not quoted by LaFeber—is even more interesting,

> I don't know of anything that we could do or should do to prevent England or other countries from socializing certain of their industries if that is the policy they wish to follow. The attempt to force such countries to adopt policies with respect to their domestic economies contrary to their wishes would, in my opinion, be an unwarranted interference in their domestic affairs.[15]

This attitude did not prevent Clayton and many others from feeling that with American economic assistance the

British would probably feel less urge to push for socialization and governmental regulations. The reasoning was that bad economic conditions disposed a country to government intervention, while prosperity would encourage continued private enterprise.[16]

The State Department even noted some advantages in a Labour government as opposed to a Conservative one. This was brought out in the Department's policy statement on Britain of June 1948:

> On the ideological level, the election of a socialist-labor government in Britain has strengthened that country's domestic position vis-à-vis Soviet propaganda. A government of this type is not so vulnerable with its own people as a conservative regime might be to charges of reactionary prejudice against the Soviets, and a socialist flavor to its policies is a good antidote to Communist appeal abroad. While the US would not adopt for her own certain of the internal economic and social legislation which the British have adopted, it is not our policy to interfere with or attempt to direct the domestic legislation or policies of the democratically elected representatives of the British people.[17]

Thus, although most policy makers in Washington certainly disliked parts of the domestic policies of the British Labour government, few direct attempts were apparently made to influence their basic direction. In the end the Attlee government did socialize the steel and coal industries, electricity and gas, railroads and airlines.

While approximately one-fifth of the British economy became state-owned, the fraction was even higher in France— between one-third and one-fourth. Again, few indications can be found that the Americans tried to prevent the French from following policies leading to such results. In the loan negotiations the State Department, as already mentioned, pressed for the liberalization of French foreign trade. However, to try to influence the domestic policies of the Blum government would probably only undermine the American goal of strengthening the noncommunist parts of this coalition.[18]

In some special cases, examples can be found of the

United States intervening to stop socialization. In Germany General Clay and the army leadership, with support from Washington, first modified local plans for socialization in Hesse in the American zone, and then maneuvered to prevent British and local plans for the socialization of the coal mines in North Rhine-Westphalia in the Bizone.[19] On the latter occasion Marshall told Clayton that the United States could not participate in any big new commitments to help Europe get back on its feet unless it knew that the problem of producing coal in the Ruhr would be licked. The Secretary continued by emphasizing that ". . . we could not sit by while the British tried out any ideas which they had of experimenting with socialization of coal mines."[20] With Britain now heavily dependent on the United States in Germany, Washington was in a strong position. Few could doubt the outcome. There would be no socialization of the coal mines.

But Germany was an exceptional case. It was an occupied country with the powers of occupation playing a much stronger role there than the United States could do elsewhere in Western Europe. It would be almost as wrong to generalize from the German case as it would be to generalize from the experience of Austria, another occupied country.

In Austria the United States apparently favored the socialization of some basic industries and preferred the Socialists to the major nonsocialist party, the Austrian People's Party. The reason for this seems fairly evident: through socialization the Americans could hope to prevent Soviet extraction of industries which had been predominantly German-owned.

Another reason for the favorable attitude of American occupation authorities to the Austrian Socialists was probably that they were seen as less nationalistic than the nonsocialists. Excessive nationalism could slow down the development of close relations with the United States.[21] A similar appraisal could be noticed in the attitude to other conservative elements in Western Europe. Thus, the State Department and the embassy in Paris definitely preferred Blum's SFIO and the MRP to de Gaulle, despite the strong anticommunism of the latter.[22] And in discussions of the relative merits of the Labour Party and the British Conservatives, the former was often seen as more open to the world and less interested in closing off the Commonwealth to American influence.[23]

Even the U.S. attitude toward communists was not always so single-minded as one would perhaps think. Washington had few complaints about communists entering into various coalition governments in Western Europe in 1944–45. Although this was to change, there was long a difference between disliking a policy and taking measures to end it. Despite the State Department and other circles in Washington being happy to see the communists out of the French government in May 1947, the United States does not seem to have pressed the noncommunist parties to take such action.[24] American influence was considerably stronger in the more chaotic situation in Italy. Unlike Ambassador Caffery in Paris, Dunn in Rome actively encouraged the noncommunists to break with the communists. Even Secretary of State Marshall made it clear that an Italian government without communist participation would meet with encouragements, for instance in the form of increased economic support.[25]

In 1947 the State Department was on the whole interested in having the communists removed from governments in Western Europe. Sometimes it also tried to split left-wing socialists from more moderate ones. While in Italy the Nenni Socialists were seen as communist "fellow travelers," the breakaway PSLI was quite acceptable from the American point of view, so much so that the State Department took an active interest in having it included in the reconstructed Italian government, but without success until December 1947.[26]

On the political right, persons and parties that had gone far in collaborating with the Fascists were long unable to establish close relations with the United States. For the first years after the war this included Franco's Spain.

Even leaders of the wartime resistance met with little sympathy if their views were unusually conservative or nationalistic. De Gaulle has already been mentioned as an example of this in Western Europe. In Eastern Europe Washington showed little or no sympathy with such right-wing movements as the Arciszewski government of the London Poles, and, after the war, with fanatic anticommunists such as Polish Generals Anders and Bor-Komarowski, and Hungarian Cardinal Mindszenty.[27] But as the attitude toward communists and left-wing socialists hardened, there was no doubt that a softening was taking place in appraisals of most right-wing movements.

Foreign Trade

The Scandinavian countries have historically been heavily dependent on trade with the outside world. Therefore, they have generally favored relatively free trade among nations. Norway, Denmark, and Sweden all had a certain interest in joining the Bretton Woods institutions, the International Monetary Fund and the World Bank. Norway was a charter member of both, while Denmark joined soon afterward. (As a neutral state during the war, Sweden was barred from becoming a charter member.)[28]

Despite general agreement on the overall principles of international trade, some differences existed between the United States and the Scandinavian countries. First, the Scandinavians put stronger emphasis than the United States on the importance of full employment. They were also much more favorably disposed to governmental controls in the form of price stabilization measures. Although these issues indicated significant differences in domestic policies, they do not seem to have created any serious U.S.-Scandinavian controversy in the planning for the International Trade Organization and the General Agreement on Tariffs and Trade.[29]

Second, and more important, the Scandinavians had difficulties in living up to the free-trade principles they supported in theory. Due to wartime damages, needs of reconstruction, and pent-up demands from the war, great problems would arise if their trade were liberalized immediately. In a transitional period it was seen as necessary to conduct trade primarily on a bilateral basis. Norway, Sweden, and Denmark all negotiated numerous agreements which provided for the bilateral exchange of commodities. The State Department agreed that such a pattern of trade might be necessary until conditions had become more normal. And yet, with respect to the Scandinavian countries as well as to most others, Washington usually felt that the bilateral agreements in question were too comprehensive. The transitional period ought to be shorter and the scope less inclusive. Naturally, one reason for this attitude was the fact that restrictions on multilateral trade would hamper American exports.[30]

In the Policy and Information statements on the Scandinavian countries prepared by the State Department in the fall of 1946, complaints could be found about the trading policies of all three of them. Washington's disappointment seemed most noticeable with Sweden. There were apparently two reasons for this. First, Sweden presumably had a stronger economy than almost any state in Europe. The need for a transition period of bilateralism was therefore seen as small. Second, the Americans disliked, as we have seen, the one billion kronor credit the Swedes promised the Russians in 1946. The credit ran for a comparatively long period, five years or more, and was seen to freeze trade in a bilateral pattern. It had been estimated that the credit would make available for shipment to the Soviet Union between 10 and 15 percent of Sweden's total exports.[31]

On March 15, 1947, the Swedish government introduced an import control program. The program would undoubtedly hamper American exports to Sweden. Officials in the State Department felt that the import controls discriminated against the United States and in favor of countries with which Sweden had bilateral agreements, such as the Soviet Union. The department hoped to use Stockholm's desire to obtain some minor economic favors from the United States to change this alleged discrimination.[32]

Treasury officials opposed any such linkage. Their attitude apparently prevailed. Swedish assets, which had been blocked in the United States during the war, were unblocked on March 28. At the end of June an understanding was reached between the two countries that provided for some degree of competition between alternate sources of supply under the import control program.[33]

In September 1947 the Norwegian government imposed emergency import and foreign exchange restrictions. Although these were undoubtedly disliked by most American officials, the embassy in Oslo had to agree that a near breakdown in Norway's import control system had resulted in an unexpectedly large volume of imports. Measures simply had to be taken to alleviate this situation. As some restrictions were maintained into 1948–49, embassy officials indicated, although not in any strong terms, that controls ought to be loosened. In particular, restrictions should not be stricter on dollar than on other imports.[34]

Ambassador Bay took an initiative of his own to strengthen Norwegian-American economic contacts. His idea was to have Norwegian producers provide U.S. industrial concerns with goods they might be in need of. This would increase exports to the United States and give Norway some badly needed dollar earnings. The scheme might also be of some advantage to the United States. Although Bay was a former businessman himself, little came out of this well-meant, but rather loose idea of his.[35]

Despite its support of the principles of freer trade, the Truman administration tried only to a rather limited extent to press these principles on Scandinavia in the period of reconstruction. Disagreements in this field were really minor. With the possible exception of the Swedish-Soviet loan, they were of a nature which made them cause only ripples in American-Scandinavian relations. As to the loan, by the end of 1949 Swedish deliveries to the Soviet Union were so small that less than one-third of the total amount had actually been utilized. The markets in the West were more attractive to Swedish industry than those in the East.[36]

In the loans to France and Britain, as well as in those to several other countries, the United States secured the agreement of the recipient to at least parts of its program of multilateralism. Little of this was found in loans to Norway, the country in Scandinavia that received the largest amounts from the United States. The only point of significance was a general understanding with regard to the 50 million dollars from the Export-Import Bank that purchases under the credit be carried out to the maximum extent possible by private importers through commercial channels.[37] This understanding was repeated in the Marshall Plan program, and its importance will be discussed in the next chapter, as will the whole issue of multilateralism versus bilateralism from 1948 onward.

Several factors explain the decision not to emphasize free trading principles in the loans to Norway. The most important were probably the relative smallness of the assistance and the generally acceptable policies of the Norwegian government with regard to international trade.

It should be noted that the Americans themselves evidenced some of the most blatant breaks with the principles of multilateralism they proclaimed so often and so loudly. The best example in relations with Scandinavia was the shipping clause in Export-Import Bank loans and in the Marshall Plan program. And, while pressing for imports through private channels, the U.S., as Clayton told Baruch in December 1946, "still retains the import monopoly on numerous commodities, for example tin, rubber, quinine, antimony etc. The United States Government continues to contract for the Cuban sugar crop and monopolizes the importation of same into the United States."[38]

The most comprehensive measure of socialization in Scandinavia was found in Swedish plans for establishing national and preferably state control over imports and trade in petroleum products. If carried out, this would mean that three American companies, Gulf, Texas, and Standard Oil, would lose their investments in Sweden. The Social Democratic government had gone far in promising that such plans would be put into effect. In late 1945 and early 1946, when the question was discussed in Washington, a committee appointed by the Swedish government was investigating questions relative to nationalization.

The American reaction was not uniform. In accordance

with the official U.S. attitude, the Division of Commercial Policy within the State Department argued that basically it was up to the Swedes themselves to decide what to do in this matter. What Washington could do would be to point out that prompt and just compensation would be expected in case of nationalization, and to express the hope that a state monopoly would base its policies on commercial and not on political considerations. The Petroleum Division, supported by the oil companies involved, wanted to go further. While acknowledging that such were the limits of the official attitude, these interests wanted to explain the American position in more general terms. Among other things, they wanted to point out to the Swedish government that "from the point of view of the United States as a whole, every narrowing of the area of free enterprise abroad is a matter of concern." The legation in Stockholm took no definite stand. While Ambassador Johnson argued against the measure in rather dramatic economic terms, he also emphasized that from a political point of view American opposition would invariably strengthen the communists and weaken the Social Democratic government.[39]

The State Department needed several months to decide on its position. At the end of March 1946, Acting Secretary Acheson finally cabled the legation in Stockholm. While recognizing Sweden's right to create a petroleum monopoly, the emphasis in Washington's reaction was on the rather general negative effects such a measure would have. Yet, Johnson was instructed not to take the matter up with the government as such, but only "informally" with some prominent members of the commission studying the question, and only if the ambassador himself thought this advisable.[40]

The United States came out against the nationalization of the petroleum trade and industry in Sweden, but its reaction can not be said to have been very strong. It seems likely that financial considerations involving compensation and political considerations relating to the strong opposition of the nonsocialists were of greater importance than American opposition when the Erlander government in 1947 finally decided that there would be no nationalization.[41]

For a while it had seemed likely that even the Norwegians would create a state monopoly. Standard Oil and the Petroleum Division were afraid that the Labor party would put into effect its promise in the 1945 elections to create monopolies for the import of petroleum, coffee, and sugar. The Gerhardsen government decided to shelve such plans relating to petroleum before Washington had expressed any reaction.[42]

The Domestic Side

Although it could be argued that a certain aloofness was the basic attitude even on the foreign trade side, this was much more clearly the case in Washington's reaction to the domestic policies of the Scandinavian countries. For instance, from May 1945 through December 1949 I have not found one single instruction from the State Department to the embassy in Oslo that gave the ambassador any significant guidance in questions relating to internal political problems. Nothing in the cables of the department directly favored one party over another. The situation was much the same toward Sweden and Denmark.

The tone of the reports going the other way—from the various embassies to Washington—was only slightly different. It is the job of an embassy to inform about all developments of importance. This can never be done with complete impartiality. Although this is so, it would not be wrong to state that even the reports from Scandinavia were characterized by the feeling that the area was of peripheral interest to Washington. This feeling was most evident in the first two years after the liberation. In August 1945 Ambassador Osborne excused his "dull" reporting from Oslo, the reason for this dullness being simply that "the material for such reports has been extremely scanty and for the most part extremely dull."[43] There was nothing to worry about as far as Norway was concerned—in fact, there was little to inform about at all.

To avoid repetition, in this part I shall concentrate on

the reaction to developments in Norway. Sweden and Denmark will be brought in mostly for comparative purposes. In dealing with antisocialism, little is lost by this since at least parts of the State Department felt that the Norwegian Labor party was the most radical in Scandinavia.[44]

Political conditions in Norway stabilized rapidly after the liberation. The fact that the attempt to form a coalition government under Liberal Paal Berg failed caused no excitement on the part of Ambassador Osborne. A certain dislike for Conservative leader Hambro could be noticed. In part this may have been due to his role in preventing the formation of a Berg government. Probably more important, Hambro was seen as nationalistic, and not particularly friendly to the United States.[45]

On June 25, 1945, a coalition government was formed under the leadership of Laborite Einar Gerhardsen. Its formation met with neither overtly positive nor negative comments from Osborne. His main point was that "Happily at no point was there apparent any danger that a solution based on democratic principles would not be found." Despite the inexperience of the new government, it was seen as a strong one. The participation of two Communists caused no comment at all on the part of the ambassador.[46]

Neither did the negotiations between the Labor party and the Communists for the formation of a united party meet with any opposition from Osborne. Basically, he only reported what took place. As far as his personal opinion went, he seems to have had no strong feelings either way. His best contact within the Labor party, Secretary General Haakon Lie, apparently took the position that noncommunists would control communists in a united party. A united party would also eliminate the threat of an independent Communist party to the left of Labor.[47]

While the main tone even in reports from the legation in Copenhagen on the Labor-Communist unity talks in Demark was one of general reporting, a slightly more critical attitude could be noticed. Despite this, there is no indication that the legation tried to influence the outcome of the negotiations.[48] The unity efforts failed in both Norway and Denmark.

The Norwegian elections in October resulted in a parliamentary majority for Labor, and Einar Gerhardsen formed a new government based exclusively on that party. Osborne's only comment on the large Communist vote, 12 percent, was that the "Communists did worse than they hoped, better than Laborites have been willing to admit." The major surprise was the 8 percent of the vote received by the Christian People's Party. The nature of this party was evidently difficult to comprehend for Americans. The Policy and Information Statement from August 1946 termed the party "mystic." After new elections in the fall of 1949 an analysis by the Research and Analysis branch of the State Department called the party "somewhat nebulous."[49]

However, at least one person within the embassy in Oslo, Assistant Military Attaché Thor B. Ellingsen, was fearful of communist strength and communist intentions in Norway. In several reports Ellingsen argued that the communists were arming and perhaps preparing for an uprising. The Military Attaché, Rayens, later Lester Johnsen, considered these reports much exaggerated. So did the ambassador and Norwegian politicians and military leaders who were asked to comment on such rumors.[50]

Relations between the Labor parties and the Communist parties in the three Scandinavian countries cooled off from the fall of 1945 on. To some extent they were nevertheless still able to cooperate in passing reform legislation. Only in the spring and summer of 1947 did an open break occur.

I have not found any examples of the local embassies urging the social democrats to start campaigns against the communists. But it was obvious that the hardening which had taken place in Washington meant that the Americans would be supporters of such a campaign once it started. In mid-1947 both the embassy in Oslo and the State Department noted with satisfaction that the Norwegian Labor party was making strong efforts to combat communist strength, in particular in the trade unions. The embassies in Copenhagen and Stockholm were reporting on similar developments in Denmark and Sweden. In the reports from Stockholm a rising dissatisfaction with the left wing of the Social

Democrats under Minister of Finance Wigforss was also noticeable. Wigforss's policy of "orthodox class ideology and his
theories about a redistribution of wealth" were seen as weakening the broad front against the communists.[51]

The increasingly anticommunist attitude of the Labor
parties in Norway, Sweden, and Denmark was one reason for
the positive evaluations the State Department made of conditions in the three countries. Yet, even before the campaigns against the communists started in full, the Department stressed that "Norway and its two Scandinavian
neighbors, Sweden and Denmark, constitute the strongest
bulwark of social democracy on the continent of Europe
today, and it is to our interest that this condition shall continue to obtain."[52]

Scandinavian social democrats were seen not only as
anticommunist and increasingly so, but also as fairly moderate and representative of the prevailing political current in
the region. This was brought out in the department's analysis
of the domestic policies of the Norwegian Labor government
in August 1946:

> In domestic matters, the present left-of-center Labor Govern-
> ment is following a moderate socialization program based
> upon a comprehensive system of planning which seeks to rec-
> oncile the interests of both capital and labor. In the opinion of
> the Labor Party leaders, this policy, which is essentially a
> continuance of the prewar evolutionary processes, comes clos-
> est to meeting the desires of the majority of the Norwegian
> people, who on the whole are more interested in honest gov-
> ernment which will institute social reform with the least pos-
> sible shock to existing institutions than in state socialism.[53]

As we shall shortly see, Ambassador Bay complained
about some of the economic policies of the Norwegian Labor
government. However, his overall analysis was not basically
different from that of the regional specialists in the State
Department. In his report of April 11, 1947, on events in
Norway in the last year, the ambassador first found "political activities here rather calm and subdued" and then concluded by stating that "the present Labor Government is ac-

ceptable and well entrenched . . . Communism is no serious
threat in the foreseeable future." In his half-yearly report
dated October 1947, it was obvious that Bay wanted the government to scale down its many controls and regulations. At
the same time he had to note that "the country as a whole is
fairly well satisfied with the Labor Government, despite increased taxes, high prices and tightening governmental controls." [54]

It was easy to maintain an attitude of noninterference as
long as the policies of the Labor party were regarded as moderate. Even so, it is incorrect to see the United States as consistently opposed to social and economic reforms, and as
always preferring conservative parties to more radical ones.
As we have seen in the British case, the State Department
found that the Labour party could be more effective than the
Conservative in combating Soviet or communist influence.
The battle could be carried on not only through vigorous
campaigns, but also more indirectly. Reforms could weaken
the very foundations of communism. In a draft Policy and Information Statement on Sweden, the Department noted that
"if the Social Democratic Party realized substantial portions
of its social reform program, the Communists' strength may
be expected to wane." [55]

As far as governmental regulations were concerned, the
Norwegian Labor party was seen as going further than its
Swedish and Danish counterparts. Since the policies of the
Norwegians met with no basic opposition, it could be expected that the response to Swedish and Danish policies
would be at least equally positive. Generally this was indeed
the case.

In 1945 the Social Democrats in Denmark had adopted a
program in favor of a planned economy with a rather comprehensive system of governmental control. It was obvious
that the legation in Copenhagen was skeptical of this program, even though it doubted that parts of it would ever be
put into effect. [56] After the elections nonsocialists, not the
Social Democrats, formed a government. When the Hedtoft
government came to power after new elections in October
1947, the embassy found little to worry about. The 1945 pro-

gram had been an effort to reduce the communist vote. It had gone too far and was now, in the analysis of the embassy, recognized by the Social Democrats as a tactical error. In his account of the situation as of November 1947, Ambassador Marvel described the attitude of the Hedtoft government in the following terms:

> No schemes of nationalization of industry or breaking up large estates will be undertaken. Effort will be made to enlarge social reforms such as old-age pensions, workman's compensation et cetera, but with an eye to what budget will bear. In short, policy of prewar Social Democrats will be followed.[57]

This could hardly frighten anyone in Washington. The situation in Sweden in the first two years after the war was described in similar terms. With the exception of the petroleum monopoly, the general appraisal of the policies of the Swedish Social Democrats was favorable. A comment made by the Office of Special Political Affairs in the State Department in August 1947 was typical. The Office thought Sweden would be exceptionally well suited for membership on the Economic and Social Council of the UN because of "its economic importance and its moderate, progressive economic and social policies."[58]

Instead of going further into the early period, the question could be asked whether the negative assessments which were made of the foreign policy of Sweden from the fall of 1947 on came to influence Washington's analysis of the domestic situation in that country. Both in National Security Council reports from August-September 1948 and in a new Policy Statement of August 1949, the tone was certainly critical of Sweden's foreign policy. On the domestic side, however, these sources contained few complaints. While the Erlander government had proved unwilling to stand up to the Soviet Union, Washington definitely recognized the willingness of the Social Democrats to fight the communists domestically.

The State Department noted that communism had not thrived in Sweden. While communist influence had risen during the war and in the immediate postwar period, the party had experienced a great decline since the end of 1947. The reasons for this were "international events, the popular recognition of the fifth column characteristics of the Party, and the anti-Communist campaign of the Swedish Social Democrats and trade unions."[59] Yet, firmness against communism on the domestic side only made U.S. disappointment over Sweden's foreign policy greater. The Swedes were seen to belong to the West. The problem was that they refused to assume the responsibilities that this entailed.

The only criticism of note was the allegation that Swedish industry was extensively organized along cartel lines in pulp and paper, mining, metallurgical, and electrical equipment. These arrangements represented a potentially restrictive influence on the free movement of international trade. As we have seen, Washington felt freer to criticize foreign trade practices as compared to domestic policies. But since the cartel arrangements in question had not yet proved to have any such restrictive influence, the State Department only noted that "US policy remains one of alert observation for possible restrictive effects."[00]

Washington generally regarded the purely domestic policies of Scandinavia as beyond the scope of official criticism. To take Norway as an example again, from 1945 to 1947 the embassy in Oslo was never instructed to present any grievances against the economic policies of the Labor government. Only with the introduction of the Marshall Plan was the influence of the United States to be of any significance. This does not mean that criticism could not be found in correspondence between the American embassy in Oslo and the State Department in Washington. The point is that until the time of the Marshall Plan such criticism was not brought up in official conversations with representatives of the Norwegian government. At least, if critical remarks were made, they were not reported back to Washington.

The part of Labor's domestic policies which met with most skepticism in the department as well as in the embassy in Oslo was the so-called Lex Thagaard. The Lex Thagaard made it possible for the government to do almost anything it liked in the economic sphere. Public authorities could set prices, decide whether a concern was to have the right to start production, to expand, to change to new articles, or to close down. It should be mentioned that little use was actually made of the most far-reaching articles in this legislation.[61]

As early as May 1945 the Division of Northern European Affairs noted that "While possibly desirable on economic grounds in order to curb inflation and to facilitate an orderly reconstruction of the Norwegian economy, this measure [the Lex Thagaard] resembles too closely the policy followed by Quisling and, for reasons of political expediency, may have to be diluted."[62] A similar kind of at least implied criticism could be found in reports from Osborne and later, more strongly, from Bay.

At the same time, until late 1947 the embassy in Oslo had to agree that the Labor government met with little opposition from the nonsocialists. As to the reasons for this, Bay noted, probably with some sympathy, that the Labor party had proved its ability to keep the trade unions in line with regard to strikes and wages. He also felt that, despite the annoyances of all the restrictions, the average citizen led a contented life.[63]

Thus, even in the reports sent by Bay, criticism of the Lex Thagaard and other far-reaching governmental regulations was muted. A more general summing-up of the attitude of the ambassador was found in that part of his long report of October 1947 where he stated that:

> . . . Norway's Labor Government, while espousing basic socialistic principles and a program of State economic planning, has tempered the implementation of its plans with a realistic recognition of practical limitations and a healthy understanding of the individualism of most Norwegians.[64]

That was not an unperceptive judgment on the policies of the Labor government. Neither could it be seen as a harsh judgment.

At this time the CIA also made a comprehensive analysis of the situation in Norway. In a long report of September 1947, the agency emphasized that despite extensive governmental control and regulation, Norway's economy was still essentially one of free enterprise. The authors of the report even thought that the notable economic improvement which had taken place in Norway after the war was "largely attributable to intelligent application of Government controls which had been agreed to in principle by all parties as temporary necessities under post-war conditions." Another positive appraisal of governmental controls was made by the agency a year and a half later, in February 1949.[65] As R. Harris Smith has argued in his book on the Office of Strategic Services, the predecessor of the CIA, those who see the OSS and the CIA as filled only with conservatives are in for a surprise.[66]

With the introduction of the Marshall Plan, American influence on Norway's foreign trade as well as its domestic policies increased considerably. This period will be dealt with in the next chapter.

5

The Marshall Plan
and Norway:
A Case Study

IN THIS CHAPTER I will study the American attitude to
Scandinavian social democrats from a different perspective
from that of the preceding chapter. Instead of analyzing the
relationship between the Truman administration and the
ruling parties in Scandinavia in general, I will deal with the
questions of how and to what extent the United States used
the Marshall Plan to influence the domestic policies of these
countries, and Norway in particular.

Washington's policy in the years from 1945 to 1947 represented a mixture of rising interest and lingering lack of
interest, of developing new contacts and commitments and
still seeing Scandinavia as peripheral to Europe, of expansion and limitations thereto. The introduction of the Marshall Plan and the participation of the Scandinavian countries in the OEEC represented an expansion of American
assistance and commitments to these countries. A new interest was taken in their domestic policies. Yet, as we shall see,
the effects of the Marshall Plan may easily be exaggerated.

A Brief Historiographic Sketch

The question of how the United States came to influence the domestic policies of the countries participating in the Marshall Plan has, not unexpectedly, received most attention from revisionist historians. From their perspective of seeing the United States as a capitalist power bent on shaping a world congenial to its economic interests, the Marshall Plan offered a golden opportunity. As usual, the most clear-cut presentation of this view is found with the Kolkos: "America's intention to shape Western Europe's economic policies was the critical fact of the plan from the beginning." There was to be no more socialization, expenditures for social welfare were to be restricted, the budget balanced, and a system of taxation established that encouraged private initiative. The result was that the position of labor and the great masses deteriorated. Apparently exceptions existed to this rule, because the Kolkos suddenly state that "[only] in England and Scandinavia did labor's relative position improve."[1] Hardly anything is said to explain why these countries differed from the rest of Western Europe.

Again as usual, Walter LaFeber holds a more moderate view. Instead of seeing the Marshall Plan as an instrument to further only economic interests, he argues that the plan offered all things to all people. And yet, in his analysis of how the United States exported its economic system through the Marshall Plan, he seems to revert to the position of the Kolkos. In a summing up of the advantages the Truman administration gained through the plan, LaFeber notes that the Marshall Plan would

> eradicate the threat of continued nationalization and spreading socialism by releasing and stimulating the investment of private capital, maintain demand for American exports, encourage Europeans to produce strategic goods which the United States could buy and stockpile, preserve European and American control over Middle Eastern oil supplies from militant nationalism which might endanger the weakened Euro-

pean holdings, and free Europeans from economic problems so they could help the United States militarily.[2]

Most traditionalists deal primarily with the immediate postwar phase. Therefore, what they write about the influence of the Marshall Plan on the domestic policies of the Western European countries should not be pressed. Nonetheless, their general perspective is clear. The United States simply helped rehabilitate the economies of Western Europe and thereby beat back the threat of a communist take-over. In their opinion, this can hardly be called interference in domestic policies.

What Herbert Feis writes in his *From Trust to Terror* about the more direct influence of the Marshall Plan on Western Europe is found in a footnote where he describes the operations of the so-called counterpart funds. In his biography of George Marshall, Robert Ferrell devotes two chapters to various aspects of the Marshall Plan, barely mentioning the spreading of American economic influence.[3]

Instead of going further into the cold war literature, I will mention some specialized studies on the workings of the Marshall Plan. The two most detailed ones are Hadley Arkes' *Bureaucracy, the Marshall Plan, and the National Interest,* and Harry Bayard Price's *The Marshall Plan and Its Meaning.*[4]

The point of view of Hadley Arkes is well summed up in his phrase of the United States being "The Imperfect Interventionist." On the one hand, the United States had many ways of influencing the economic policies of Western Europe. Washington had to consent to any use of the counterpart funds, all kinds of clauses were introduced to promote U.S. exports, limitations were imposed on trade with Eastern Europe, private channels of trade were favored over those controlled by the government, investment plans had to be submitted to American authorities.[5]

On the other hand, while the Kolkos see the United States as not only having these as potential instruments, but also as actively exploiting them, Arkes concludes that they were all circumscribed in different ways. Disputes arose among various authorities over exactly what to demand in

return for the assistance given, Washington agreed to leave
many of the basic decisions to the Western Europeans themselves, and in many cases the Europeans simply opposed
American initiatives with success.[6]

Harry Price regards the United States as even less interventionist than does Arkes. His general perspective is one
that sees the United States and Western Europe working
together for a set of common goals. In a typical statement,
Price writes (about the way in which the Economic Cooperation Administration [ECA] could control the dollar assistance) that "this 'leverage' in negotiations was not abused; it
was employed solely in support of mutually agreed principles
and objectives."[7] Very seldom is the United States seen as
interfering in the economy of a Western European country
against the wishes of the local government.

Communism and Socialism

It had long been a basic argument in American foreign
policy that while chaos and economic dislocation would tend
to further the spread of totalitarian ideologies, prosperity
would make such ideologies fade away. After fascism had
been crushed, communism was of course the new benefactor
of chaos.

This argument contributed much to the introduction of
the Marshall Plan. Even George Kennan, the Director of the
Policy Planning Staff, who emphasized that the plan should
not aim at combating communism as such, took most of this
back when he stated that the United States should instead
combat "the economic maladjustment which makes European society vulnerable to exploitation by any and all totalitarian movements and which Russian communism is now
exploiting." When the Secretary of State warned in his
famous Harvard speech that governments or parties "which
seek to perpetuate human misery in order to profit therefrom
politically or otherwise will encounter the opposition of the
United States," there was little doubt as to who represented
the target of his phrase.[8]

Washington expected to reduce communist strength not only by promoting economic growth. A rather direct use of the Marshall Plan money could be seen in Italy where the State Department made it clear during the 1948 election campaign that American aid would be suspended if the communists and their allies won the April elections. Even in countries where communist influence was much weaker than in Italy it was obvious that Washington wanted the local governments to take active steps to combat such influence.[9]

In Norway, however, there was really little need for further action. As we have seen, after the Labor party had started a campaign in the spring of 1947 to reduce communist influence, the State Department had little to complain about. After the take-over in Czechoslovakia communists were more or less branded as potential traitors in case of a Soviet attempt to gain control in Norway.[10]

In July 1948 two of ECA's labor advisers in Paris arrived in Oslo to discuss the trade union situation and the influence of the communists. On July 24 they had a meeting with the leadership of the Norwegian Federation of Labor (LO) and with Haakon Lie, the Secretary General of the Labor party. When the ECA representatives inquired about communist influence, Lie and Nordahl, the leader of LO, answered that "the Communists had little influence in the Norwegian labor movement, were identified, and in process of being weeded out." The two did not stop there. They even indicated that "they would be in a position to offer suggestions to the American labor movement as to how to combat Communism in the unions."[11] With such an attitude prevailing in the leadership of the trade union movement and in the Labor party, the Norwegians could not be accused of any lack of resolve in combating communist influence.

While the attitude toward communists was generally satisfactory, Ambassador Bay complained in January 1948 about the fact that the Norwegian labor leaders issued few public statements in praise of the Marshall Plan. He did not doubt that they were strongly in favor of the plan, but they should come out openly with their support.[12]

Yet, at the very time Bay made his comment to the

State Department in Washington, the situation was in the process of changing. On January 30 the main paper of the Labor party, *Arbeiderbladet,* printed an editorial which was seen by Bay as a forthright endorsement of the Marshall Plan.[13] A few days later the representative board of the Oslo Labor party, with several prominent party leaders present, came out strongly in favor of the European Recovery Program (ERP).[14] Finally, Secretary General Lie had for some time been planning a determined campaign to convince union and party members that the program was in the best interest of the labor movement. A pamphlet was issued by Lie and the Workers' Educational Society (Arbeidernes Opplysningsforbund) describing the ERP in very favorable terms. As a matter of fact, the publication was an almost direct translation of some American material. This fact was not mentioned, which represented a break with copyright laws. The American embassy took responsibility, since it was felt that "the value of the pamphlet might be considerably lessened if it bore any indication of United States inspiration or collaboration which might be exploited by opponents of the European Recovery Program."[15]

Bay had been working for a mission to Norway by a prominent trade union representative, James Carey of the CIO. The purpose was to strengthen Norway's support for the recovery program. In late February the ambassador no longer thought such a mission necessary. The reason given by Bay himself for this change of attitude was simply that Norwegian support for the ERP was now quite strong and consolidated.[16]

After the introduction of the campaign in favor of the Marshall Plan and the repercussions of the Czechoslovak coup, there was no lack of open support for the European Recovery Program. In early April Bay analyzed the Norwegian attitude in the following terms, "Beginning cautiously, the Norwegian attitude toward the ERP has been increasingly appreciative, understanding and energetic." Even more approvingly, in a report made in July the embassy stated that "it may be said that every step in the development of the European Recovery Program since Secretary Marshall's speech at Harvard June 5, 1947, has received satisfactory coverage in every medium of publicity in Norway."[17] The report not only indicated that the embassy was satisfied with what was being done at the moment. The initial skepticism the Plan had met with had even been forgotten.

The question of to what extent Marshall aid was distributed so as to encourage changes in the foreign policies of the countries in Western Europe will be discussed later in this study. Only one aspect of East-West relations will be dealt with here, namely that of East-West trade. (It should be pointed out that many of the findings of this chapter are of a somewhat more tentative nature than are those in other chapters of this study. This is in large part due to the poor state of the files for the Economic Cooperation Administration and its mission in Norway.)

The initial plans of the recovery program were based on an increase in trade between the two halves of Europe. Western Europe badly needed to increase its exports while Eastern Europe could supply some resources which the West wanted. Such imports from the East would also relieve the burden of the United States in providing for the needs of Western Europe.[18]

Largely due to the ever-widening scope of the embargo policy, American trade with Eastern Europe declined very rapidly in the period from 1948 to 1952. Soon the United States even wanted the Marshall Plan countries to limit their trade with Eastern Europe. Washington did not try to have Western Europe adopt quite as restrictive policies as it had itself. What the Americans wanted was to prohibit the export of items contributing "importantly" to the war potential of the Soviet Union and the Eastern European countries (the 1-A list), and to limit, but not prohibit, the export of items contributing less than "importantly" to the potential of these countries (the 1-B list).[19]

Negotiations with the members of the ERP started in September 1948. In 1947 the Scandinavians had been reluctant to agree to anything that might limit their trade, however small, with Eastern Europe. A year later this attitude had been modified as far as Norway and Denmark were concerned. Although the two countries objected to certain items on the lists, in general they agreed to American desires.

State Department reports from November 1948 and July 1949 on the status of the embargo negotiations noted that Denmark had indicated its basic support for the U.S. program. The Norwegian government had agreed to exclude all 1-A items in future transactions. One reason for Denmark's and particularly Norway's compliance with the 1-A list was that few of their products were involved.[20]

The problematic country from the American point of view was Sweden. The policy of neutrality, the limited ERP assistance to Sweden, and its volume of trade with Eastern Europe all made negotiations with Sweden more difficult than with Norway and Denmark. Stockholm was unwilling to go any further than to give vague assurances of agreement in principle with American efforts to limit trade with Eastern Europe.[21]

At least in 1948–49 Washington did not threaten to withhold assistance if the Swedes did not comply. Instead the State Department and the ECA warned that they might have to scrutinize U.S. exports to Sweden from a security standpoint. Such a scrutiny would not relate to all U.S. exports, but to those products that supported Swedish trade with the East. It might also affect Sweden's arms production.[22]

The Swedes agreed to modify their position somewhat. The Erlander government remained unwilling to make any commitment not to export the items on the American lists. It was ready, however, to receive the lists for its own information in negotiations with the countries in Eastern Europe. In addition Stockholm agreed not to export any products received under the recovery program. Despite these concessions, every now and then Sweden's trade with Eastern Europe and its lack of effective cooperation would provoke negative comments from the American side.[23]

On the basis of my limited material, it is difficult to come to any definite conclusions as to the 1-B list. Congress in particular tried to reduce Western Europe's trade in the non-strategic as well as in the strategic field. General trade between Denmark-Norway and Eastern Europe did decline significantly. To a large extent this may well have been due to the American-sponsored embargo policy.

Yet, Scandinavia's trade with Eastern Europe declined little compared to the drop on the American side. It also fell off less than the Western European average. Sweden's trade in some fields even increased. On the whole it can probably be said that at least Norway and Denmark tried to follow the American lead if substantial economic interests were not involved. In that case, not only the Scandinavians, but also most other Western Europeans were loath to follow Washington's signals. They could do this since the administration applied rather limited pressure on the Europeans to make them conform with American standards.[24]

There was little in the legislation of the European Recovery Program that could be interpreted as American opposition to socialization as such. The National Association of Manufacturers, with some support in Congress, had wanted Washington to insist that nations that received economic aid from the United States should undertake no further nationalization programs or "initiate projects which have the effect of destroying or impairing private competitive enterprise."[25] Clauses of this nature were rejected by the Truman administration since they represented obvious interference in domestic affairs. Nonsocialism was not something that the United States could force upon the Europeans against their will. And yet, as we have seen, a widespread feeling existed that perhaps the same objective could be reached more indirectly. The argument was that outside assistance would lessen the need for restrictions and controls in Western Europe.

The American attitude in these matters may be illustrated by an examination of that attitude toward the government-owned industries being established in Norway in 1948–49: the national iron and steel works in Mo i Rana, and the aluminum plant at Årdal.

With regard to the iron and steel works one might have thought that Washington's dislike for government enterprises would be strengthened by the probability that the new plant would lead to a decrease in imports from the United States.[26] This argument, however, is countered by the fact that it was a primary goal of the ERP to obtain a balance in Europe's trade with the dollar area when the four-year period of the plan was over. The iron and steel works would help Norway achieve such a balance.

The reports from the ECA mission and from the embassy in Oslo which I have been able to examine contain only a few indications of American opposition to the works. Conversations the embassy had with government officials were largely informative in nature. A slight criticism might perhaps be seen in questions as to whether the project was to be financed in part by Marshall Plan money, but that can not be taken for granted. At least some U.S. officials in Oslo were much impressed by the savings Norway would make compared to importing steel from abroad.[27] In January 1948, after a visit to the United States, the director of the iron and steel works reported that he had not met with any opposition to the Norwegian plans. Norwegian officials I have interviewed express a similar point of view.[28]

On the other hand, there are firm indications that at least some persons connected with the ECA in Paris and some legislators in Washington disliked the iron and steel works because they were not seen as logical from a European integrationist point of view. Western Europe had more than sufficient capacity to produce whatever steel and iron it needed, and a new plant in Norway would only add to the overcapacity. In the end, however, these objections were not so strong as to prevent the Norwegians from completing the project, and apparently the ECA even financed a small part of it.[29]

While there was a problem in adjusting new to existing capacity in iron and steel, this was less of a problem with regard to aluminum. The new metal was needed in a military production which was becoming of increasing concern to both the United States and Western Europe. The State Department and the embassy noted this fact in their analyses of Norwegian plans for an increase in the production of aluminum.[30] My sources are few, but I have found no evidence that the United States opposed the plant at Årdal for the reason that it was state-owned as opposed to private, in the way most of the nonsocialists in the Storting did.

After the outbreak of the Korean war, the demand for aluminum increased considerably. In part as a result of this, a new state-owned plant was established, this time at Sunndalsøra. With aluminum now being an important strategic material, Washington, through the Economic Cooperation Administration, agreed to lend the Norwegians up to 24 million dollars to help finance the new government project. Most of the nonsocialists in the Storting not only voted against the plant as such, but also against the American loan even after it had been decided that the plant was to be built.[31]

In connection with the enactment of the ERP, Congress had made it clear to the participating countries that Washington preferred that private channels be used to the maximum extent possible in importing goods under the program.[32] This could no doubt be seen as interference in the domestic policies of Western Europe in favor of free enterprise. Nevertheless, little was evidently done to see to it that the Europeans actually conducted their foreign trade through private channels. Often ECA bodies themselves acted contrary to this general line of policy. This was sometimes the case in Norway. Neither in Britain nor in France was it really possible for the United States to circumvent state trading organizations.[33]

For all their initial hesitation about the Marshall Plan, Norwegian government leaders soon felt there had been little reason for their doubts. To an ever-increasing extent, the plan was regarded as a success, both in general and as far as benefits for Norway were concerned.[34] Every now and then rumors circulated that Washington and ECA Administrator Paul Hoffman would no longer tolerate measures of socialization in the countries participating in the recovery program.[35] But, at least in the case of Norway, the United States never intervened directly against what few moves the Norwegians made in this direction.

The OEEC and Bilateral Agreements

On Washington's insistence the Western Europeans had agreed that the Paris conference in the fall of 1947 would result only in a temporary report. A new conference was to be convened to strengthen cooperation among the ERP countries along the lines desired by the State Department.

When the new Paris conference opened on March 15, 1948, it soon proved evident that the differences between the United States and the European countries least inclined toward integration had diminished considerably.[36] As to Scandinavia, the firm American attitude, the region's increasing Western orientation, and economic problems had considerably modified the positions of Norway and Sweden. Nothing whatsoever was left of the initial view that once the first Paris conference was over, further cooperation ought to be handled through the ECE.

Even if those least inclined toward integration had modified their attitude greatly, the United States and most of the continental European states still wanted to advance further than did the United Kingdom, Scandinavia, and Switzerland. This issue was closely tied to that of government controls in foreign trade. To encourage integration at least this part of the system of controls had to be liberalized. On March 28 Ambassador Caffery, who was in charge of the American delegation in Paris, complained about the British attitude. He told Marshall that Britain was an obstacle to economic unification through the progressive removal of trade and financial barriers among the ERP group. Although Caffery did not specifically mention the Scandinavians, they stood for similar policies.[37]

The ambassador's suggestion that Washington try to bring the British—and indirectly the other skeptics—around to a more integration-minded position was only in part supported by the State Department. The Truman administration had come to realize that the British simply would not go as far as the continental powers, due largely to their commitments in other parts of the world. This was "inescapable." At the same time as the United States was abandoning its most comprehensive schemes, it insisted that the Organization for European Economic Cooperation be given effective powers. Washington wanted to avoid having the various countries, supported by their local ECA missions, come before the ECA administrator with competing claims. The coordinating job should be taken care of by the OEEC in cooperation with the special United States representative in Paris.[38]

Agreement was worked out along these lines. On April 16 the final act of the conference was signed and the Organization for European Economic Cooperation created. Paul Hoffman had already been appointed ECA administrator. Averell Harriman became the special representative in Paris.

Not only did the United States promote its objectives through the Paris conferences. After considerable doubt as to how to organize the aid program, the decision had been taken to proceed along two lines at the same time. In addition to the OEEC and the multilateral approach, the United States wanted to conclude bilateral agreements with all the participating countries. These were to provide the basis for the enforcement of the Economic Cooperation Act, which was passed by Congress in April 1948.[39]

The bilateral agreement between the United States and Norway was signed on July 3, 1948. It was quite similar to those for the other ERP countries. That was to be expected. First, the Economic Cooperation Act gave the basic outline of the agreements. The necessary money had to be granted by Congress. That body wanted to make sure that the act was followed and American interests protected. Second, the negotiations between Norway and the United States were carried out concurrently with those for the other countries. The Western Europeans kept in close contact and alterations in the American draft obtained by one country had to be granted to the others as well.[40]

In article II of the Norwegian-American agreement, Norway had to promise "to stabilize its currency, establish or maintain a valid rate of exchange, balance its governmental budget, create or maintain internal financial stability, and generally restore or maintain confidence in its monetary system." The language in this article reflected the language Congress had used in passing the Economic Cooperation Act. The Norwegians could do little to alter it.[41] Depending on how the article was interpreted by the ECA, it could clash with existing policies not only in Norway but also in several other countries. The United States did not try to exploit this article to the maximum extent possible to shape the economic policies of Western Europe. Washington agreed to interpretations that lessened the impact of the article. The obligation to balance the budget was not to mean that the budget had to be balanced every year, but only "in the long run." Yet even this form was disliked by Secretary of Commerce Brofoss. The Norwegians also managed to avoid a specific provision in the agreement relating to exchange rates.[42]

This does not mean that the article was without influence on the policies of the ERP countries. In Norway it is likely that its emphasis on financial stability was one of several factors which strengthened a policy of budgetary surpluses. The first two budgets after the war had been made up with considerable deficits, despite full employment and pressure on prices. This practice was changed with the budget for 1947–48. Since this budget was submitted before the American-Norwegian agreement was negotiated, it is most likely that the American attitude served to strengthen an already existing policy, and not to introduce a new one.[43]

It has been suggested that the devaluation of its krone on September 18, 1949, was forced upon Norway—and other Scandinavian countries—by the United States.[44] As with many of the questions discussed in this chapter, the contention is difficult to analyze in any detail without going quite far into the decision-making process of the Norwegian government, something which would be beyond the scope of this book.

To express an opinion based on American sources, it appears to be true that the United States wanted many of the Western European countries to devalue their currencies in relation to the dollar. A devaluation would help increase European exports to the United States and thereby tend to reduce the dollar gap. A devaluation could also, by improving the terms of trade in favor of the Europeans, lead to a reduction in barriers to American trade with Europe.[45]

In March 1949 Hoffman began to press for a devaluation of the pound. It was foreseen that at least most of the smaller countries would have to follow a British decision to devalue. The Truman administration on several occasions suggested that the British take such a step.[46]

When forces within the British government wanted to increase planning and cut imports instead of devaluing, Washington decided to step up its pressure. The State Department promised assistance through the International Monetary Fund if London agreed to devalue. This was done despite a rule excluding ERP countries from access to the fund. Conversely, if the British did not agree to devalue, no assistance would be granted.[47] The *Foreign Relations* volumes, on which this account of British-American relations is based, indicate that the American attitude was instrumental in bringing about the British devaluation of September 18.

There is little in the American sources relating specifically to the situation in Norway. The conclusion of the country study on Norway prepared by the ECA in February 1949 was that "the existing rate is not hampering recovery and that no change in the rate which would balance Norwegian international transactions would be desirable or even feasible at present." However, this was before a British devaluation was seen as urgent. The key was what the British did. If they devalued, as Washington was coming to insist they should, the Norwegians would probably follow. Furthermore, if Norway's extensive use of subsidies, price controls, and rationing was to be modified, then that would tend to create a pressure on prices and increase the need for a devaluation.[48]

From the sources available it can not be concluded that the United States intervened actively to make the Norwegians, or the other Scandinavians, devalue their currencies. But indirectly, through their influence on the British, the Americans had a most important impact on the monetary decisions of Scandinavia.

In another part of article II of the bilateral agreement, the Norwegian government had to promise "to cooperate with other participating countries in facilitating and stimulating an increasing interchange of goods and services among the participating countries and with other countries and in reducing public and private barriers to trade among themselves and with other countries."[49]

Again, a conflict could easily be foreseen between the American desire for far-reaching European integration and the Norwegian attitude of skepticism, if not outright opposition, to any such development. The United States strongly supported the liberalization of trade within Western Europe. This liberalization could go all the way from a reduction in some tariffs to a European customs union. The latter was preferable, but definitely a long-term objective. A more immediate goal would be the establishment of regional customs unions. Washington also strongly supported the idea of a European Payments Union to facilitate trade among the ERP countries and thereby lessen the demand for assistance from the United States.

In the field of regional liberalization, considerable discussion arose about a Scandinavian customs union. Washington wanted such a group established along with other regional unions, such as the one for the Benelux countries (where the initiative had been taken before the Marshall Plan), and one for France and Italy.[50]

While Sweden and Denmark were willing to advance considerably toward a liberalization of trade within Scandinavia, Norway held back. Oslo's basic objection was, as Foreign Minister Lange told Bay in February 1948, that the reduction of Scandinavian trade barriers "would flood Norway with Danish agricultural products and Swedish industrial goods whereas Norway has little to export those countries in exchange."[51] This attitude on the part of the Norwegians remained a basic obstacle to any large-scale liberalization of Scandinavian trade.

Although Washington hoped to see a Scandinavian scheme come to fruition, little active policy guidance seems to have been supplied. This was particularly the case until October 1949 when Hoffman delivered his important speech to the Ministerial Council of the OEEC. As long as discussions were going on among the Scandinavian countries, the State Department was apparently satisfied. At least in the period of this study, no instructions were issued asking the local embassies to push this kind of cooperation.

Despite the well-known fact that the Norwegians were holding back, even the ECA mission in Oslo apparently did little to prod the Norwegian government. On one occasion the mission even contributed to creating a wrong impression about the Norwegian attitude. In his testimony before the Senate Foreign Relations Committee in February 1949, the Chief of Mission to Norway, A. E. Staley, Jr., told the committee that Norway was undertaking discussions with Sweden and Denmark looking toward closer economic integration among the three countries.[52] Nothing was said about the reluctance shown by the Norwegians in these discussions.

The fact that the United States put more emphasis on liberalization within the entire ERP area than on regional cooperation was undoubtedly one reason why the latter was not pushed more actively on the American side. The free lists within the OEEC and the European Payments Union represented the most important steps in the direction of liberalization within the entire area. With their economies heavily dependent on foreign trade, the Scandinavian governments in principle welcomed a liberalization of European trade. Yet, like the Americans, the Scandinavians did not always live up to the general principles they proclaimed. For instance, the comprehensive system of regulations set up to control exports and imports certainly conflicted with multilateralism.

The reservations of the Scandinavians led to negative comments in Washington. In July 1949 after a tour of some European countries, Secretary of the Treasury John Snyder summed up his impressions for President Truman by stating that the British policy "is likely to mean more planning and further discrimination against American and Canadian products. Although still giving lip service to convertibility and multilateral trade, the steps which they are taking at present appear to be leading them in the opposite direction. The Scandinavian countries are aligned with the British in this approach." As was so often the case, the Scandinavians followed the British. That gave them some protection in their dealings with Washington. If the British could maintain their system of regulations, so could the Scandinavians.[53]

In the negotiations leading to the creation of the European Payments Union in 1950, the northern countries were not as reluctant to support a comprehensive scheme of integration as they were on many other occasions. The point of view of the Norwegian government was that it favored any proposal in the direction of multilateral payments as long as it did not interfere with Norway's emphasis on full employment and as long as it did not create serious difficulties in the country's balance of payments.[54]

The usual division between most of the continental states and Britain-Scandinavia was not very prominent in the EPU negotiations. Other lines of cleavage interfered with this traditional division. In May 1949 the Europeans split on the important issue of automatic flexibility. Most countries supported the principle. Norway opposed it, but Sweden and Denmark did not take positions. Norway had the support of Britain, but also of France.[55] Furthermore, after the frustrating experiences of the years of bilateral payments, there was little opposition to the creation of a more effective organization as such. The main question was in what ways the system of payments could be made more effective.

The establishment of the EPU did not create any debate in Norway. It was much too technical a matter to cause any excitement outside the narrow circle of experts and politicians directly involved. It was different with the free lists for trade within the OEEC. Again, the government supported the basic principle. In practice, however, the Norwegians had great difficulties in accepting the lists as they were worked out. It was felt that on the scale favored by the OEEC they would result in a loss of control over imports and thereby make it much more difficult to continue the policy of favoring investment over consumption. The government also argued that the lists could interfere with the policy of full employment.[56]

The first Norwegian free list was published in November 1949. It was expanded at the end of the year so that by January 1950 nearly half of all private imports into Norway were included. Further liberalization took place thereafter. This slow process led to repeated disputes between the Labor government and Hoffman and Harriman in Paris, and the ECA and the State Department in Washington. The ECA mission in Norway often showed more sympathy with the problems Norway faced in freeing trade than did authorities in Paris and Washington. In the end, however, concessions had to be made by the government in Oslo.[57]

The Truman administration was willing to make economic sacrifices, at least in the short run, to achieve some measure of integration in Western Europe. This attitude was most pronounced in the Economic Cooperation Administration and in parts of the State Department, while the Treasury and strong business interests often pressed for maximum economic benefits for the United States even in the short run. Despite suffering many setbacks, the latter interests were able to insert several clauses, meant to bring about certain business advantages, in the Marshall Plan legislation.[58]

The one of most immediate interest to Norway was the shipping clause, which provided for at least 50 percent of ERP goods shipped to Norway (or to any other country) having to be transported on American vessels. As had been the case with the similar provision in the Export-Import Bank loan, this met with strong opposition from the Norwegian government. The opposition was of no avail, despite the fact that Norway's attitude coincided with that of both the ECA in Paris and the State Department in Washington.[59]

Another important clause in the legislation of the ECA related to strategic materials that were in short supply in the United States. Article V of the bilateral agreement required the Norwegian government to facilitate the transfer to the United States of such materials. In theory this might have had quite far-reaching consequences. In practice it did not. The main reason was quite simply that Norway had few materials of interest to America. It presented no great problem to the Norwegians to agree to this article, especially after they had been able to secure an addition to the agreement which further modified chances of American interference.[60]

As of February 1949 no purchase had been made of Norwegian materials of this nature. Copper was the only commodity in which the Americans had taken an interest, but nothing had been sold as of February.[61] During the parliamentary debate on the bilateral agreement, Communists had raised the question of U.S. acquisition of molybdenum. Again, nothing was apparently bought and all of Norway's molybdenum was destined under contract for delivery to the Soviet Union. This provoked some negative comments from the American embassy, but no great controversy, since this material was not really in short supply in the United States.[62]

After the outbreak of the Korean War, America's interest in strategic materials increased greatly. Deliveries of copper, zinc, and aluminum were either stepped up or initiated. (The last product was also sold to Eastern Europe.) Somewhat later magnesium was added.

The counterpart funds represented the instrument with the greatest potential for interference into the economies of Western Europe. According to ECA legislation and the bilateral agreements, each government had to deposit local currency funds equal to the amount of assistance received. This counterpart fund could only be used with the consent of the United States. (Five percent was to be applied toward administrative and other expenses by the Americans.)[63]

By far the greatest part of the counterpart funds in Norway was used for retirement of the German Occupation Account. This application of funds was a Norwegian idea, to which the ECA missions in Oslo and Paris and the National

Advisory Council in Washington gave their consent. There was no initial interest on the American side in using the funds for investment purposes, as was done in most Marshall Plan countries. Inflationary pressure was so strong in Norway that Hoffman in particular would have preferred that the Norwegians undertake additional action to reduce this pressure, but the mission in Oslo argued with success that the government was already doing what was possible.[64]

Obviously debt retirement gave the Americans little or no influence on local economic policies. From late 1949 on, however, circles within the ECA in Washington and Paris wanted the Norwegians to use the counterpart funds for various investment projects, while sterilizing equal amounts in other ways. The argument was that the Marshall Plan should be used for visible productive purposes and not for rather unspectacular deflationary policies. This rather complicated bookkeeping operation did not meet with much favor either with the Gerhardsen government or the ECA mission in Oslo, and hardly anything came of it in 1950–51.

From 1951 to 1953 a minor part of the funds was used in industrial projects in northern Norway while another somewhat larger share went into strengthening Norway's defenses. The background for this change was that ECA now insisted that the funds be used for purposes other than debt retirement alone. This created a conflict with the Norwegian government, while parts of the Labor parliamentary group had long wanted to use some of the money for investment projects. The new policy gave ECA some influence on where the money was spent. It seems likely, however, that Norwegian authorities had at least as much say as ECA on the way in which these parts of the counterpart funds were used.[65]

The parts not being used for debt retirement were rather small. Until 1952, 1,275 million kroner had been used for debt retirement and almost nothing for investment purposes. In 1952 656 million was used for debt retirement and 243 million for investments in defense and production. In the first half of 1953 168 million kroner was being spent on defense in northern Norway and nothing on the German Occupation Account.[66]

Norway was possibly the country where the influence exerted by ECA through the counterpart funds was most limited. Only Britain came close to Norway in almost exclusively using the funds for debt retirement, with the concomitant circumscription of American interference.[67]

In other countries the ECA missions exerted strong influence. The Western zones of Germany, Austria, Greece, Turkey, and France are the best examples. Too much should not be made of the first four, however. Germany and Austria were under occupation—that made the question of interference somewhat academic. In Greece and Turkey national administration had broken down to such an extent that Americans were actually involved in running the national bureaucracies. That created a different situation from that of the rest of the ERP countries.[68]

In France an opportunity for effective intervention clearly existed since more than half of the counterpart funds was used for productive investment purposes. Nevertheless, the French apparently had most of the projects staked out through the Monnet Plan or through their own administrative machinery. ECA recognized that its leverage in this case was limited. If releases from the counterpart funds were withheld, the French usually found alternative sources of finance.[69] In spite of this, interference was actually much more frequent in France than in other "normal" ERP countries.

In November 1948 Secretary of State George Marshall and French Prime Minister Henry Queuille agreed upon some basic measures that had to be taken to correct the situation in France. These were a "purge of Communists, economic rehabilitation, the fiscal reform, a balanced budget, etc." If this was accomplished, it would, in Marshall's words, "strengthen my case when I went before Congress" to obtain ERP money.[70]

The United States could not hope to achieve the goals mentioned by Marshall through the recovery program alone. The role of the counterpart funds alone had to be moderate. But, again and again in 1948 and 1949 representatives of ECA and the American embassy in Paris told the French government that at least a program of financial stability was necessary if the French were to use the counterpart funds in the way they wanted. Through a system of monthly releases the Americans hoped to make sure that the French would live up to expectations.[71] When the Queuille government fell in October 1949 even the monthly releases were temporarily stopped in expectation of a new French government with a satisfactory fiscal policy.[72]

Yet the State Department and ECA recognized that if they wanted to strengthen the moderate forces in France, they must not go too far, since too direct intervention would only weaken these forces. The fact that American representatives kept complaining all through 1948 and 1949 about the nature of French financial policies certainly indicates that ECA and the State Department were not able to persuade the French to the extent hoped for.[73]

The Economic Cooperation Act and the bilateral agreements were the most important formal instruments with which the ECA missions and Washington influenced domestic policies in the various European countries. In addition, other less formal ways existed. The creation of the ECA missions and the increasingly close contact between the United States and Western Europe meant that through a constant flow of day-to-day impulses American influence would spread in the European countries.

It is fairly easy to establish what attitudes ECA authorities in Norway and in Paris stood for. Their analyses of the Norwegian scene were not much different from those the embassy had been making for some years already. A typical example was found in the ECA country study on Norway dated February 1949. After having praised the rapid recovery after the war, the study noted that this had only been made possible

> by heavy taxes, which may limit incentives to produce and which contribute to the decline in individual savings. The suppression of inflation has involved the establishment of arbitrary controls, and of price relationships that themselves tend to produce unfortunate consequences. While there is no

evidence of a large diversion of resources to uncontrolled domestic services, there is undoubtedly some leakage of this sort. It is possible that consumption has been so drastically restricted as to encourage absenteeism and labor turn-over. There is no indication as yet that Norway has been able to develop an amount of voluntary saving large enough to maintain the reconstruction program and at the same time to begin a gradual relaxation of detailed economic controls.[74]

This was a mixture of criticism, some rather implicit praise, and an attempt at objective analysis. Most Americans would certainly oppose the Norwegian system of taxation, which was perhaps the most progressive in Western Europe. Negative comments were often heard about the comprehensive system of regulation, which certainly did not resemble anything in America, and Americans also criticized the fact that almost all Norwegians took their vacations in July and thereby caused a break in production. Most Americans agreed that not enough was done to attract tourists to increase dollar earnings.[75]

Finally, ECA considered the Norwegian four-year plan too ambitious. Norway simply would not have the resources to accomplish all that was set down in the plan. The expansion in shipping and especially in export industries was in accordance with America's desire that all possible effort be made to obtain self-sufficiency in dollar earnings at the end of the four-year period. If curtailments were to be made, ECA apparently wanted these to go further into nonpriority areas, primarily inland transport and domestic industries.[76]

ECA authorities certainly did not meet with success in modifying Norwegian policies on all these points. When policies were changed, this usually resulted from many factors, not simply the consideration that ECA wanted a change. Sometimes the mission in Oslo defended Norwegian actions, even on the points here mentioned, with some success.

Taxation remained quite progressive. The system of regulation was modified through the free lists as far as exports and imports went. By necessity that led to changes in other areas as well, but much of the system continued at least into the early 1950s. The national program for 1949–50 was substantially more modest than what could have been expected from the plan for the period from 1948 to 1952. Further cuts in investments were planned for 1950–51. Some efforts were made to attract tourists, and Norwegians continued to take their vacations in July.[77]

Influence in Reverse

While the Marshall Plan meant a considerable stepping up of American influence on the economies of Western Europe, too much should not be made of this. U.S. influence became less than what could have been expected from the Economic Cooperation Act and the bilateral agreements. It was also less than what is either implied or directly stated in most revisionist writings. The economies of the "radical" Western European countries, Britain and Scandinavia, in many ways remained different from the continental, not to speak of the American model, although some narrowing did take place. On the whole, Arkes's characterization of the United States as the "imperfect interventionist" seems fairly apt for this period.

We should not stop by analyzing how the Marshall Plan came to strengthen American influence and further conservative policies. After all, some interesting impulses could be found in the other direction as well. First, occasionally the United States favored policies that were more appreciated by the parties of the left than by those of the right. Second, the European Recovery Program in some ways meant that European influence on Washington would also increase. Again, I will analyze this primarily in terms of the American-Norwegian relationship.

It has already been mentioned that the American loan to the state-owned aluminum plant at Sunndalsøra was better liked by the Labor party than by the nonsocialists. The most clear-cut case of the Marshall Plan coming to strengthen nonconservative policies is found in the four-year plan itself. The United States insisted that the ERP countries work out plans for the period of the aid program. These were to show

how the assistance would be used and how the various national economies would become self-sufficient at the end of the period. Washington wanted to make sure that the job would be done this time. The Europeans were not to come back asking for even further aid.

Such long-term plans were quite in line with economic thinking within the Labor party. The first full-fledged national, as opposed to government, budget had been worked out by the Labor government for the year 1947. The four-year plan was only an enlargement of policies which the Labor party had already come to stand for. Although differences existed between ECA and the Norwegian government over the exact contents of the plan, the introduction of the plan as such created no controversy.

The main nonsocialist parties in Norway had been strongly opposed to the introduction of any national budget that was to be anything more than a forecast for the coming year. They did not want the government to strengthen its influence over the private sector of the economy. A four-year plan was therefore contrary to the policies the nonsocialists wanted to pursue. It is likely that these parties, along with industrial, financial, and banking interests, were disappointed at what looked like support from the United States for the planning principles of the Labor party.[78]

Yet the nonsocialists in the Storting did not actually oppose the four-year plan. This was certainly unexpected. There seem to have been two primary reasons for their stand. First, the nonsocialists were definitely pro-Western. It was somewhat difficult for them both to criticize the government for not being sufficiently pro-Western and at the same time oppose a central element in the Marshall program. Second, in the tense atmosphere of early 1948 it was recognized as important to stand together against the Communist party. Therefore, a compromise was worked out: the nonsocialists would not go against the government and the four-year plan, but this would not be interpreted by the government as a stamp of approval of the economic policies of the Labor party. In fact, no directly affirmative or negative vote was to be taken on the four-year plan. In the end two members of the

Agrarian party followed the Communists in voting against the government, despite the noncommital way in which the motion had been phrased.[79]

The Truman administration and ECA not only wanted the participating countries to work out national four-year programs—they wanted a similar plan even for the entire area encompassed by the European Recovery Program. Nothing came of this. The difficulties in working out national programs were multiplied manifold in the attempt to establish a regional one.

It was an essential element in the planning of the Labor party, and also in the four-year plan, that on the import side priority should be given to equipment essential for recovery, primarily industrial recovery, rather than to consumer goods. Norwegian officials even complained to ECA representatives about the fact that some of the continental countries acted differently and thereby put pressure on the Oslo government to modify its policies.[80]

Washington and ECA preferred the Norwegian attitude to that of emphasizing consumer goods, although concern existed that the Norwegians might have carried this policy too far. Some persons within ECA placed Norway at the very top as far as effective handling of assistance was concerned. As one important official phrased it, the Norwegians "knew exactly what they were going to do and received the maximum benefit. The country that benefited the most and used the Marshall Plan help most skillfully was unquestionably Norway; way out ahead of any of the other countries." At the other extreme were Greece, Turkey, and Portugal. In these countries ECA had to use considerable time and money simply to furnish an administrative apparatus.[81]

Americans were surprised that the Norwegian government possessed the political strength necessary to give such high priority to investments. Although this policy would probably result in maximum benefit in the long run, it was unpopular from a short-term political point of view. (As it turned out, due to the rapid growth in production the government was able to give more to consumers than originally planned.)

The emphasis on investment was to a considerable extent dependent upon close cooperation between the government and the trade union movement. An intimate relationship existed between the leadership of the government, the Labor party, and the trade unions. This cooperation could be seen in another fact that impressed American observers—the peace prevailing on the labor scene. Very few days were lost to strikes. Sometimes strong measures were taken against the leaders of illegal strikes.[82] This policy would have been much more difficult to pursue for a nonsocialist government.

Then, although Washington and ECA undoubtedly came to have considerable influence on Norwegian economic policies, at the same time, impulses often went in the other direction. The ECA missions became instruments that strengthened the various European countries in their dealings with the United States. Some examples of this have been noted already.

The most important way in which the ECA mission and the U.S. embassy tried to strengthen the Norwegian case was with regard to the amounts of assistance given to Norway. On several occasions American representatives in Oslo proposed to their superiors that amounts which had been cut from Norwegian requests be restored. I have not found any example that the opposite took place—that cuts were recommended. It is difficult to find out exactly what effect such intervention had. Most likely the effect, if any, was small. At this time ECA generally followed the advice of OEEC as to how the assistance was to be distributed within the financial limits set by Congress.[83]

Despite the fact that support from the ECA mission and the embassy did not in any way guarantee that the Norwegians would be able to settle disputes in their favor, it is interesting to note the extent to which local Americans became supporters of the Norwegian government. The shipping clause was another example. The unanimous dislike this provision met with in Norway was to some degree reflected in dispatches from the embassy and the ECA mission.[84]

But again no change took place in Washington's policy.

As we have seen, domestic shipping interests were strong with good connections in Congress. In fact, one reason, but not by any means the only one, for the sharp curtailment in Norwegian shipbuilding in 1949-50 was probably the attitude of the Truman administration and of Congress. While the Americans seem to have supported the rebuilding of the merchant marine as a necessary part of Norway's dollar-earning efforts, their attitude apparently changed when the issue arose of expanding beyond the level of the prewar period. Even the partial support of ECA in Paris could not modify Washington's attitude at this time.[85]

In January 1949 the embassy and the ECA mission took another initiative to help the Norwegians. This time the question concerned duty-free entry and defrayment of inland transport charges on American relief packages to Norway. This had been a matter of some concern to the Oslo government. Again, Washington refused to heed the advice of the local Americans. Not only that, but this time the State Department also openly complained that the initiative in matters of this nature should be taken by the Norwegians themselves, not by the embassy or the ECA mission.[86]

The embassy and the ECA mission also had sympathy with Norwegian government complaints that the United States included domestic Norwegian taxes in determining the value of imports from Norway for customs purposes. Again, Washington was not willing to alter its practice. The United States recognized that its attitude had to change when General Agreement on Tariffs and Trade (GATT) entered into effect, but before that happened nothing would be done to satisfy the Norwegians.[87]

Washington and ECA made an effort to develop friendly relations with the ERP countries. One way of doing this was to staff the various missions with suitable representatives. In Norway officials with a trade union background could be expected to be most welcome. Close contacts developed between the trade union and Labor leadership and some of the advisers attached to the embassy and the ECA mission. When former businessman A. E. Staley resigned in the spring of 1949, John Gross became the new ECA chief in

Norway. Gross had been ECA Labor Advisor in Norway and Denmark and came from union ranks. He felt at home with the labor movement and the Norwegian government was quite satisfied with the work he did.[88]

Being a trade union man was no prerequisite for getting along with the Labor government. The Norwegians certainly appreciated the job done by businessman Staley. When he left he was awarded a high Norwegian order, the St. Olav. Secretary of Commerce Brofoss argued that Staley be given this because it was due to him that "Norway has received as favorable treatment as it has when it comes to ERP assistance."[89]

Expansion with Limitations

American interest in and commitments to Scandinavia and Norway grew in the period under study here, 1945 through 1949. American exports increased sharply compared to the years before the war. That increase was to a considerable extent temporary and due to the reconstruction needs of the Scandinavian countries and the shattered state of other sources of supply. As Western Europe revived, imports from the United States fell. Exports to the United States from Scandinavia also increased, but not sufficiently to keep up with the sharp rise in imports.[90]

The expansion of the commitments and influence of the United States was seen in other areas as well. American assistance became of great significance to the Scandinavian countries. In the period 1945 through 1949, Norway received approximately 155 million dollars, Denmark approximately 215 million, and Sweden approximately 80 million. By far the largest share came in 1948–49 with the ERP. With increased assistance came an influx of personnel attached to the ECA missions. At the end of January 1950, twenty-three persons worked for the ECA mission in Norway in administrative positions. The numbers in Sweden and Denmark were twenty-five and twenty-six respectively.[91]

The rise of America cannot be analyzed only through

numbers. Washington had specific goals it wanted to promote in Western Europe. On the economic side these were most explicitly stated in the Economic Cooperation Act of 1948 and in the bilateral agreements with the ERP countries. As we have seen, these related among other things to the promotion of freer trade, to the pursuit of what Americans called "sound" financial and monetary policies, and to the sale of strategic materials. The countries in the recovery program had to agree to establish counterpart funds which could give the United States great influence over their economic policies. Traditionalists who deal with this period have undoubtedly paid too little attention to how the United States influenced the policies of the Western Europeans. Strings were certainly attached to most U.S. assistance. Depending upon the attitude of the country in question, these strings would interfere to a greater or lesser extent with its existing policies.

Nevertheless, American influence through the Marshall Plan can easily be exaggerated. While the generalizations of some revisionists, the Kolkos in particular, would fit with some of the countries in the European Recovery Program, they would not apply to others. Highly developed states with stable and democratic regimes were able to pursue more independent policies than were countries like Germany, Greece, and Turkey.

With the Marshall Plan the United States certainly became more of an interventionist in Western European affairs, but still an "imperfect" one. This "imperfection" was evident both on the national level and with regard to the wider aspect of European integration. Despite free lists, the European Payments Union, and the machinery of OEEC, the process toward integration stopped far short of what Washington would have liked. Nothing became of the customs union desired by many Americans. With the exception of the Benelux, which originated before 1947–48, very little even became of more limited regional unions. While much was done to abolish quotas in Western European trade, little was accomplished in this period in the field of tariff reductions.

The integrated four-year plan for the entire ERP area which ECA promoted in 1948–49 came to nothing.[92]

On the national level one should distinguish clearly between the economic conceptions held by American policy makers and the extent to which they tried to make Western Europe adhere to these conceptions. Former businessmen Bay and Staley were able to get along well with the Norwegian Labor government. As we have seen, in some cases the embassy and the ECA mission became advocates of the Oslo government before the ECA in Paris and the administration in Washington. It is another matter that they were hardly ever able to change U.S. policies according to Norwegian desires.

Similarly, despite Washington's dislike of measures of large-scale socialization, it was possible to socialize sectors of the economy without seriously disturbing relations with the United States. It was definitely possible to pursue progressive social policies and to maintain systems of taxation that were outrageous from an American point of view.

Points could easily be found where the Truman administration and ECA were at odds with the Norwegian Labor government. The best examples were the scope of the organization to administer the recovery program, some of Norway's many economic regulations, and the speed with which the free lists were expanded in 1949–50. Especially in the last two cases American policies were closer to nonsocialist sympathies than to those of the Labor party.

On the other hand, issues undoubtedly existed where ECA and Washington could be said to come closer to the Labor government than to the nonsocialist opposition. The most important one was U.S. insistence on the working out of national four-year plans. Another was the American willingness to grant a loan to the state-owned aluminum plant at Sunndalsøra, a plant which was built against the wishes of most nonsocialist members of the Storting.

Washington maintained close relations with Britain and had few significant objections to the domestic policies of the Scandinavian social democrats. This illustrated that left-of-center governments could be acceptable. To establish state enterprises and comprehensive economic regulations represented only elements in the policies of a country. America's attitude had to be adjusted according to the overall performance of the country in question. If its general foreign policy orientation was satisfactory, then relations with the United States need not be greatly affected by socialization. This was especially the case if the question of compensation was satisfactorily solved from the American point of view. If a country's general foreign policy orientation was not seen as sufficiently close to the United States, then that country's degree of socialization would receive more attention in Washington, and relations would deteriorate.[93]

What disturbed the relationship between the United States and Scandinavia in late 1947 was the foreign policy orientation of the Scandinavians, and not their domestic policies. In 1948 when relations with Norway and Denmark again became satisfactory, while Washington's opposition to Sweden's attitude only became more pronounced, the decisive factor was again foreign policy orientation.

In most instances it appears to be wrong to conclude that the business climate in a certain country was what primarily shaped the American attitude. On the other hand, the treatment accorded U.S. business no doubt represented parts of the picture that constituted the total American relationship with that country.

This balance between economic and other interests was brought out in the Statement of United States Credit and Investment Policy approved by President Truman on August 23, 1948. The most pertinent sentence read that

> While it is not the policy of this Government to refuse credits to countries simply on the ground that they are conducting state enterprises or are pursuing nationalization programs, or on the ground that enterprises to be assisted are in greater or lesser degree controlled by the foreign government, the treatment accorded United States property owners by countries engaged in nationalization programs is of concern to the United States and is taken into consideration when those countries seek loans from the United States.[94]

In other words, the business climate certainly counted when the United States determined its attitude to a country seeking favors from Washington, for instance in the form of loans. But the business climate was far from the only thing that counted, and in fact usually it was not even the most important factor. In relations with Scandinavia the foreign policy orientation of the social democrats was the primary concern of American policy makers. True, no comprehensive socialization took place in these countries. They did have, however, a set of government regulations which could hardly be described as conducive to U.S. investments.

Washington was able to develop rapport with left-of-center governments. As long as socialists and social democrats were willing to break with the Soviet Union and with communism, Washington could indeed have close relations with them. In fact, sometimes reasons existed for preferring such governments to more conservative ones.

It is dangerous to generalize about American foreign policy. An exception will almost always be found to any broad generalization. If I should venture upon a conclusion as far as the attitude to various kinds of governments is concerned, I would argue that American policy makers generally felt most comfortable with politicians located around the so-called middle of the political spectrum.[95]

After the end of World War II politicians of the far left soon met with sharp opposition from the United States. Yet, Tito was to prove an exception when he showed that a form of communism firmly independent of the Soviet Union could be created.[96] Often Washington felt uncomfortable with politicians of the far right as well, although the growing struggle with the Soviet Union was to blur the dislike most policy makers felt for such politicians in the immediate postwar phase.

In Western Europe the United States could usually base its policies on governments that were anticommunist, democratic, and moderate. If circumstances did not permit such ideal combinations and a choice had to be made between left and right, Washington preferred staunch anticommunists to anyone tinged with communism, and authoritarian reactionaries to left-wing revolutionaries. American policies in great parts of Latin America and Asia were to illustrate that. In Western Europe, however, Washington normally did not have to consider the extremes, since more ideal types could be found.

6

The Origins
of NATO

WE HAVE EXAMINED Washington's attitude to the social democrats in Scandinavia in general and in Norway in particular. Now let us consider the foreign policy side again. This, then, will be the story of what role the United States foresaw for Scandinavia in the formation of the North Atlantic Treaty Organization (NATO). This chapter will attempt to establish the larger framework within which the American policy toward Scandinavia operated, for despite the increasing attention paid to this region in 1948–49, Washington's policies still represented only a small part of the larger picture constituted by the policies toward the whole of Western Europe. After sketching in that larger picture here, in the next chapters I will analyze in detail the American policy toward Scandinavia as such.

A Historiographic Sketch

As already touched upon, traditionalist as well as revisionist historians have generally concentrated on the very first years after World War II. Few of them write in any de-

tail about the period from 1947 to 1949. Nevertheless, two
main interpretations can be established for the transforma-
tion of American foreign policy from the Marshall Plan to
the NATO alliance.

On the traditionalist side Herbert Feis' *From Trust to
Terror: The Onset of the Cold War 1945–1950,* is a representative work for these years. As so often with Feis, there is
little explicit discussion of why events took place. Mostly he
is satisfied with giving his version of what actually happened. Even so, his implicit analysis of motive forces in
American foreign policy is clear enough. As with traditionalists in general, his main theme is one of U.S. reaction
to Soviet initiatives. On a few occasions Feis brings this underlying premise out in the open. In discussing the change in
American policies from 1939 to the formation of NATO ten
years later, he states that "Hitler had propelled the American people along the first long swing of this arc of change,
and Stalin had hurtled them to its end." American security
interests and democratic ideals were challenged first by Hitler's Germany and then by Stalin's Soviet Union. This
German-Soviet analogy is something that Feis keeps coming
back to. Two pages after the statement quoted above, he
reminds the reader that "American troops who had first been
placed in Europe to fight Hitler were going to remain there
to deter or fight Soviet Communism."[1]

Like most U.S. diplomatic historians, Feis pays relatively little attention to the policies of other countries, nota-
bly those in Western Europe. His point of view is nonetheless
quite obvious. Instead of seeing the United States as thrusting itself upon Western Europe, his argument is that the
Western Europeans actively encouraged the United States to
take an active interest in their affairs to balance the looming
Soviet-Communist danger. Most of Feis' analysis of the origins of NATO is really a description of to what extent the
Truman administration and Congress were willing to take
on the responsibilities which the countries in Western
Europe wanted the United States to assume. His point of
departure is that even in May 1948 Truman and his advisers
"had not resolved in their own minds the nature and range of

the obligations to be accepted in the contemplated mutual defense pact or the military arrangements for making it effective."[2]

Louis Halle, although less of a clear-cut traditionalist than Feis, basically follows the same line of analysis. The opening statement in his chapter on the formation of NATO reads, "The winter of 1947–1948 was a winter of crisis for the nations of western Europe. Their economies had broken down, the Communist parties under orders from Moscow had embarked upon an all-out effort to wreck their political structures, invasion by the Red Army seemed an imminent possibility." An economic recovery program was under way. What remained was for Western Europe to rehabilitate itself militarily. And, again, the Europeans had to call on the Americans to help in that task.[3]

On the revisionist side less agreement exists on what led to the formation of the NATO alliance. As usual, the extreme version is found with the Kolkos. In their opinion not only was there little danger of a Soviet attack on Western Europe, but American policy makers were well aware of the improbability of such an attack. To the Kolkos the Soviet danger was something that successive administrations in Washington fostered "to maintain a sustaining tension to enact extremely costly legislation generally desired for reasons having little, if anything, to do with Russia."

The advance of U.S. capitalism was what counted, now as always. NATO was in part promoted as a means of crushing left-wing movements in Western Europe, in part to subjugate Western Europe to the interests of the United States. In a typical passage the Kolkos state that while the Europeans concentrated on the danger from a resurgent Germany, the United States desired to "strengthen Western Europe's ability to cope with internal revolt as well as to sustain a psychological mood of anti-Soviet tension that the administration thought functional."[4]

Yet, there is one element of moderation in the interpretation presented by the Kolkos. They do not argue that only the United States pressed for the creation of NATO. As we have seen, the Kolkos indicate that the Europeans too wanted such an alliance, although for different reasons than the Americans. They even go so far as to write that "the Europeans were now subjecting the United States to a polite degree of blackmail by exploiting its fear of losing allies."[5] Therefore, although Washington certainly did not have to be dragged into the affairs of Western Europe, it did not thrust itself upon Europe either.

A critical attitude toward the foreign policy of the United States does not necessarily have to lead to a defense of Soviet actions. Yet it is true that on the part of most revisionists, criticism of American policies has led to a corresponding playing down of Soviet intentions. Few, if any, go as far as the Kolkos in this respect. William Appleman Williams states only that "American leaders were not motivated *solely* [italics mine] by fear of Russian military attack."[6] He does not entirely discount the danger of a Soviet attack, but argues that Washington exaggerated this threat.

The revisionist perspective is generally one of the Americans pressing for the new alliance in order to strengthen their influence in Europe. Nothing, or a brief mention at most, is written by most revisionists about the extent to which the Western Europeans encouraged the United States to take a more, rather than less, active interest in their affairs. This seems to be true of Gardner, Fleming, and Horowitz. Even a moderate such as LaFeber hardly deals with the attitudes of the Western Europeans. In rather general terms he states that "Now that the Marshall Plan was reviving Europe economically, the United States, in the full splendor of its postwar power, was attempting to strengthen its ties with, and influence over, Europe by creating military institutions which would provide fresh channels for American aid and policies."[7] The United States is seen as the creator of the new alliance. The origins of NATO are found in Washington, not in Western Europe.

A postrevisionist interpretation of a somewhat peculiar type is found with Stephen E. Ambrose. On the one hand, Ambrose apparently agrees both that the Soviets posed a threat to Western Europe and that the Europeans actively sought to involve Washington in their affairs. On the other hand, he appears to go further than many revisionists when he argues that the objective of the United States in entering the NATO alliance was that "Europe would become, for the American businessman, soldier, and foreign policy maker, another Latin America."[8] Western Europe would now be as firmly subjected to Washington's domination as Latin America had been.

Who Pulled Upon Whom?

After the war London feared that the United States would once again withdraw from the affairs of Europe. To both the Churchill and the Attlee government it was a primary goal to try to prevent any such development. In 1947 there could no longer be any doubt that the United States would take a strong interest in the affairs of Europe, unlike what had been the case after World War I. With the Marshall Plan America was helping to reconstruct Europe economically on a more lasting basis than was possible through the less coordinated assistance given so far. On the political level Washington was considering itself the leader of the "free world." The Truman administration was coming to insist that countries which wanted to be included among the friends of the United States break both with the Soviet Union and with any form of cooperation with communists.

In late 1947 the British were stepping up their efforts to involve the Americans on a third level as well, the military. In March 1947 London and Paris had concluded the treaty of Dunkirk, but this treaty had not sufficiently served the purposes of the British government. It was formally directed only against the possibility of a renewed attack by Germany and not against the Soviet Union. It was quite narrow as far as membership went—not even the Benelux countries were included. Finally, the Dunkirk treaty was in no way connected with the United States.[9]

After the ending of the London meeting of the Council of Foreign Ministers on December 15, 1947, Bevin presented his thoughts about military cooperation to Secretary of State

Marshall. The thrust of his presentation was that first Britain, France, and the Benelux countries would establish an arrangement of regional military cooperation. This group was then to be linked in some way or another to other countries in Western Europe, to the Dominions and, most important, to the United States. The Foreign Secretary did not go into specifics in his talk with Marshall. What they discussed was not a formal alliance, "but an understanding backed by power, money and resolute action." On this level the Secretary of State signaled his general agreement with Bevin's ideas.[10] When the British wanted to show French Foreign Minister Bidault a record of the talks, the State Department replied that this was acceptable if it was made clear that Marshall had not definitely approved any particular course of action.[11] Thus, although Bevin was trying to draw the United States out, Washington only indicated its general sympathy with the British idea of closer military cooperation in Western Europe.

Bevin and the British were not the only Europeans who wanted to involve the United States quite closely in the defense problems of Western Europe. Belgian Prime and Foreign Minister Paul-Henri Spaak was even more outspoken in that respect.[12]

When Bevin delivered his famous speech in the House of Commons on January 22, 1948, a discussion had already started in Washington as to what role the United States was to play in the efforts toward military cooperation in Western Europe. Two main views could be found. One emphasized the need for intimate cooperation between Western Europe and the United States. The best example of this was found in the memo Director of the Office of European Affairs Hickerson sent to the Secretary of State on January 19. It was an unstated premise in Hickerson's memo that the problems of Europe had to be analyzed in military terms. He was quite explicit about the role of the United States: "In my opinion a European Pact modelled on the treaty of Rio de Janeiro is the best answer to the security problem for Western Europe. For such a pact to be really effective, the United States would have to adhere. I believe that this country should and could adhere to such a treaty if it were clearly linked up with the UN."[13]

Basically, this was to be Hickerson's line of action all through the weeks and months of tangled negotiations which followed. Congress and public opinion might react against the United States being directly involved in a military pact with Western Europe. Concessions might have to be made to this opposition. But as far as his own feelings went, Hickerson wanted the United States to participate directly in a pact with Western Europe on the pattern of one for all, all for one. He was opposed to what he understood was Bevin's first step, the extension of the Dunkirk treaty to the Benelux countries. The membership ought to be wider than that and the new security system should refer not to Germany, but to the Soviet Union as the outside threat.[14]

The other American view was expressed in a memo Director of the Policy Planning Staff George Kennan sent to the Secretary a day later than Hickerson's, on January 20. Kennan was quite explicit that the danger to Western Europe was not primarily military. Thus, "Military union should not be the starting point. It should flow from the political, economic and spiritual union—not vice versa." He was emphatic on the point that if military arrangements were to be established, then the initiative had to come from the Europeans. As far as the role of the United States was concerned, he no doubt wanted the United States to support a Western European military group. Washington's atomic monopoly would be a deterrent to Soviet military aggression, American troops would remain in Europe, and military supplies had to come from the United States. Kennan's point, however, was that "People in Europe should not bother their heads too much in the initial stage about our relationship to this concept."[15] It was evident that he did not want the United States to take direct part in plans for European military cooperation, at least not in the initial stage.

The differences between Hickerson and Kennan were quite similar to those between Clayton and Kennan over the Marshall Plan. Clayton and Hickerson wanted to see the United States directly involved from the very beginning.

Only that would guarantee the effectiveness of the effort and make certain that the Americans got the proper return for the resources they invested. Kennan, on the other hand, feared the consequences of Western Europe being forced to rely on the United States.[16] As had been the case in the preparation of the Marshall Plan, the basic discussion about the American attitude to European defense was going on within the State Department. The military exerted little influence in this early phase and President Truman and his personal staff also were largely on the outside.

On January 20 George Marshall replied to a letter he had received a week earlier outlining the ideas Bevin was to present to the House of Commons. The reply was meant to encourage the British while at the same time being noncommittal as far as the role of the United States was concerned. The British ambassador was told to inform Bevin that "his proposal has deeply interested and moved me and that I wish to see the United States do everything which it properly can in assisting the European nations in bringing a project along this line to fruition."[17] Marshall said nothing about the direct role of the United States and it was made clear that the initiative had to come from the European side.

In the conversation Hickerson had with British Ambassador Lord Inverchapel on January 21, the Director of the Office of European Affairs went quite far in suggesting that if the Europeans insisted upon the direct participation of the United States, "this country would be sympathetically disposed and would at least give it very careful consideration." Yet, when he more formally expressed the State Department's preliminary position, Hickerson agreed that the initiative had to lie with the Europeans. Only after further information about their plans and after consultations with Congress could the Truman administration present any more definite views.[18]

The United States did not take any clear-cut position in these first contacts with Britain. Some officials in the State Department had their own private opinions about how far the United States should go in encouraging European military cooperation, and about the extent to which the United

States should participate in such arrangements. Hickerson and Kennan represented two different lines among prominent policy makers. But most officials did not express definite views at this stage. Too many uncertain factors existed for that, not only on the European side but even more as far as Congress and U.S. public opinion were concerned.

Nevertheless, the British pressed on. On January 27 Ambassador Inverchapel informed the State Department that he had received instructions from Bevin to request that informal talks be held between the United States and Britain on the whole question of Western security. His objective was obvious: "the treaties that are being proposed cannot be fully effective nor be relied upon when a crisis arises unless there is assurance of American support for the defense of Western Europe. The plain truth is that Western Europe cannot yet stand on its own feet without assurance of support."[19]

Bevin's renewed effort to draw the United States into a more affirmative position failed. After discussions with Marshall, Under Secretary Lovett informed the British Ambassador, in stronger terms than Hickerson had, that it was most important that the initiative rested with the Europeans. Only after they had agreed on a military arrangement would the United States be in a position to "carefully consider the part it might appropriately play in support of such a Western European Union."[20] It was evident that the United States would support a military arrangement in Western Europe, but it was not agreed that this support would be in the form of direct participation.

Bevin was not to be stopped by such a response. On February 6 Ambassador Inverchapel informed the State Department that it was Bevin's opinion that a vicious circle was being created. The United States would not define its position as to participation before an arrangement had been worked out. The British government argued that an arrangement could not be worked out at all without American participation since the Western Europeans would then see little point in such plans.[21]

This alleged vicious circle did not make the State Department change its attitude. Lovett again pointed out that the United States wanted to encourage military cooperation in Western Europe. But as long as Washington did not have a clear picture of what it was going to support, it was impossible to decide how to extend support. Furthermore, Lovett informed Inverchapel that "if it became known in Congress that in addition to the economic commitments involved in the European Recovery Program the United States is asked to assume new and extensive military and political commitments it might well adversely affect the prospects for the approval by Congress of the European Recovery Program."[22] No decision could be expected at least until the ERP had been cleared through Congress. That would still take a couple of months.

Then came the crisis in Czechoslovakia, resulting in a communist government, and a letter from Stalin to Finnish President Paasikivi asking for a defense agreement between the two countries. These events, in particular the first, were to strengthen Bevin's pressure on the United States. They would also somewhat weaken America's reluctance to adopt a clear-cut position. What is most remarkable, however, is how little the American attitude actually changed.

Washington's main worry about the coup in Czechoslovakia was the effect it would have in France and Italy, the two countries in Western Europe with the strongest communist parties. As a result of this, Marshall instructed the U.S. ambassador in Belgium to sound out the representatives of the Benelux countries, France, and Britain, meeting in Brussels on March 4, about their views on the inclusion of Italy in the planned Western Union. The Secretary of State also asked for their appraisals of the problem of meeting "fifth column aggression on Czech model." The State Department was obviously worried about the pattern of events in Czechoslovakia being repeated elsewhere. A most exposed country in that respect was Italy.[23]

On March 4 French Foreign Minister Bidault joined the efforts of Bevin and Benelux representatives in pressing for military talks with the United States. While noting the beneficial results achieved through the Marshall Plan initiative, the French Foreign Minister stated that the time had come to extend cooperation to the political and military fields.[24] Hickerson was also coming to press for further developments on the American side. In his memo to the Secretary of State of March 8 he recommended that consultations be started immediately with the National Security Council and with Congress about the security of the European countries. A main question to be dealt with was the possibility of American participation in "a North Atlantic-Mediterranean regional defense arrangement."[25] On February 26 George Kennan had left Washington for a tour of the Far East. That diminished the influence of his insistence on Europe taking the initiative. When he came back to Washington almost two months later, the American position had changed considerably.

General Clay's famous warning of March 5 about Soviet intentions also contributed to the changing climate in Washington. While its influence on the State Department was no more than moderate, its impact was considerably greater on circles within the Defense Department and the military. Important policy makers felt that chances of war had increased, although the general appraisal even at this time was that it was unlikely that the Soviet Union would launch any form of direct attack on Western Europe. Strong indications also exist that the cable represented a dramatic presentation of Clay's views to be used in strengthening the hand of the military in their presentation of the budget before Congress.[26]

A message of March 11 from Marshall to the embassy in Rome indicated that Washington's attitude was being modified. The American public, and thereby indirectly Congress, were regarded as prepared for new initiatives to contain Soviet-Communist influence. The Secretary stated that the regional security arrangements that were being worked out would have American support. On the other hand, the basic position was still that "form and extent of our relationship to them cannot be determined until we can study final product Brussels talk."[27]

Threats to Norway

Despite the coup in Prague, Clay's warning from Germany, and pressure from Western Europe, and from the Office of European Affairs, Marshall's cable to the embassy in Rome showed that Washington had far from made up its mind as to what kind of support the United States would give to the European defense effort. However, on the very next day, on March 12, the Secretary of State notified Lord Inverchapel that "we are prepared to proceed at once in the joint discussions on the establishment of an Atlantic security system." This was certainly a surprising turn of events. First, the United States was willing to enter into talks right away. Marshall suggested "the prompt arrival of the British representative early next week." Even the British were somewhat taken aback by this sudden feeling of urgency on the American side. Second, Marshall now referred to an "Atlantic security system." This indicated a high degree of involvement on the part of the United States. No longer was the emphasis on the United States supporting a Western European arrangement.[28]

What can explain this change in attitude on the American side? There can be little doubt that events relating to Norway contributed strongly to the change. On March 11 the British Foreign Office delivered an aide-mémoire to the State Department, dealing with the situation in Norway. The British ambassador in Oslo had been informed by Foreign Minister Lange that the Norwegian Foreign Office had received reports from three different capitals that Norway might be faced with a request to negotiate a pact on the Soviet-Finnish model.[29] The Norwegian government had already decided that if such an eventuality arose, the request would be refused. However, the Norwegians wanted to know what kind of assistance they would receive in case of Soviet pressure or, worse, an attack. Lange had also informed Ambassador Bay of these developments.[30]

The British based their aide-mémoire on the assumption that a Soviet offer would in fact be made. The rumors about a Soviet-Norwegian pact can be seen as most welcome to the British in their efforts to involve the United States more actively in the defense of Western Europe. The Foreign Office depicted the threat to Norway in a most pessimistic way. London warned Washington that "all possible steps should be taken to forestall a Norwegian defection at this time, which would involve the appearance of Russia on the Atlantic and the collapse of the whole Scandinavian system. This would in turn prejudice the chance of calling any halt to the relentless advance of Russia into Western Europe." Bevin's solution was the conclusion of an Atlantic pact in which all the countries directly threatened by a Russian move to the Atlantic could participate. He specifically mentioned the United States, the United Kingdom, Canada, Eire, Iceland, Norway, Denmark, Portugal, and France.[31]

The American policy was now conducted along two lines at the same time. On the one hand the United States wanted to enter into immediate talks on an Atlantic security system. These talks were to be conducted with Britain and Canada. On the other hand Washington still maintained that a decision on the degree of support to be given to the Brussels powers could be made only after the United States had studied the agreement they would reach. This was clear from letters Marshall sent Bevin and Bidault on March 12. Thus, the Atlantic system was seen as a supplement and not as an alternative to the Western European arrangement. This had been Bevin's idea as well. In addition the Foreign Secretary foresaw even a Mediterranean system.[32]

The Norwegian situation did not create the Atlantic security system, but it speeded up the process of clarification in Washington and it illustrated quite decisively that a five-power arrangement would not be sufficient for Western Europe. Other countries had to be brought in as well. Those bordering on the Atlantic were of particular interest both to the United States and to Britain.

The role of Norway hardly received any public attention at the time. An informed source like the *New York Times* did not deal with it except in vague generalities.[33] In his speech to Congress on March 17, President Truman referred primarily to Czechoslovakia, Greece, and Italy. About Scandinavia he stated only that "Now pressure is being brought to bear on Finland, to the hazard of the entire Scandinavian peninsula."[34]

This reticence was to be expected at least on the part of Truman. Information about a Soviet-Norwegian pact was of course dealt with on a top-secret basis. Any publicity about a possible Soviet offer might actually serve to provoke such an offer or seriously affect relations with Moscow.

Historians have paid little or no attention to the role of Norway.[35] A strong objection to an interpretation placing considerable influence on the rumored pact proposal as a trigger for the Atlantic security system is the fact that even the memoirs of policy makers in Washington do not mention the Norwegian situation. Hardly anything is found about the "threat" to Norway in the memoirs of Truman, Bohlen, Kennan, and Acheson. Does this mean that it had little or no influence on evaluations in the U.S. capital?

I do not think so. The State Department papers certainly indicate, as we have seen, that the British aide-mémoire of March 11, probably together with reports from the American embassy in Oslo, were of considerable importance. Other sources support such a conclusion as well. First, on the Canadian side, the memoirs of the then Under Secretary of State for External Affairs, Lester B. Pearson, and those of his second-in-command, Escott Reid, are explicit about the role of Norway. Both men were involved in the development of the Atlantic system from the very start. In discussing the background of the American-British-Canadian talks in Washington in March, Pearson specifically states that "Soviet pressure on Norway was particularly disturbing." Reid stresses the Norwegian picture even more and comments that the "fact that the incident which precipitated the talks on the treaty was a Soviet threat to Norway seems to have been kept secret for ten years or more."[36]

Second, Marshall right away informed Secretary of Defense Forrestal about the British aide-mémoire. The dispatch to Forrestal, who was at Key West, summarized the tripartite British proposals for a Western European system with

American backing, an Atlantic, and a Mediterranean system. The Secretary of State noted that he had already discussed the matter with his closest advisers, Lovett, Hickerson, Bohlen, Armour, Douglas, and Thompson. Forrestal was informed that the President would be notified. This surely indicates that the situation in Norway was looked upon with great concern.[37]

The primary reason for the lack of attention which the "threat" to Norway has received in memoirs and among historians is that the rumored pact proposal did not materialize. As a result of this, other matters were soon seen as more important. As early as March 22, in the first meeting of the American-British-Canadian representatives, Hickerson noted that "Italy, more even than Norway, is most directly menaced."[38]

As to Italy, Ambassador Dunn in Rome was reporting that the communists and their supporters might well receive 40 to 45 percent of the vote in the upcoming elections. On March 15 George Kennan suggested to Marshall that the best course was for the "Italian Government to outlaw Communist Party and take strong action against it before elections." If the communists responded with civil war, as Kennan expected they would, then the United States should intervene. No action was taken along such lines. Even Hickerson cautioned against following Kennan's advice. However, the embassy in Rome and the State Department only gradually became more optimistic about the likely results of the April 20 elections in Italy.[39]

To conclude, there was never any doubt that the United States would support in some way or other the security arrangements that were evolving in Western Europe. America's commitment to these arrangements was stepped up as a result of the increased international tension in the first months of 1948. Yet, despite the situation in Norway soon being pushed into the background again, in the crucial phase around the middle of March the rumors about the Soviet pact proposal to Norway contributed greatly to basic changes in Washington. Spurred by the fears of the British as to Norway's position, the State Department rather suddenly became willing to start immediate talks with the British and the Canadians. Equally significant, although the one did not exclude the other, Washington agreed that these talks were to focus on an Atlantic security system instead of on American support to a Western European arrangement.

Creation of the Atlantic Security System

On March 17 Britain, France, the Netherlands, Belgium, and Luxembourg signed the Brussels treaty. It was a treaty of mutual assistance—the participating countries promised military and other aid in case of an attack on one of them. The only power specifically named as a potential aggressor was Germany. Yet it was evident that the Soviet Union and not Germany had been foremost in the minds of those who had negotiated the agreement.[40]

On the very day the treaty was signed, President Truman promised in his speech to Congress that "the determination of the free countries of Europe to protect themselves will be matched by an equal determination on our part to help them do so."[41] The United States would support the Western Union which had now been established. Truman said nothing in his speech, however, about the likelihood of the United States entering directly into a defense arrangement with Western Europe. In a joint message after the President's speech, Bevin and Bidault indicated their strong interest in talks with the United States to determine the nature of America's support for the Western Union.[42] Such talks were not to start before July.

Unknown to France and the Benelux countries, the emphasis had shifted from the idea of the United States backing a Western European arrangement to that of creating an Atlantic system. The British had all along preferred this alternative, but had proceeded along the European line in part to encourage the United States to decide on its degree of involvement. With the Canadians being brought in, the supporters of the Atlantic idea received further strength. When the American-British-Canadian talks, which Washington had agreed to on March 12, began ten days later, the Canadian and British representatives indicated at the very first meeting that they preferred an Atlantic pact to an extension of the Brussels treaty. An Atlantic pact would make the inclusion of the United States and Canada, as well as other countries, easier than would an extension of the Brussels system.[43]

It was up to the State Department to formulate an American negotiating position. Several ideas were tossed around. Four lines of action received particular attention. The first was a treaty of reciprocal military assistance based on Article 51 of the United Nations Charter. Such an arrangement would make it possible to include selected countries even outside Western Europe. Greece, Turkey, and Iran were apparently foremost in mind. This approach was temporarily favored by those in the State Department who dealt with matters relating to the United Nations Organization. Hickerson also briefly toyed with this idea.[44]

The second approach was a unilateral assurance by the United States to the Western Union members and other countries in Western Europe to the effect that Washington would consider a Soviet attack on any of them an attack upon the United States. This course was favored by the staff of the National Security Council[45] and had the strong sympathy of George Kennan. At this stage, however, Kennan was still away in the Far East.

The third possibility was an extension of the Brussels pact. This was an idea which received broad support in the State Department. The problem was the position of the United States and Canada under such a scheme. If the two countries were to enter on the same basis as the other members, that would destroy the basis for further European integration in the military field.[46]

The fourth possibility was an Atlantic pact. This was what the British and the Canadians supported, and what the United States came to favor. A treaty under Article 51 of the UN Charter was abandoned at the second meeting of the American-British-Canadian group. It would be too cumbersome, too long in implementation, and would involve the

United States more intimately in the affairs of the Middle East and Asia than Washington desired. A unilateral assurance by the United States was long favored as a short-term measure, to give the Europeans some protection while a more comprehensive system of reciprocal guarantees was negotiated between Western Europe and North America. The idea of extending the Brussels treaty was accepted by all three countries, but as a means of strengthening the European end of the security system, not as an alternative to the close association of the United States and Canada.[47]

In the second meeting of the American-British-Canadian group, the representatives of the three countries reached general agreement on the primacy of an Atlantic (Western) mutual defense pact. In the third meeting it was agreed that the "objective is a Security Pact for the North Atlantic Area, plus an extension of the Brussels agreement. The US would be a member of the North Atlantic Pact along with all nations bordering the North Atlantic (including Iceland) and Italy, except that Spain would not be immediately eligible." This idea was then, in slightly altered form, written into a draft agreement from the conference.[48] The last meeting was held on April 1.

Hickerson, Chief of the Western European Division Achilles, Ambassador to Britain Douglas, George Butler of the Policy Planning Staff, General Gruenther, and Colonel Griffin had been the negotiators on the American side.[49] Hickerson was undoubtedly the most influential. He was Director of the Office of European Affairs and had been intimately involved in the planning process in Washington from the very beginning. He also chaired at least four of the six meetings of the whole group. Achilles was a firm supporter of his Atlantic ideas.[50] The same was probably true for Ambassador Douglas and, to a less extent, Butler.[51] The two military representatives were only marginally involved in the negotiations. Without clear guidance from the Defense Department, they do not seem to have exerted any significant influence.[52]

Hickerson's leading role was enhanced by his insistence that the talks be held on what he called the "pick and shovel level." He did not want the participants to have to seek instructions daily from their capitals. Their superiors would be free to comment on the draft afterward. Unlike British and Canadian practice, it is possible that Hickerson conferred only marginally with Lovett and Marshall. Such independence was made easier by the fact that Lovett was away on holidays for most of this period, while Marshall was busy preparing for his trip to South America—he left on March 30, not to return until April 24.[53]

At the beginning of April significant parts of the foreign policy establishment in the United States, Britain, and Canada had reached agreement on the need for a North Atlantic defense arrangement. The list of countries to be invited to participate included the United States, Britain, Canada, France, Norway, Sweden, Denmark, Iceland, the Netherlands, Belgium, Luxembourg, Eire, Italy, and Portugal. Reservations were still held concerning Western Germany, Austria, and Spain. The participants in the Washington talks had also accepted the basic principle that an attack on one of the member countries was to be considered an attack on all of them. Finally, they had agreed that in addition to participating in the North Atlantic arrangement, the countries in Western Europe were to be encouraged to join the Brussels treaty as well.[54]

If the draft from the Washington talks had represented the agreed position of the three governments, a final pact could probably have been worked out fairly rapidly. But it did not. Few problems existed on the British and the Canadian sides. The question was whether first the State Department, then the executive branch, primarily the President and the Defense Department, and finally Congress would accept the draft from the Washington talks.

At this stage the State Department was led by Lovett and Hickerson. Kennan was still away, and even Secretary of State Marshall himself seems to have been left somewhat on the outside. His agreement to conduct talks with Canada and Britain on an Atlantic security system was apparently taken by Lovett and Hickerson as the Secretary's consent to proceed along the lines they desired. This they did despite the fact that a Policy Planning Staff report which Marshall had transmitted to the National Security Council on March 24 was rather noncommittal about the role of the United States, holding several options open.[55] After the Secretary of State left Washington on March 30, he evidently received little information about the Atlantic negotiations. Only on April 20 was he given a full report of what had been accomplished so far. With the report went a statement that the basic agreement of Forrestal and President Truman had already been obtained.[56]

In his answer from Bogotá on April 23, the Secretary made only a few comments on the information he had received. The most important one concerned his opposition to a declaration aimed at discouraging a possible armed attack against Greece, Turkey, and Iran, three countries which would be left outside the North Atlantic system but toward which the United States had already taken on important commitments. In addition, the Secretary expressed his hope that "If the matter can wait until I return, I suggest we discuss it at more length then."[57]

By the time Marshall returned to Washington on April 24 the executive branch had already come far in deciding on the main features of the American policy. Basically, the results of the American-British-Canadian talks had been accepted by the State Department and the National Security Council. A report prepared on April 13 by representatives of the State Department, the departments of the Army, the Navy and the Air Force, and the National Security Resources Board closely followed the outcome of these talks. The report, NSC 9, dealt with the position of the United States with respect to support for the Western Union and a North Atlantic military arrangement. This paper was then forwarded to the National Security Council where it seemingly met with sympathy on the main points.

The Joint Chiefs of Staff and the Defense Department under Forrestal supported the idea of a collective defense arrangement for the North Atlantic area. Probably little substantial disagreement existed between the prevailing military attitude and that of Lovett and Hickerson. Some differences in emphasis were to be expected. The JCS did not want an Atlantic arrangement to reduce their freedom of action in determining American strategy. They also wanted to be sure that European requirements would not interfere with those of the United States itself. Indirectly this represented a plea for an increased defense budget. With these exceptions the military still largely left the initiative in working out Washington's position to the State Department.[58]

The President had agreed to the initiation of talks with Britain and Canada. That fact and his speech to Congress on March 17 could be seen as his general approval of the policies followed by the State Department. But the speech was short on specifics and until mid-April President Truman was really only marginally involved in the discussions on the role of the United States. This certainly irked some of his White House advisers.[59] With the decision to start talks with Congressional leaders, in particular Senator Vandenberg, the President was brought in more directly. The fact that the National Security Council also became involved meant a further enlargement of the role of departments and persons outside the State Department.[60]

In May significant changes took place in the American position with regard to direct U.S. participation in a North Atlantic security system. The two NSC papers completed on April 13 and April 23 had stated that the United States was to issue invitations to the list of countries agreed to in the Washington talks "with a view to the conclusion of a collective Defense Agreement for the North Atlantic area."[61] However, in NSC 9/2, dated May 11, this point had been dropped. Now the accent was on inducing those countries which were not already members to join the Western Union. About the role of the United States, the May paper only stated that

> If, as a result of its diplomatic talks with the British, French and Benelux representatives, the U.S. Government became convinced that some further political commitment was necessary at this time to bolster public confidence in Western Europe, the U.S. Government should discuss with the parties

to the Brussels Treaty some form of association by the U.S.,
and if possible Canada, with them along the lines recommended in the Senate resolution.[62]

This recommendation was accepted by the National Security
Council.

Even if Washington was still prepared to become a
direct participant in a North Atlantic security system, the
emphasis had once again shifted in the direction of the Europeans doing as much as possible for themselves and the
United States only later making up its mind about what role
it was to play. This did not mean that Washington had re-
verted to its attitude of January-February. Compared to that
period the United States now had no qualms about entering
into direct talks with the Western Union countries. Washington must also have expected that the Europeans would
press for the maximum participation of the United States
and Canada. Most important, if the expected pressure occurred, the United States was evidently ready to yield.

What explains this change in the direction of emphasizing the role of Europe once again? Several factors have to be
taken into account. One had to do with changes in the situation within the State Department. Until mid-April not only
had Kennan been away from Washington, he was also less
determined in his analysis of the nature of the Soviet challenge than he had been earlier and was soon to become
again. In March he had warned that the United States had
to be prepared for all eventualities, including an armed attack.[63] As we have seen, at this time he even argued in favor
of persuading the Italian government to outlaw the communists before the upcoming elections.

In his memoirs Kennan has argued that what he saw as
the ideal solution for the security problems of Western
Europe was a "dumbbell" arrangement where the United
States and Canada cooperated closely on one side of the
Atlantic and the Europeans on the other. The two units
should not be linked with a treaty, but the Americans would
supply the Europeans with the military equipment they
needed and guarantee U.S.-Canadian assistance in case of a

Soviet attack.[64] In internal discussions in Washington, Kennan was not to press for this ideal solution. On the other hand, although after his return to Washington he at first tried to introduce only marginal changes in the outline resulting from the Washington talks, this soon changed. Kennan's initial comments on NSC 9 and 9/1 did not break significantly with the general State Department attitude. His memorandum to Lovett of April 29 did. The Director of the Policy Planning Staff was now trying to bring back some of the ideas he had presented before the March crisis and before he had left for the Far East. He again argued that too much emphasis was placed on a military approach to security. He stressed the need for the Europeans to play a stronger role in the working out of an arrangement. In the memorandum to Lovett, Kennan stated that he had discussed his ideas with Bohlen, who in the main agreed with him.[65]

The return of Secretary of State Marshall served to strengthen those who wanted to reopen discussions about the role of the United States. As Marshall had had hardly any influence on deliberations in Washington while he had been away in South America, quite likely he now wanted to make his voice heard again.

These changes within the State Department led to renewed discussions between the main protagonists, Hickerson on the one side and Kennan and Bohlen on the other. On May 7 the three were able to present an agreed position. This position was very similar to that presented to the National Security Council a few days later.[66]

Probably even more important for the changes on the American side was the increased attention which was being paid to Congress in general, and to the Republican chairman of the Senate Foreign Relations Committee, Arthur Vandenberg, in particular. The administration had long been willing to take on stronger commitments in Western Europe than had Congress. The initiative in working out the Truman Doctrine, the Marshall Plan, and now U.S. support for a European military arrangement had lain with the executive. Although the administration had so far basically got what it wanted, care had to be taken that Congress was informed and modifications agreed to without altering the substance of the measures involved.

On April 11 talks had been initiated between Senator Vandenberg and Under Secretary Lovett. Vandenberg and important Republican foreign policy spokesman John Foster Dulles, who was also brought into the talks, again and again pointed out that the Western Europeans had to do their maximum to help themselves. They often referred to the pattern of the European Recovery Program. The United States would come in to fill those needs which Western Europe could not satisfy on its own.[67] The importance of following this advice was underlined by the fact that little was known at this stage about how Congress would react to taking on substantial new commitments in Europe shortly after the ERP had been passed.[68]

The possibility, even the likelihood, that there would be a change of administrations after the November elections had to strengthen the position of Vandenberg and Dulles further. In case the Republicans won their expected victory, much of the work might have to be redone if the Truman administration had not cleared its views with the GOP foreign policy leadership. The United States could enter into no major commitment without bipartisan approval.[69]

Changes in the international climate also contributed to the somewhat revived aloofness on the American side. After the building of tension in March, a lull occurred. The Soviets did not come to propose a pact with Norway. The one concluded with Finland proved less ominous than what could have been expected from the original Soviet proposal. The Christian Democrats won a surprisingly large victory in the Italian elections. Until the imposition of the Berlin blockade on June 24, both Washington and the Western European capitals experienced a diminishing sense of urgency which contributed to the slowdown in the defense talks.[70]

NSC 9/3, completed on June 28 and approved by the President on July 2, followed the lines of NSC 9/2 of May 11. Compared to the NSC papers of April, the emphasis remained on the role of the Western Union, and the point about the United States only making a decision about direct membership in a North Atlantic arrangement at a later stage was upheld.[71] This, then, was the American negotiating position when the Washington exploratory talks between the representatives of the United States, Canada, Britain, France, and the Benelux countries began in Washington on July 6.

When the talks started, it immediately became clear that the British and the Canadians wanted the United States to enter a North Atlantic arrangement on as close a basis as possible. Their views could hardly come as a surprise after what had taken place in March. But the positions of France and the Benelux countries were more complicated. Unaware as they generally were of the March meetings, they saw the working out of an Atlantic treaty as more of a long-term development than did the Americans, the British, and the Canadians. The French were not opposed to a treaty, but they wanted to make quite sure that the process of concluding it would not interfere with a rather immediate American commitment both to defend the continent of Europe and to reequip the French forces. These problems of coordination with France being supported by Belgium and in part even by Holland were not solved before early September.[72]

Despite these differences, the attitudes of the Europeans, the British in particular, and the Canadians had to strengthen the position of those in the State Department who had all along wanted the United States to join an Atlantic arrangement on an equal footing with the other participants. This group was strongly represented on the American negotiating delegation. Hickerson and Achilles were both there. To an increasing extent Hickerson was becoming the key man on the U.S. side. He had participated in the March talks, and he hardly missed an important meeting in the new round of talks which lasted from July 6 to September 10. As Director of the Office of European Affairs he handled most significant conversations with the ambassadors of the various European countries.

Marshall played only a minor role in the Washington exploratory talks. With great confidence in Lovett, the Secretary of State was content to leave the leadership to the

Under Secretary. Although Lovett may have had his doubts about the need for the United States to commit itself to Western Europe in the form of a treaty, he did not voice such doubts openly. Generally, he was much closer to the position of Hickerson than to that of Kennan and Bohlen.[73]

While Kennan and Bohlen did not participate in all the meetings of the Washington exploratory talks and had nothing like the contacts with the Europeans as had Hickerson, they did take part in many of the conversations with Canada and the Western Union countries. The point is that their influence was being reduced, once again. Not only that, but they both also modified their positions considerably in view of the attitude of the British and the Canadians in particular.

The Kennan-Bohlen ideas did not represent any clear-cut alternative to the prevailing attitude in the State Department. Their "dumbbell" concept had never been spelled out in any detail and they both agreed that the United States had to back up Western Europe militarily. When Britain and Canada pressed so hard for the direct membership of the United States in an Atlantic organization, a refusal would mean a considerable loss of prestige for them, especially after the round of negotiations in March. When the Europeans simply refused to believe that the Soviet threat should be met primarily through political and economic measures, that too greatly undermined the position of Kennan and Bohlen.[74]

After the passage of the Vandenberg Resolution on June 11 in favor of the association of the United States with a regional defense organization, the outcome of the Washington talks could be foreseen.[75] With the Europeans and the Canadians in favor of American membership and with Congress and even most Republicans ready to agree to such participation, there was little room for opposition to the North Atlantic concept. The United States would participate directly in an Atlantic treaty system based on the Rio principle of one for all, all for one, but with due respect for the role of the American Senate.

The differences between the Europeans and in part the

Canadians on one side and the representatives of the United States on the other never disappeared entircly. Washington continued to insist that the Europeans do as much as possible to help themselves.[76] Nevertheless, with the main lines of the American position clearly established, little need exists to go into the further details of the negotiations in Washington. After the exploratory talks were temporarily completed on September 10, the negotiators took a two-month break for consultations with their home governments. The new round then started on December 10 and was to last for two weeks, while the final stage went on from January 10 to March 28, 1949. The formal signing of the North Atlantic Treaty took place on April 4, 1949.

Expansion with Limitations

In the postwar period the United States took up commitments in most parts of the world to an extent unprecedented in time of peace. On the military side America's participation in the occupation of Japan, Germany, Italy, and Austria was of great importance. U.S. troops did not withdraw from Western Europe within two years as Roosevelt had told Stalin at Yalta they would. On the contrary, in his Stuttgart speech of September 1946 Secretary of State Byrnes made it clear that the troops would remain in Germany as long as there was an army of occupation. President Truman and leading officials in Washington also pointed out to Western European leaders that the atomic bomb ought to give pause to those who might be planning moves of aggression. In the talks among the Western Europeans in early 1948 about arrangements of military cooperation, little doubt existed that the United States would support such arrangements in some way or another. After a period of uncertainty, the United States even chose to come in as a full participant in a North Atlantic treaty system. The creation of NATO temporarily capped the growth in U.S. military commitments to Western Europe. These had in turn been preceded by an increase in Washington's political and economic commitments to Western Europe. Therefore, the main theme of America's policy toward Western Europe in the period from 1945 to 1949 was undoubtedly one of expansion in commitments, influence, and interest.

On the other hand, the overall picture of expansion on the part of the United States should be modified somewhat. Interesting limitations could be found on America's expansion into the affairs of Western Europe. Most important, it was not true that the United States thrust itself into Western Europe against the will of the Europeans. As we have seen, not only the British government but also those in France and the Benelux countries actively encouraged the Truman administration to take a more immediate interest in first their economic and then their defense problems. They hardly worried about U.S. domination over Western Europe. Instead they tried to make Washington abandon its half-hearted encouragement of efforts toward military cooperation in favor of more decisive support.

Most Western European leaders feared an expansion of Soviet influence. The concentration on a threat from Germany in the treaty of Dunkirk as well as in the Brussels treaty was primarily for French domestic reasons. As French Foreign Minister Bidault told Ambassador Caffery in early March 1948, in the ambassador's words, "what he really wants more than anything else, is a concrete military alliance (against Soviet attack) with definite promises to do definite things under certain circumstances. He does want explicit mention of Germany in some way purely for domestic political reasons. The French public would expect that, not only expect it but would attack him, if he left it out."[77]

A strong fear existed not only in Washington, but also in noncommunist quarters in most capitals in Western Europe, that events were moving in favor of the Soviet Union and the local communists. A combination of Soviet pressure, short of war, and internal upheavals on the whole worried policy makers in Washington, London, and Paris more than did the possibility of a direct Soviet attack on Western Europe.[78]

Nevertheless, an attack could not be entirely ruled out. In cases like these one wishes the margin of safety to be rather large. Governments prepared for the worst. The leaders in the Kremlin had undoubtedly done unexpected things. Perhaps they did not understand what they could get away with and what they couldn't. In March-April 1948 such fears were particularly strong both in Washington and in Western Europe. Even policy makers who normally stressed the political and economic nature of the Soviet challenge did not feel so certain at this time that their analyses had been right.

As had been the case in the Marshall Plan negotiations, Washington was also interested in limiting its commitments to Western Europe. On the economic side, the United States had pushed for the establishment of the OEEC and the EPU. These organizations would band the Europeans more closely together and thereby limit the American role. There was little desire in Washington to spend more dollars than necessary on European recovery.

Similarly, on the military side representatives of the Truman administration were to stress again and again that the more the Europeans could do on their own, the better for the United States. That was the primary reason why the Americans wanted to maintain and strengthen the Western Union at the same time as the Atlantic security system was established. At the second meeting of the American-British-Canadian talks on March 23, 1948, Hickerson had made it clear that the United States and Canada should not join the Western Union since the U.S. "hopes to see the eventual development of a United States of Western Europe . . . and the Brussels pact offers the hard core for such a development."[79]

This was to remain a constant theme in further negotiations. Washington never tired of reminding the Europeans of the advantages of integration, even if this would work against the economic interests of the United States, at least in the short run. The important memo of September 9 from the Washington exploratory talks noted that although the United States and Canada had to be brought into a North Atlantic system, "The establishment of the O.E.E.C. and the signature of the Brussels Treaty are important achievements which indicate the intent of the peace-loving countries of

Europe to work together in their common interest, and additional steps designed to bring about a substantial and permanent degree of cooperation and unity among these countries would materially improve the present position."[80] Washington struggled to make the Europeans cooperate more closely, not to create a Western Europe more dependent on the United States. The more the Europeans did for themselves, the less the Americans would have to do.

Other interesting limitations could be noticed at this time. The United States did not press for the widest possible participation in the new security system. Quite the contrary, Washington was against the membership of countries like Greece, Turkey, and Iran.[81] There was even considerable doubt about the role of Italy. On the whole the United States wanted the Italians to come in, but then by force of membership in the Western Union. When no such membership materialized, the Truman administration was long reluctant to admit Italy directly into the North Atlantic pact. Italian participation would break with the geographic framework of the alliance and make it difficult to refuse the strong requests of the Greek and Turkish governments for membership.[82] Both the State Department and the JCS were also quite skeptical about the insistence of the French to include Algeria under the treaty.[83]

Despite some interest on the part of the American military in the inclusion of Spain, the Truman administration agreed that Franco's Spain should not be permitted to participate at this time.[84] Thus, limits still existed on the extent to which anticommunism and base interests could serve as sufficient criteria to secure the friendship of the United States. Neither were there at this time any immediate plans for the rearmament of West Germany and that country's participation in the Atlantic alliance. The time could be foreseen when this question would be brought up, but no attempt was made in the negotiations leading to the NATO treaty to bring about the rearmament of West Germany.[85]

Some final signs of the limitations in America's policies should be mentioned although they do not relate to Western Europe. In late 1949 the Truman administration was prepared to leave the whole of China to the Chinese Communists. The United States had adhered to its policy of giving only quite limited support to the Chiang regime. After the fall of the mainland, Washington was preparing for the fall even of Taiwan. It would not commit large resources to prevent such a development.[86] However, in that part of the world, as in Europe, the outbreak of the Korean War would lead to great changes in the policies of the United States. The Korean War would also bring an end to the period of defense budgets below the 15 billion dollar mark. In the course of a few years the defense budget would triple.[87]

7

Scandinavia: Neutralism or Western Orientation?

Before proceeding to look at the attitudes of various American policy makers to the role of the Scandinavian countries in an Atlantic security arrangement, we have to examine foreign policy events in these countries in the first half of 1948. This was a period of widening differences between the orientation of Norway on the one hand and Sweden on the other, with Denmark falling somewhere in between. I will examine how these differences developed and, in particular, Washington's reaction to this development. To what extent did the Americans try to promote such a split among the three Scandinavian countries?

Neutralism or Western Orientation?

The most important foreign policy initiative in Western Europe in early 1948 was the speech delivered by British Foreign Secretary Ernest Bevin in the House of Commons on January 22. Bevin stressed the need for the countries in

Western Europe to unite against the Soviet threat. As a first step the Foreign Secretary wanted France and the Benelux countries to join Britain in a defense alliance.[1]

Nothing was explicitly stated in the speech about the role of the Scandinavian countries. It was obvious that Scandinavia was included in Bevin's general references to Western Europe. In the summary of his views which the State Department had received before the speech, the Foreign Secretary had indicated that the British would "seek to form with the backing of the Americans and the Dominions a Western democratic system comprising Scandinavia, the Low Countries, France, Italy, Greece and possibly Portugal." It was equally clear, however, that the Scandinavians were not seen as initial members of the new security arrangement. In line with earlier British comments on the hesitant nature of Scandinavian foreign policy, it was considered most likely that they would prefer to wait before making up their minds about joining or not. Bevin did not really object much to this, since it was questionable what protection the British and the French could offer Scandinavia.[2]

Washington, in keeping with its low profile at this time, offered little advice. But it was obvious that the Americans wanted a broad base since this would make the arrangement more effective and more attractive to the United States. Washington, as well as London, would like to see the Scandinavians involved in a Western European security project.

Again, chances of the three countries making such a choice in the near future, if at all, were seen as small. In his memo to Marshall of January 20, George Kennan argued that to emphasize military defense, instead of economic and political cooperation, would frighten the Scandinavians rather than attract them.[3] Those more skeptical than Kennan of Scandinavian policies expressed even stronger views. Neither Theodore Achilles of the Western European Division nor Republican foreign policy spokesman John Foster Dulles thought that the Scandinavians would want to join a European political arrangement.[4] In his memo of March 8 Hickerson stated that it was necessary to keep a security program separate from the European Recovery Program "to avoid driving the Scandinavians, Swiss and possibly others out of the ERP."[5] Hickerson feared that if a choice had to be made, the Scandinavians would leave the ERP rather than become involved in a military arrangement. His juxtaposition of Scandinavia with Switzerland illustrated his attitude to the three countries.

Despite all these generalizations about Scandinavia, in early March the State Department had definitely become aware of basic foreign policy differences among the Northern states. The reactions of Denmark, Sweden, and Norway to the ideas of Bevin represented a turning point in this respect. In his speech to the Riksdag (the Swedish Parliament) on February 4, Foreign Minister Undén strongly supported the policy so far pursued by the Swedish government and refused to take sides in the way Bevin wanted. In his reports on the speech, Ambassador Matthews was at least as interested in attacking the opinions expressed by Undén as in reporting them. It made little difference to Matthews that the policy proclaimed by the Foreign Minister had the strong support both of the Riksdag and of public opinion.[6]

Prime Minister Hedtoft of Denmark also came out against his country joining any kind of bloc. An open split between the Great Powers was seen as a catastrophe and something which Denmark had to do what little it could to avoid. It was evident, however, that the Danes desired to keep a somewhat lower profile in this matter than the Swedes.[7]

Reactions were different in Norway. On February 3 the steering committee of the Oslo Labor party gave its support not only to the Marshall Plan, but also to the ideas of Bevin.[8] Although this statement had not been agreed to by Foreign Minister Lange, and was disliked by him, even the Foreign Minister adopted an attitude different from that of the Swedes and the Danes. In his speech to the Storting on February 12, Lange balanced between two opposing poles. On the one hand, he stated that Norway would not want to join any bloc at this time. On the other, this refusal to join the Bevin plan was couched in language which made it clear that this attitude might soon have to be reexamined. Thus,

Norway's "no" to the ideas of Bevin was different from those of Denmark and Sweden in substance, and even more so in style.[9]

This difference was noticed with pleasure on the American side. In his report on Lange's speech, Ambassador Bay praised the attitude of the Foreign Minister and of noncommunists in general: "Until barely a few months back, references to Norway's East or West leanings were made in whispers and with furtive glances. Today the seal-and-ball juggling act seems to have lost much of its attraction."[10] More and more Norwegian politicians were coming out in open praise of the West. The impression conveyed by Bay of the situation in Norway was dramatically different from that presented by Matthews from Sweden.

Matthews saw himself as conducting a campaign of education against neutralism. Again and again he would tell representatives of the Swedish government that it was wishful thinking to believe that Sweden would be able to stay out of a third world war. Although Sweden would undoubtedly choose the West if a choice had to be made, that was no consolation to Matthews. Those who felt they belonged on this side had to take their stand now, when the West needed all the support it could get. And it might be too late for the Swedes to choose once a major conflict had erupted.

To some extent the ambassador was able to agree with Undén when the Foreign Minister argued that Sweden's policy had changed in the direction of the West in the last year. This change could best be seen in the attitude to participation in the European Recovery Program. Like Norway, Sweden had moved from very halfhearted approval of a modest organization to more solid support for a quite comprehensive one. Matthews and others still complained that Sweden did not show the proper spirit of gratitude and cooperation on every point. Nevertheless, no doubt existed about the basic support given to the recovery program by the Swedish government.[11]

It all came down to the point that in East-West terms the Swedes were simply not willing to take a break with neutralism. In his cable of February 16, Matthews enumerated the fallacies of neutralist thinking in twelve points. His conclusion was that although the pressure of events might modify Sweden's attitude, the evolution would be slow at best. In part this was apparently blamed on special features in the national character: "As Department is well aware, Swedes are slow to think and slow to move."[12]

The most likely means of bringing Sweden around to break with neutralism was, in the analysis of Matthews, to induce Norway to join "a western union." That would give the Swedes a feeling of being isolated not only from the West, but also from their Scandinavian neighbors. As to the possibility of Norway joining such a union, he concluded on March 3 that "I gather from the telegrams of our Oslo Embassy and recent Norwegian public statements that this development is not beyond the realm of possibility. I hope that any steps the Department and Ambassador Bay can take to hasten this process will be taken."[13]

A rapidly growing impression that the policies of Norway and Sweden were becoming less and less alike was based on more than their different reactions to Bevin's speech of January 22. An important event had taken place on February 17 when Norwegian Defense Minister Hauge had called the American Naval and Air attachés to his office. At their meeting he expanded on a theme which had been on his mind for some time, the possibilities and probable nature of U.S. assistance to Norway in case of war. Hauge inquired about the role of Norway in American air strategy, what aid might be expected in a war, and at what stages in an international conflict the United States would want to establish air, sea, and land bases in Norway.[14]

Reports received by the State Department on the meeting of the foreign ministers of Sweden, Denmark, Norway, and Iceland on February 23–24 further underlined the differences between Norway and Sweden. Although no definite plans for joining a Western bloc had been discussed, a split between Norway, supported by Iceland, and Sweden, generally supported by Denmark, was seen to exist in their analyses of the international situation.[15]

The next step in the rapprochement between Washington and Oslo was the speech delivered by Prime Minister Einar Gerhardsen on February 29, the so-called Kråkerøy speech. Influenced by the events in Czechoslovakia, the Prime Minister pointed out in very strong language that to combat communist influence represented the most important part of the struggle to maintain Norway's independence.[16] The speech dramatically strengthened the established Labor policy of reducing communist influence, a policy which the State Department had long observed with pleasure. Although the Swedish Social Democrats were also fighting communist influence in the trade unions and elsewhere, they were not so blunt as Gerhardsen. To Washington, others ought to take a strong stand as well. A case in point was the Czechoslovak socialists who had never been able to take a clear stand against cooperation with the communists. At this time the fate of Czechoslovakia often cropped up in contexts such as these.[17]

The growing differences among the Scandinavian countries, and between Norway and Sweden in particular, were noticed beyond the level of the regional experts in the Division of Northern European Affairs. On February 17 the Norwegian ambassador in the United States, Wilhelm Morgenstierne, reported that the State Department was adopting a more favorable attitude to Norway. He mentioned that Assistant Secretary Armour had praised Lange's speech on the Bevin plan while he had been highly critical of Undén. One week later Morgenstierne reported that Hickerson had expressed a similar position. The Director of the Office of European Affairs had praised the attitude of the Norwegians in maintaining a front against the communists while he condemned the views of Undén and the Czechoslovak Socialists.[18]

Both Marshall and Lovett indicated to the Norwegian ambassador that willingness to defend itself against domestic and foreign threats represented a most important criterion for the United States in deciding how much to support another country. In this context Morgenstierne noted that

Lovett was familiar with the contents of Gerhardsen's speech against the communists. Senator Wiley had even praised it on the floor of the Senate.[19]

Matthews' transfer to Sweden contributed to the increased involvement of the State Department leadership in the affairs of Scandinavia. From his period as Director of the Office of European Affairs he knew both Lovett and, in particular, Hickerson well. It was quite natural for the ambassador to conduct his campaign against the evils of Swedish neutralism not only in Stockholm but in Washington as well. In February-March 1948 he sent semiofficial letters to Lovett and Hickerson where he explained his attitude to Sweden's policy. He also asked the Under Secretary to meet with Swedish financier Mark Wallenberg on the latter's visit to the United States to "give him some straight-from-the-shoulder talk on the facts of life."[20]

On the whole Matthews enjoyed the support of the State Department in his denunciations of Swedish neutralism. On January 31 a cable had been sent in Marshall's name specifically commending him for a presentation of his position to Defense Minister Vougt. Lovett did meet with Wallenberg and apparently had a frank conversation with him. Hickerson supported Matthews with few, if any, reservations.[21]

Yet, Matthews was not completely satisfied with the attitude shown by Lovett. He did not like the fact that the Under Secretary had told Wallenberg that Washington was not writing off the Swedes as unreliable. He felt the American attitude should be less reassuring. Despite professing to Lovett that he had adjusted his tactics to a more indirect approach, he had told Hickerson that he was pointing out in "friendly fashion" in Stockholm that even if Sweden were able to stay neutral in a new war, it would probably have to deliver vitally needed industrial goods to the Soviet Union. In that case, Matthews told the Swedes, ". . . it is inconceivable that the United States with its duty of self-preservation and its presumed obligations to its Western allies would not, albeit with reluctance, be compelled to destroy Swedish industry from the air." This was being rather explicit.[22]

Matthews was not the only ambassador with contacts

within the State Department leadership. In February Bay resumed his correspondence with Assistant Secretary Armour on the question of bringing a prominent American speaker to Norway and possibly to the other Scandinavian countries as well. As we have seen, nothing had come of a similar idea in October 1947. The ambassador was quite direct about the purpose of such a visit. On February 6 he had told Armour that the purpose was "lining up the doubtful elements of labor in support of the Marshall Plan." He suggested that Jim Carey, the Secretary of the CIO who was already on his way to Europe, would be a suitable person. Bay was even willing to handle expenses from his own personal money. After the debate in the Storting in mid-February which showed broad support for the Marshall Plan, he told Armour that there was no great need for such a visit after all. That, in addition to Carey's crowded schedule, led to the idea being dropped.[23]

Armour and the State Department had apparently considered the planned visit a good idea. Even after Bay's report on the debate in the Storting, Armour indicated that "Although I agree that the importance of such a visit has diminished in respect to Oslo in particular, I think such a project is a good idea as regards Scandinavia in general."[24] Sweden was probably foremost in his mind.

The information about Hauge's rather far-reaching questions and his interest in military assistance from the United States also led to important discussions in Washington. Assistant Secretary of State Norman Armour sent letters to the Secretaries of the Army, the Air Force, and the Navy, respectively Kenneth C. Royall, Stuart Symington, and John L. Sullivan, asking for their reactions to the Defense Minister's questions.[25] As we shall see, this was to provoke high-level discussions about the strategic role of Norway. The Norwegian government was not, however, to receive any answers for some months yet.

The underlying reasons for the increased interest in Scandinavia, within the State Department in particular, were the deteriorating climate between East and West, and Washington's growing involvement in the affairs of Western

Europe on the political, economic, and now also the military level. As a border area to the Soviet Union Scandinavia commanded some special attention.

The interest in Norway reached its climax with the reports about the possibility of Norway being offered a pact with the Soviet Union on the Finnish model. These reports in turn led to the important aide-mémoire of March 11 from the British Foreign Office to the State Department.

The formation of an Atlantic defense system was meant to take care of the security needs of the Norwegians, among others. The long-range response to the Soviet threat to Norway was therefore, as Bevin indicated to Marshall on March 14, the working out of an Atlantic arrangement. Norway and the other two Scandinavian countries were included on all the lists of possible participants in an Atlantic system resulting from the American-British-Canadian talks.[26]

The inclusion of Norway in the Atlantic security arrangement was the answer on one level to Oslo's feelers for support from the West. However, no information could be given at this time to the Norwegian government about the discussions conducted in Washington. These were handled on a most confidential basis. Until such information could be presented to them, other means had to be relied upon to encourage the Norwegians to adopt a firm attitude to any Soviet offer which might materialize. On this level the answer to the rumors about a Soviet pact proposal was given in a telegram from the Secretary of State to the embassy in Oslo on March 12. The telegram only vaguely hinted at the contacts with the British government which led to the talks in Washington. The substance of the cable was the insistence that "If Soviet demands are made on Norway, in our opinion it is imperative that Norway adamantly resist such demands and pressure. Events in Czechoslovakia and elsewhere demonstrate futility of any other course. Soviet demands on Turkey and Iran were resolutely and successfully resisted by those countries. The American Government supported both Turkey and Iran in resisting the Soviet demands."[27] The countries Norway was compared with illustrated the seriousness with which Washington appraised the situation in

Norway. The answer was clear: any Soviet offer should be refused.

Foreign Minister Lange had pointed out in his contacts with the American and British ambassadors that the Norwegian government would reject any proposal for a Soviet-Norwegian pact. Washington's advice primarily strengthened a policy which had already been decided upon. Ambassador Bay nevertheless noted that Prime Minister Gerhardsen, who was acting as Foreign Minister while Lange was attending an OEEC meeting in Paris, received the American message "with obvious appreciation."[28]

In his talks with Bay the Norwegian Foreign Minister had also indicated the interest of the Norwegian government in acquiring military supplies from the United States. This represented a strengthening of the feelers put out by Defense Minister Hauge in his meeting with the Naval and Air attachés on February 17. On this level Hickerson tried to show a forthcoming attitude when he told Ambassador Morgenstierne on March 17 that military supplies were not limited to the countries of the Brussels treaty. He implied that the United States would probably be favorable to a formal Norwegian request, although he could not say anything about the specifics of an answer.[29]

Denmark and Sweden also discussed what stand they would take if they should receive Soviet pact proposals. Representatives of both the Swedish and the Danish governments indicated that their replies as well would be negative. A major difference existed between refusing to side with the West and entering into a special relationship with the Soviet Union. There was no desire for the latter either in Sweden or in Denmark.[30]

Neutralism or Western Orientation?
Spring-Summer, 1948

In the fall of 1947 Denmark had been seen as the most Western-oriented of the Scandinavian countries, to the extent that differences were made in the State Department among the three. This had changed by March 1948—now Norway was regarded as most Western-oriented. No one apparently felt certain about the position of Denmark, except that it lay somewhere between that of Norway and that of Sweden.

Little changed in this picture in the next few months or, for that matter, in the rest of the period being studied here. Therefore, we do not have to go into any great detail in the analysis of American evaluations of the Scandinavian countries in the spring and summer of 1948.

Dislike of Sweden's neutrality only became more pronounced in the spring and summer. In report after report Matthews denounced the policy of the Swedes. The attitude of the embassy in Stockholm was well summed up in the conclusion that "Swedish political neutrality at the present time is working contrary to United States political and strategic interests; that budging Sweden from neutrality will be difficult but not impossible; and that a calculated policy to that end should be undertaken."[31]

The most noteworthy high-level denunciation of Swedish neutrality was presented in a memorandum from Marshall to Truman dated June 3. In the opening statement the Secretary of State wrote that "Sweden has followed stubbornly a policy of neutrality which since the end of the war has been of more benefit to the Soviet Union than to the Western countries." The reason for this harsh judgment of Sweden's policy was evident. The Swedes were unwilling to recognize that the struggle between the Soviet Union and the United States was not a traditional Great Power conflict, but "rather the question of the survival of nations which believe in freedom and democratic processes." By not supporting the West, Sweden revealed "a division among the free nations of the world [which] can only serve to invite aggression."[32]

Sweden was still felt to belong to the West, by democratic tradition and by its domestic anticommunism. American policy makers felt that the Swedes should therefore see it as their duty to stand up and be counted in the defense of democracy against Soviet aggression. The fact that the United States itself had only recently abandoned its aloofness to the troubles of Europe did nothing to reduce the intensity of such feelings in Washington—quite the contrary, this only increased it. Americans admitted they had made mistakes in the past. Others ought to do the same. American representatives often came back to the lessons the United States had learnt. It would be too late for Sweden to change when its neutrality was no longer respected.[33]

Washington recognized the special position of Finland, and no attempt was made to induce Finland to become associated with the Western security arrangement. The State Department continued its policy of support for the Finns even after the conclusion of the Soviet-Finnish treaty in April 1948. Care was taken that this was done in an inconspicuous manner so as not to irritate the Soviet Union. Due to its history and geographic position, Finland's policy met with considerable sympathy in Washington.[34]

The Swedes met with no similar understanding. In Washington's analysis, there was little chance of the Soviet Union taking reprisals against Sweden if it joined the West. Most policy makers argued that the stronger the Western Powers were, the smaller the chance of any aggressive Soviet move.[35] Sweden could contribute significantly to the strength of the West.

The Danes maintained their low profile throughout 1948. Yet, while in the winter indications had been found that Denmark was sometimes regarded as following the lead of Sweden—as for instance in reports from the meeting of the Foreign Ministers in late February—in the following months the impression emerged that Denmark was opting for a more independent course or even moving in the direction of Norway.

In March the government in Copenhagen and particularly the Danish embassy in Washington were quite worried about the international situation. Measures were taken to guard against any communist plans of violence and against the possibility of a Soviet invasion. The State Department appreciated this "awakening to realities." The Danes not only pointed out that they would refuse to enter into any kind of agreement with the Soviet Union, but they also urgently requested various kinds of military equipment from the United States. They were particularly anxious to obtain 60,000 rifles.[36]

In addition Foreign Minister Rasmussen showed interest in obtaining a guarantee of military support in case of a Soviet attack, a topic which had first been brought up by the Norwegians. Rasmussen's presentation of Denmark's attitude tended to place that country on a course quite different from Sweden's. The alleged reason for this was that the Foreign Minister was satisfied that "Sweden will maintain its neutral attitude and therefore Denmark must determine independently its own course." In two analyses presented to the Secretary of State by the CIA, a similar picture emerged. No sharp break in Denmark's foreign policy was foreseen, but a slow and gradual drift in the direction of closer association with the West was expected.[37]

The Norwegians and the Danes were to come back to the point that the best solution to their security problems might be a guarantee by the United States to defend their countries.[38] While unilateral guarantees had been discussed in the American-British-Canadian talks in March, in particular as a temporary measure to protect Western Europe while a more comprehensive arrangement was being worked out, the idea was soon discarded. One major reason for this was the opposition of Senator Vandenberg to any one-sided American guarantee, especially when it was to be issued by the President and thereby leave the Senate on the sidelines. A U.S. guarantee would also break with the principle of reciprocity in American-European relations.[39]

In late April Foreign Minister Rasmussen told Marvel that if the United States became associated with the Brussels treaty and the Scandinavian countries were invited to do likewise, then "Denmark would join even though Sweden refused." Although Rasmussen, as so often, emphasized that this was his personal opinion not yet confirmed by the government, his remarks constituted an important signal about Denmark's growing affiliation with the West.[40]

The important point to policy makers in the State Department was that the Danes had once again established a line clearly separate from the Swedes and were approaching that of the Norwegians. This analysis on the part of a key person such as Hickerson had been brought out in his private message to Matthews on March 27. There the Director of the Office of European Affairs stated that "Norwegians and Danes both beginning to show encouraging awareness of facts of life."[41] The two countries had not taken as strong positions as Hickerson and Matthews had hoped, but they were definitely moving in the right direction.

Norway continued to be considered the most Western-oriented of the three Scandinavian countries. True, Bay's reports from Oslo in April indicated that the Norwegians were still not willing to join a Western group. The picture he presented was nevertheless one of the government slowly working itself toward a decision to join the West. On April 9 he cabled Washington that Foreign Minister Lange would still avoid joining a Western group "pending obvious security advantage." However, if an emergency arose, then Norway "will strike alone for shore if Denmark and Sweden procrastinate and remain aboard obviously sinking ship." Bay reported that Lange was doubtful about what choice Sweden would make, while "Denmark would likely follow Norway's lead under such conditions."[42]

After Lange's speech to a meeting of the Oslo Military Association on April 19, the ambassador became even more optimistic. Bay now wrote that "I personally feel he [Lange] so chose his language as to prepare the way for a progressively closer association with the West, including the possibilities of practical military arrangements and an eventual role in the evolution of the Western Union now in process of development under the Bevin Plan, even if Sweden or Denmark or both should be unprepared to take such steps."[43]

Norway's growing orientation toward the West, in particular as witnessed by Lange's speech to the Oslo Military Association, made the Swedish government fear that Norway would join a Western military system in some form. This would create a serious split in Scandinavia. In consequence Foreign Minister Undén arrived in Oslo on May 3 with a proposal that the three Scandinavian countries consider how they could work out their own joint military arrangement. The Swedish government made it clear from the very start that any common defense effort would have to be based on neutrality. The Danes were apparently willing to accept talks on this premise.[44]

The Norwegian government was not. It could agree to discussions with Sweden and Denmark, but not on the conditions laid down by Undén. As a result, formal talks were postponed. But in September the Norwegians did consent to the setting up of a defense committee with representatives from the three countries to examine only the possibility of a Scandinavian association independent of the West. Barring any unexpected situation, the three also agreed that no negotiations would be carried out with the Western Powers for the purpose of association with them before the defense committee had finished its work (probably in February 1949).

These concessions did not mean that the Norwegians had abandoned their Western orientation. Nothing was stated publicly about the fact that only a neutral association was being examined. If agreement could not be reached, the three countries were free to strike out on their own. Finally, the Norwegian members of the defense committee were largely pro-Western in attitude.[45]

While the discussions about the defense committee had been going on, Foreign Minister Lange and other pro-Western politicians had emphasized that they would never agree to any form of Scandinavian cooperation based on the Swedish neutrality model. Lange also pointed out to Ambassador Bay that he was disappointed at the weak stand taken by the Danes. As a result, he would try to stiffen the attitude of the Danish government against Scandinavian cooperation on the basis of neutrality.[46]

Norway's Western orientation was probably exaggerated by the embassy in Oslo and thereby also by Washington. The impression was easily created that the Norwegians had agreed to formal discussions with the Swedes only for tactical reasons. Chances of Norway and Sweden finding a common platform were regarded as small. If the talks failed, Lange would recommend Norway's association with the West.

As the Foreign Minister pointed out, after talks had broken down, then it would be easier to convince "die-hard party members and Norwegian people" that Norway had no alternative to joining the West.[47]

The embassy had no clear perception of the opposition to the policies of Lange and others with a Western orientation. A strong group within the cabinet preferred cooperation with Sweden to a Western association. Even stronger opposition existed within the parliamentary group of the Labor party. The fact that Prime Minister Gerhardsen in May had gone quite far in accepting the idea of a neutral Scandinavian group was also largely unknown to the embassy. From Stockholm Matthews reported that the Prime Minister had been most displeased by "Swedish attempted pressure to detach Norway from the west."[48]

In Bay's defense it should be argued that the extent of the opposition was known to very few observers at the time. It also seems likely that Lange played it down. On May 18 Bay reported that Lange had told him that one reason why the government had let "matter simmer for time being" was to "avoid alienating *small* [italics mine] minority within Labor Party which believes Norway should make every possible effort collaborate Sweden."[49] Similar comments were made on other occasions.

While Americans had no good channels to the opposition within the Labor party, they had excellent contacts with Norwegians who were even more pro-Western than the Foreign Minister. The two most influential ones were Secretary General of the Labor party Haakon Lie and Ambassador Morgenstierne in Washington. Lie openly presented the talks with Sweden as an attempt to win the Swedes over to alignment with the West. In Washington Morgenstierne was conducting his own little private campaign to prevent Scandinavian cooperation on the basis of anything other than strong association with the West. When at the beginning of June he feared that the Swedes were having some success in persuading the Norwegians, the ambassador asked a representative of the Division of Northern European Affairs whether "there weren't some way by which the United

States could express its disapproval to Sweden concerning
such interference in Norwegian affairs."[50] Proceeding from
Morgenstierne's comment and the fact that the Truman administration was strongly interested in promoting the Western orientation of the Scandinavian countries, we might ask
what means Washington used to further their desired break
with neutralist policies.

Encouragement through Use of the Marshall Plan

The United States had many instruments at its disposal
with which to influence the foreign policy of the Scandinavians. A major one was the extension or refusal of financial assistance. In this context the question arises of whether,
and, if a positive answer is given, to what extent the United
States used Marshall Plan aid to encourage the Western orientation of certain states.

Richard Freeland has argued that political considerations played a very minor role in determining amounts of
assistance. The basic factor was a country's balance of payments with the dollar area. Norwegian historian Magne
Skodvin has argued even more strongly, with reference to
Norway, that the degree of Western orientation was of no
importance in the distribution of Marshall Plan assistance.
The major reason, in the opinion of Skodvin, was quite simply that the Americans had little influence over this aspect
since it was handled by the Organization for European Economic Cooperation.[51]

No doubt distribution was based primarily on economic
criteria. Most important was a country's balance of payments
with the dollar area. In addition, while the United States
itself decided on the amounts for the second quarter of 1948,
the OEEC was largely responsible thereafter. Although the
Economic Cooperation Administration made the final decision, it usually introduced only marginal changes in the
amounts proposed by the Europeans through the OEEC.[52]

All in all, the possibilities for bringing political criteria
into the distribution were small, in particular after the sec-

ond quarter of 1948. This does not mean that assistance was never influenced by political purposes, only that such considerations were of minor importance compared to economic criteria.

The best example of political considerations influencing the distribution of assistance is found in the suspension of aid to Indonesia through the Netherlands in late 1948. While the State Department was not willing to stop assistance to Holland itself, Congressional pressure led the department to warn the Dutch that it might even have to do that if policies in Indonesia were not altered. Similar warnings were issued in connection with the delivery of arms to the Netherlands. This issue disappeared only with the independence of Indonesia.[53]

Other examples can also be found. In the first year of the program there was actually one example of the ECA raising an allotment beyond what had been requested. That was for the French zone of Germany. In this case the Americans reacted against the stern policies pursued by the French. Washington and the ECA favored a more lenient attitude.[54]

Before the establishment of the OEEC and the ECA, the crucial body in determining aid to the various countries was the National Advisory Council on International Monetary and Financial Problems. The NAC was made up of representatives of the departments and agencies dealing with foreign aid, primarily the State, Treasury, and Commerce departments, the Federal Reserve System, and the International Monetary Fund and Bank. Quite often NAC representatives were influenced by somewhat different factors. It was most important that the "political" divisions of the State Department were not represented on the Council. These could be expected to show more interest than the economic divisions in letting criteria other than economic ones influence decisions.

Since Norway was emerging as the most Western-oriented of the Scandinavian states, it should be expected that considerations related to the East-West conflict would show most clearly in attitudes toward that country. Ambassador Bay often argued in favor of the Norwegians being treated as favorably as possible under the ERP. While he found it difficult to go into the complex economic factors involved, he showed little hesitation in presenting political arguments for assistance to Norway. On February 11 Bay told the department that he would not refrain from mentioning one aspect "of considerable importance, namely the desirability of avoiding any development which might in any way retard what seems to be the increasing orientation of Norway toward the West. The situation in that respect appears to be entirely different from that in Sweden." He was to repeat the same argument in later reports. In general terms Ambassador Matthews took the same attitude.[55]

What influence did recommendations of this nature have on the State Department and the NAC in Washington? On February 13 Hickerson informed Ambassador Morgenstierne that the department would recommend that Norway be moved from the category of countries that would receive only loans (Sweden and Ireland) to that of countries that would get part loans and part grants. No reason was given for this change. Morgenstierne thought it was related to the unfavorable terms under which Norway sold fish to the Western zones of Germany.[56]

There had been some debate within the NAC as to whether Norway should receive only loans. At the time Hickerson talked to the ambassador the issue had not been settled, although it seemed likely that the Norwegians would obtain 15 percent of the assistance for the first fifteen months in the form of grants.[57] When Hickerson found it necessary to inform Morgenstierne before a final decision had been made, it seems likely that he wanted to make sure that the ambassador understood that at least the State Department was trying to deal with the Norwegians in a friendly way. Apparently the same could not be said about the U.S. military in Germany who were responsible for the fish contracts.[58]

On March 22 the department informed Ambassador Bay that 15 million dollars was the tentative estimate of what Norway would receive for the April-July 1948 quarter. No decision had evidently yet been made as to the grant percentage. Denmark would also get 15 million while 10 million had been set aside for Sweden. In May, however, it was decided that Norway would obtain 20 million dollars, 25 percent of which as a grant. Denmark would receive the same amount, while Sweden would get nothing.[59]

It is not possible to state with certainty what determined these changes in May as compared to the March estimates. They can well be explained in terms of changed economic circumstances. In April the Norwegian government had informed the embassy in Oslo that Norway's balance of payments situation was not as good as had been estimated in Washington. Similarly, only in April did the Norwegians really begin to press for part of the ERP assistance being given as a grant instead of receiving the entire sum as a loan. The State Department's assumption that a substantial part of Norway's dollar deficits could be financed by borrowing from the World Bank was also now recognized as too optimistic.[60]

It is significant that in the NAC deliberations the Federal Reserve Board representative actually proposed that Norway should receive half of its assistance in the form of grants. Evidently he based this on an estimate of Norway's ability to pay. He also argued that the countries in the 100 percent loan category should be those which had been neutral during the war, since they were much more able to pay than were the others. At a staff meeting of the NAC on April 13 tentative agreement was even reached that while Sweden would receive only loans, Norway would get 50 percent grants and Denmark 75 percent.[61]

It is not necessary to bring in political considerations to explain the amounts set aside for the Scandinavian countries in general and for Norway in particular. Yet, although the influence of the political divisions of the State Department was quite limited on this question, it seems likely that their attitude was one of the factors which strengthened the position of Norway and Denmark and weakened that of Sweden.

On several occasions the political divisions were anxious to integrate Marshall Plan assistance with overall political relations. On March 5 Benjamin M. Hulley, Acting Chief of the Northern European Division, argued that while the division was willing to go along with an amount of 15 million dollars for Denmark, "Political considerations make it desirable not to cut Denmark's allotment below the $15 million figure." The day before he had made a similarly political recommendation as to the assistance Iceland ought to receive.[62] In more general terms, on April 15 the State Department representative on the NAC staff concluded that "Sweden could get along without ERP assistance and could live on her reserves."[63] He therefore wanted the 10 million set aside for Sweden to be transferred to other countries.

As to Norway, in connection with the press release of the tentative amounts for the first fifteen months of the ERP, Under Secretary Lovett cabled Bay on April 19 that the State Department was "seriously concerned re above figures and effect their publication will have in NOR[way]." The figure for Norway, 32.8 million dollars, was received with much disappointment by the Norwegian government. Lovett pointed out that the figures were tentative and would be revised on a quarterly basis. According to the April estimate Denmark was to receive 130.8 million and Sweden 28.4 million in the fifteen-month period.[64]

One reason for the low estimate for Norway was, as Lovett told Bay, that the Norwegians had still not used all of their old Export-Import Bank credit. The "National Advisory Council insists that countries use outstanding Eximbank loans to fullest extent possible."[65] Lovett's cable should be interpreted as an attempt by the State Department to soften the impact of figures which bore no relationship to the political orientation of the Scandinavian countries.

The announcement of the amounts for the fifteen-month period again led Ambassador Bay to urge a more favorable treatment for Norway. On May 8 he strongly supported an upward revision of the estimates. He warned that the Norwegians might well relapse into political apathy if they felt they were not properly treated in the ERP. Bay argued that ". . . Norway's future decisions and actions will have important influence on evolution of Danish and even Swedish policies and Scandinavian trend may largely determine whether Russia will have important Atlantic outlets."[66] Matthews in

Stockholm had also, as we shall see, stepped up his campaign in favor of giving Norway the best possible treatment as a way of indicating to the Swedes what they had to do to obtain similar favors.

The reports from Matthews and Bay, as well as the growing interest of the State Department in encouraging the Scandinavian countries to break with neutrality, probably made the department favor changes in the March figures. On May 18 Marshall not only cabled the embassy in Oslo that Norway would receive twenty million dollars for the April-July period, he also informed Bay that the State Department had recommended to the ECA that Norway be given another 20 million for the next quarter. This telegram was sent in response to Bay's strong complaints of May 8. "At this rate . . . Norway should receive approx. $80–90 mil ECA assistance for first year."[67] Eighty to ninety million dollars a year was not bad when the Department had first indicated that Norway might receive only 32.8 million for the fifteen-month period.

At this time, however, American influence on the distribution of assistance diminished drastically due to the role of the OEEC. For the period from mid-1948 to mid-1949 the OEEC recommended for Norway, Denmark, and Sweden respectively 84, 110, and 47 million dollars. The ECA agreed to 83.3, 109.1 and 46.6 millions.[68]

But while Washington had little influence on total allotments for the various countries after the second quarter of 1948, the ECA, and thereby indirectly to some extent the State Department, carried more weight on decisions as to the percentage given as grants as opposed to loans. However, it is difficult to discern any tendency related to the stand of the various states in the East-West conflict in the percentages given as grants. Through December 1949 Denmark received 48.2 percent of its ERP assistance as grants while Norway got only 30.2 percent. Sweden received nothing in grants. The country that got the most as grants was Austria, with 69.9 percent.[69]

It seems evident that the distribution of assistance through the Marshall Plan was only to a very small extent influenced by political considerations related to the East-West conflict, particularly after the second quarter of 1948. Furthermore, Britain and the Netherlands, which were hardly threatened by domestic communism, together received almost as much as did France and Italy. This indicates that even the threat of domestic communism had little influence on the distribution of ERP aid.[70]

Nevertheless, at least with regard to the amounts for the second quarter of 1948, State Department circles and especially the American embassies in Oslo and Stockholm tried to bring in the political orientation of the Scandinavian countries as one criterion for distribution. Norway, the most Western-oriented of the three, seemed likely to receive little aid if economic criteria only were taken into account. In all probability political evaluations had some influence in gradually bringing about a more favorable treatment for Norway.

This conclusion is supported by the impression most Norwegians who were in touch with American representatives had of the decision-making process in Washington. The close connection between Norway's Western orientation and the favors it received in the form of economic assistance was pointed out by such people as Ambassador Morgenstierne, his Chargé Eigil Nygaard, Norwegian economic representative in Washington and participant in the OEEC talks in Paris Ole Colbjørnsen, Director of the Norwegian Bank Gunnar Jahn, and Under Secretary in the Defense Department Dag Bryn.[71] Some of the members of the cabinet itself appear to have had a similar impression. It should be mentioned, however, that Foreign Minister Lange was apparently not among these.[72]

How to Reward Friends and Punish Enemies

The European Recovery Program was to a considerable extent controlled by the Europeans themselves and the open introduction of East-West political considerations might have had serious repercussions in relations with the neutral states participating in the ERP. Any American desire to re-

ward friends and punish enemies could therefore be expected
to show much more strongly in other areas.

Matthews in Stockholm felt that the American attitude
ought to be based on an overall evaluation of relations with
the Scandinavian countries. On April 21 he brought out in
full thoughts which he had long been developing. The ambassador recommended that "in our policy we should carefully distinguish between 'neutral' Sweden on the one hand
and Norway and Denmark on the other. Any gestures of aid
to the latter coupled with refusals to aid Sweden will help
shake Swedish neutrality."[73]

Matthews generally regarded chances of Sweden joining
the West as fairly small. If, however, his "process of education" with regard to the Swedes were to have any chance of
success at all, maximum encouragement ought to be given
Western-oriented Norway and Denmark, while Sweden
should receive no support. As the ambassador was to repeat
again and again, "The cure for isolationism is isolation." By
shaking the Swedes in their belief that they would be helped
by the United States in an emergency even if they stayed
neutral, he hoped to energize those in the military, in the
press, in the business world, and elsewhere who argued in
favor of Sweden following a course similar to Norway's and
Denmark's. There was nothing to lose in following such a
strategy, since the likelihood of Sweden orienting itself toward the East was so small that it hardly had to be taken
into account.[74]

There was general sympathy in Washington for Matthews' approach. On June 18 Hickerson told Lovett that "I
am in full accord with the work which Ambassador
Matthews has been doing to cause the Swedes to change
their neutrality policy."[75] He was not the only one. In early
September the National Security Council concluded that

> The United States should endeavor by all appropriate mea-
> sures:
>   a. To strengthen the present tendency of Norway and Den-
>   mark to align themselves with the Western Powers.
>   b. To make perfectly clear to Sweden our dissatisfaction
>   with the apparent failure to discriminate in its own mind

and in its future planning between the West and the Soviet Union.

The National Security Council also discussed how Norway and Denmark were to be strengthened and American dissatisfaction made evident to Sweden. The agreed recommendation was that

The United States should *continue* [my emphasis] to support Norway and Denmark by measures such as the following:
a. Extension of economic aid by means of favorable U.S. foreign trade policies.
b. Providing equipment first to strengthen Norway and Denmark's military posture as a deterrent to Soviet armed aggression, and second to enable the Norwegian and Danish forces to resist actively an actual attack.[76]

The National Security Council can be said to have given its general approval to the strategy Matthews had been advocating for the last half-year. Not only that, but the NSC did not see this as a new policy, but as a continuation of existing ones. Military assistance was to be used to induce Norway and Denmark to associate themselves with the West. Economic instruments in the form of American trade policies were to be exploited for the same purpose.

At this stage I will look into the extent to which such policies were in fact pursued in the period leading up to the NSC meeting and shortly afterwards. What special favors did Norway and Denmark receive from the United States? Was Sweden actually punished for its policies?

Matthews and the State Department tried to influence the Swedes to break with neutrality in many different ways. Special attention was paid to deliveries of military equipment and other forms of military contact. The Swedes should not be encouraged to believe that their neutrality would still allow them to receive military assistance from the United States. On April 8 Matthews, both in a private cable to Hickerson and in a more official one to the Department, intervened strongly against a planned naval visit to Sweden. He argued that "The fact that our naval vessels visit Norwegian and Danish ports and omit Swedish ports will not be lost on the Swedes." Hickerson agreed with the ambassador and was able to make the Navy cancel that part of the trip which included Swedish harbors.[77]

The next step in the process of discrimination among the three Scandinavian countries was Matthews' intervention against the delivery of American radar ground warning equipment to Sweden. The ambassador wanted it made clear to the Swedish government that the reason for withholding the equipment was quite simply that the United States disliked its neutrality policies. He was to repeat his advice as long as the case was under consideration.[78]

Again the department supported the ambassador. The American attitude made the Swedes refrain from presenting an official request, but it seems they were able to obtain some similar equipment from Britain. Washington had no objections to selling commercial-type radars to Sweden even though these were used for military purposes. The argument was that they were surplus, obsolete, and available on equal terms to all bidders.[79]

The most important military transaction between a Western country and Sweden in 1948 concerned the delivery of up to 210 Vampire planes from Britain to Sweden. Matthews objected strongly to the proposed sale and asked the department to take the matter up with the British. Again Hickerson supported the ambassador and even asked Lovett, "Why the hell should we spend money to rearm the Brussels Pact countries when they are selling jets to neutrals?"[80]

The State Department did present an aide-mémoire to the British along the lines proposed by Hickerson. In rather blunt language the department made it clear that London's recent sale of fifty Spitfire planes to Sweden had been bad enough. An even larger order for jet planes would have to "be reviewed in light of the military requirements of the Brussels Pact signatories." The background for this not so implied threat was the department's fear that American attempts to modify Swedish policies would be nullified by the British sales. If the "endeavor to influence Sweden toward eventual alignment with other Western Powers in such a form as may be found collectively acceptable" were to succeed, then Washington and London would have to coordinate their policies.[81]

The State Department persuaded the Joint Chiefs to take the Vampire sales up with their British counterparts. The JCS agreed with the department's objections to the sales, but saw little purpose in protesting since it was known that the Royal Air Force had already dissented.

On the British side, the military had been overruled by the Ministry of Supply. London had considerable economic interest in such a large deal, and since the delivery to Sweden did not interfere with the military procurement of the Western Allies, London saw no need to cancel sales which had already been fulfilled in part.[82]

In August the Swedish Air Force showed interest in having secret military talks with its American counterpart. On the advice of the State Department this was rejected by the U.S. Air Force in view of the policies of the Swedish government. To such lengths did Matthews carry his campaign that he even intervened against a proposed "hunting trip" by Air Force General LeMay in September. The continuation of routine intelligence talks was acceptable, but not the establishment of new contacts with the Swedish military. The ambassador thought continued pressure would in the end lead the military to urge changes in the Swedish attitude.[83]

Circles in the Northern European Division argued differently. Thus, Charles Rogers of NOE felt that the Swedish military were already accomplishing slight modifications in Sweden's policies and that their feelers for increased contact with the United States should not be rebuffed.[84] Such advice carried little weight in view of the attitudes of Hickerson and Matthews.

Denial of favors to Sweden was one side of the coin. The other was a forthcoming attitude toward Norway and Denmark. On April 16 the Norwegian embassy in Washington formally presented an aide-mémoire to the State Department listing Norway's desires for military equipment from the U.S. Ambassador Bay urged prompt and favorable action on the request. So did the Office of European Affairs under Hickerson. As a result, on April 26 Under Secretary Lovett told Secretary of Defense Forrestal that "the Department of State attaches great importance, from the political viewpoint, to the fulfillment of the Norwegian request to the greatest extent practicable."[85]

The Norwegian feelers from February on had prompted the American military to initiate an analysis of the strategic importance of Norway to the United States. Since this study had not been completed when Norwegian Under Secretary of Defense Dag Bryn arrived in Washington in late April, and since the United States was receiving demands for military assistance far in excess of what it could deliver, representatives of the Defense Department at first apparently adopted a rather lukewarm attitude in their conversations with Bryn. This was only in part changed as a result of the intervention of the State Department.[86]

On June 10 the Joint Chiefs of Staff concluded their analysis of the role of Norway, and Forrestal expressed his agreement with their analysis four days later.[87] The JCS concluded that they favored providing the Norwegians with military equipment, both to strengthen Norway's military posture as a deterrent to Soviet armed aggression, and to enable the Norwegians to resist actively an actual attack. A small amount of equipment should be furnished "promptly" from U.S. surplus property "as an immediate measure of encouragement to the Norwegian Government." The JCS emphasized that further provision of military assistance should be dependent upon the attitude of Congress, the availability of equipment, the world-wide priorities of the United States, and "Norwegian participation in the Western Union or some similar collective defense arrangement."[88]

Thus, the military signaled that association with the West would be of importance in deciding on large-scale requests. As for the matériel requested in April, it appears that it was primarily the supply situation and legal obstacles that prevented the United States from delivering what Norway desired. The legal obstacles did not relate to the Vandenberg Resolution, but to requirements both about the proceeds of surplus sales and about the demilitarization of surplus equipment. As to supply, the United States was not able to furnish the type of tanks wanted by the Norwegians. Instead the Americans were willing to sell another light tank type. Of the 750 bazookas the Norwegians had asked for, the United States could only deliver 350. A conclusion that Norway's nonmembership in the Western Union counted little for Washington's difficulties in supplying the desired equipment at this time is supported by the fact that the needs so far indicated by the Norwegians were smaller than those of most other nations. Yet, with considerable exaggeration the military argued that delivery of the matériel would be "a small price for Norway's firm allegiance to the Western Powers." By granting as much as possible of the Norwegian request, the United States could further Norway's Western orientation.[89]

The State Department felt that the limited quantities the United States could deliver might easily discourage the Norwegians. Therefore, the department contacted the British to see if they might be able to furnish some of the equipment asked for. The British, however, could do little, since Oslo's request in many ways competed with Britain's own defense needs.[90] An embarrassing situation had arisen for the two governments. They undoubtedly wanted to encourage the Norwegians in their present orientation. This could be done by delivering military equipment, but the fact remained that it was only possible to meet the Norwegian request to a very limited extent.

Ambassador Bay, supported by Matthews, reacted strongly. With the Swedes obtaining a large number of Vampires from Britain and the Norwegians getting little of what they wanted, Bay told the State Department that "I fail to comprehend how we can expect them [the Norwegians] to hold out against Swedish exhortations to eschew foreign commitments and adhere to a Scandinavian mutual defense pact on Swedish terms. This is time if ever there was one to give Norwegians a shot in the arm."[91]

The State Department could only reply on August 27 that "We have tried hard to meet request more fully but regret we simply do not have supplies to make possible a

more favorable reply now." Marshall did advise Bay, however, that the department was certainly aware of the considerations he had advanced. It hoped to meet further Norwegian requests either from commercial sources or, more
likely, through Congressional consent to reactivate American military production. The Norwegians were also to be told
that the State Department highly appreciated the stand they
had taken with respect to self-defense, and their refusal to
compromise with neutrality proposals.[92]

In the end the Gerhardsen government informed the
State Department that the light tanks offered by the United
States were not of a suitable type. As to the bazookas, the
Norwegians stated that while interested, they now preferred
to await America's reconsideration of the whole question of
military supplies to Norway as well as to the other Scandinavian countries. Oslo evidently received only twenty sets
of radar from the United States at this time.[93]

The Danes met with the same difficulties as had the
Norwegians. On the one hand, the State Department wanted
to show a forthcoming attitude to encourage the Danes in
their westward orientation, even if Denmark did not take
quite as clear a stand in this respect as Norway. On the
other, problems existed in providing the equipment in question. The rifles in which Denmark was particularly interested were not surplus, but reserve in the United States,
which meant that they would have to be taken out of stock,
later to be replaced. This the American military were not
willing to do. Some machine guns, which the United States
offered to sell instead, were rejected since they would only
add to the existing undesirable variety of weapons in the
Danish Army.[94]

The military's analysis of Denmark's role differed from
their appraisals of Norway in two important respects. One
was the ever-present connection between Denmark and
Greenland. Delivery of arms to Denmark might hasten the
conclusion of a satisfactory new agreement on bases on
Greenland.[95] This factor would indicate that the military
were more favorable to the Danish as compared to the Norwegian requests. This was not the case, however. In fact,

the military stated, with reference to some substitute rifles for the Garands that had been requested, that they were opposed to making these rifles available. Only overriding political considerations would make them change their mind.

The other difference between the military's appraisal of Norway and Denmark lay in their feeling that it would make little strategic sense to supply the Danes. The machine guns were to be delivered only because of the Greenland connection. As to the rifles, in the words of General Wedemeyer, Director of the Plans and Operations Division within the Department of the Army, "A strategic analysis would indicate that Denmark might be overrun very quickly should the Juggernaut to the East decide to move Westward. Any equipment that we make available to Denmark might then become the property of said potential enemy and might be used against our own forces. If the Juggernaut does not roll, the equipment would not be required in Denmark." [96]

So despite the Greenland argument, the military were against the delivery of most equipment to Denmark. The State Department only in part invoked the overriding political considerations referred to. Unlike the case of Norway, the attitude of the military has to be counted among the main reasons, such as supply shortages and legal difficulties, for the refusal of the United States to supply large quantities of assistance. [97] Again, the State Department contacted the British to make them satisfy the Danes at least in part, but no deal was made. In the end Denmark bought rifles from Sweden. [98]

NSC 28/1, which was approved by the President on September 4, recommended that action on the delivery of arms to Norway and Denmark be delayed pending base negotiations with respect to Greenland and Spitsbergen. This provision was revoked on December 3. It is unlikely that the provision had much effect even in the period from September 4 to December 3. The American attitude had been clarified and communicated to the Norwegians and in part to the Danes before September 4. The planned sale of radar to Norway was not held up in the September-December period. [99]

The indication that the United States might now desire

bases on Spitsbergen illustrated that the situation had changed as compared to 1945 and even early 1947. Apparently Secretary of the Air Force Symington had suggested that the Air Force might be interested in such bases. After further study the National Security Council, in line with earlier analyses, concluded that the United States did not at present require any base rights on Spitsbergen.[100]

The State Department wanted to encourage the Norwegians and the Danes in their westward orientation through the supply of military equipment, but was only able to do this to a very limited extent. Yet, other ways existed in which Washington could encourage friends and punish the Swedes.

One example can be found in the American attitude to the question of representation on the UN Security Council in 1949–50. The problem was which one of the Western European countries was to be represented. Washington felt that the Netherlands would be the best choice. This was ruled out, however, due to opposition from other states. One of the Scandinavian countries was then the most likely candidate. In August Lovett told the complaining Dutch that the United States would support the Norwegians. The Under Secretary argued that "since April Norway has followed a commendable strong line."[101] A couple of weeks later Marshall cabled the embassy in Oslo that "among the Scandinavian countries Iceland too small, Sweden in Dept's opinion too disinclined to take stand on issues, Denmark was considered but Norway on balance considered better." The Secretary of State even emphasized that should the Norwegians indicate any reluctance to having a seat on the Security Council, the embassy should stress the duty of states such as Norway to undertake UN obligations even though onerous.[102] All this showed that although Washington promoted Norway's candidacy in part to encourage the Norwegians, the American attitude was even more the result of a desire to have the country most friendly to the United States represented on the Security Council. In the end Norway was elected.

As we have seen, the positions taken in the UN by the

Norwegian and Swedish governments in the fall of 1947 had led to sharp expressions of indignation on the part of several important policy makers in the State Department. This had changed in at least two ways by the fall of 1948. First, in 1947 the voting behavior of these governments had been studied with some urgency. One year later the UN constituted only a small part of a large picture. Now there were so many other ways in which the attitude of the Scandinavian countries could be registered.

Second, the Scandinavians had modified their positions somewhat. The resolutions voted upon in 1948 were not identical to those of the previous year. Nonetheless, while they had abstained in 1947 on the American-supported resolutions in the Greek and Korean questions, Norway and Denmark now backed the United States on both issues. Sweden followed the United States in the Greek matter, but still abstained with regard to Korea. As to the interim committee of the General Assembly, the three Scandinavian countries all voted with the Americans, as they had done in part even in 1947.[103]

A Partial Conclusion: Pressure Within Limits

The embassies in Oslo and Stockholm, as well as leading circles in Washington, wanted to pursue policies which clearly discriminated between Norway and Denmark on the one hand and Sweden on the other. Military and economic favors were to be granted to Western-oriented Norway and Denmark and withheld from neutral Sweden.

Nevertheless, definite limits existed on the extent to which the United States was willing and able to use its aid policies to reward friends and punish enemies. On the military side the United States was simply unable to furnish most of the equipment desired by Norway. The positive attitude of the State Department toward Denmark was modified by the reluctance of the military to extend assistance to a country which was seen as almost impossible to defend.

With regard to Sweden, the military did not really have

any strong influence on policies until the NSC took all of Scandinavia under consideration in late August. Then, if anything, they wanted to pursue an even more hostile course than did the diplomats. While the State Department generally favored holding the option open of considering Sweden's military needs after those of the countries cooperating with the United States had been taken care of, the JCS argued that even if there should be anything left, the Swedes should not receive any assistance.[104]

But even in the Swedish case, American pressure did not amount to much. Sweden asked for little from the United States. Commercially available equipment which was in surplus, like some types of radar, was not withheld. The basic reason, however, for the failure of American pressure was the lack of coordination with the British. Since London was able to grant Sweden much more assistance than the United States gave Norway and Denmark combined, there could be little effect in Washington's policy of rewarding friends and punishing enemies.

Even stronger limits existed on the extent to which the United States used its economic leverage to reward Norway and Denmark and punish Sweden. Washington made no serious attempt to interfere with normal trade with Sweden. With a possible exception for the amounts extended in the second quarter of 1948, the European Recovery Program was generally administered on the basis of economic criteria. The ERP could only to a very small degree be integrated with overall foreign policy goals toward Scandinavia.

The United States had, as Edmund A. Gullion, Special Assistant to Robert Lovett, told Marshall in March 1948, "at all times a powerful lever on them through our ability to cut off aid under the Act." This was stated with relevance to ERP assistance to Western Europe in general. But this lever could only be applied in extreme situations. The Americans never actually threatened the Swedes with stopping Marshall Plan assistance. Neither was this even recommended by Ambassador Matthews. The only time this possibility was discussed at all was in January 1949 in connection with Washington's efforts to limit exports of strategic importance from the ERP countries to the Soviet Union and to Eastern Europe. Then Matthews in fact warned the department against presenting such a threat. The State Department in turn made it clear on January 14, 1949, that "We do not consider advisable at present withholding ECA assistance as weapon of bargaining or retaliation in connection East-West Trade Negot[iation]s."[105]

There were many reasons why the United States held back from fully exploiting what leverage it had in attempting to move the Swedish government away from neutrality. On the military side the United States simply possessed little leverage. On the economic side no strong sentiments could be found in favor of anything resembling economic warfare against a country which, although neutral, could not be described as a threat to the United States. In addition, the risk always existed that overt pressure might prove counterproductive to American objectives not only in Sweden itself, but also in other parts of Western Europe.

One rather interesting, although temporary, reason existed for the American reticence. This had to do with the "uranium problem." As Hickerson told Lovett on June 18, 1948, he agreed with what Matthews had done to make the Swedish government abandon its attitude of neutrality. "He [Matthews] has not, however, taken into account this uranium problem and the time has come when we must fit this into the general picture."[106]

The uranium problem was really two problems in one. First, Washington wanted the Swedes to refrain from selling atomic energy equipment to the Soviet Union or to countries dominated by it. Second, the United States itself might want to purchase significant quantities of uranium from Sweden. The Swedes had been experimenting with the extraction of uranium from oil shale and were at this time apparently seen as potentially the second largest producer of uranium in the world.[107]

If the United States would want both to purchase uranium from Sweden and dissuade the Swedes from exporting equipment to the Soviet Union, these objectives might easily conflict with a strong campaign against Sweden's foreign policy. On July 2 Lovett told Matthews that "In considering our policies toward Sweden, we must at all times recall that it is, both relatively and absolutely, an important source of uranium." The Under Secretary argued that "if we are to make a request for uranium it would be unfortunate, if the Swedes had been forced into a reaffirmation of their neutrality position so categoric as to preclude their making it available to us."

On the other hand, Lovett did point out that the department had not quite figured out how the uranium problem could be fitted into the overall relationship with Sweden. He even concluded that he did not believe that relaxation of U.S. pressure was desirable or that it would advance chances of getting uranium.[108]

Despite Lovett's conclusion, to Matthews in Stockholm this was news of a most discomfiting kind. He had received the impression, in briefings before he left Washington in October 1947, that Sweden was not a very likely source of uranium. He now felt that the uranium question could upset his entire strategy of isolating Sweden. Therefore, he wrote back to Lovett on July 15, "if our need for uranium is so urgent, we must be prepared to take very drastic action to modify Swedish policy."[109] His argument was that if the United States really needed Swedish uranium so badly, then it would only be possible to obtain it if the Swedes abandoned neutrality and associated themselves with the West.

The ambassador also reacted strongly against a paragraph in Lovett's letter which, quite unexpectedly, raised the question of whether the United States was best served by Sweden following a policy of association with the West or one of neutrality. Matthews told the Under Secretary that if he saw any validity in the argument that it was best for the West to have Sweden sitting on the East-West fence, then "I think I have been wasting my time in trying so persistently to point out the fallacies of Swedish neutrality."[110]

In late August-early September the uranium issue was finally clarified. The Americans concluded that there was little risk of Sweden exporting any atomic energy equipment to the Soviet Union. On two occasions the Swedish government had on Washington's suggestion stopped orders to the Soviet Union. The question of securing uranium for the U.S. was determined to be of little immediate importance, since it would still take considerable time before Sweden could export any. Thus, the issue could be handled within the limits of the existing policy toward Sweden. No revision was needed.[111]

Even after the decision had been made that the uranium question could be fitted into the existing overall policy, Washington still felt that it might become necessary some time in the future to ask Sweden for uranium. In a National Security Council report of March 1949, the American sources of supply were listed as Belgium—the Congo—and in the future South Africa and "eventually Sweden."[112]

The uranium issue did not stop the United States from putting pressure on the Swedes to break with neutrality. This policy had been initiated before June, when the uranium was really brought to the attention of the leadership in the State Department. It is likely, however, that the question may at least have helped to prevent a further stepping up of American pressure. This was most noticeable in the summer of 1948, a period of great importance in American-Scandinavian relations.

8

Scandinavia and a Western Military Arrangement in 1948

GRADUALLY THE UNITED STATES became the predominant Great Power in matters relating to the Scandinavian countries. In the economic field the United States had been a main source of financial assistance from the very end of the war, although its role was considerably modified because of Sweden's large-scale aid to both Norway and Denmark. With the introduction of the Marshall Plan, Washington's position was strengthened. Scandinavia's share of U.S. assistance to Western Europe increased and an institutional setup was worked out which gave the United States much greater influence than before on the economic policies of the region.

Along with the strengthening of the American role in Scandinavia and in Western Europe as a whole went a relative decline in Britain's influence. It was becoming more and more evident that Britain would have to rely upon the United States not only in the economic field, but also in the military. In March 1948 the Americans finally agreed to talks with the British and the Canadians for the purpose of establishing a North Atlantic security system. This meant that the leadership even in military matters was definitely being transferred to the other side of the Atlantic. In talks with Foreign Minister Lange in mid-March, Bevin pointed out that the Scandinavian countries ought to adapt themselves to this fact.[1]

In the first years after the war the defense planning of Norway and Denmark had been based on the support of Britain.[2] In 1948 this was beginning to change. The British could no longer satisfy Norwegian and Danish requests for military equipment. It was becoming obvious that in the future the Scandinavians would have to obtain most of their defense matériel from the United States. As the Norwegians and the Danes began to press for such assistance, the United States took on a new importance in the defense planning of the two countries.

The United States was also to a very large extent deciding the contents of the defense arrangement to be set up in the North Atlantic region. In this chapter I will examine the conceptions held by prominent American policy makers as to the role of Scandinavia in this arrangement. How closely did Washington want Scandinavia integrated in the security system which could be foreseen? What alternatives existed and what support did the various alternatives have?

A Brief Historiographic Sketch

Little interest has been shown by American historians in the question of Scandinavia's position within the North Atlantic security system. Herbert Feis mentions in passing that Norway and Denmark were two of several countries which the United States, Canada, and the Western Union members wanted to include in the planned Atlantic scheme. Then, in February 1949, when faced with Soviet pressure not to join the pact, Foreign Minister Lange hurried to Washington. "There Acheson told him that unless Norway joined, the Americans could not promise military equipment. Thus, bluntly faced with a choice, the Norwegian Parliament had authorized Norwegian participation. Denmark, rather than be alone, followed, as had Iceland."[3]

In Feis's short and somewhat misleading account, two elements stand out—the Soviet threat and the crucial role of the United States. As could be expected, the Kolkos are most concerned with the latter, although they too pay very little attention to the position of Scandinavia within the Atlantic arrangement. Their perspective is clear, however: the United States wished NATO to emerge, and did this "even to the extent of threatening to cut off arms sales to the reluctant Danes and Norwegians should they not join."[4] Thus, Washington at least in part forced the two countries into NATO.

While American historians have shown little interest in this, the role of Scandinavia has received more attention within the region itself. The leading studies have been written by Norwegian historians Magne Skodvin and Knut Einar Eriksen, and by Swedish political scientist Krister Wahlbäck.

In his analysis of the American attitude, Skodvin focuses almost exclusively on the question of membership in NATO versus a neutral Scandinavian defense arrangement. There is no discussion in his book *Norden eller NATO?* of the extent to which other alternatives existed on the American side. In this respect Eriksen's perspective is very similar to Skodvin's. He too sees the attitude of the United States as clear-cut. Washington strongly favored the membership of Norway and Denmark in NATO and worked against a Scandinavian neutrality pact. As to the many strategic reasons for this, they both emphasize the interest of the U.S. military in the Arctic regions.[5]

Even Krister Wahlbäck analyzes the American attitude rather exclusively in terms of NATO membership versus neutrality. In his account, significant military reasons explain why Washington wanted Scandinavia, and Norway and Denmark in particular, to adhere to the North Atlantic arrangement. In time of war bases in Norway and on Greenland would be of great importance. And if the Scandinavian countries were to receive assistance from the United States in case of war, this had to be prepared for before hostilities broke out.[6]

Wahlbäck pays only slightly more attention than Skodvin and Eriksen to discussions within the State Department and other circles in Washington about the role of Scandinavia. Little more is stated than that Kennan was more favorable to Scandinavian cooperation than was the rest of the State Department leadership.[7] In later writings both Wahlbäck and Eriksen have somewhat strengthened their analyses of the situation within the State Department.[8] But on the whole, the internal American debate is of little interest to the three Scandinavians. They have all dealt primarily with the Scandinavian side, not with the American attitude.

I will attempt to show that there was considerable American discussion about the relationship of the Scandinavian countries to a North Atlantic security arrangement. In 1948 and early 1949 Scandinavia was of greater interest to U.S. policy makers than has been indicated by American or Scandinavian writers. The discussion in Washington did not focus only upon full membership in NATO and neutrality. Various forms of attachment to the West were discussed, and several of them were acceptable to most policy makers. While there was general agreement that neutrality ought to be opposed, considerable differences existed as to how much neutralists had to modify their policies before harmony could be reestablished.

The Majority Position: Full Participation

John Hickerson was undoubtedly the best example of a prominent policy maker who pressed for the inclusion of the Scandinavian countries in a Western military arrangement on a comprehensive basis. The Director of the Office of European Affairs played an important part in all discussions about the nature of such an arrangement and the role Scandinavia was to have within it. His overall concept—that of an Atlantic system with as many Western European countries as possible involved—appears to have remained the same throughout 1948 and 1949.

In the preparations for the Washington Security Conversations in March, Hickerson participated in the discussions of the Policy Planning Staff on the American position. Although it is difficult to specify his views in these discussions, it is obvious that he agreed with the general recommendations which resulted from them. The first draft of these recommendations argued that the defense against the Soviet Union should include every possible independent European nation. "Special effort should, therefore, be made to break down the neutrality attitude of both Sweden and Switzerland."[9]

After a few meetings the group was able to present its report to the Secretary of State. This report contained important nuances compared to the first draft, but the basic objective remained the same: a very inclusive membership on the European side. The Policy Planning Staff paper (which should not really be seen as a PPS document since Kennan had not participated in the discussions while many officials outside the Staff had), stressed that the United States should press for the "immediate inclusion" in the Western Union of Norway, Sweden, Denmark, and Iceland, with Portugal to follow speedily thereafter. Italy should be invited to participate as well and "eventually" the Union should also include Eire, Switzerland, Germany, Spain, and Austria.[10]

In the March talks, as the emphasis shifted from the Western Union to an Atlantic system, the three Scandinavian countries were still seen as desirable participants. Norway, Sweden, and Denmark were included on all the various lists of countries to be invited to participate in the planned Atlantic arrangement. The final draft from the American-British-Canadian conversations recommended that the President announce that invitations were to be issued to "the United Kingdom, France, Canada, Norway, Sweden, Denmark, Iceland, The Netherlands, Belgium, Luxembourg, Eire, Italy, and Portugal (provided that secret inquiries had established the fact that these countries would be prepared to accept the invitations) to take part in a conference with a view to the conclusion of a collective Defense Agreement for the North Atlantic Area."[11]

From his contacts with Ambassador Matthews, Hickerson was well aware of the difficulties in trying to bring about a change in Swedish policies. Although it might prove difficult to bring Sweden into an Atlantic arrangement, Matthews and Hickerson saw this as their goal. They also agreed that the key to any change in Sweden's attitude was to be found in Norway's and Denmark's participation.

In the rounds of talks between the representatives of the United States, Canada, and the Western Union countries which began in Washington in July, Hickerson again argued in favor of a most comprehensive European membership. On July 28 he suggested "Iceland, Ireland, Sweden, Norway, Denmark (including Greenland) as possible candidates in the near future, with Italy perhaps also a candidate but in a somewhat different category, at least insofar as time of entry is concerned." The Director of the Office of European Affairs even indicated that he thought Austria, after the conclusion of a peace treaty, and possibly Switzerland ought to be considered for inclusion.[12]

In late August his disagreements with Kennan forced Hickerson to state in some detail his position on the role of the Scandinavian as well as the other countries considered for membership. Hickerson favored the double membership concept. He wanted as many as possible of the European countries to take part in the Western Union by acceding to the Brussels treaty. The Western Union states would then participate in the North Atlantic system together with the United States and Canada.

However, the possibility could well arise of some European countries being primarily interested in the Atlantic system and not so much in the Western Union. Indications existed that this was the attitude of Norway and Denmark. In response to such an eventuality, Hickerson agreed that a special arrangement could be made for "Portugal, Iceland, Denmark, Norway and possibly Ireland (unless and until they were prepared to become full members of the Brussels Treaty)."

This special arrangement would not be as comprehensive as full membership in the Brussels treaty/Atlantic alliance. The members of the North Atlantic group would agree to collectively regard an armed attack on any of these countries as an attack against themselves. In return the countries in question would make facilities on their territory available to the Atlantic group in order that its members might effectively protect and defend them.[13]

Sweden was not among the states explicitly mentioned by Hickerson. This did not mean that it had been forgotten. He made it clear that any country willing to accept the obligations referred to above could enter into such association with the North Atlantic group—this included Sweden. The Director of the Office of European Affairs obviously thought chances greater of the Swedes agreeing to join if this could be done on the basis of limited commitments instead of through full membership in the Brussels treaty. He was ready to grant Sweden this form of association, although he preferred that it entered on the basis of full membership.

In fact, Hickerson even employed a third category in his August proposal. With reference to the members of the OEEC which did not join the North Atlantic alliance either through full membership or through the special arrangement mentioned, he argued that "The members of the North Atlantic Security group would issue a joint statement at the time of the conclusion of the Pact, to the effect that any threat of aggression, direct or indirect, against any of the OEEC countries would be regarded by all members of the group as a development calling for the consultation envisaged in the Pact."

This meant that those OEEC members which did not join the Atlantic pact in any of the two forms mentioned, were to be covered by an advance statement promising consultations within the alliance in case of aggression against them. The outcome of such consultations might possibly be that armed assistance would be extended, although no obligation existed to take such action.

This third category of association was meant to apply primarily to Greece and Turkey, which would not be admitted in the form of full membership or through a special arrangement even if they wanted to do so. Presumably, this category would apply also to Sweden if no other arrangement already existed for that country. No reservation was made on this point when Hickerson stated that all members of the OEEC not otherwise mentioned would be covered by such a statement. Thus, if Sweden could not be induced to become either a full member or a member with limited commitments, a third category of association was accepted even by Hickerson. For that matter, under such circumstances this category would probably apply to Denmark and Norway as well. However, it should be emphasized again that he preferred full membership in the Atlantic alliance for all the Scandinavian countries, including Sweden.[14]

The fact that Hickerson considered Sweden a desirable member of the Atlantic group was explicitly brought forth in a memorandum he sent to Kennan on November 26. At this time the dispute between the two primarily concerned the position of Italy. Kennan was of the opinion that any country "unwashed by Atlantic waters" should not be eligible for membership. Hickerson, on the other hand, argued that Italy ought to be included. He asked Kennan not to "forget Columbus and millions of his descendants in this country." Most important in this context, he also pointed out that "Sweden and Germany were natural members of the Atlantic community."[15]

Who, among the policy makers in the State Department and elsewhere, supported Hickerson's position that the Scandinavian countries, in particular Norway and Denmark, ought to enter the Atlantic alliance on the basis of full membership? Hickerson had the strong support of the Chief of the Division of Western European Affairs, Theodore Achilles. Achilles worked closely with Hickerson and the two held quite similar opinions both on the need for the United States to become intimately involved with the Western Europeans in a common defense effort, and on the desirability of having an inclusive alliance. True, even they did not show any particular interest in bringing in Greece, Turkey, Northern Africa and other areas outside Europe, but with regard to Italy and the Scandinavian countries they argued strongly in favor of their full membership. In later years Achilles was full of admiration for the work accomplished by Hickerson. He even called the North Atlantic treaty a "one-man Hickerson treaty." [16]

Another supporter of Hickerson was the Chief of the Division of Northern European Affairs, Benjamin Hulley. Since his Division was in charge of Scandinavia, he had considerable contact with the embassies of the Scandinavian countries. His influence in the decision-making process, however, was smaller, and he did not enjoy as close a relationship with Hickerson as did Achilles. [17]

Although in favor of the Scandinavian states becoming full members of the North Atlantic system, Hulley was not so emphatic on this point as were Hickerson and Achilles. This was particularly the case with his early analyses of Sweden's position. Thus, on June 10 he sent Hickerson a memorandum which must have disturbed the Director of the Office of European Affairs. In the memorandum Hulley denounced Sweden's neutrality and its attempts to persuade the Norwegians and the Danes to align themselves with Sweden. Yet, at the same time he argued that "the Swedish proposal of a Scandinavian defense bloc offers several possibilities which should be explored." Hulley reconciled this with his denunciation of Swedish neutrality by pointing out that the offer of a defense pact, even though based on neutrality, appeared to be a long step away from past Swedish policies. He reasoned that in a future war the Soviet Union would probably attempt to secure control over at least Norway and Denmark. In that case Sweden would also be involved if a Scandinavian pact was concluded. [18] No indications exist that Hulley presented such views after June 1948.

A crucial person within the State Department in most of the North Atlantic discussions was Under Secretary Robert Lovett. Lovett should be included among the "hardliners" in this question. At the same time, even he occasionally presented views which showed that his convictions were not so single-minded as those of Hickerson and Achilles. We have already noted that Lovett shocked Matthews with his statement in early July that it was a matter of opinion whether the interests of the United States were best served with Sweden staying on the fence or being firmly aligned with the West.

Achilles has asserted that Lovett was instrumental in implementing Hickerson's recommendation that Counselor Charles Bohlen be transferred out of Washington in late 1948, thereby reducing the influence of those opposed to an Atlantic treaty and the idea of a very inclusive membership.[19] With Marshall away for several extended periods, it is most likely that the Director of the Office of European Affairs had to enjoy the support of at least Lovett to present the views he did to the representatives of the Western European, including the Scandinavian, governments.

Lovett was the ranking American in the conversations with Canada and the Western Union countries from July onward. To the extent that personal nuances can be found in the comments made by members of the American delegation, it appears that Lovett concentrated on having Norway and Denmark as effective participants in the Atlantic alliance. Apparently he took little interest in Sweden. However, since he stressed the importance of including Norway and Denmark, it would follow that he must have been opposed to Swedish attempts to bring about a form of Scandinavian military cooperation largely independent of the West.

On August 20 Lovett was asked by the representatives of Belgium and the Netherlands what constituted the U.S. minimum of member countries in a North Atlantic scheme. In addition to the Western Union members, the Under Secretary answered that he would "guess" that "Greenland, Iceland, the Azores and Norway would be the minimum, ideally and perhaps practically also."[20] The bases on Greenland, Iceland, and the Azores were considered the most essential of all bases outside the United States itself. For Lovett to mention Norway in this context was a sign of great importance being attached to its participation.

The fact that this was not a casual remark by the Under Secretary was underlined in the joint memorandum of September 9 which summed up the Washington talks. The paper noted that the American representatives had emphasized that if an Atlantic system were to be effective, it had to include "the North Atlantic territories of Denmark (Greenland), Iceland, Ireland, Norway and Portugal (the Azores)."[21]

From the importance attached to Norway and Denmark, it was obvious that the Under Secretary preferred that they become full members of the Atlantic alliance. Yet, Lovett was apparently more interested than Hickerson in the question of gradated membership. In the discussion on July 9 he pointed out that there were all sorts of gradations of interests among the various possible adherents. The solution to this varying interest "might lie in different degrees of membership." On August 20 Lovett reminded the Washington group that he had argued in favor of gradated membership. He seems to have had three primary categories in mind, called "resident members, non-resident members, and summer privileges." These were not further defined, but very likely corresponded to the categories adopted by the U.S.-Canadian-Western Union meeting on September 9. As such they will be dealt with later.[22]

While the Under Secretary seemed more open than Hickerson to the possibility of less comprehensive forms of membership, it should not be forgotten that the latter too agreed to the limited commitments concept if the countries concerned did not accept his first choice, full membership in the Atlantic system through participation in the Western Union. It was all a matter of emphasis—Hickerson saw the limited forms as even more of a fallback position than did his superior.

Important persons in Congress also wanted Scandinavia to become associated with the West on a close basis. Most noteworthy in this respect was Senator Arthur Vandenberg, the influential chairman of the Senate Foreign Relations Committee. In his talk with Marshall and Lovett on April 27, Vandenberg stressed the importance of having Scandinavia associated with the Atlantic arrangement. The reason he gave was that this would have great appeal in the Senate because of the high proportions of Scandinavian voters in some districts.[23] For Vandenberg it must have been significant that much of the opposition to America's close military involvement with Western Europe was expected to come from the Midwest. With Scandinavia included, he probably figured that opposition in this area would be reduced.

In the April 27 talk the senator did not specify in what form Scandinavia ought to be included. According to Lovett's memo of the conversation, he only stated that Scandinavia should be brought in "in some way."[24] Later Vandenberg came to stress the strategic importance of Norway and Denmark. He apparently argued that without Denmark (Greenland), Iceland, and Norway, the pact would not fulfill the requirements of the Vandenberg Resolution in the sense of contributing to U.S. security. Greenland and Iceland were of primary concern. He seems to have felt, however, that the inclusion of these areas depended on the stand taken by Norway and, of course, Denmark.[25]

This underlining of their strategic importance indicated that the senator wanted Norway and Denmark intimately involved in the Atlantic security system, and this was the way in which his comments were interpreted in the State Department. Nevertheless, Vandenberg's attitude was not seen as barring looser forms of association. As we shall see, the idea of gradated membership remained part of the American negotiating position throughout almost the whole of 1948, long after the Vandenberg Resolution had been passed.

During most of 1948 the military left the initiative to the State Department in formulating an American position on the role of Scandinavia in the Atlantic security system. In the March talks in Washington the military had played a marginal role. Only on June 10 did the Joint Chiefs of Staff have their answers ready to the questions put forth by Norwegian Defense Minister Hauge in mid-February. And not before late August, in connection with the deliberations in the National Security Council over NSC 28, did the JCS express any specific views concerning Denmark and Sweden.

In their June 10 memorandum to the Secretary of Defense, the JCS stressed that Norway was of considerable strategic importance to the United States and the Soviet Union alike. This indicated that the military wanted Norway to become closely associated with the West, a view which was further supported by their conclusion that provision of large-scale military assistance to Norway should be dependent upon "Norwegian participation in the Western Union or some similar collective defense arrangement."[26]

The JCS memorandum also dealt with another problem of great importance in American-Norwegian relations in 1948–49, the question of bases on Norwegian territory. In general the U.S. military wanted the Europeans to understand that an effective defense meant that the United States had to obtain base and transit rights. With regard to Norway, however, the JCS pointed out that "our strategic interests lie primarily in the denial of Norwegian bases to the Soviets, rather than utilization of such bases ourselves." Bases in Norway could too easily be knocked out from Soviet air fields in the Murmansk area or even in East Germany. The military also argued that "The development of allied bases in Norway prior to outbreak of war would tend to precipitate a Soviet armed invasion of Norway." This analysis only applied in time of peace and in the early stages of a war, because in later stages the JCS indicated that Norway would be quite useful as a base area for retaliatory strikes against the Soviet Union.[27] It was obvious that the need for bases in Norway was of a more limited nature than on Greenland and Iceland.

In the National Security Council discussions on The Position of the United States with Respect to Scandinavia, it was evident that the strategic role of Norway and Denmark, as appraised by the military, became an argument in favor of the close association of Scandinavia with the North Atlantic alliance. The conclusion of both NSC 28 and NSC 28/1 was that the United States should examine with the Western Union countries the problem of increasing the security of "Norway, Denmark, and if appropriate, Sweden, through their integration into or *association in some form* [italics mine] with the Brussels Treaty system or otherwise."[28]

Until September 1948 the concept of limited commitments was circulated largely within the State Department. Few Americans outside the department had any knowledge about the various categories. Yet, although the military did not express their opinions in terms of full membership versus limited commitments, the recommendation agreed to in NSC 28 really left most options open. It could not be said to preclude arrangements short of the full membership of the three countries in the Atlantic alliance or the Western Union. Most likely category two, that of a special arrangement, in Hickerson's memorandum of August 31 would be within the limits set in NSC 28 and 28/1. Quite possibly even category three, that of a still looser arrangement, would suffice as far as the Western orientation of at least Sweden went.

There could be little doubt what solution the JCS preferred. Their objectives might have been obtained under forms other than full membership, but that was not the point. To the military it was evident that this kind of association—full membership—would be the most effective way of securing their goals. Nevertheless, the principle of gradated membership would probably have been an acceptable fallback position for the military, as it was for other important policy makers in Washington. The basic point of the second category was that the countries involved would agree to defend their territories and make available to the full members of the North Atlantic group such facilities as were within their power.[29] This fitted in quite nicely with the military requirements with regard to Norway and Denmark proper. Sweden was not considered of great importance from a strategic point of view. Even looser arrangements might therefore be acceptable for that country.

The position of the United States was not only determined by domestic influences. The views presented by the other countries in the Washington talks also had to be taken into account. Britain and Canada both argued most strongly in favor of the close association of Scandinavia with the West. The two wanted to establish intimate cooperation between North America and Western Europe. In this context Norway and Denmark were of great importance. Again and again the representatives of Britain and Canada emphasized that Norway and Denmark were essential within an Atlantic system.[30] But this emphasis did not preclude even London and Ottawa from accepting the principle of gradated membership. In the September summing up of the conversations between the United States, Canada, and the Western Union members, all countries agreed to the relevance of this principle in relation to Norway and Denmark. A looser arrangement could be accepted for Sweden than for the other two.[31] Both the Canadians and the British preferred that the Norwegians and the Danes came in as full members. Yet, if they were not prepared to take on the obligations of this more comprehensive form of association, the possibility of limited commitments arose.

Why a Close Association?

Many different reasons were advanced by those in the United States who supported the close cooperation of Scandinavia with an Atlantic security system. Those of a military nature will be dealt with first.

The Scandinavian countries were of strategic value to Washington in several ways. Although the polar strategy was not yet of essential significance, it was certainly increasing in importance. The Arctic route represented the shortest distance between the central interiors of the United States and the Soviet Union. In addition, this approach would represent the greatest element of surprise in case of an attack. Greenland was essential in an Arctic scenario, but even Norway, particularly Spitsbergen, was of importance.

Despite its growing significance, in November the National Security Council concluded that at present the United States required no base rights from Norway on Spitsbergen, and no move was actually made to encourage the Norwegians to grant such bases. The recommendation that armed assistance be withheld from Norway pending base negotiations was withdrawn. The main American objective with regard to Spitsbergen was still to prevent Soviet bases or military installations on the island.[32]

But more important at this time than the polar strategy

was the fact that the Scandinavian countries were midway on the air route between London and Moscow. Not only that, but the shortest route between Moscow and Washington-New York also passed over the southern parts of Norway and Sweden. In the wording of the National Security Council in August-September 1948, Scandinavia "lies astride the great circle air route between North America and the strategic heart of Western Russia."[33]

The JCS maintained that a major strategic interest in Scandinavia was the denial to the Soviets of air and submarine bases in Denmark and Norway and their island possessions. This objective might have been obtained without the Scandinavians in the Atlantic alliance, since there was little doubt that even a neutral Scandinavia would defend itself in case of a Soviet attack. But the U.S. military feared that a neutral Scandinavian arrangement could be forced by the Soviet Union to grant concessions which would jeopardize Atlantic lines of communication as well as the security of the British Isles.[34]

As we have seen, the JCS did not take any interest in bases in Norway in time of peace and in the early stages of a war. Norway's insistence that it would be impossible for domestic reasons to grant bases to the United States or even to Britain therefore created no difficulties in Norwegian-American relations. Basically, the same analysis applied to Denmark.

What counted more than peacetime bases was, for instance, that an early warning of a Soviet attack on North America and Britain would be facilitated by the inclusion of Scandinavia. The Western Powers would also be denied the right to overfly their territory in a retaliatory strike against the Soviet Union if the Scandinavian countries were to remain neutral. The United States and the Western Allies should also have the opportunity to use Norwegian and Danish bases in time of war.[35] This point was brought up in the conversations Foreign Minister Lange had in Washington in February 1949. On that occasion, the State Department again stated that there was no question of bases in time of peace. It was underlined, however, that a distinction should be made between bases and "the implications of common defense arrangements with regard to coordinated disposition of facilities." The point seems to have been that if Norwegian territory was to be used in time of war, some preparations had to be made in time of peace to make such use effective. Among other things, important equipment had to be on the spot in advance.[36]

The long Norwegian coastline was another factor of great importance to the United States, Britain, and Canada when they pressed for Norwegian membership. Soviet control over Norway would give the Soviets easy access to the Atlantic and thereby represent a great threat to communications between North America and Western Europe. In the talks in Washington, Norway was often described along with Iceland, Portugal (the Azores), Denmark (Greenland), and Ireland as "stepping stone countries." They were stepping stones for communications between America and Europe and thus essential to an Atlantic arrangement.[37]

A neutral Scandinavia could not be expected to cooperate in time of war with the Western Powers to maintain control over the Atlantic. Great Britain in particular, but also the United States and Canada, paid special attention to the role of the southwestern part of Norway. From there the distance across the North Sea to Britain was short. The establishment of Soviet air or naval bases in that region would be most dangerous.[38]

While Norway—in part through its possession of Spitsbergen—controlled the exit from the Barents Sea, Denmark and Sweden controlled an even more important waterway, the exit from the Baltic. It would be easy for the Western Powers to close the Soviets off in the Baltic if Denmark or Sweden were members of an Atlantic alliance. If a neutral group did this, it would have to be seen as a hostile act by the Soviet Union.[39]

These were all significant strategic advantages in having the Scandinavian countries tied to the West. The most important of all, however, would be the status of Greenland. Greenland was absolutely essential for the defense of the United States and for communications across the Atlantic. Washington would never permit an arrangement which did not in effect give it military control over the island. In some form, and the Danes understood this, Denmark would have to grant the United States base rights on Greenland.[40]

Finally, the National Security Council noted in its reports on The Position of the United States with Respect to Scandinavia that both Norway and Sweden possessed an industrial potential of some importance. The NSC placed special emphasis on the extensive oil shale and kolm deposits in Sweden. These, as we have seen, were regarded as potential sources of uranium. And the Norwegian merchant marine was possibly even more important from an economic point of view than potential deposits of uranium in Sweden. This fleet had been a significant asset for the Allies during World War II. In the deliberations in 1948–49, it was once again recognized that it would be of great value in future conflicts. If Norway remained neutral, the Allies would not be able to use this fleet, one of the largest in the world.[41]

There were not only military and economic, but also foreign policy reasons for wanting the Scandinavians in an Atlantic alliance. It would be interpreted as a loss to the West if these states remained outside. Most policy makers in Washington were also of the strong opinion that zones of neutrality were zones of uncertainty. They would represent an invitation to the Soviet Union to try to strengthen its influence.

Chances of the Soviet Union risking a military confrontation with the West were generally regarded as small. What is of interest in this context, however, is that in Washington's analysis zones of neutrality might tempt Moscow into moves it probably would have refrained from had it known that a war could be the outcome. With Scandinavia clearly a part of the West, the Soviet Union would not take aggressive action. If Scandinavia remained outside a Western military arrangement, the response of the West would not be known in advance and the Soviets might be tempted to believe that the risks involved were small. Therefore, the Swedish argument that East-West relations were served by some countries standing in the middle was strongly rejected by most policy makers in Washington. The contrary was seen to be true.[42]

As we have seen, a general aversion to neutrality could be found in Washington. Neutrality was not only dangerous, it was also wrong. It was particularly wrong for a country which was really oriented toward the West. Sweden even relied on the West to come to its defense in case of an attack, but it did not want to bear the costs of defending Western democratic ideals. It was one thing to be more or less forced into neutrality, as the Finns were considered to be. It was something different to adopt such a policy quite voluntarily.[43]

Finally, the State Department was well aware of the fact that the foreign policy choices of the Scandinavian countries were closely tied together. Norway was seen as the key country, since it was the most Western-oriented of the three. If Norway could be brought into the Atlantic alliance, this would have important bearings on both Denmark and Iceland. Thus, in a report on the Washington talks dated January 13, 1949, it was affirmed that Norway would be interested in joining an Atlantic pact. If, on the other hand, ". . . Norway accedes to the Scandinavian alliance, Denmark will follow suit." The paper did not explicitly state that Denmark would join the West if Norway did, but such an outcome seemed likely. The report also concluded that Iceland in turn would probably follow the lead of Denmark with reference to the North Atlantic pact.[44]

Chances of Sweden joining were generally seen as small. The factor which might possibly bring it in would be its isolation from its Scandinavian neighbors. However, the January report noted that "Whether or not Sweden comes into the Pact is of relatively little importance."[45] Norway, Denmark, and Iceland were all of greater strategic importance than Sweden.

The Minority Position: Affiliation

Although even Hickerson agreed that the possibility of association through limited commitments ought to remain open for those countries which did not come in as full members, he and most other policy makers preferred that Norway and Denmark in particular joined as full members. Yet, some not only accepted the principle of gradated membership, but even preferred that Scandinavia became tied to the Atlantic system in such a less comprehensive way. The strongest and most prominent spokesman for this position was George F. Kennan, the Director of the Policy Planning Staff.

Kennan had been among those who early and strongly warned against the Soviet danger. Well before the war ended, he had on numerous occasions tried to correct what he saw as illusions about the possibility of cooperating with the Soviets. In Kennan's opinion, there was bound to be conflict between the Soviet Union and the United States. His Long Telegram of February 1946 was his most famous effort in the direction of educating the State Department. The telegram, in Kennan's own words, read "exactly like one of those primers put out by alarmed congressional committees or by the Daughters of the American Revolution, designed to arouse the citizenry to the dangers of the Communist conspiracy."[46]

In 1944–45 Kennan had been more critical of Soviet intentions than had most other policy makers. In 1946, the reception the Long Telegram met with was primarily due to its expressing what policy makers had already come to feel, but had not yet placed in such a comprehensive perspective as had Kennan.[47] In 1948 the State Department and military leaders were becoming even more pessimistic than Kennan about Soviet intentions.

In his attempt to arouse official opinion, many nuances had been lost, not only by his readers but also by Kennan himself. His early analyses did not really examine in what ways the Soviet Union represented a threat to the West. This was only done later. From 1948 onward, Kennan was to be more explicit than most others in emphasizing that the threat was not military, but primarily political and economic.

The differences between this and the predominant view in Washington should not be exaggerated. On the one hand, frequently even Kennan recognized that the Soviet danger was in part of a military nature. In March 1948 he was quite explicit on that point. On the other hand, most policy makers agreed that the danger of a Soviet attack on Western Europe was limited.[48]

Nevertheless, in the discussions about Atlantic security Kennan generally came to feel that the proposed solutions to the problems of Western Europe concentrated too much on the military side. If the East-West struggle was primarily political and economic, why then focus on military solutions? Not only was it a waste of resources to rely primarily on military instruments to block Soviet expansion, but it would also have other decidedly negative effects. First, countries which already cooperated with the West through the European Recovery Program might refuse to join a military alliance, thus causing an unnecessary split. The Russians could be expected to make political capital out of such a split. Second, the establishment of a military alliance in Western Europe would "amount to a final militarization of the present dividing-line through Europe." Kennan thought that the hardening of the division between East and West would materially reduce chances of arriving at political settlements for Austria and Germany and make it impossible for the Eastern Europeans to loosen their ties with the Soviet Union.[49]

Kennan had been forced by the climate in Washington and by the British-Canadian attitude to abandon his "dumbbell" concept of the United States and Canada cooperating in North America and the Europeans working closely together on their side of the Atlantic. He had to accept that the two parts would be bound through a treaty of mutual assistance, and not only through a unilateral American guarantee of support and deliveries of equipment to Western Europe.

Although he accepted a mutual treaty, the Director of the Policy Planning Staff continued to argue against the concept of including as much as possible of Western Europe in an Atlantic alliance. First, he went against the inclusion of any country not "washed by Atlantic waters" if this country was not part of a union of states which generally met this criterion. Second, Kennan didn't want "to extend this alliance as far as possible—to jam it, so to speak, as close as possible to the Soviet borders."[50]

On the other hand, even Kennan agreed that it was difficult to leave a country out if it wanted to participate in the security system. Then, there was always the danger that Moscow would misinterpret the nonparticipation of certain countries and take this as an opportunity to try to extend its influence.

Kennan's solution to these conflicting factors was the concept of gradated membership. While most policy makers regarded this as only a second-best solution, Kennan saw it as the best. This led to several important differences with Hickerson and those who supported him. The two differed sharply over the role of Italy in the North Atlantic alliance. On this issue Kennan had strong support in Washington.

Of more interest in our context were their differences over Scandinavia. Kennan actually preferred that neither Norway nor Denmark came in as full members of the Atlantic group. He made that clear on several occasions. Thus, in his dispute with Hickerson in late August, he specifically stated that Portugal, Iceland, Denmark, Norway, and Ireland should not be considered members of the group.[51]

To Kennan these countries ought to be associated with the alliance through an arrangement whereby the members of the North Atlantic treaty—i.e., the United States, Canada, and the Western Union—agreed to regard an attack on any of them as an attack on themselves. The stepping stones would in return agree to make military facilities available to the alliance so they might be more effectively defended.

On September 2 Kennan was specifically asked by the British representative in the Washington talks about the role of Norway. He answered that Norway properly belonged in this "second category" of the gradated membership concept. The reason he gave was that "its principal role in the event of a war would be to provide certain facilities and bases," adding that "the size of its army required its presence in the homeland for defense of its borders."[52]

Kennan was not more specific than others about what exactly would be the differences between full membership and this second category. Some points were clear, however. In time of peace the countries in the second group would have little to do with the Atlantic alliance, since they were not to be members, and therefore presumably would take only a very limited part in discussions within it. In time of war Kennan's comments probably implied that the second category states would not have to participate in the fighting unless their own territories were attacked. Even then their role might be limited in the sense that they would not have to send troops to other areas to fight. In case of a limited Soviet attack, they might thus be able to stay out of war altogether since they would not be under the same general obligation as the full members to come to the assistance of any member country which was attacked.

Hickerson wanted to have Sweden included in the Atlantic alliance on as close a basis as possible, but was ready to accept looser arrangements in case his first choice could not be accomplished. Kennan did not want to have Sweden as either a full member or a second category country. On July 8 the Director of the Policy Planning Staff gave Sweden as an example when he argued that "the United States [which in this case must have meant primarily himself] had doubted the advisability of pressing certain countries close to the Soviet Union into making military engagements when their neutrality might in certain circumstances be more desirable."[53]

In this case Kennan defended neutrality as preferable to close association with the Atlantic alliance. His more general line was that any member of the OEEC not specifically mentioned as either full member or second category associate should be included in a third category. The links between the states in this category and the Atlantic treaty would be quite weak. The members of the North Atlantic group would only issue a statement at the time of the conclusion of the pact to the effect that "any threat of aggression, direct or indirect, against any of the OEEC countries would be regarded by all members of the Group as a development calling for the consultation" envisaged elsewhere in the pact.[54] This was a rather loose way of tying these countries of the OEEC to the Atlantic arrangement, since it was unknown what such consultations would lead to.

Kennan employed three categories of association with the Atlantic alliance. These were only basic models, however, since he evidently thought that even finer nuances could be developed. On September 9 he told the representatives taking part in the Washington talks that "it would be unwise to prejudge today the exact terms on which certain countries might later be admitted to the Pact; furthermore, the capacities and requirements of nations varied so widely that they could not be fitted into one or two precisely drawn categories."[55]

Who Supported Affiliation—and Why?

Very few persons outside the State Department had any detailed knowledge about the position advanced by Kennan. Therefore, when referring to those who supported his ideas, I do not by this mean that these persons held views identical to Kennan's. The point is that several prominent policy makers either generally supported his concepts or, quite independently, developed a similar perspective of their own.

The most prominent supporter of Kennan within the State Department was Counselor Charles Bohlen. The common starting point for Soviet experts Kennan and Bohlen was their analysis of the Soviet threat to Western Europe. Since, in their opinion, the threat was more political and economic than military, it was wrong to concentrate so much on military defense. Politically, the issue of whether or not to join the pact would tend to create divisions not only between members and nonmembers, but also within the participating countries.

For much of 1948 Bohlen was either out of Washington or working on the Berlin question. He was only intermittently able to have any influence on the Atlantic negotiations. There are also indications that in 1948 he did not press his views on membership in the alliance with the same conviction as did Kennan.[56] His attitude was to become more clear-cut and his influence stronger when Dean Acheson took over as Secretary of State in January 1949. Bohlen's absence from the negotiations served to strengthen the position of Hickerson. As we have seen, his absence had been favored and possibly even pushed for by Hickerson and Achilles.

While Senator Vandenberg was a supporter of Scandinavia's close participation in the Atlantic security system, important Republican foreign policy spokesman John Foster Dulles had greater doubts about the role of that region. In his book *War or Peace,* published in 1950, Dulles wrote that "The inclusion of Norway seemed to some unnecessarily provocative of the Soviet Union, as Norway has a common frontier with the Soviet Union and the Soviet Union would have strongly, and understandably, resented the establishment along that common border of air bases that were open to use by the United States."[57] The pronoun "some" applied to the author himself. As we have seen, on several occasions Dulles had exaggerated Soviet influence in Scandinavia. This probably helps explain his lack of interest in the region's membership in the Atlantic alliance. Granted this analysis, Scandinavian participation would be even more of a provocation to Moscow than if Soviet influence were seen as more limited.

While Dulles, then, to a considerable extent agreed with the position of Kennan and Bohlen, few indications exist that he actively pushed his view. Yet, in February 1949 he told the ambassadors of Norway and Denmark that he thought the best solution would be for the Scandinavians to establish a joint arrangement whereby the three countries would be tied to the Atlantic alliance in more indirect ways than through direct participation.[58] The State Department must have been as aware of Dulles' position as were the Scandinavian embassies in Washington.

A more vocal critic of the idea of "jamming the alliance with countries close to the Soviet Union" was columnist Walter Lippmann. In his opposition to bringing the Scandinavians into the Atlantic security system, Lippmann could be seen as continuing his battle against the version of containment which Kennan had propagated through his famous "Mr. X" article in *Foreign Affairs* of July 1947. By 1948–49, however, Lippmann and Kennan had come to stand for ideas which were quite similar.[59]

While the Canadians and the British supported the concept of bringing the Scandinavian countries, Norway and Denmark in particular, into the North Atlantic system on as close a basis as possible, the European continental nations were skeptical or directly opposed to this. The French, especially, argued that Scandinavia held little strategic importance to them. There would even be some negative effects if the Scandinavians joined the alliance. A strengthening of the northern flank might result in less attention and equipment for the continental states.

The French came to push for the early inclusion of Italy. Developments there were seen as of much greater significance than what took place in Scandinavia. To buttress their position, the French used some of the arguments advanced by others skeptical of bringing the Scandinavian countries too closely into the Atlantic pact. Thus, on July 8 Ambassador Bonnet somewhat rhetorically asked the other participants in the talks whether it would be wise "to enlarge the system in such a way that could, however wrongly, be considered by Russia as encirclement?" His answer was obvious, ". . . it would be well to strengthen the present consolidation of nations in the case of peace and not enlarge membership too rapidly."[60]

The French received support from the Belgians and, in part, the Dutch. On September 9 the representative of Belgium in the working group suggested that the participating countries only state that it "might be desirable" instead of "it would be desirable to have Norway, Denmark, Portugal, Iceland and Ireland as members" in the Atlantic alliance.[61] And, at least in the first round of talks in Washington in the summer of 1948, Ambassador van Kleffens of the Netherlands argued, like the French, that it would be best to permit the Brussels treaty members to strengthen their ties with each other and with the North Americans before admitting other states.[62] The Dutch, however, did not maintain this view with the same strength of conviction as did the French and the Belgians.

One of the arguments used most often by the Swedes in defense of their policy of not joining the Atlantic alliance was the effect such a move would have on the delicate position of Finland.[63] As we have seen, in the fall of 1947 this argument had met with sympathy at least in parts of the State Department when the more modest idea of Scandinavian military cooperation had been discussed. The Division of Northern European Affairs reasoned, as did the Swedes, that any move in the Scandinavian area which the Soviet leaders would regard as hostile might very well serve to increase Soviet control over Finland. At the worst, Finland might become absorbed by the Soviet Union through political pressure or even military occupation.

In 1948 this argument was still accepted by those opposed to having the Scandinavian countries as full members in the Atlantic alliance. Kennan argued that the inclusion of Sweden in particular could quite likely lead to a strengthening of Soviet influence in Finland. The membership of Sweden in the pact might lead to an expansion of Soviet influence, instead of the opposite.[64]

In his conversation with Undén on October 14, Secretary of State Marshall condemned Swedish neutrality. He did not, however, give any answer to the Foreign Minister's contention that for Sweden to join the West would lead to changes in favor of the Soviet Union in Finland. "The Finnish argument" was undoubtedly a difficult one to handle for those who pressed most strongly for a change in Swedish policies. Ambassador Bedell Smith in Moscow, who probably favored the line of Hickerson and Matthews in relations with Stockholm, had to admit that there might well be some truth to the claim that Moscow's policy toward Finland was moderated by a desire to prevent Sweden from joining the Atlantic alliance. Even Hickerson himself told Swedish Ambassador Boheman in November that his "argument about possible effects in Finland struck a very responsive cord with us."[65]

NSC 28 and 28/1 both argued that while the United States wanted Sweden to align itself with the West in "such form as may be found collectively acceptable," it should at the same time "refrain from forcing Sweden into an attitude which would be unnecessarily provocative toward the Soviet Union." Although it was far from clear what this compromise statement actually meant, most likely it did reflect a certain uneasiness about Finland's position in case Sweden joined the Atlantic pact, at least as a full member.[66]

Nevertheless, those who argued in favor of Sweden becoming closely associated with the West generally tried to play down the significance of the Finnish argument. They pursued three main lines of argument. First, the Swedes, in their opinion, used the argument as an alibi. It was only a tactical device to make the best out of a policy they would have pursued anyway. Second, if the Soviet leaders decided that it would be in their interest to draw Finland further into their orbit, relations with Sweden would not bar them from such action. Third, the inclusion of Sweden and the other Scandinavian countries would strengthen the Western Powers. The stronger the West, the less likely any aggressive move on the part of the Soviet Union would be.[67]

To sum up, several important policy makers in Washington were skeptical of the idea of bringing the Scandinavian countries into the Atlantic alliance on the basis of full membership. The skeptics were supported by the continental European states, in particular by France. It should be noted, however, that with the possible exception of Lippmann, their alternatives were not based on acceptance of the neutrality policies of the Swedish government. The question was *how* Scandinavia was to be associated with the West, not *whether* it was to be tied to the wider Atlantic framework. This was at least true with regard to the position of Norway and Denmark. To the extent that the Scandinavians would choose to follow a common policy, this evidently meant that even Kennan and those who supported ideas similar to his were opposed to Stockholm's attempts to persuade Oslo and Copenhagen to adopt a neutralist attitude.

Kennan's alternative was to have Norway and Denmark

as participants in the Atlantic alliance on the basis of limited commitments. Sweden should be covered by the consultation clause foreseen for those members of the OEEC which were not tied to the pact in other ways. In case the three countries were to establish uniform policies, the best solution, according to this group of policy makers, would be to have the Scandinavian arrangement tied to the Atlantic alliance in more indirect and less comprehensive terms than through participation in the pact itself. At least this was what Dulles told the ambassadors of Norway and Denmark, and it would seem that this represented the general view of the wider group as well.

Marshall's Position

Within broad lines the policies followed by the United States toward Western Europe in 1947–48 conformed with the personal viewpoints of Secretary of State Marshall. He personally launched the European Recovery Program through his famous speech at Harvard on June 5, 1947. The Secretary did not just deliver the speech. He was personally involved in its drafting and actually made some changes in the version prepared by Bohlen immediately before the speech was delivered.[68]

On the military side, the Secretary of State in general terms agreed with the ideas presented by Bevin after the meeting of the Council of Foreign Ministers in November–December 1947. He also gave his approval to the opening of talks with the Canadians and the British on the establishment of an Atlantic security system. Marshall on several occasions strongly condemned the neutrality policies of Sweden.

Yet, evidence can be found that the Secretary did not share the views of those who pressed most strongly for the inclusion of Scandinavia in the Atlantic alliance. Despite his repeated denunciations of neutrality, Marshall did not agree with the attitude of Hickerson and Matthews.

On October 12 Hickerson told Swedish Ambassador-

Designate Boheman that the United States was "worried, distressed and shocked by the adherence of Sweden to the policy of neutrality, a word which was really offensive to us." This was too much for Marshall. In a move which was most unusual on his part, he administered a rebuke to the Director of the Office of European Affairs. In a cable to Lovett from Paris, the Secretary of State pointed out, with reference to the quotation above, that "it seems to me that such obvious pressure at present time does more harm than good." He instructed Lovett that if reasons did not exist of which he was unaware, department officials should lay off on "such outspoken pressure tactics with Sweden."[69]

Here, however, Marshall's views on the various forms of association between Scandinavia and the Atlantic alliance are of most importance. We have few sources to any private position before the fall of 1948. In late April, while he was still in Bogotá, he had warned the department against the United States spreading its resources too thin in a military arrangement. But that had referred to the proposed Anglo-American statement on Turkey, Greece, and Iran designed to protect them against a possible attack when they were left out of the Atlantic system. Although this argument might be used against the inclusion of the Scandinavian countries as well, there is no evidence that the Secretary had this in mind. In 1947 Marshall had been somewhat skeptical of the wording of the Truman Doctrine speech. He felt it was "a little too much flamboyant anti-Communism." Interestingly, he had similar doubts about the President's foreign policy address to Congress just about a year later.[70]

In the fall of 1948 indications are that Marshall had some sympathy with ideas similar to those of George Kennan. At least it can be stated that the Secretary projected an attitude which was different from that of Hickerson. This was revealed in conversations with Lange and, in particular, with Danish Foreign Minister Rasmussen. These conversations were held in Paris in connection with the General Assembly of the UN meeting there. It is quite possible that Marshall was at this time influenced by Charles Bohlen, who was the most important adviser with him in Paris.

In his meeting with Lange on September 29, the Secretary of State was quite noncommittal when the Norwegian Foreign Minister brought up the topic of a Scandinavian defense arrangement and its ties with the West. He expressed misgivings about the Swedish attitude, but he did voice the opinion that if the Scandinavian countries could prevent the Russians from gaining control over the important southwest coast of Norway, a Scandinavian arrangement could have real value.[71]

On the very same day that Marshall and Lange talked together in Paris, Hickerson met with Ambassador Morgenstierne in Washington. The Director of the Office of European Affairs pointed out that the United States wanted Norway to join both the Brussels pact and the North Atlantic system. He even indicated that such participation would be the only form under which countries like Norway and Denmark could qualify for assistance from the United States under the Vandenberg Resolution.[72]

It is interesting to note that Marshall told Lange that he was not aware of the fact that on September 23 the Norwegians and the Danes had received some information about the planned Atlantic system from Hickerson. Instead of replying directly to questions on the American attitude to Scandinavian defense cooperation put to him by the Norwegian, Marshall cabled the State Department for recommendations on what to answer.

Lovett recommended that the Secretary of State tell the Foreign Minister that "provided it contained no impediment to Nor and Dan cooperation with West for defense, Scand defense arrangement would be asset and valuable supplement to Nor and Dan participation in Atlantic arrangement. We would welcome eventual Swed participation in latter if and when Swed prepared participate."[73] This had to mean that the United States would be favorable to Scandinavian defense cooperation only to the extent that such an arrangement did not break with the overriding goal: that of bringing at least Norway and Denmark into the Atlantic alliance on as close a basis as possible.

Before this reply was presented to Lange, Marshall

talked with Danish Foreign Minister Rasmussen. In their conversation on October 5, the Secretary made a most intriguing statement about Scandinavia's relationship with the Atlantic system.

The American himself took the initiative in discussing "the relationship of a Scandinavian defense arrangement with whatever broader North Atlantic arrangement might be worked out." After some general comments about the atomic bomb having provided the major deterrent influence on the Soviet Union, the development of Western Europe's economic strength through the European Recovery Program, and the need to reinforce Europe militarily, Marshall got down to the topic he had announced. According to his own memo of conversation, he stated that "there were many ways in which the Scandinavian group might provide strength toward the development of Western Europe. I said that I could even see the possibility of a neutral group, provided such a group could ensure that the straits leading from the Baltic to the Atlantic could, and would be, closed in the event of trouble."[74] This was a rather sensational statement. Marshall seemed to open the way for the United States to take a favorable view of a Scandinavian pact with no other link to the Atlantic alliance than the support the Western Powers would get from the closing of the exit from the Baltic in case of an international crisis.

Was this an isolated slip of the tongue, or can other indications be found that the Secretary may have been willing to look with sympathy upon an arrangement with such limited ties with the West? There are some. The day before Marshall talked to Rasmussen, he had discussed the role of Scandinavia with Bevin. Then he had dealt with the question from a different angle. He made some comments on why the United States was opposed to a Scandinavian arrangement based on neutrality. Marshall told Bevin that "there was certain danger in a Scandinavian netural [sic] bloc since there were facilities and important waterways controlled by the Scandinavian countries to say nothing of Greenland which was of vital importance to the United States, which, if neutralized, would be most damaging."[75]

This seemed to signify that a Scandinavian bloc had to do more than just promise to close the straits from the Baltic to meet with American acceptance. Nevertheless, the Secretary's wording was certainly less hostile to the idea of a Scandinavia with weak ties to the West than was typical of Hickerson and those who supported him. A separate arrangement might well be worked out for Greenland. That being so, a Scandinavian promise to close the Baltic exits would probably go a long way in meeting the criteria for acceptance suggested even in Marshall's conversation with Bevin.

When the Secretary's adviser, Hayden Raynor, later gave Lange the answers to his questions, he followed the line suggested by Lovett.[76] Therefore, Marshall's statement of October 5 had to be seen by Rasmussen (and, to the extent that he informed them, by the Norwegians and the Swedes as well) as an isolated expression of the American attitude. (There is no indication in the files of the Norwegian Foreign Office that Lange was informed by Rasmussen of what Marshall had said.) The Danish Foreign Minister apparently made no attempt to bring out further details in what he had been told.

Marshall's conversations with the Scandinavian foreign ministers in September-October were important in at least one other respect. As to the question of what information to give to the Swedes about the Atlantic pact, an interesting shade of difference could be detected between the State Department in Washington and Marshall in Paris.

Lovett had told the Secretary that ". . . we could not offer advice on question informing Swed of our conversations. It would seem preferable to delay doing so for present." This was a somewhat curious recommendation, with a discrepancy between its first and second part. Marshall, through Hayden Raynor, brought this message to Lange with the implication that although there might be reasons for not informing the Swedes, the Norwegians had to decide for themselves whether they wanted to do so or not.[77] Lovett and Hickerson, on the other hand, placed most emphasis on the second part of their recommendation. Lovett even asked

Morgenstierne to check with his government that there was no misunderstanding on the point that the Swedes, if informed at all, were to be given no details.[78]

When Lange met Marshall again on November 20, he once more brought up the question of the American attitude to Scandinavian defense cooperation. Reflecting Swedish reluctance on this point, the Norwegian inquired about the likely response to an arrangement with no ties with the Atlantic alliance. Marshall answered mostly in generalities, saying, among other things, that this was something he would like to turn over in his mind before making any further reply.[79] No further reply was, however, given by the Secretary directly to this question.

There is one final indication that Marshall viewed a Scandinavia with limited ties with the West in a more sympathetic way than did the hardliners in the State Department and the military. On November 24 Kennan submitted to the Secretary and the Under Secretary a paper on "Considerations Affecting the Conclusion of a North Atlantic Security Pact." There Kennan, in somewhat diluted form, also presented his ideas on the territorial scope of the pact. His main argument was again that an Atlantic alliance should embrace only those countries whose homeland or insular territories were washed by the waters of the North Atlantic, or which were part of a close union of states that met this description.[80]

Kennan did not explicitly refer to countries that would not be eligible if this principle were accepted. Primarily he was against the inclusion of Italy, but the argument was relevant for the situation of Sweden as well. At least this was how both Hickerson and later Bohlen interpreted the meaning of this principle.[81]

What stand did Marshall and Lovett take on Kennan's paper? Apparently no formal record was made of their views. There is, however, a handwritten note referring to Kennan on the cover page which reads that the "Secretary indicated orally his agreement to the second part of the paper. On the first there was no disagreement anywhere."[82] The second part dealt with the territorial scope; the first discussed the significance of concluding the pact.

This could be interpreted as another sign that the Secretary of State was opposed to making the scope of the alliance as inclusive as Hickerson wanted. Most likely it meant that Marshall was less interested than Hickerson in bringing in Italy, but his comment may even have had some relevance for Sweden's relationship with the pact.

Although the Under Secretary as well had his doubts about the role of Italy, he was probably closer to Hickerson on this point than was the Secretary.[83] Since Kennan had submitted the paper also to Lovett, it would seem most natural that he had noted his approval if it had been obtained. Furthermore, in his memo to Kennan of November 26, Hickerson stated that the Under Secretary and the Defense Department (National Military Establishment—NME) agreed with the opinion that Italy must be included in the Atlantic pact, although he did not specify in what form. In fact, the Director of the Office of European Affairs put it the other way around, "EUR[opean Division] fully shares Mr. Lovett's and the NME view that Italy must be included."[84] It is unlikely that Hickerson would have written this, if Lovett had not actually supported him at this time.

To sum up, it is not possible to conclude with certainty what the position of Marshall was on the relationship between the North Atlantic system and Scandinavia. It might well be that he did not stick to one specific view all through 1948. Few of the policy makers in Washington did. Changes had to be made reflecting discussions with Canada and the Western Union members, contacts with the countries interested in some sort of association with the Atlantic alliance, and changes in the domestic and international climate in general.

What is evident, however, is that on several occasions Marshall showed less interest in urging arrangements which would link the Scandinavian countries firmly to the wider Atlantic framework than did Hickerson and other hardliners in this question. Once he even indicated that a Scandinavia merely willing to block the exits from the Baltic in time of crisis might meet with favor in Washington.

If Marshall favored such looser ties, why was this view not adopted by the Truman administration? There are several answers to this question. First, the American attitude was, as we shall see, in reality more flexible than historians have assumed. Not only Marshall but the Truman administration were willing to consider arrangements falling short of the full membership of the three Northern countries in the Atlantic pact.

Second, although Scandinavia was of some importance to the United States in 1948, it was only one of many areas which the State Department had to deal with. Except for brief periods, as in mid-March, the affairs of the region were never at the center of attention in Washington. In short, the Secretary of State had more important problems to consider than the details of the relationship between the Atlantic system and the Scandinavian countries.

Third, there is reason to doubt not only the extent to which the Secretary held a clarified position on Scandinavia's role, but also the extent to which he was effectively in charge of the whole Atlantic question in 1948. There is strong evidence that his leadership was slipping in the course of the year. He was away for long periods at a time, in March and April in South America, and in most of September through December in Paris. He was losing touch with events in Washington. Marshall was also becoming an ill and very tired man. His failing health compelled his retirement after a kidney operation in December 1948. As his official biographer writes, "He had remained in office during the last months only out of loyalty to President Truman who was in the hectic election campaign."[85]

Marshall did not personally take part in any of the rounds of talks with the Canadians, the British, and the other Western Union nations from March onward. Just as Truman had strong confidence in Marshall, the Secretary in turn put great trust in Lovett, whom he knew and respected from their close cooperation during the World War. From July on the Under Secretary seemed to be effectively in charge, with Hickerson as his close adviser. This was demonstrated by the fact that when in late August Hickerson and Kennan disagreed sharply over the territorial scope of the Atlantic system, the two asked Lovett, not Marshall, to re-

solve the dispute, although the Secretary was in town.[86]
When Marshall held talks with other foreign ministers, he
consistently asked the department in Washington for recommendations on what to say. More remarkable, almost without exception he followed the lead of his advisers. It must
have been a pleasure to work under Marshall, especially in
the first part of his term, in particular for officials accus-
tomed to the highly personal leadership of Byrnes.

Finally, even if Marshall had possessed the will to carry
out a more personal policy, strong countervailing pressure
existed to a policy favoring a Scandinavia with very limited
ties with the West. There was the attitude of Lovett and
Hickerson within the State Department itself, supported by
the embassies in Oslo and Stockholm. The military were also
beginning to play an increasingly stronger role. Last, but not
least, crucial Senator Vandenberg was seen as in favor of the
Scandinavians becoming closely linked with the Atlantic alliance.

The Official American Position—1948

Important disagreements existed among policy makers
as to how closely the Scandinavian countries were to be tied
to the Atlantic system in preparation. Hickerson and Kennan disagreed. There was a split—only in part opened—
between Marshall and other State Department leaders. Differences remained between Vandenberg and Dulles. The
British and the Canadians stressed the Atlantic approach
and the importance of Scandinavia, while continental states
led by France preferred a Scandinavian arrangement that
would not take resources away from themselves. Despite
these differences, Washington as well as the other capitals in
the North Atlantic talks had to formulate an agreed position.

In April the National Security Council began its deliberations on the Atlantic security system. In NSC 9 of April 13,
entitled The Position of the United States With Respect to
Support for Western Union and Other Related Free Countries, the departments involved agreed that Norway, Swe-

den, Denmark, Iceland, and Italy "if the results of the Italian elections are favorable" should be approached for the purpose of "ascertaining whether they would be prepared . . . to accede to the Five-Power Treaty in the near future and to enter into negotiations for a North Atlantic Collective Defense Agreement."[87]

Thus, in this preliminary stage of planning the National Security Council apparently foresaw a double role for the Scandinavian countries and other potential participants in the new security arrangements. They would join both the Western Union and the Atlantic system. However, the NSC paper also dealt with the possibility that the countries mentioned would not at this time wish to accede to either the Brussels treaty or the Atlantic system. In that case, the report noted, consideration would have to be given to extending an assurance of immediate support if an armed attack took place. The idea was still to do this through a presidential statement amounting to some sort of U.S. guarantee, in preparation for the establishment of the Atlantic security system.[88] Thereby the report actually contained at least two categories of association with the Atlantic arrangement. Those states which chose not to come in on the "normal" basis could still be given protection from the United States in the form of the presidential statement. No specific alternative was mentioned for the three Northern countries in this respect, although the NSC planners undoubtedly preferred that Norway, Denmark, and Sweden all joined as members of the Brussels treaty and the Atlantic system.

NSC 9/1 of April 23 followed the lines of the April 13 report. The role foreseen for the Scandinavian nations was still a double one, membership both in the Western Union and in the Atlantic arrangement. However, in NSC 9/1 nothing was explicitly stated about any sort of presidential guarantee in case a country chose not to join the Western system. The idea of a guarantee remained, but not as an alternative to membership. Greece, Turkey, and Iran were not thought of as members of the Atlantic system. They would therefore have to be protected in this other way.[89]

As we have already noted, NSC 9/2 of May 11 differed

from its predecessors in the important way that it emphasized that the initiative had to remain with the Western Europeans. Forms of association on the part of the United States with the European defense effort would only be discussed if Washington became convinced that some further political commitment was necessary to bolster public confidence in Western Europe.[90] This change of emphasis had to have consequences for the role of the Scandinavian countries. In case they wanted to join the West, they would have to rely primarily on participation in the Brussels treaty since it was unclear what kind of Atlantic arrangement would be created, if any.

The relevant passage of NSC 9/2 stated that "The Department of State should explore with the five Governments [the Brussels treaty members] the problem of increasing the security of Norway, Denmark, Iceland, Italy and perhaps Portugal and Sweden through integration into or through some form of association with the Brussels Treaty system or otherwise."[91]

This recommendation opened the door for a number of different relationships between the Scandinavian states and the Western Union. They could become full members or they might become more loosely associated with the Brussels treaty. The word "otherwise" meant that even other alternatives might be open. Yet, this option probably referred primarily to the possible association of the Scandinavian countries with the Atlantic system which Washington—despite its more hesitant attitude at this stage—still expected would be created.

The quotation also illustrated that a distinction was now made for the first time between Norway and Denmark on the one hand and Sweden on the other. Although nothing was directly stated about this, two main reasons probably existed for this distinction. Norway and Denmark were more important from an American strategic point of view than was Sweden, and chances were smaller that Stockholm would break with neutrality.

The recommendation of NSC 9/2 was repeated word for word in NSC 9/3 of June 28, which was approved by the

President on July 2.[92] This then was the basis on which the United States started the talks with Canada and the Western Union states on July 6 (the Washington Exploratory Talks on Security). Representatives of the seven countries summed up their position in a provisional draft, dated July 22, entitled Territorial Scope of a North Atlantic Security Arrangement and its Relationship to the Security of Other Nations. The paper was primarily a description of the discussions in progress, not a presentation of final conclusions. Nevertheless, it comes closer than any other document to setting out the dominant mood in the Washington group as a whole in mid-1948.[93]

In its first paragraph the paper stated that the problem was to devise an arrangement which would meet the security needs of the nations represented without overextending their military capabilities. The working group then agreed that to be fully satisfactory the North Atlantic system would have to provide for the security not only of the nations taking part in the Washington talks, "but also for the defense of the North Atlantic territories of Denmark (Greenland), Norway, Iceland, Portugal (the Azores) and Ireland, which, should they fall into enemy hands, would jeopardize the security of both the European and the North American members and seriously impede the flow of reciprocal assistance between them."[94]

The emphasis on the importance of the stepping stones was primarily the product of views expressed by the American, British, and Canadian representatives. On the other hand, they all agreed that the resources of the group would be limited and should not be spread too thin. It was also evident that both the interest of the various countries in participation and their circumstances and capabilities varied widely. Referring to these "circumstances and capabilities," the working group concluded that "Taking these variations into account rather than attempting to fit each nation into a uniform rigid pattern may provide the solution." Thus, different forms of association could be foreseen, taking into account the peculiarities of the individual state.[95]

Three main categories were explicitly mentioned. The

first one, naturally, would be full membership. This would involve undertakings for mutual assistance in the event of an armed attack upon any party; provision for consultation if the security of any party was otherwise threatened either directly or by a threat to a nonparty; and participation in the agencies set up to implement the treaty. The original full members would be the United States, Canada, the parties to the Brussels treaty, "and such other members of the North Atlantic community as are ready to undertake the requisite obligations and are acceptable." [96]

The dominant countries in the Washington talks preferred that Norway and Denmark came in as full members. However, the paper noted that "While it would be desirable to have Norway, Denmark, Portugal, Iceland and Ireland as full members, these countries may not now be prepared to accept fully the requisite responsibilities." If they were not willing to join the pact as full members, "they should be invited to accede to the Pact with limited commitments, the exact nature of which would be determined in negotiation with them."

Although the nature of their commitments might vary from country to country, the general framework would be the same. The full members would agree to regard an attack on any of these stepping stones as an attack against themselves. The stepping stones would in turn agree to defend their own territories to the limit of their capabilities and "to make available such facilities as are within their power, when required, in order to provide for the protection of the North Atlantic area." The countries in this second category would not be represented on the agencies of the Atlantic alliance responsible for military decisions. Such an exclusion would even be possible for some of the full members. [97]

Finally, the paper described a third category of association with the Atlantic pact. In case a country whose territorial and political integrity was of concern to the wider group did not come in either as a full member or with limited membership, it could be invited "to accede to the treaty on conditions to be agreed between them [the members of the group] and the state so invited." Very little was stated about the nature of the ties between the Atlantic alliance and the countries in question except that they might come in "under such special arrangements as might be necessary owing to their geographical position or to their international obligations (Sweden, Italy)." Thus, Sweden and Italy were mentioned as the two countries most likely to fall into this third category. In a long-term perspective it was also recognized that West Germany and Spain might be eligible for participation in one of the three categories.[98]

This paper was written before the disagreements between Hickerson and Kennan over the status of Italy in particular, but also the Scandinavian countries, became fully manifest. To the extent that it can be placed within the framework of this struggle, it represented a compromise between the concepts of the two policy makers. The paper held open the status of full membership for all the countries mentioned, including even Italy and Sweden. It specifically stated that it would be desirable to have the stepping-stone countries as full members of the Atlantic group.

On the other hand, the concept of gradated membership was accepted, a concept which Kennan felt more comfortable with than did Hickerson. Although the three categories were outlined only in a most rudimentary form, making further comment on them very difficult, they were clearly seen as separate. If they refused full membership, Norway and Denmark could enter with limited commitments. Sweden would have both this option and the one under the third category, a category which possibly was open even to the other two. Finally, nothing was mentioned about the Scandinavians becoming members of the Western Union, as Hickerson undoubtedly wanted them to.

The next authoritative statement is found in the National Security Council reports 28 and 28/1, The Position of the United States With Respect to Scandinavia, dated August 26 and September 3. The most relevant paragraph in the two papers was identical and read that ". . . the United States should explore with the members of the Western Union the problem of increasing the security of Norway, Denmark, and if appropriate, Sweden through their *integra-*

tion into or association in some form with the Brussels Treaty system or otherwise." [italics mine][99]

The wording was almost identical to that of NSC 9/2 and 9/3 of May and June. This was keeping all avenues open. The three countries apparently still had the option of coming in through full membership or through some looser association with the Western Powers. What was different compared to the July paper was primarily the fact that association or membership under the Brussels treaty were again emphasized. But participation in the Western Union would also bring the Scandinavians into the Atlantic system.

The difference is best explained in terms of who had participated in drafting the various papers. The NSC documents were purely American, while the July paper represented the joint thinking of all the countries participating in the talks. Washington wanted the Europeans to carry as much of the burden as possible, with the United States then coming in to perform what they could not do on their own. The Europeans on the other hand tried to strengthen the American role. They generally preferred new members to participate directly in the Atlantic system, and not under the Brussels treaty. The peripheries of Europe could only be defended, if at all, with America intimately involved.

While these discussions were going on, the United States actually made no serious attempt to induce the Scandinavian countries to join the Western Union. Matthews took an interest in bringing at least Norway in and he had the sympathy of Hickerson, but the predominant feeling was that this should not be done until the American role had been clarified and the relationship of the Western Union with the wider Atlantic system decided upon.[100]

The National Security Council reports on Scandinavia were vague on the various forms of association open to the Scandinavians. Around this time, however, another paper was produced which gives a clearer idea of the discussions in Washington and the other capitals.

On September 9 the participants in the Washington Security Talks agreed on a memorandum which was meant to sum up the results of the talks which had been going on since July 6. The paper represented an agreed statement on the problems discussed and was submitted to the participating countries for further study and comment. Although it presented no final conclusions, the representatives had been keeping in touch with their home governments and more work had been put into the September memorandum than the preliminary summing up of July.

Like its predecessor the September paper contained a section entitled Territorial Scope of a North Atlantic Security Arrangement and its Relationship to the Security of Other Nations. The two documents were really quite similar, showing that there had been few developments of significance since July. The analyses both of the inadequacy of the resources of the alliance and of relations with the stepping stones were almost word-for-word the same. The three major categories which had been outlined in July were maintained. The further statement that "The division of nations between these categories need not be rigidly fixed but should permit flexibility" was found in both papers.[101]

The group of full members was still seen to consist of the United States, Canada, the parties to the Brussels treaty, and such other countries of the North Atlantic community as were ready to undertake the requisite obligations and were acceptable to the group. The stepping stones were undoubtedly eligible for full membership, but if they chose not to come in under such terms, the second category of limited commitments remained open. These commitments were as vague as they had been earlier. Neither had the third category with its special references to Italy and Sweden changed. There were, however, a couple of changes that deserve notice. The July paper had emphasized that "it *would* be desirable to have Norway, Denmark, Portugal, Iceland and Ireland as full members." The September 9 paper only stated that "it *might well* be desirable" [italics mine] to have these countries as full members.[102] This was a weakening of the position taken in July. The new wording left it more open as to which was preferable, to have the stepping stones as full members or included in the second category. As we have seen, Kennan preferred that at least Norway, and probably

Denmark as well, came in under the second category and not as full members.

This apparently significant change was written into the document on the very day it was completed. The proposal was made by the Belgian representative and he gave no reason except that his government was not positive as to the wording of the July paper which had been maintained on this point until September 9. His suggestion led to few comments from the other participants. The British representative only stated that he would not object to this change in language although he "believed the United Kingdom desired the inclusion of Norway and Portugal in the Pact." [103] This seemed to indicate that to London, Norway and Portugal were the most important of the stepping stones.

The American delegation at this meeting was led by George Kennan, with neither Lovett nor Hickerson present. Kennan said nothing directly to the point raised by the Belgian. Somewhat later in the meeting, however, he emphasized that "it would be unwise to prejudge today the exact terms on which certain countries might later be admitted to the Pact; furthermore, the capacities and requirements of nations varied so widely that they could not be fitted into one or two properly drawn categories." [104] This certainly was a statement in favor of flexibility in determining the conditions under which the various countries would become associated with the Atlantic alliance.

The working group agreed to the change proposed by the Belgian representative. It is not likely that this reflected any shift in attitude in London, Ottawa, and in dominant circles in Washington as to the role of the stepping stones. The alteration in favor of more open-ended language was probably made so that all the participants could accept the paragraph in question without any great difficulties. The change did illustrate, however, that at least as far as the association of Scandinavia with the Atlantic alliance went, no hardening of terms had taken place.

Two other changes in the September paper should also be noted. While the July document had stated that "Denmark (Greenland), Norway, Iceland, Portugal (the Azores) and Ireland" were of considerable strategic importance, the corresponding sentence now read that "Denmark (especially Greenland), Norway, Iceland, Portugal (especially the Azores) and Ireland" were of such importance.[105] This reflected a certain upgrading of the strategic value of the Danish and Portuguese home territories. But the roles of Denmark and Portugal were still seen primarily in terms of their island possessions, Greenland and the Azores.

The other alteration concerned the statement from the July document that "The limited members would certainly not, and some full members possibly not, be represented on the agencies responsible for military decisions." This sentence was dropped in the September memorandum.[106] Too much significance should not be attached to this either. It could be argued that the deletion represented a sign of flexibility. Although limited members might prefer not to be represented on the agencies responsible for military decisions, they could conceivably want such representation. According to this theory, taking the statement out simply left the question more open than it had been in July. On the other hand, it might be that the deletion represented an attempt to bring the limited members more closely into the Atlantic alliance by opening the way for their participation in military decisions. It is possible that this was the way Hickerson reasoned on this point.[107]

On the whole the situation in September was quite similar to what it had been in July. Full membership was open to all the Scandinavian countries. The strategic importance of the stepping stones had again been emphasized. The value of the Danish homelands was somewhat more pronounced in September than in July. All these points underlined the close interest the United States took in the position of Scandinavia.

It cannot be said that those who stood for the less expansive concept—an arrangement short of full membership and thereby also a somewhat smaller role for the United States in the northern region—had lost significant ground. The main features of the July paper had been maintained. The changes made in September did go in both directions.

What happened to the concept of gradated membership after September? The next step was for the September 9 document to be discussed within the various governments. On November 6 President Truman approved its "general principles." Lovett and Vandenberg apparently also agreed with its main lines.[108] There is nothing in the available sources as to their views particularly on the section on the territorial scope of the Atlantic arrangement and its relationship to the security of other nations. Most likely they approved at least the broad ideas of this section, since these ideas must be included among the general principles of the paper.

Therefore, the gradated membership concept probably remained in force in November. This is strengthened by the reply Acting Secretary Lovett gave to inquiries from the embassy in Copenhagen about the nature of limited commitments. Ambassador Marvel had received information about something he called the "French approach," which he understood as the possibility of varying obligations among the members of the North Atlantic pact. Marvel supported this since he felt it would make it easier for Denmark to participate. Lovett's answer to Marvel's cable confirmed that in the exploratory talks the "possibility of limited commitments for certain countries including Norway and Denmark . . . was envisaged. . . ." However, the Acting Secretary went on to state that "this should under no circumstances yet be intimated to anyone in view [of the] desirability [of] Norwegians and Danes becoming full members if possible." He even indirectly rebuked French representatives in Copenhagen by his comment that it was important that the French gave no hint of possible limited commitments to Norway and Denmark at this time.[109]

Lovett's cable was most important. It set the tone for the American attitude to limited commitments in late 1948. Washington continued to recognize that it might be possible for the stepping stones to join on a limited basis, but it was becoming increasingly evident that the State Department leadership preferred that these countries came in as full members. Not only that, they were to receive no information about the concept of limited commitments since such information might lessen chances of their becoming full members.

This attitude revealed differences over the idea of gradated membership which had existed all along, but were only
now brought to the forefront. Key policy makers in Washington all agreed to the *possibility* of the stepping stones entering into arrangements with the Atlantic alliance short of full
membership. But was this to represent the first choice of the
United States, or was it a fallback position? Kennan and those
who agreed with him thought the first. They were supported
by the French. Those increasingly in charge in the State
Department preferred that limited commitments be no more
than a fallback position, only to be considered if all efforts to
bring the stepping stones in as full members failed.

Similar ideas prevailed in London and Ottawa. Both the
British and the Canadians, while accepting the main lines
of the September 9 memorandum, thought that everything
should be done to bring in the Norwegians and the Danes as
full members. Only if that failed should the concept of limited commitments be brought to life.

This development was given added force by the response
a British proposal to accommodate the Scandinavians met
with. In October the Foreign Office had suggested that while
Norway and Denmark come in as full members of the Atlantic alliance, they could at the same time join with Sweden in
a Scandinavian military arrangement. Under such a scheme
an attack on, for instance, Belgium would require full assistance from Norway and Denmark, but not from Sweden. If
Norway and Denmark were attacked, they would receive assistance from both the Atlantic alliance and from Sweden. In
case of an attack on Sweden, the British thought that not
only would Norway and Denmark have to help as members
of the Scandinavian arrangement, but the Atlantic group
should also be committed to help.[110]

After discussions with Prime Minister Gerhardsen and
Defense Minister Hauge, Foreign Minister Lange rejected
the so-called Hankey plan. Three main reasons could be seen
for the Norwegian rejection. First, the plan would, as Lange
told Norwegian Ambassador Prebensen in London, "be very
dangerous from a Norwegian domestic point of view [*indre-*

politisk standpunkt]." If the Norwegian public were to understand that Sweden would in fact receive the same guarantees
as Norway while maintaining a looser relationship to the
West, that would serve to undermine the position of the Gerhardsen government and in particular those within it who
argued most strongly in favor of a Scandinavia closely associated with the West. Second, such a plan would very
likely have the effect of encouraging the Swedes in their
belief that they could get something for nothing. As a result
they would stick to their established policies as firmly as
ever, and Norway's desire for a joint Scandinavian solution
on the basis of association with the West would be effectively
undermined. Third, chances were probably seen as small
that Sweden would agree to such a plan. In conversations
with their neighbors, the Swedes were showing little willingness to accept degrees of Western orientation considerably short of what was implied in the Hankey plan.

Hankey had informed only the Norwegians about his
plan. Nothing was to be done which could embarrass the
government in Oslo. The sharp Norwegian opposition therefore meant that no information would be given to Danes and
Swedes about the proposal.[111]

The British had forwarded the plan to the State Department on October 12. At the time the Americans gave their
response to it, on November 15, the Norwegians had already,
unknown to the department, rejected it. The reply was written by Hickerson and was said to represent "working level
views," probably signifying that it had not been discussed
with the Secretary of State and persons outside the State
Department.[112]

Hickerson informed the British embassy in Washington
that on this level the department agreed with the substance
of the plan "and particularly with the view that every effort
should be made to induce Norway and Denmark to become
full parties to a North Atlantic Security Treaty. If these two
countries do become parties, the problem of Sweden might
well be solved if that country were prepared to enter into a
satisfactory Scandinavian Defense Treaty." The Director of
the Office of European Affairs did have one major reserva-

tion, however. If the Swedes were to obtain a guarantee of assistance from the Atlantic alliance without membership in it, this would be a one-way guarantee. Not only was that wrong in itself, but if the Norwegians and the Danes heard of it, they might well hope to obtain a similar solution. This argument corresponded to the reaction of the Norwegian government. The department therefore proposed that the plan be modified so that in case Sweden was attacked, only Norway and Denmark would be bound to assist. The Atlantic powers should not be required to help, but could, after consultations, choose to give assistance. In this way the Swedes would not, in the opinion of the State Department, receive any favored treatment.

Before sounding out the Norwegians and the Danes, the department wanted the reaction of the British and U.S. ambassadors in the Scandinavian capitals. Ambassador Marvel in Copenhagen was largely in favor of the plan and offered only minor additions to it. Ambassador Matthews and the embassy in Oslo were both strongly opposed.[113] They argued along the same lines as had the Norwegians. First, the plan was still slanted in favor of the Swedes. The reason for this was that the North Atlantic states would be bound to support Norway and Denmark if the two intervened to help Sweden. That obligation would in reality involve the Western pact in war even if only Sweden were attacked. Second, Matthews did not think that Stockholm would agree to the proposal. Third, to grant a favored status to the Swedes would only induce Norwegians and Danes to seek similar arrangements and thereby reduce chances of their coming in as full members.

Matthews summed up his attitude in the following terms, along the lines he had been arguing for months:

> It seems to me that instead of trying to entice Sweden into indirect semi-participation with the West now, it is better tactics to concentrate on Norway and Denmark and, especially important, give them military equipment, while stimulating Swedish fears of being left all alone in a completely exposed position, and allowing Swedes to believe that Sweden is of little military importance to the West. Thus and thus only, I

think, may the Swedes seek participation in North Atlantic pact as a form of insurance.[114]

Thus, Matthews evidently still had some hope that Sweden might in the long run come to take part in the Atlantic pact. The ambassador's strategy to reach this goal was the same as always: favors to Norway and Denmark, and isolation of Sweden.

Through the American embassies in Scandinavia, the State Department was now informed about the Norwegian opposition to the Hankey plan, an opposition which had led to the plan being shelved, although not rejected. This, in addition to the attitude of Matthews and the embassy in Oslo, made the State Department put even its own plan away.[115] Hickerson probably did not feel too bad about this, since the American proposal had only been developed reluctantly in response to British ideas.

Planning in Washington concentrated on the relationship between each of the Scandinavian countries and the Atlantic alliance. Little attention was being paid to the question of what ties a joint Scandinavian arrangement would need to be acceptable to the Western Powers. This might seem somewhat surprising since the three states were trying to reach agreement on such a joint Scandinavian solution.

Yet, little doubt could exist about the views of those increasingly in charge in the State Department. Norway and Denmark were most important from the American point of view. What counted was to bring these two countries into as close a relationship as possible with the Atlantic alliance. Due to Sweden's attitude, a joint Scandinavian arrangement would necessarily be based on limited ties with the West. But if the unexpected should happen, if Norway and Denmark should refuse to come in as full members, even Hickerson and those who supported him were ready to agree to more limited arrangements.

On December 9, the day before a new series of meetings began in the Washington exploratory talks, Hickerson met with Hoyer-Millar, the British minister in Washington. The two concluded that it be the "working-level views" of the United States and Britain that they should not urge Norway and Denmark to accept an arrangement less advantageous than the one Sweden was offered. The two also agreed that "In forming Atlantic Pact forget Sweden for the present; concentrate on Norway and Denmark."[116] This meant that the United States and Britain would not again present a proposal which might only complicate Oslo's and Copenhagen's decisions in favor of full membership in the Atlantic pact.

In discriminating between Norway-Denmark and Sweden there was always the danger that the first two might want the same limited arrangement as Sweden. This was not desirable. Furthermore, the best chance of breaking Sweden's neutrality lay in increasing its isolation from its Scandinavian neighbors. Even then it was recognized that the possibility of a definite break might be small.

With Marshall away, then ill and hospitalized, Lovett was more than ever in charge of the State Department. The Under Secretary, Hickerson, and Achilles handled all important contacts with the embassies. Bohlen was not back from Paris before December 14, and the influence of Kennan was being reduced—he was becoming more and more of an outsider in the department. Even Kennan agreed on the strategic importance of the stepping stones, including Norway and Denmark. The difficulties in working out one arrangement for Norway and Denmark and a separate one for Sweden eroded his position still further.[117]

Although the military still played a less significant role than the State Department in formulating the American policy toward Scandinavia, there was little doubt that the Joint Chiefs preferred that the northern countries, in particular Norway and Denmark, be brought into the Atlantic pact on as close a basis as possible. That had to strengthen the views of Lovett and Hickerson.[118] The attitude of Senator Vandenberg was probably equally important. Vandenberg continued to favor the close association of Norway and Denmark with the Atlantic alliance. He apparently felt that without Iceland, Denmark (Greenland), and in part Norway, the pact would not fulfill the requirements of the Vandenberg Resolution in the sense of contributing to the security of the United States. At least this was how Charles Bohlen presented the senator's position to Dean Acheson, after the latter took over as Secretary of State.[119]

Therefore, the round of talks which began on December 10 was different from earlier meetings, at least concerning the role of Scandinavia in the Atlantic arrangement. On December 13 the Canadian representative, Ambassador Wrong, started off by stating that Canada would like the original members of the North Atlantic pact to include Norway, Denmark, Sweden, Iceland, and Ireland. He wished every effort would be made to persuade these countries to join as full members. Thus, Canada wanted not only Norway and Denmark, but also Sweden to join on this basis. But if these efforts of persuasion failed, then the Canadians were apparently still willing to consider fallback arrangements based on some degree of reciprocity.[120]

Lovett followed up by emphasizing more strongly than ever the importance of the stepping stones. The Under Secretary stated that "if the treaty were to appeal to American opinion, membership should not be confined to the seven countries now represented at the talks. From the point of view of the Western Atlantic powers, the desirability of an association limited to these seven governments would be materially less, if it existed at all." He wanted the stepping stones to join as soon as possible. If they could not sign the treaty by February 1, they should at least give some definite indications that they would soon be ready to do so.[121]

Lovett argued sharply against Scandinavian neutrality. Although it might be unlikely that Sweden would join the Atlantic alliance, no step should be taken which might exclude any of the northern countries. But, again, the most important thing was the membership of Norway and Denmark. The Under Secretary felt confident that the Scandinavians would never be able to agree on a neutrality solution: "It is apparent there will be no neutrality pact; if there is no neutrality pact you have got a chance for two out of three."[122]

With the United States, Britain, and Canada holding to such views, there was little the continental states could do. The French argued that the Scandinavians did not really negotiate about a neutrality pact and Bonnet still showed an interest in bringing the three northern countries into the Atlantic arrangement on a limited basis.[123] However, Belgian Ambassador Baron Silvercruys signaled that he no longer saw any particular advantages in limited commitments for the Scandinavian countries. Instead, he used the fact that Norway and Denmark would be approached for membership as an argument in his opposition to bringing French North Africa and even Italy under the scope of the Atlantic alliance. He argued that Norway and Denmark would be opposed to the inclusion of these areas, and that any decision in this direction might complicate their participation.[124]

There could be no doubt as to the outcome of the discussions in Washington. No one objected when Hickerson on December 22 summed up the fate of the limited commitments concept by stating that ". . . it had been decided that the best thing was to have only one type of membership in the pact."[125] Every effort should be made to bring the Scandinavians in as full members.

However, even Hickerson did not close the door to different responsibilities within the category of full membership. But he argued that special situations could be provided for in the specialized bodies set up, instead of by making formal distinctions in the pact itself. With specific reference to Norway and Denmark, he stated that it might well be in the interest of the alliance that the two should not have an obligation to declare war in case of an attack on just any one of the member countries. "We would want them to make certain facilities available and to do certain things, but not necessarily to declare war unless they were invaded."[126] There was also the problem that although Hickerson was pressing hard for the full membership of Italy, he was running into strong opposition both within Washington and from other capitals. This might make it necessary for Italy, at least, to enter on a more limited basis.[127]

Although the concept of limited commitments had not been completely killed and buried, with respect to the Scandinavian countries the outcome of the Washington talks was clear. In annex D of the draft treaty of December 24, the participants agreed that "Iceland, Norway, Denmark, Ireland and Portugal should be invited to join the Pact if they are willing." Although this was not specifically stated, they would be invited to come in as full members. With regard to Sweden, the group concluded that it was doubtful whether an approach should be made. Chances were small that it would want to join, but if she did, "she should be welcome—the Norwegians and Danes being at liberty to pass this information on to the Swedes."[128] It would be up to Norway and Denmark to decide what information they wanted to give the Swedes. Washington did not want to do anything that could embarrass the two countries.

The United States was to be responsible for extending the invitations to the stepping stones to join the alliance. The Americans should also handle contacts in general with these countries. (Portugal was an exception in that the United States and Britain were to hold such responsibility together.) This could be seen as formalizing what had already become increasingly evident: that the United States was taking the lead even in Scandinavian affairs. To some extent this arrangement was an indirect rebuke to the French. They were not to be given any chance to present their diverging views directly to the Scandinavians, thereby causing possible embarrassment to the efforts to bring Norway and Denmark in as full members.

The Washington group even determined the time when the stepping stones were to be invited to join the pact. Invitations were to be extended after the wording of the Atlantic treaty had become reasonably definite but before it had become final. This was to be done in order to avoid confronting these countries with a definite text on a "take it or leave it" basis.[129]

Yet, the idea of arrangements short of full membership even for Norway and Denmark had not died. Interesting changes were soon to take place on the American side.

9

Climax:
The United States,
Scandinavian Cooperation,
and NATO

The Karlstad Meeting

THE AMERICANS HAD generally reconciled themselves to the timetables worked out for the Scandinavian talks. According to these, the talks would be over by February 1949. Washington as well as London would have preferred that the Scandinavians did not take quite so long in making up their minds, but since the United States, Canada, and the Western Union powers were still trying to work out the principles of the Atlantic treaty, there was little need for hurry. The main points were that the United States and Britain be kept informed about developments in Scandinavia, and that chances of Norway and Denmark joining the Western alliance were not reduced through their talks with Sweden.

Therefore, it came as a surprise to Hickerson and the State Department that Ambassador Morgenstierne contacted him on December 29 asking rather detailed questions about the contents of the pact. This was done under instructions from the Foreign Office in Oslo, the ambassador for once having counseled that it might be better to wait a little since this kind of information was expected within a week or so anyway.[1]

The reason for such haste on the part of the Norwegians was that the Scandinavian talks were approaching a climax. Before any final decision was made, the Norwegian government wanted to obtain as much information as possible about the Atlantic alternative. On December 31 Hickerson tried to make available the information Morgenstierne desired. A rough outline of important parts of the foreseen Atlantic pact was given. Hickerson also made it clear that the United States intended to sound out Norway and Denmark, in addition to Iceland, Ireland, and Portugal, as to their willingness to participate in the Atlantic alliance. Once again Washington emphasized that the question of military bases would not be raised with the Norwegian government.[2]

In rather vague terms Hickerson repeated to Morgenstierne what he had said on December 22 about the possible advantages of some countries staying out of war unless directly attacked, but this was now stated without any direct reference to the situation of Norway and Denmark. No other indication was given that variations in form of association would be possible. Some days later similar information was presented to the Danes and the Icelanders.[3]

On January 5-6, 1949, the prime ministers, foreign ministers, and defense ministers of Sweden, Denmark, and Norway met at Karlstad, Sweden, to discuss a Scandinavian defense pact. The Norwegians preferred an arrangement where each of the three participating countries was free to enter into whatever association with the North Atlantic pact it wanted. The Danes aimed at creating a grouping where its members could not at the same time enter into pacts with the Atlantic alliance. The Danish government did not, however, exclude other and weaker ties between the Scandinavian arrangement and that for the North Atlantic. It was obvious that whatever agreement Norwegians and Swedes could reach would be acceptable to the Danes. Sweden wanted a Scandinavia with no ties with the West except for delivery of arms, primarily to strengthen the weak Norwegian and Danish forces.

Despite these initial differences, the participants in the Karlstad meeting were in the end able to agree on major provisions of a Scandinavian defense pact. The Karlstad formula remained vague, but it appears that no explicit ties with the West were foreseen. Yet this fact was not to exclude assistance in case of an attack on any of the three countries. The participants were also to be supplied with weapons from the Western Powers, primarily from the United States.[4]

Major concessions were made on both sides. The Swedes accepted that the arrangement was to enter into force immediately. They agreed that the Americans and the British were to be asked about their attitude to a Scandinavian defense system, in particular their stand on delivery of arms to the countries involved. It was even possible that Greenland might be able to enter into a special arrangement with the North Atlantic powers without Denmark doing so. The Norwegians agreed to make the opening to the West much smaller than they preferred. Instead of membership in the Atlantic pact, Norway would at best only obtain arms and some measure of understanding from the West.

Some differences remained, the most important concerning the question of timing. Which was to come first, the establishment of the Scandinavian pact or the approach to the Western Powers inquiring about their attitude? The Swedes and the Danes evidently preferred the pact to come first, the Norwegians the approach to the Western Powers. But if the approach came first, what would happen if the United States and Britain stated that they could not furnish the Scandinavians with weapons? In addition, significant differences existed within the Norwegian and Swedish delegations. On both sides there were those, with strong support in their home countries, who thought too many concessions had been made.

What was the American attitude to the Karlstad formula? It could surprise no one that ambassadors Matthews and Bay reacted strongly against the compromise.[5]

Matthews lashed out against it: "I feel strongly that acceptance of the Karlstad formula by us would be generally interpreted in Sweden, in Moscow and elsewhere as a diplomatic setback for us of the first order and that it might well have serious consequences for the whole Atlantic project and for our success in the vital task of coordinating the defensive strength of all western countries now living in fear of Soviet aggression." It was only slightly more surprising that the embassy in Moscow supported this analysis by the ambassador in Stockholm.[6] Yet, the Soviet Union attacked a Scandinavian pact almost as vehemently as it attacked membership in the Atlantic alliance.

Ambassador Marvel in Copenhagen came out in support of the Karlstad compromise. While at first somewhat hesitant about it, on January 12 Marvel cabled Washington that "on reflection and in consideration Karlstad formula is based on assumption only Russia can be considered potential aggressor, I believe problem should be reconsidered in view Karlstad developments." Not only did he recommend that the problem be restudied, but it was also implicit that he wanted the Karlstad formula accepted. To Marvel it was better to have the Scandinavians united and only indirectly supporting the West than to have only weak Norway and Denmark reluctantly joining the Atlantic alliance. Since the compromise applied only to the mainland areas, the ambassador thought Greenland could be taken care of through a separate agreement with Denmark.[7]

Given the situation within the State Department in January 1949, there could be little doubt about Washington's reaction. Lovett and Hickerson effectively handled the security question between themselves. Since their view was supported by Vandenberg and the military, their position was strong. An additional factor served to strengthen their negative attitude to the Karlstad plan. At the time the State Department informed the Scandinavian countries about the American position, it already knew from Bay's reports that the Norwegian government would probably reject the Karlstad formula. Too many concessions had been made to the Swedes.[8]

On January 14 Acting Secretary Lovett cabled the American embassies in Britain and the three Scandinavian countries that "We favor Scand defense Pact provided its members are not impeded thereby from entering larger regional pact. Scand group alone clearly would not have enough strength protect its members against aggression." If at least Norway and Denmark were free to enter the Atlantic alliance, then they might also join with Sweden in a Scandinavian defense association. Without such ties to the West, they would not receive support from the United States in the form of military supplies. "We hope Scand Govts entertain no illusions on these points."[9]

This was a restatement of the Lovett-Hickerson position in terms more direct than those used on October 1 when Lovett had recommended to the Secretary of State that he tell Lange that "provided it contained no impediment to Nor and Dan cooperation with West for defense, Scand defense arrangement would be asset and valuable supplement to Nor and Dan participation in Atlantic arrangement."[10] In the period between the two messages the American attitude to limited commitments had been clarified—clarified to the point that the concept was completely rejected as a first choice option.

Nothing was to be done that might prevent Norway and Denmark from becoming full members of the Atlantic pact. With Washington rejecting the Karlstad formula, chances were seen as quite good that the two countries would agree to join as full members. Bay had made this clear with respect to Norway in his cable of January 12.[11] On the same day even Marvel had cabled the department that "By political pressure Danes and presumably Norwegians can be brought into North Atlantic pact." The ambassador in Copenhagen would personally be willing to accept the Karlstad formula, but he did not dispute that it was possible to bring the two nations into the Atlantic alliance. The latter opinion was of most importance to a State Department where Marvel had never carried much weight. In the meeting of the working group in Washington on January 13, it was evident that the participants expected Norway to join. If Norway did, Denmark was expected to follow.[12]

The Karlstad formula and the American reaction to it represented an interesting episode in American-Scandinavian relations. On the one hand, never did the Swedes make so many concessions. After Karlstad the government in Stockholm was indeed to doubt whether it had not conceded too much, as did the Norwegians. On the other hand, never was the American attitude less flexible. The result was that even at this time the Swedes and the dominant circles in the State Department were far from developing mutually acceptable positions.

American Doubts

Neither Skodvin nor the early Eriksen have indicated that there was any change in U.S. policies after Karlstad. In his 1976 article "USA i Skandinavien 1948–1949," Wahlbäck mentions that the American position on delivery of arms to a Scandinavian pact did not seem as inflexible when Lange visited Washington in February 1949 as it had been earlier. This apparent softening was most clearly implied in some comments made by Charles Bohlen. The arms question is, however, seen as largely isolated from the American attitude in general, which Wahlbäck describes as clearly in favor of Norwegian and Danish membership in NATO.[13] (Since the following represents an enlargement of arguments I have presented earlier, I will not in this brief historiographic sketch include my own writings and the response they have met with.)[14]

But there are many indications that the American position changed after Washington's presentation of its answer to the Karlstad formula. Most startling are some comments made by new Secretary of State Dean Acheson to the representatives of the Western Union countries and Canada when the Washington exploratory talks resumed on February 8. Acheson stated that "Looking at it from all points of view,

it might be that a certain kind of Scandinavian agreement involving arrangements between some Scandinavian
countries and the Atlantic Pact countries, and staff conversations and the supply of arms, would add up to something
more valuable than the alternative of having Norway alone
in the North Atlantic Pact."

This was not an isolated statement. The day after, on
February 9, Acheson indirectly indicated to Swedish Ambassador Boheman that he might reflect upon the possibility of
supporting a Scandinavian arrangement with no stronger
ties to the Atlantic pact than delivery of arms from the
United States and Britain, and staff talks between the military of the Western Powers and their counterparts on the
Scandinavian side.[15]

On the same day, February 9, the Secretary asked the
National Security Council Staff and the Joint Chiefs of Staff
several questions dealing with the position of Scandinavia in
regard to the North Atlantic system. These questions were
meant to assess the pros and cons of, on the one hand, Norway and Denmark taking part in the Atlantic pact and, on
the other, "A Scandinavian defense pact committing Norway, Sweden and Denmark to go to war in the event of an
armed attack on the metropolitan territory of any of them,
but precluding any association, either by treaty or through
military conversations, with the parties of the North Atlantic Pact." The Canadians and the Brussels powers would
urgently put the same questions to their military authorities.[16]

The United States and the other participants in the
Washington talks were in fact opening again the problem of
the basis of Scandinavian association with the West. Evidently it was no longer taken for granted that this had to be
in the form of full membership in the Atlantic alliance for at
least Norway and Denmark. Perhaps forms of association of
a more limited scope ought to be acceptable to the United
States and the other countries represented in the Washington talks?

This reappraisal was initiated *after* Norwegian Foreign
Minister Lange had arrived in Washington to seek informa-

tion about the North Atlantic pact and to discuss questions of Scandinavian defense. After the Karlstad meeting Scandinavian talks held in Copenhagen and Oslo had shown that the parties were moving away from each other. The road seemed to be open for Norway and probably also for Denmark joining the Atlantic alliance. This was a result Washington had come to favor ever more strongly. Why reconsider the U.S. position at a time when its goal was about to be achieved?

Several factors explain the reappraisal. A major one related to changes within the State Department after the inauguration of Truman for a second term on January 20, 1949. First, Dean Acheson became the new Secretary of State. Acheson had been on the outside of the Atlantic discussions. After Truman had informed him in late November that he was to become the new Secretary, he had of course been preparing himself for the job. However, Lovett would give Acheson little information of significance until he had been formally installed as Secretary of State, and after that had been done, Lovett left Washington almost immediately. Therefore, even in late January Acheson was somewhat in the dark about past discussions.[17]

Acheson's style of operating was probably one reason for the reappraisal after he had taken over. He liked to have different opinions presented and then decide from the options laid before him. This was now done with respect to Scandinavia's relations with the Atlantic alliance. As part of his process of education, he wanted the advantages of the various alternatives spelled out.[18]

Second, as already mentioned, Robert Lovett left. The Under Secretary had become a driving force for bringing about the close association of Scandinavia with the West. James Webb, the new Under Secretary, had little to do with the final phase of the Atlantic negotiations.

Third, and probably most important, Acheson made Bohlen his primary adviser on the security question, not Hickerson.[19] As we have seen, Bohlen had been in and out of Washington in 1948, and thus had little say in internal discussions. To the extent that he had exerted any influence, he had usually sided with Kennan. Now, being in the number two spot, he definitely made his voice heard. The line Acheson took in the meeting with the Atlantic pact ambassadors on February 8 had been directly suggested to him by Bohlen. On February 10 he wrote a memorandum to the Secretary declaring, about Kennan's November study on the North Atlantic pact, that "Although I was not here at the time I wish to state that I share entirely the views expressed here which last spring and summer I had talked over at considerable length with Mr. Kennan."[20]

What Kennan had written about the territorial scope of the North Atlantic pact related primarily to the situation of Italy. But as Bohlen himself pointed out, "some of the general considerations advanced particularly as to the real meaning of the pact, apply with force to the problem of Scandinavia we are now considering." He argued that the Atlantic treaty was primarily a political instrument, not a military one, as most others in Washington understood it to be. In Bohlen's analysis, the pact would not achieve its purpose if it operated in such a way as to cause divisions within a participating country or between countries. With this in mind he recommended that the Secretary read Kennan's November paper "because I think the general comments are extremely pertinent."[21]

In his memorandum to the Secretary, Bohlen implicitly referred to another, more indirect reason for the reappraisal undertaken on the American side. He told Acheson that the main reason for the inclusion of the stepping-stone countries in the Atlantic pact had been the insistence of Senator Vandenberg that this be done. Vandenberg's views had been expressed primarily in talks with Robert Lovett.

But the senator's attitude was somewhat less important in February than it had been some months earlier. In the November elections, instead of the expected Republican victory, the Democrats had bounced back with unexpected strength. After those elections, Tom Connally had replaced Vandenberg as Chairman of the Foreign Relations Committee. Connally was considerably less interested in foreign policy than was Vandenberg and there is no indication that he cared particularly about the importance of the stepping stones. Some uncertainty could even be detected as to whether Norway should now be included among these countries. On February 10 Bohlen included it only indirectly, for the importance its choice had on decisions in Iceland and Denmark (Greenland). Norway's role was similarly played down in his memorandum of February 14 to Acheson in preparation for discussions with Senators Connally, Vandenberg, and George. And this he did while discussing Vandenberg's concept of the stepping stones.[22]

The Karlstad formula apparently did not exclude Greenland from having a status separate from that of the Danish homeland. This was recognized in Washington as being of significance. Thus, in the questions he put to the military, the Secretary of State asked how the situation would be affected if, despite a Scandinavian defense pact with no explicit ties with the West, Iceland became a member of the Atlantic alliance and Greenland was covered by a special arrangement. The JCS only answered that this would be "advantageous."[23]

One reason for the insistence on membership for Norway and Denmark had been that it was generally thought that both countries would agree to come in as full members, especially if they were not given any reason to believe that less comprehensive forms of association would be acceptable to the Atlantic powers. This assumption was not surprising taking into account the reports the State Department had been receiving from the embassies in Oslo, Stockholm and in part Copenhagen, and the fact that Norway's fear of the Soviet Union was seen to have contributed greatly to the Atlantic discussions in March 1948.[24] The complete rejection of the limited commitments concept on the part of Lovett and Hickerson probably also reflected an increasing certainty on their part that there would be little need for a fallback position.

In late January-early February, however, considerable doubt arose as to whether Norway's and in particular Denmark's participation could be taken for granted. On February 1 Hickerson had to admit that "I don't know what Danes will do," but he added that "We want and need Denmark, tho." He also mentioned Norway's impression that the Danes would probably join the Atlantic pact, but only after "considerable soul searching."[25]

Denmark might choose to remain outside the Atlantic alliance. The fact that this fear was real had been illustrated by Acheson's already quoted comment to the representatives in the Washington exploratory talks. The Secretary of State had posed the alternatives of either having a Scandinavian arrangement with some ties with the West or "having Norway alone in the North Atlantic Pact."[26]

There was even some doubt about the position of Norway. All through 1948 the embassy in Oslo and the State Department had no clear impression of the scope of the opposition within the Labor party to Norway's association with an Atlantic alliance. Ambassador Morgenstierne had on many occasions stated that he was sure Norway would join the North Atlantic pact.[27]

Occasionally Foreign Minister Lange argued that something short of full membership would be the best solution for Norway. Yet, not even he did give the Americans any clear understanding of the size of the opposition to Norway joining the alliance. When the Foreign Minister explained the reasons why Norway had agreed to talks with Sweden and Denmark about a Scandinavian defense arrangement, the impression was evidently created with many policy makers that this was done for the sake of public opinion. Thus, in a summing up of Lange's attitude on November 20, Hayden Raynor told the Secretary of State that "Norwegian public opinion would not accept a breakaway from the Swedes without this final effort to bring them along."[28] When agreement had proved impossible, and this was the expectation both on the part of the State Department and the Foreign Minister, Norway would be free to join the West.

At the end of January this picture was modified. In several reports the embassy in Oslo dealt with the opposition to the Atlantic alliance much more fully than had been done before. Although these reports were based primarily on public sources and therefore gave far from complete information, the opposition within the Labor parliamentary group and in other Labor party circles was seen as quite widespread.[29]

In a summing up on February 1, Ambassador Bay concluded that in the last week

> there was an upsurge in public opposition to Norwegian participation in the Atlantic pact. This opposition was more vociferous than effective but in the event an invitation to Norway to join the pact is long delayed or if the balance between obligations and benefits flowing from participation is not clearly advantageous to Norway, this opposition could against the background of probable domestic political developments, conceivably threaten Norwegian membership.

The report concluded that "unless the unforeseen should occur," the Labor party leadership would be able to secure a strong majority for its pro-Western position in the Storting. Bay mentioned Lange, Hauge, and Secretary General Lie as the driving forces within the party. Since this group had the strong support of almost all nonsocialist representatives, there was little danger that Norway would reject membership in the Atlantic alliance.

Yet, Bay would not entirely discount the possibility that such a rejection could take place. It was not absolutely certain that even Norway, the most Western-oriented of the Scandinavian countries, would join the alliance. If it did join, as was still most likely, the Labor party would probably lose its parliamentary majority. The embassy foresaw—incorrectly—great losses for Labor in the upcoming fall elections if the party leadership came out strongly in favor of the North Atlantic pact. In this analysis, such a loss might well bring the opponents of Western cooperation to power within the party.[30]

The February 1 report met with more interest in the State Department than was usually the case with embassy reports from Oslo. Acheson commended the author on the "comprehensive and timely report concerning opposition to Norwegian participation in the Atlantic Pact."[31] Although it is uncertain whether this specific report had been seen by the department leadership at the critical phase of the re-evaluation period, reports which had certainly been received also created a better picture of the scope of the opposition in Norway than Washington had ever had before.

The State Department would have preferred that Lange had delayed his Washington visit somewhat. Considering the confusion on the American side, this was a natural desire on the part of the department. However, the Americans would not do anything to make Lange postpone his visit once it had been planned.[32]

If a Scandinavian arrangement with limited ties with the West were to meet with approval, the Foreign Minister would have to be told this. As we have seen, even those who had most vehemently argued in favor of Norway and Denmark coming in had had their fallback positions if the two countries refused to join as full members. Now the period of probing and examining was over. When Lange returned from Washington, the Norwegians would probably make their final decision on whether to join the alliance or not.

Finally, on February 5 John Hickerson had informed Acheson that the purpose of Lange's visit was "to obtain authoritative information on the North Atlantic Treaty in order to obtain a strong majority in the Norwegian Parliament for taking part in the Treaty."[33] If this was seen as the purpose, then some of the Foreign Minister's comments in conversations on February 7 and 8 must have proved surprising to department officials. On the first days of his visit Lange made a final effort to explain the advantages to the Western Powers of having a united Scandinavia. Even he, who was considered the most Western-oriented of all major politicians in Scandinavia, argued at this late stage in favor of the West supporting the Scandinavians with weapons even if their joint arrangement had only a few other ties with the West.[34]

The Final Phase

In the first round of the American-Norwegian conversations, on February 7 and 8, the Norwegian Foreign Minister did most of the talking. That was natural for several reasons, one of them being that Washington had not yet been able to decide on a clear-cut policy. The pressure under which the foreign policy establishment worked is perhaps best illustrated by the contacts between the State and Defense departments. Only on February 9 did the Secretary of State request the views of the Joint Chiefs of Staff on the relationship between Scandinavia and the North Atlantic pact. The JCS answered the next day, Secretary of Defense Forrestal stating in his covering letter that "Because I understand from your letter that time is of the essence, I am forwarding these views before having thoroughly studied them myself."[35]

On February 10–11 Washington made up its mind. Basically, the State Department, after consultations with the military and the countries represented in the security talks, concluded that the established policy had to be continued. It was still preferable to have Norway and Denmark as full members of the Atlantic alliance. With reference to the Norwegians, Acheson told Truman on February 10, "We would assure them that an enthusiastic welcome awaited them either as participants in the drafting of . . . a pact or if they did not wish to do this in acceding to it later on."[36]

Two changes would be made on the American side, however. They were both primarily changes in style rather than content. The first was to make it quite clear to Lange that the decision on whether to join the Atlantic alliance or a Scandinavian pact was a decision the Norwegians had to make themselves. The purpose of this point was to play down somewhat America's involvement in Norway's choice. Washington was not to choose for the Norwegians. To the extent that this advice served to undramatize the situation, it could be seen as a sign, however small, of flexibility on the American side.

The other change was to emphasize that the United States would not "use the granting of military supplies as an instrument of pressure." The Norwegians were only to be told that "all other questions being equal," the nations that were associated with the United States in defense agreements would have priority over those that were not. The countries in the Atlantic alliance would still stand first in line as far as supplies of military equipment went, but participation in the alliance would not alone be of such overriding importance as had generally been indicated before.[37] (The American position on delivery of arms to Scandinavia will be more fully dealt with shortly.)

Many reasons can be found for the decision to stick to the established policy, with the modifications mentioned above. The most important one was undoubtedly that it was difficult, if not impossible, for the United States to change policy at this late stage. This was most concisely summed up on February 11 by Hickerson and Bohlen in a joint memorandum to the Secretary of State:

> After careful consideration of the problem involved in regard to Norway and the North Atlantic Pact as against a Scandinavian preclusive pact, we have come to the general conclusion that we cannot at this time, without most serious consequences, attempt to retrace our steps and indicate to the Norwegians that a Scandinavian pact of the only type Sweden would be willing to conclude would have the blessing of this country or, for that matter, of the other participants in the North Atlantic conversations. Therefore, the first recommendation which we will make to you is that, as a matter of policy, we still desire Norway and Denmark to join the Atlantic Pact.[38]

Hickerson's position had, with minor modifications, been upheld. Despite the fact that he wanted a more accommodating policy toward a Scandinavian arrangement with limited ties to the West, Bohlen had to agree that it was too late for the introduction of basic changes. Nonetheless, the quotation above revealed that the two had discussed the possibility of the United States agreeing to a Scandinavian pact on a model acceptable by Sweden.

The opinions of the military also had to count. The Joint Chiefs of Staff made it clear in their answers to the questions asked by the Secretary of State that they wanted Norway and Denmark to join the Atlantic pact. Only in that way could the United States be sure that bases would be effectively denied the Soviet Union and facilities made available to the United States. A Scandinavian defense pact on the Swedish model would not be acceptable. If Greenland could be included under a separate arrangement, that would in itself be advantageous. It would not, however, compensate for the disadvantages in a Scandinavian pact.[39]

It was of great importance for Washington's attitude that the British and the Canadians preferred that Norway and Denmark come in as full members. In the meeting of the Washington exploratory talks on February 8, even Britain and Canada had shown some openness for other solutions. Ambassador Wrong had stated that Canada would be "happy to see a Scandinavian defensive arrangement on the lines proposed by the Swedes, provided there could be some organic connection between the Parties to the Atlantic pact without this involving any of the Scandinavian countries in full participation in the Pact." Oliver Franks of Britain had declared that it would be a new situation requiring careful study if it was really possible to establish a Scandinavian defense pact which did not preclude special arrangements for overseas dependent territories, primarily Greenland.[40]

However, at this late stage there was little time for further clarification. A choice had to be made. If the entire issue was not to be reopened, the alternatives were either full membership in the Atlantic alliance for Norway and probably Denmark, or a Scandinavian pact on the Swedish model. Under the circumstances there could be no doubt what Britain and Canada preferred. Even the Netherlands, which had earlier shown some sympathy for a Scandinavian solution, now felt it was difficult to change course. The only one who still argued in favor of a Scandinavian pact was Bonnet of France, with lukewarm support from the Belgian representative.[41]

To Acheson and probably to other policy makers as well, it must have counted that the Swedish position seemed to be rather inflexible. Despite the diplomatic qualities of Ambassador Boheman, when asked directly by Acheson on February 9, he had to conclude that the Swedish government would not agree to staff planning with countries outside the Scandinavian group. This seemed to be the minimum which the Swedes would have to accept if the United States were to support a Scandinavian arrangement.[42]

A change of course at this late stage would also seriously affect the Norwegian government. It would undermine the position of those who had been fighting for Norway's participation in the Atlantic pact if the United States now suddenly indicated that it could support a Swedish formula. The most spectacular evidence of Norwegian fears of a reappraisal had been given on February 7 when the Secretary of the Norwegian embassy, Sivert Nielsen, had contacted Charles E. Rogers of the Northern European Division. The two had also earlier been in contact in cases of a particularly delicate nature. According to Rogers' memorandum of conversation, Nielsen stated that "The Norwegian Government now considers that it requires all-out support from the United States in order to save itself, and the decision of Norway which can no longer be postponed depends upon that support." Nielsen went on to say that "it was now up to us: that insofar as Norway was concerned we were in a position to bring about any arrangement that we wished." Rogers could not on his own calm the Norwegian and did not make any reply. He just notified Hickerson of what had taken place.[43]

Some questions arise in relation to the statements made by Nielsen. First, what had made the Norwegians fear that changes might be under way in the American policy as this had been proclaimed on several occasions? When the Scandinavian ambassadors in the United States had analyzed the American attitude on January 29–30, no such changes had been foreseen. Kauffmann and Morgenstierne then agreed that although Washington might be open to other solutions than full membership in the Atlantic alliance, the Truman administration preferred this latter alternative. Even other solutions would have to be premised on a degree of Western orientation clearly unacceptable to Sweden. Boheman took one significant exception to what his colleagues had stated. He maintained that if the Scandinavians just went ahead and formed their arrangement without asking the Americans, Washington would probably come to reconsider its established position.[44]

No definite answer can be given to the question of what had created such Norwegian fears. It might be that Nielsen's statements simply represented a precautionary measure. What had probably happened, however, is that the Norwegians had gained further information about previous discussions inside the administration. Hickerson has indicated that Kennan even advised the Norwegians not to join the Atlantic pact. Nielsen has only stated that the embassy had at this time become informed of the broad outline of discussions within the State Department.[45]

A second question is on whose behalf the Secretary made his rather startling statements. Nielsen himself said to Rogers that he came on the initiative of Morgenstierne and without the knowledge of Lange and other members of the Norwegian delegation. Considering some of Morgenstierne's earlier statements and initiatives in this question, this was certainly a possibility. Yet, it would seem more likely that Nielsen presented his views at least with the knowledge of the Foreign Minister and that he pointed to Morgenstierne to create some distance from Lange and thereby make it possible to be more blunt in his comments. Even for Morgenstierne, it would have been out of the ordinary to have taken such an initiative without Lange's knowledge and with the Foreign Minister in town.[46]

On February 9 Nielsen again contacted the State Department. This time he talked with Achilles and said that he came with the knowledge of both Morgenstierne and Lange, but not with instructions to do so. The reason for his visit was the fact that doubts were still lingering within the Norwegian delegation about the American position. Some of the wordings used in the official talks were more open-ended than before with regard to a Scandinavian solution. Rumors were also circulating. Just by reading the *New York Times* indications could be found of the discussion going on within the State Department. As so often, some in the bureaucracy thought it to their benefit to leak information to the *Times*.[47]

Nielsen was worried if "there had been any lessening of our interest in the Atlantic Pact." He also felt that "our position on furnishing arms was perhaps not quite so firm as the

Embassy had previously understood." Achilles denied that there was any change in policy, either with regard to the Atlantic alliance in general or to the supplying of arms to Scandinavia. On Nielsen's question about the American attitude to a Scandinavian pact on the Swedish model, but with special arrangements for Greenland and Spitsbergen, Achilles answered that this was "largely hypothetical"—a response could not be given without more precise information as to the nature of the arrangements foreseen.[48]

Although many questions can be raised in connection with the two visits Nielsen paid to State Department officials during Lange's visit, there can be little doubt that they indicated fear on the part of Western-oriented Norwegians that the United States would change course. Despite his presentation of the Scandinavian alternative, even Foreign Minister Lange had declared in his very first conversation in Washington that Norway was ready to face a break with Sweden and that "the Norwegian Government had . . . made all necessary preparations to put before the Norwegian Parliament the question as to whether or not Norway should indicate its willingness to accept an invitation to join the preparatory talks on the Atlantic Pact." Such a way of presenting the Norwegian case had to put the answer on Acheson's lips. Not unnaturally, the Secretary of State had the clear impression that Lange wanted Norway to participate in the Atlantic pact.[49]

One other factor related to Norway also had to support a policy of having at least that country as a full member in NATO. On January 29 and again on February 5 the Soviet ambassador in Norway had delivered written communications to the Norwegian Foreign Office. Moscow warned Norway, although in restrained terms, against joining the Atlantic alliance. In particular the Soviet Union was concerned about the possibility of Norway opening up bases to the Western Powers. The Norwegians replied that they would not do so unless attacked or threatened with attack.

The Soviet communications made Norway's choice even more of a question of prestige than it had already become. For Norway and Denmark not to choose NATO would in many circles be considered a defeat for the alliance. Not only that, it would also be a victory for the Soviet Union. At this stage of the cold war the one was almost automatically becoming the other.[50]

Thus, on February 8 even Dutch Ambassador van Kleffens argued that the establishment of a Scandinavian arrangement with only loose ties to the West would be construed as a great success for Soviet policy. In their joint memorandum Bohlen and Hickerson also referred to these prestige factors when they summed up why the United States had to adhere to its basic policies: ". . . in the circumstances, and given the past history of the negotiations, the approaches already made, and the public interest aroused as well as the Soviet pressure on Norway, there seems to be no other feasible course for us to take."[51]

One final reason could be found why the United States still came to support the full membership of Norway and Denmark in the Atlantic alliance. This was the position of Iceland. Iceland was even more important than Norway as a stepping stone for communications between North America and Western Europe. Special arrangements could be made for Greenland under a Scandinavian pact. In Iceland, however, such a pact would quite likely affect American interests in a most negative way. Although the State Department did not have much information on the position of Iceland, it was apparently assumed that if Norway and Denmark did not come into NATO, Iceland would probably remain outside as well. In the February 8 meeting of the Washington talks, Hickerson stated that the American minister in Iceland had been informed by the Foreign Minister that it might be difficult for Iceland to join if Norway and Denmark did not do so.[52]

Arms Assistance to Scandinavia

The arms question has received considerable attention in Scandinavian literature. Both Skodvin and Eriksen see the negative American attitude to the delivery of arms to

Scandinavia as a major reason for the breakdown of the Scandinavian talks. They both interpret Washington's position as quite narrow. With the exception of certain specified countries, such as Greece and Turkey, the United States would give priority to the members of the North Atlantic alliance. Other countries, such as the Scandinavian ones, would have to compete for whatever would be left after the needs of the priority states had been filled. Most likely nothing would be left, since the requests for assistance far surpassed what the United States had available.[53]

Krister Wahlbäck, in line with official Swedish policy at the time, interprets the American attitude as somewhat more flexible. He implies that the position of giving priority to the Atlantic pact members was not fixed. A Scandinavian arrangement, once formed, would probably have received assistance from the United States after all. After the initial disappointment over not having brought Norway and Denmark into NATO had subsided, Washington would have recognized it as in its interest to cooperate with Scandinavia. It was obvious that a joint arrangement would be directed solely against the Soviet Union. To support his argument, Wahlbäck mentions that Sweden did in fact receive arms from the United States after Norway and Denmark had joined NATO.[54]

The present analysis plays down the question of defense supplies somewhat. The key to the American attitude lay in the larger question of the acceptable minimum in terms of the foreign policy orientation of the Scandinavian countries. Washington's attitude to the delivery of arms was to a great extent determined by the stand of the various policy makers in the debate over limited commitments. This debate is the most important aspect, and the question of arms should not be seen in isolation from this wider framework.

Two factors may modify this assertion somewhat. First, it was undoubtedly true that it was impossible for the United States to grant all requests for armed assistance. In late 1948-early 1949 it was estimated that the requests were three to four times higher than America's capacity to deliver. There was definitely at least a temporary shortage on the part of the United States. With Washington speeding up both its rehabilitation of surplus weapons and the production of new ones, this shortage could eventually be alleviated, but this would take some years.[55]

Second, to Congress the question of arms was separate from, although closely related to, the establishment of the Atlantic pact. The financial resources to increase arms production would have to be appropriated by Congress and dealt with separately from the approval of the North Atlantic treaty as such. A most important criterion for Congress would be the extent to which the country in question met the standards of the Vandenberg Resolution.

Yet the Vandenberg Resolution was not very precisely formulated. Its language had to be interpreted by Congress and by the executive branch. The categories of states allied with the United States or toward which the United States held special responsibilities were not clear either. If the Scandinavians were able to form an arrangement which met with the general approval of Washington, then the United States would presumably agree to supply them with arms.

Neither the shortage of weapons nor the Vandenberg Resolution was interpreted in such a way as to bar the stepping stones from entering the Atlantic pact with limited commitments. According to the September 9 memo from the Washington exploratory talks, these countries would have to agree to defend their territories to the limit of their capabilities. This provision would have been somewhat meaningless if the United States were not willing to supply them with the necessary equipment to make such a defense effective. The same could probably be said about the special status foreseen for Italy and Sweden in the September 9 memo.

With this in mind, those who argued in favor of a Scandinavia with limited ties with the West had to conclude that such a grouping would also receive armed assistance from the United States. Anything else would make the American approval illusory, since the furnishing of arms was the most important way in which Washington could support such an arrangement.

This relationship was brought out in the conversation

Morgenstierne had with Dulles in mid-February 1949. Dulles then argued that a Scandinavia associated with the West by means short of a treaty was the best solution. He did not define exactly what this association was to be, but it fell considerably short of full membership in the Atlantic pact. The point in this context is that Dulles thought that even such a grouping would receive arms from the United States.[56]

The Vandenberg Resolution did not actually prevent the United States from giving assistance to countries not taking part in the North Atlantic talks. As we have seen, in the summer and fall of 1948 the United States was willing to furnish Norway and Denmark with some military equipment. The Americans simply did not have available for anyone the kinds most desired by the two Scandinavian countries. Reasons of capacity and legality—not related to the Vandenberg Resolution—more than reasons of policy prevented the United States from fulfilling at least the Norwegian request. In 1948 the United States also gave substantial assistance to Italy, another country whose association with the North Atlantic pact was uncertain.[57]

In line with the Vandenberg Resolution, the Scandinavians were repeatedly told that priority would be given to countries "associated with the US in regional or other collective defense arrangements based on continuous and effective self-help and mutual aid and affecting our national security."[58]

How did State Department officials in effect interpret the language of the resolution? With the American attitude not quite determined on the crucial point of what exactly constituted the acceptable minimum of Western orientation on the part of the Scandinavian countries, it could be expected that the position on arms would reflect Washington's uncertainty on the larger question.

This was in fact what happened. Washington's attitude to the delivery of arms generally followed its vacillations in the question of Scandinavia's relationship to the Atlantic alliance. Thus, Hickerson tended to present the American position in more narrow terms than did most other policy makers. According to Morgenstierne's memo of conversation, on September 29 the Director of the Office of European Affairs emphasized that participation in the Atlantic pact "would be the form, under which countries like Norway and Denmark could implement association with the United States in the sense of the Vandenberg Resolution."[59]

This was a more narrow version than the official one, which Acting Secretary Lovett had communicated to the Embassy in Oslo on September 22. Then Lovett had stated that ". . . any rigid neutrality provision would appear incompatible with the intent of the Vandenberg Resolution and might well disqualify signatories from getting U.S. aid, at least until the requirements of members of collective arrangements such as that contemplated for the North Atlantic area had been met."[60]

To some extent the narrowness of Hickerson's version can be explained by the less formal nature of his communication. But that probably does not explain everything. Despite the priority given to the members of the North Atlantic pact even in the official statement, most likely its ambiguity reflected some real differences of opinion as well. What was meant by "rigid neutrality provision"? What exactly would be the degree of Western orientation necessary to obtain arms from the United States? Two months later Lovett cabled Matthews in terms almost identical to those used in September. Just to be sure the ambassador reflected the official attitude, the Under Secretary added that "we know you will be careful to avoid any appearance of desire bring pressure and on contrary to give impression of disinterest in anything Sweden may do."[61] Despite this warning, indications are that Matthews presented the American stand in narrower terms than he had been instructed to.[62]

In this as in most other questions, the Secretary of State generally followed the lead of the department officials, which usually meant Lovett and Hickerson. When on November 20 Lange asked Marshall about the American attitude to arms deliveries, he replied that this could not be answered offhand and that the role of Congress had to be taken into account. In typical fashion he cabled Acting Secretary

Lovett for advice. Lovett's answer was a general version of the Vandenberg Resolution. Lange was then informed along these lines.[63]

The only indication we have of a more personal viewpoint on the part of the Secretary is a short preliminary comment he made to the Norwegian Foreign Minister. In response to Lange's question about the American attitude to a Scandinavian arrangement without formal ties with the West, Marshall answered that "in view of the limited availability of military supplies and in light of the many claimants . . . I questioned if such an arrangement would be feasible."[64]

Marshall's answer was somewhat vague and is difficult to interpret in any detail. Since no other tie with the Atlantic alliance was foreseen than the delivery of weapons, a very forthcoming attitude could hardly be expected. Yet the Secretary's reply was a retreat from his surprising comments made to Rasmussen a month and a half earlier.

In the fall of 1948 Norwegians and Swedes disagreed in their interpretations of the American position. The Foreign Office in Oslo thought it quite evident that a Scandinavian arrangement without ties with the West would not receive armed assistance from the United States. Stockholm was not so sure about that. In this connection Foreign Minister Lange and some other Norwegian representatives took an interest in having U.S. officials explain Washington's attitude in more explicit terms. On September 7, before a meeting of the Scandinavian foreign ministers, Lange had told Bay that he "felt his position in Foreign Ministers meeting might be fortified should answer suggest restriction of aid under these conditions." (By "these conditions" Lange meant a "defense pact with rigid neutrality provision, excluding defense alliance with any other foreign power under any foreseeable conditions.")[65]

Such Norwegian attempts to clarify and buttress the U.S. stand seem to have had little influence. As we have seen, even in November Washington did not spell out in any detail what its position would be in relation to various arrangements.

A harder line could be noticed in December. This, then, would be in accordance with the sharpening in Washington's attitude to forms of association short of full membership in the Atlantic pact. The lead in modifying the existing policy was taken by the embassy in Stockholm and by Lovett and Hickerson.

On December 2 Chargé Cumming in Stockholm told an official in the Swedish Foreign Office that the "aid" from which Sweden would be disqualified until the requirements of the North Atlantic pact members had been met, might include not only arms but also raw materials which were essential to the Swedish armament industry. Such a restriction would develop if deliveries to Sweden came into conflict with those to the allies of the United States. The day after this had been stated, Lovett cabled the embassy that this interpretation was supported by the State Department. On December 7 Hickerson told Ambassador Boheman that "if we undertook a program of military supply, the demands would be as great that only qualified nations would receive any, that shortages in raw materials such as steel would develop, and that unqualified nations would probably be unable to obtain supplies from us." [66]

Hickerson told Boheman that this attitude was not meant as a punitive measure, but simply reflected limitations of supply. The ambassador protested strongly against the inclusion of raw materials for arms production. He stated that if this were to be Washington's position, the result would probably be that the plans for Scandinavian defense cooperation had to be given up for the time being. [67] That was not much of a threat to Hickerson.

In December-January the American opening to an independent Scandinavian arrangement was smaller than ever. The three northern capitals were informed, in response to the Karlstad formula, that they should entertain no illusions on the point that limitations of supply would in the foreseeable future preclude the furnishing of weapons to countries not qualified for assistance. In interpreting this position, Hickerson was more blunt than before. On January 13 he and Achilles told Morgenstierne that there could be no question of a Scandinavian arrangement which was not part of the Atlantic pact receiving any military equipment from the United States. Similar comments were made to Boheman one day later.[68]

Hickerson's wording was different from that which had been used by Lovett as late as January 11. Then the Acting Secretary had told the Norwegian ambassador that although members of the alliance would be given priority, this did not preclude other countries as well from receiving assistance from the United States. Italy was specifically mentioned as a possible recipient even if it did not become a member of the alliance.[69]

In view of the hardening of Washington's position, it is remarkable that Morgenstierne feared that the American attitude was not so firm as to entirely preclude deliveries to additional states even if they remained outside the Atlantic pact, at least not after a certain time had passed. On January 13 he asked Hickerson "whether it might develop that the United States in a year or so, perhaps on the urging of our own military, might supply arms to countries which are not in a regional association of interest to U.S. defense." In that case, the ambassador added, "the Norwegian Government would be thrown out of office immediately." Hickerson replied that "so far as I could judge such action would be out of the question." In reports to the Foreign Office in Oslo, Morgenstierne made similar analyses. Although the American position seemed clear, he reported, the possibility existed that it might change later. To prevent this, he wanted to obtain guarantees in Washington that such action would not be taken.[70]

There was reason for some doubt about the American attitude. Below the official surface, signs of relative flexibility remained. In their answer of February 10 to the questions from the State Department, the Joint Chiefs stated that even with a Scandinavian neutrality arrangement "some degree of military assistance might be provided by the United States prior to the outbreak of war to strengthen Scandinavian military potentiality." On February 8 Bohlen told Lange that "we were anxious to avoid using the question of military supplies as a pressure weapon. Membership in the Pact will be one factor but not the only one in allotting military supplies. It does not follow that countries not in the Pact would be excluded."[71]

After Bohlen had presented this open version of the U.S. position, Lange pointed out that "it is very important that we be clear on this point."[72] The day after, Nielsen expressed to Achilles his fear that the Americans had softened. The Norwegians could not at this time be said to encourage a flexible stand.

Washington in the end decided that it wanted Norway and Denmark as members in NATO. Despite the new and ambiguous wording, the Norwegians did not feel that the State Department position had really changed. There would not be enough for everyone and priority would still be given to America's allies.

The question should be asked of the extent to which the "hardliners" in Washington used the delivery of arms as an instrument to discourage an independent Scandinavian arrangement and instead bring at least Norway and Denmark into the Atlantic alliance on as close a basis as possible. To a considerable extent it seems likely that they did exploit the arms question in such a way.

There was little doubt in Washington about the importance of the supply problem for the fate of the Scandinavian negotiations. Lange and other Norwegians had repeatedly made it clear that Norway would not join a Scandinavian pact unless this could be done with the understanding and support of the United States and Britain. A crucial sign of such approval would be their willingness to supply weapons. It was of great significance that the Western Powers be willing to give such requests priority in terms of time of delivery and payment.[73] It would be difficult indeed for Norway and Denmark to afford weapons on a purely commercial basis. To the more prosperous and self-sufficient Swedes these questions were not of the same importance.

On January 13 the International Working Group in Washington noted that the Norwegians were aware of the fact that if they signed a Scandinavian alliance, they would be unlikely to qualify for aid from the United States. This was seen as a basic reason for the Norwegian government's strong attitude in favor of membership in the Atlantic pact. On January 21 the U.S. military attaché in Oslo cabled the State Department that "I believe Norway will join Atlantic Union unconditionally . . . if US stand is firm regarding military help to Atlantic Union nations only."[74] Ambassador Bay had long been of the same opinion, as had the British.[75] Finally, on February 1 Hickerson noted that "dimness of the prospect of getting arms from the west for such a grouping [a pact on the Karlstad formula] continues to turn Nor and Den to the west. We have gotten the idea across that first priority for military assistance will go to pact countries."[76]

With the hardliners definitely aware of the importance of the arms question for the outcome of the Scandinavian negotiations, and strongly in favor of Norway's and Denmark's participation in the Atlantic alliance, the temptation must have been strong to present a narrow version of the American position on the delivery of arms. It can hardly be seen as a coincidence that Hickerson and Matthews took such an interest in presenting Washington's attitude in the way they did.

To some extent it was official policy to use the arms problem in such a manner. As we have seen, NSC 28 took as its point of departure the desire to strengthen the tendency of Norway and Denmark to align themselves with the Western Powers, while making clear American dissatisfaction with Sweden's policies. In the first case to provide and in the second to withhold military equipment was seen as an important instrument to reach this objective.[77] This was even more directly brought out in the American aide-mémoire to the British of September 21 which explicitly stated that the arms question was used "as a means of influencing Sweden to modify its position of neutrality."[78]

To point out that the arms question was used to promote the Western orientation of the three northern countries does not necessarily mean that a Scandinavian arrangement without explicit ties with the Atlantic alliance would have obtained weapons if it had materialized. Again, even Kennan and Bohlen preferred that Scandinavia broke with neutrality although this break did not have to be so sharp as Hickerson and the military wanted it to be. History cannot be rerun and it is therefore somewhat futile to speculate on what would have been the American position under such circumstances. As we shall see, the fact that Sweden did receive some assistance from the United States does not have to signify that a neutral Scandinavia would have been supported in the same way.

Norway and Denmark Choose NATO, Sweden Remains Outside

After Lange had left Washington, the State Department received reports that the Foreign Minister was not quite satisfied with the results of his visit. The Norwegian had probably gained the impression that the American position was not as inflexible as he had earlier understood. Toward the very end of his visit it had also become evident that Senate leaders Connally and Vandenberg would insist that the United States could not be automatically committed to go to war in case of an attack on one of the member countries in NATO.[79]

Other factors must have contributed to Lange's wariness. What would Moscow's reaction be when the Norwegian government rejected the second Soviet note? Fears were expressed that this might lead to hostile—even armed—actions.[80] And, although the Labor leadership felt fairly sure that the party would support Norwegian membership in NATO, there was the question of how to handle the opposition to minimize injuries in an election year. Finally, although the British would support an immediate invitation to Norway, London was not really too happy to have Norway as a founding member. This would only create pressure from others to enter on a similar basis, and thereby probably delay the conclusion of the pact.[81]

Lange counseled that Norway take its time to make the decision in favor of membership. Other policy makers, with

Prime Minister Gerhardsen now in the lead, insisted that the issue be resolved as soon as possible. The result was that the question would be decided at the Labor Party Conference on February 17–19. There the party leadership won a resounding victory.[82] In his report on the conference, Bay stated that "Congress was masterfully handled by party leadership which was determined obtain favorable vote but to avoid charges of railroading only after giving opposition full opportunity express itself."[83]

After the conference Foreign Minister Lange inquired of the State Department, through Ambassador Morgenstierne, whether Norway was certain of being allowed to take part in the pact discussions once it asked to be invited. Hickerson answered by repeating what Acheson had told Lange, that Norway would be welcome to join whenever it wanted to. If a more precise answer was desired, the question would have to be put before the governments participating in the Washington talks.

That was then done in the meeting of the Washington exploratory talks on February 25. The representatives declared themselves ready to ask their capitals for immediate approval of Norway's participation. There was one exception, French Ambassador Bonnet. He insisted that all the countries under consideration for membership be invited simultaneously. In particular he argued in favor of membership for Italy.[84]

The French attitude met with sharp opposition from the United States. Washington was more or less supported by all the other capitals. As Acheson informed Ambassador Caffery in Paris, Bonnet "was reminded by various persons present of Lange's problem with Storting and Moscow, that Nor and Ital participation had never previously been linked, that present Nor situation represented crisis which must be met and that rebuff would be catastrophic." In terms quite unusual for Acheson, he informed Caffery that he had told Bonnet that the French ambassador "appeared ready, in order to get Italy in, to run extreme risks over Norway, risks to which he was not entitled to subject all of us and that if French govt insisted on this position I would not take responsibility for consequences." The U.S. ambassador in Paris was instructed to intervene with the French government and inform it of the necessity of promptly giving the Norwegians an affirmative reply to their request for participation in the Washington talks.[85]

The question of Norwegian participation would be discussed in the Storting on March 3. It was seen as most desirable, both by the government in Oslo and by the State Department, that the Norwegians be told by that time that they would be welcome to enter whenever they wanted to. Any other reply might cause difficulties for the Gerhardsen government. In addition, Norway's decision would have considerable impact on the choices to be made by Denmark and Iceland. Presumably, the better treatment the Norwegians received, the more encouraged Danes and Icelanders would be to follow suit.[86]

The inclusion of Italy would break with the North Atlantic concept geographically. Those in the State Department and among the military who favored full membership for Italy argued primarily that it come in indirectly, by its participation in the Western Union. But this had not yet been accomplished. Furthermore, at this time Norway was again seen by the Truman administration as more threatened than was Italy.[87]

Both President Truman and the Senate leadership agreed with the State Department that a firm stand be taken in the matter of Norwegian participation. The Italian case ought to be held open and only decided later. Truman and the senators even mentioned that it might possibly be better not to have Italy in the pact at all.[88] When Acheson presented this position to the ambassadorial group on March 1, he was again supported by all except Bonnet.

In the end Bonnet did yield, but only after he had secured some concessions. It was agreed that the Norwegians immediately be told that they would be most welcome to join in the discussions whenever they wanted to. This was communicated to Morgenstierne after the meeting. The same would apply to Denmark.

On the other hand, the Italian question would be taken

up shortly. The French insistence on Italian membership would weigh heavily when the decision was made. In fact, even despite the attitudes of Truman and Senators Vandenberg, Connally, and George, on March 1 Acheson signaled his readiness to take Italy in. In this he no doubt had the strong support of Hickerson and the Joint Chiefs. The Benelux representatives and Ambassador Wrong, the latter on doubtful authority, also indicated their acceptance of Italian participation, while the British made it clear that they would not object if the others were in favor. After this Truman and the senators reconciled themselves to Italy's participation, the former obviously with some regret.[89]

Norway would be told that the other countries had practically agreed on Italian membership. Thus, it would not be possible for the Norwegians, who were skeptical of Italy's participation, to delay its inclusion.[90] The French decision to yield in the Norwegian matter hastened the way for bringing even Algeria under the Atlantic treaty. The State Department, the Senate leadership, and the JCS had all been unwilling to include any part of Africa. In the end, however, Washington gave in to the view that since Algeria was part of France, it should not be excluded from the pact.[91]

On March 3 the Storting, in a secret meeting, voted in favor of Norwegian participation in NATO. Norway had made its decision. One day later Morgenstierne took his place in the Washington exploratory talks.

Now interest focused on Denmark. At this time, however, there was not much doubt about the outcome even in that country. After it had become evident that Norway would join, the Danes were preparing to make a similar decision. This was reflected at the meeting of the Social Democratic leadership on February 28. On March 2 Prime Minister Hedtoft told Ambassador Marvel that all efforts to create a Scandinavian pact had been exhausted. He would recommend that Denmark join the Atlantic alliance. The State Department was informed that Foreign Minister Rasmussen would want to make a trip to Washington.

The purpose of the trip was to obtain as much information on the pact as possible before the final decision was

made. The State Department thought the visit somewhat su-
perfluous, in particular since the Dane would receive the
same answers as had Lange. The Danish government had
been notified of the results of the Norwegian-American
talks.[92]

In his memoirs Acheson described Rasmussen as a person who moved "like a sparrow with careful watchfulness."
While Lange had impressed the State Department and the
Secretary with his courage to take a clear stand, Rasmussen
obviously made less of an impression.[93] The fact that Denmark was ruled by a Social Democratic minority government, with opposition to NATO being found even in nonsocialist circles, serves to explain the hesitancy of the Danes.
Denmark's choice was more than ever seen as influenced by
what the Norwegians had done.

An important point in the talks held by Rasmussen concerned the status of Greenland. As we have seen, Greenland
was of greater significance to the United States than was
the Danish homeland. All along the Americans had insisted
that their wartime bases on Greenland be maintained. This
had been quietly accepted by the Danish government. The
talks now led to agreement on the principle that the bases
should be considered primarily a question for the Atlantic alliance as a whole, and not primarily a Danish-American one.
This did not really change much and its agreement to allow
Washington to maintain bases on Greenland was by far the
most important contribution Denmark made to the alliance.
With the State Department being willing to issue a statement that proclaimed that the island would never be used for
aggressive purposes, the Greenland matter no longer presented any problem in Danish-American relations. As they
had with regard to Norway, the Americans affirmed that
they had no desire for bases in the Danish homeland in time
of peace.[94]

A few days after Rasmussen had come to Washington,
Foreign Minister Benediktsson of Iceland arrived. He too
had come to prepare the ground for a final decision on his
country's relationship with the Atlantic pact. Again, it was
rather obvious what choice the Icelandic coalition govern-

ment would make. With Denmark and Norway having made clear their intentions to join, Iceland was seen as sure to follow.[95]

The maintenance of its base rights was the primary interest of the United States in Iceland. The Americans did not at this time press for an expansion of these rights. They were satisfied to note that the Icelanders agreed that in case of war the Allies would be granted rights similar to those they had enjoyed during World War II. The fact that Iceland had no armed forces and did not intend to establish any did not really present any problems for the Americans.[96]

Unlike Norway, Denmark and Iceland did not take part in the final stage of the Washington exploratory talks. But along with Italy and Portugal, they did join NATO as original signatories of the treaty on April 4.[97]

Only Sweden remained outside the Atlantic alliance. As we have seen, on numerous occasions Matthews had expressed the hope that by encouraging Norway and Denmark to join the pact and thus isolating Sweden, the United States could induce the Swedish government to break with its policy of neutrality. This was not purely a hope on the ambassador's part—he thought there might be some chance that this strategy would succeed. The State Department generally considered this possibility smaller than did the ambassador, and in addition was really less concerned than Matthews about Sweden's position as long as Norway and Denmark chose to enter the Atlantic alliance.[98]

On January 28 Matthews had cabled that if Norway and Denmark joined the alliance, then Swedish accession "within areas" was not impossible.[99] Led by influential military leaders and journalists, the Swedes would come to feel the strains of isolation and enter into a closer relationship with the Atlantic powers. One month later the ambassador reported that the Swedish public was beginning to "feel increasingly isolated and consequently more drawn toward western association." This, then, was to be taken as an indication that his earlier predictions might be coming true.[100]

But even Matthews must have had his serious doubts. In the February 28 cable he also stated that he had always felt certain that Sweden would not join "at this time." The Swedes would need time to reevaluate their attitude. When it came to concrete signs of change, there were few. The ambassador also had to respond to various charges that he had been exerting undue pressure in Stockholm—such accusations had been presented by prominent columnists Walter Lippmann and James Reston. Matthews went to great lengths to deny these charges, but he was not able to remove entirely the impression of having used undue tactics, even from the mind of Secretary of State Acheson himself.[101]

It was gradually becoming evident that, in matters of arms deliveries, the State Department no longer adhered to the strategy of isolation of Sweden as strictly as the embassy in Stockholm would have wished. In 1948 Washington had licensed delivery of various kinds of less important radar equipment, as well as of minor amounts of aviation spare parts and components, radio gear, and small quantities of electronic testing and research matériel. This continued in 1949 despite considerable initial skepticism on the part of the Pentagon, and evidently even increased after it had become clear that Norway and Denmark would join the Atlantic alliance. The State Department and the military also tried to replace damaged or missing parts of ammunition on deliveries started in 1946–47, until it was discovered that this was not possible since the ammunition in question was either not surplus or not in production. Contacts between American and Swedish armed services representatives increased.[102]

The embassy in Stockholm was not always informed about these small modifications in U.S. policies. What it came to know about, it generally disliked, and told Washington so. The State Department replied that the equipment was commercially procured and in large part for commercial use.[103] It was a further blow to Matthews that the Norwegians, instead of supporting the policy of isolation, now argued that it would benefit even them if Sweden was able to build up its defenses. Ambassador Bay came to support the Norwegian line of reasoning on this point.[104]

On May 26 John Hickerson was appointed Assistant

Secretary of State for United Nations Affairs. That meant that Matthews' most influential supporter in Washington had been transferred to work where he would have little or nothing to do with Swedish affairs. Therefore, when in August the ambassador again tried to further his views through his contacts within the department, he wrote to Llewellyn Thompson, Deputy Assistant Secretary for Europe, urging that the contemplated visit to Sweden of the Senate Armed Services Subcommittee on Appropriations be stopped. Such a visit would be interpreted as a lessening of opposition to Swedish neutrality and would "reverse any trend—now being so articulately advocated by Swedish military authorities—toward closer association and closer planning with the West." [105]

It was left to Theodore Achilles to answer. The Director of the Office of Western European Affairs made it clear that the visit would take place. The only concession was that the committee would be billed not as an Armed Services Subcommittee, but as members of the Appropriations Committee. Achilles concluded his letter by expressing the hope that Matthews would be able to "manage the activities of the group as to cause you no embarrassment." [106]

There were even those who openly argued that no attempt should be made to bring Sweden into the Atlantic alliance. In late March Charles Rogers of the Division of Northern European Affairs, who even in 1948 had shown some sympathy for Sweden's position, indicated that in his opinion that country served as a stabilizing influence in northern Europe. To have Sweden in NATO might be seen by Moscow as a provocation. Instead Washington should strengthen its "silent partnership" with Stockholm, and, through a loosening of restrictions on arms exports and intelligence contacts, bring about closer relations. [107]

While the department did agree to some of the small steps favored by Rogers, his analysis of Sweden's role in general was only in part supported by leading policy makers. At least implicitly the August 15 policy statement on Sweden reaffirmed the objective of bringing it into the alliance, although it was noted that "it is against our policy to exert pressure on Sweden to join the North Atlantic Pact." The hope was expressed that Norway's and Denmark's participation, together with a growing Swedish opposition to communism and the Soviet Union, would bring about closer ties with NATO, if not actual membership. But, as the policy statement recognized in its very last sentence, this evolution "will be slow at best unless Russia takes some overt action."[108]

Despite signs of a more accommodating attitude to Sweden among the U.S. military, skepticism still prevailed among the Joint Chiefs. In an emergency war plan of mid-1949, approved by the JCS on December 8, Sweden was seen as one of the neutral countries least friendly to the West. In case of a Soviet attack on them, the military expected that Turkey and Spain, as well as Ireland and Switzerland, would ally themselves with the Western Powers, while "Sweden and Afghanistan may submit to occupation by the Soviets."[109]

Some months later the formal objective of bringing Sweden into the Atlantic alliance was abandoned. In February 1950 Acheson informed a disappointed Matthews that while the United States would be favorably disposed to a Swedish application for membership, "We do not seek such application and barring some unforeseen development would not expect to do so for at least several years." This did not mean that Washington accepted Swedish policies entirely as they were. Acheson emphasized that considerable scope existed for moving away from neutrality without joining NATO. But instead of withholding military equipment to obtain such a result, as Matthews still wanted, the State Department was now ready to loosen restrictions further, unless Sweden's desires conflicted with those of the NATO allies.[110]

It was only appropriate that in late May Matthews was transferred to Washington to become Deputy Under Secretary of State for Political Affairs. With Norway and Denmark in, the United States had realized its most important objective in Scandinavia with relation to NATO. It was recognized that the policy of neutrality continued to have broad support in Sweden, and that major changes were unlikely. Moreover, the United States already had its hands tied up in satisfying the demands for military equipment from the present members of NATO, without having to take Sweden's full needs into consideration. Finally, the argument about the effects on Finland of Sweden joining the West, never entirely discarded in Washington, was now seen to have increased validity.[111]

10

Conclusion:
Expansion
with Limitations

THERE ARE SEVERAL strands in this study. On the one hand, I have tried to place the policies of the United States toward Scandinavia within the larger framework constituted by policies toward other parts of the world, in particular toward the rest of Western Europe. On the other, I have also tried to establish the relevance of my own findings in relation to what has been written by other historians about the foreign policies of the United States. It is time to try to weave these strands together as explicitly as possible.

A New Role for the United States

The years after World War II witnessed a tremendous expansion in American commitments toward most parts of the world. Not only did the United States formulate policies for almost every region of the globe, but Washington now had considerable means to reach its objectives.

The term "isolationism" as applied to the period up to

World War II may easily give a wrong impression of American policies. True, the United States did not join the League of Nations and it did not play a very active role in European Great Power diplomacy in the interwar period. Yet there had been little isolationism on the part of the United States toward Latin America and the Pacific. And even in other parts of the world American influence was spreading.[1] Throughout the twentieth century American exports and imports had been growing, although not so rapidly. Investments had increased more dramatically. The total value of investments abroad has been estimated at $0.7 billion in 1897. This increased to $5.0 billion in 1914, and $34.3 billion in 1940.[2]

Nevertheless, there can be no doubt that in the postwar period the United States took on far more extensive commitments than it had earlier. This development was, in fact, least striking in the economic field. There was of course a continued strong increase in trade and investments in absolute figures. The sum of investments abroad increased from $36.9 billion in 1945 to $54.4 billion in 1950. But in terms of Gross National Product percentage in this century, at least the foreign trade of this period came out rather on the low side. Furthermore, both in trade and investments the Western Hemisphere was still more important to the United States than was Western Europe. Naturally, as far as grants and credits went, then the Western European countries received by far the most.[3]

The change was more striking in the military and political fields than in the economic. After the war the Americans came to take on occupational responsibilities in such widely scattered countries as Germany, Italy, Austria, and Japan— in Japan the United States even took great care to protect its role as the only power of importance. The United States established a network of bases in the most diverse parts of the world. The bases on Greenland and in Iceland were of particular interest in the context of relations with Scandinavia.

To an ever-increasing extent the United States came to use its vast resources to combat Soviet and communist influence in various parts of the world. (Until Tito's break with the Soviet Union in 1948, few policy makers in Washington made any distinction between Soviet and communist influence. The two were seen as identical in most cases.[4]

As early as the spring of 1945 most of the State Department leadership as well as many other policy makers had become convinced that the Soviet Union could not be trusted. In the final weeks of his life even President Roosevelt came to modify his belief in the possibilities of getting along with Stalin and the Soviet leaders. FDR had for some time been opposed to sharing the secrets of the atomic bomb with the Soviets. He also held back on economic assistance in the form of a loan, at least in part to attempt to temper the foreign policy behavior of the Soviet Union.[5]

After Roosevelt's death the anticommunism of Washington's policies became only more pronounced. Truman spoke most strongly to Foreign Minister Molotov when the two met in Washington in late April. Political questions came to take precedence over military ones, and the United States came to adhere ever more strongly to policies which were meant to reward its friends while punishing those who would not cooperate to further American objectives. Long before the introduction of the Marshall Plan the predominant place of Western Europe had become evident. On a yearly basis the Western Europeans had received at least as much assistance before the Marshall Plan as they did under it. Washington's purse strings had indeed tightened toward Eastern Europe well before the spring of 1947. On the other hand, the organization of America's assistance to Western Europe would be different with the Marshall Plan, a fact which was to be of great importance in relations with Scandinavia.

A similar perspective can be applied to the formation of NATO. Significant as was the participation of the United States in a military alliance outside the Western Hemisphere, that step as well had to some extent been prepared in preceding years. The atomic bomb had long been seen by policy makers in Washington as a deterrent to moves of aggression on the part of the Soviet Union. Although the new weapon could not actively be used to bring the Soviet leaders to accept U.S. foreign policy goals, its mere existence was thought to temper Soviet behavior.

Furthermore, by way of its forces of occupation in Germany, the United States was actually committed to the defense of Western Europe from the very end of World War II. After Byrnes' speech in Stuttgart in September 1946, it was obvious that these forces would remain as long as the other Great Powers maintained troops in Germany. Since any Soviet attack would probably come through that part of Europe, the United States would most likely be involved in the defense of Western Europe from the first shot. Finally, the intervention of the United States in two world wars had shown that the Americans would not tolerate the domination of Europe by a hostile power.

In the final analysis the expansion in commitments after the war was the result of the tremendously enhanced power of the United States. While all other major powers suffered great material and manpower losses, America came out of the war with a much stronger economy than ever before and with few casualties. No victorious Great Power suffered anything like the losses of the Soviet Union.[6]

To the extent we can generalize, this point about the overwhelming power of the United States is much more strongly brought out by revisionists than by traditionalists. My argument that the changes brought about in Washington's policies with the Marshall Plan and NATO can be exaggerated is obviously directed against the position of most traditionalists. In somewhat less clear-cut terms, the circumstance that the danger of a Soviet attack on Western Europe was generally seen as small by the Truman administration also fits in better with a revisionist attitude than with a traditionalist one.

Even if American policies in the period from 1945 through 1949 can be described as defensive in the sense that policy makers felt they reacted against the spread of Soviet influence, some further comments should be made on this point. First, it can be taken for granted that most countries will tend to assume that their actions represent an answer to actions by others. From Moscow's point of view I think it can be postulated that the Soviet leaders felt themselves in an inferior position compared to the United States. The Soviet expansion in Eastern Europe was probably at least in part seen by them as a defensive move to safeguard essential strategic and political interests.[7]

Second, even if spurred by its fear of communist expansion, the United States came to expand its own commitments and influence on a larger scale than did the Soviet Union. Moscow established firm control in Eastern Europe and North Korea. The communists were also victorious in China, although the Soviet Union did little to produce that result. But what about the rest of the world? Most other parts witnessed a significant strengthening of American influence. This was not so much seen in Latin America, where U.S. hegemony had long been evident, but in Western Europe and in parts of Asia. Of course, the means of expansion applied by the United States were usually different from those of the Soviet Union. The leaders in the Kremlin often had to turn to rather direct action. The Truman administration possessed not only military means, but had at its disposal an arsenal of economic and political instruments as well. Yet, these usually made America's influence no less effective, especially since Washington's forms of control were generally much more in accordance with the will of the local populations than were Moscow's.[8] Unlike the United States, the Soviet Union did not really become a global power in this first period after the war. America's influence could be felt in almost all corners of the world. With only a few exceptions, the Soviet Union counted for little outside its border areas.

Despite the feeling of the Truman administration that its actions were defensive, the increase in American influence in many different parts of the world is a significant fact in world history after 1945. Therefore, although historians generally agree that the United States expanded its role in the postwar years, I tend to feel that this expansionist side is more in accordance with the views held at least by moderate revisionists than with those of most traditionalists.

But although expansion was the main tendency in the policies of the United States, there were many limitations on this expansion. These limitations have received little attention from most revisionists. Revisionists tend to argue that not only was the United States by far the strongest power, but that Washington was also "aggressively" intent on playing the predominant role in every important part of the globe.

If these two assumptions are pressed as hard as they usually are by most revisionists, they easily come into conflict with what we otherwise know about this period. How could it be that communists gained control in Eastern Europe and in China if the Truman administration was bent on using the vast means at its disposal to stop the spread of Soviet influence? Obviously not all regions were of equal importance to Washington. The many levers which in theory were available to American policy makers had to be attuned to this fact. The strongest levers, the atomic bomb and ground troops, could hardly be actively used to further U.S. goals. They were simply too drastic for that, not only in marginal Eastern Europe, but even in China. In addition, to secure more basic objectives the United States entered into agreements which served to strengthen Soviet influence in the two regions mentioned. In another context I have dealt with the many examples of this with regard to Eastern Europe.[9] In China the Yalta Agreement could possibly be seen as a similar example. There Roosevelt made considerable concessions to the Soviets at the expense of the Chinese. In return the Americans secured Soviet assistance in bringing about the defeat of the Japanese.

Many other limitations also existed on American actions. Revisionists like to dwell on the might the atomic bomb bestowed upon the United States. Traditionalists dispose of this element more quickly. The reverse is true with the demobilization of American forces after World War II. To me the implications of the bomb and the demobilization of the armed forces are both important parts of U.S. policies. It is a fact that the United States demobilized quite quickly after the war. In view of what we know about Soviet demobilization, this process went considerably further than it did in the Soviet Union.[10] It is also a fact that American defense budgets were comparatively small until NSC-68 and the outbreak of the Korean War. Only the air force had some success in obtaining financial support; the army in particular fared rather badly. But even the air force did not in this period achieve its cherished goal of 70 groups.[11]

Despite the growth in absolute figures in trade and investments, the United States remained one of the countries least dependent upon the outside world. This would tend to give some pause to arguments about rather absolute U.S. needs to obtain essential materials abroad and to maintain growth through exports and profits through foreign investments. I do not mean to imply that economic considerations did not exert influence on Washington's foreign policy. They often did. The point, however, is that such considerations represent no universal key to American policies. Sometimes economic influences were quite important; more often they represented one of many factors contributing to a certain course of action. Occasionally such considerations had little or no influence whatever.

Finally, revisionists tend to see the expansion of American influence as something forced upon other countries. Undoubtedly that was sometimes the case. In Western Europe, however, it was generally not so. In large part the expansion of American influence there was so dramatic and went so deep exactly because the Western Europeans desired an increase in U.S. commitments in the form of grants, loans, or military guarantees. The United States did not force itself upon Western Europe. More often than not, the Western Europeans wanted Washington to increase its interest in their affairs. In some cases the Truman administration even felt that the Europeans were not doing enough on their own and were relying too much on the Americans. In connection with the organization both of the Marshall Plan and of NATO, Washington tried to make the Europeans work together as closely as possible and thereby at least indirectly reduce the role of the United States in their affairs. The administration was only in part successful in its efforts. Frequently it was easier for the Europeans to rely on the Americans than to take drastic steps toward integration.[12]

Sometimes prominent persons in Washington argued that the Western Europeans were paying too much attention to the Soviet military threat and too little to the danger of communism spreading from economic and political circumstances. Nevertheless, although chances of a direct attack on Western Europe were seen as small, this eventuality could not be entirely discounted. In cases such as these, the tendency is to prepare for the worst.[13] In addition, despite the danger being small, it had kept rising in the years after the war.

Although a direct attack was seen as unlikely, it does not follow, as many revisionists think, that the Soviet threat was largely nonexistent and artificially created for tactical purposes. From the proclamation of the Truman Doctrine on, it is true that the administration often presented the Soviet danger in more dramatic terms than was done in internal meetings. But policy makers still felt that the threat existed. Of more concern than a direct attack was the fact that communism might well expand in other ways. In 1948–49 the experience of Czechoslovakia was felt to be particularly relevant, but the Finnish pact model and the strength of the French and Italian communists were also worrisome. The shadow thrown by Moscow's control over Eastern Europe, Soviet political pressure, and economic chaos could perhaps lead to the establishment of communist governments even in crucial Western Europe. What worried Washington most about the communist takeover in Czechoslovakia in February 1948 were not consequences in Czechoslovakia itself. That country had been written off as within the Soviet sphere well before 1948.[14] The main concern related to consequences in Western Europe in the form of individuals and political parties adapting to a Soviet wave instead of being willing to take action to combat communist influence.

The 1945 to 1949 period was one of flux and development. In some areas and fields the pieces of American foreign policy fell into place quite rapidly. In others it took considerably longer. In some parts of the world U.S. interests were of such importance that great efforts were made to minimize Soviet influence. In others, where the costs of attempting to gain control would be out of proportion to the interests involved, less was done to minimize Soviet or communist strength. There is no doubt that the United States was gradually stepping up its involvement abroad, but it is important to recognize that this was a gradual process.

The same evolutionary perspective should be applied in analyzing the means with which the United States tried to influence events in a direction favorable to its interests. Some levers were such that they could hardly be actively exploited at all. Others were less dramatic and could therefore be applied more easily. The United States was not ready to do everything in its power to stop any expansion of Soviet-Communist influence. While the Truman administration became skeptical of Soviet intentions at an early stage and soon thereafter shaped its economic aid policies in this light, it took longer before Washington was ready to take up explicit military commitments in Western Europe.

In pointing out that measures like the Marshall Plan and NATO represented no fundamental breaks with the past, revisionists have generally gone too far in the direction of concluding that few if any important developments took place on the American side after the end of the war. The American-Soviet confrontation even in mid-1945 is analyzed in such stark terms that little room is left for its further enhancement. This is particularly true for the analyses of both Kolko and Alperovitz, although the two hold different opinions on many points.

This study has tried to stress three factors as being of primary importance in explaining the gradual development of America's policies. First, the nature of the Soviet threat was seen to change. Although Washington reacted against the expansion of Soviet-Communist influence in Eastern Europe in 1945–46, it was quite a more serious matter when, in 1947–48, this influence was seen to threaten even crucial Western Europe. In this context it mattered less that the threat was more political and economic than military.

Second, little need existed for the United States to intervene dramatically in European politics as long as other powers protected basic American interests there. Although Britain and the United States had far from identical goals on all points, they did have a common objective in the containment of Soviet-Communist influence. As long as the British were able to take care of the needs of the various Western European countries, the Truman administration could keep a lower profile than would otherwise have been the case. As Britain's powers declined, the United States had to step in to take over much of the same role as Britain had tried to play. The ease with which this was done illustrated that the ground had been well prepared. There was little debate within the administration as to the necessity for Washington to take over in Greece and Turkey, to relieve London of some of its burdens in Germany, or to become closely involved in the European defense effort. But especially in the last case some real differences existed as to exactly how closely the United States was to become involved.

Third, it was one thing for the Truman administration to recognize the need for an active economic and military role in Western Europe, but it was another to have its analysis approved by Congress and by public opinion. Congress was seen as limiting U.S. freedom of action as far as expenditures were concerned. Although gradually becoming even more hostile to any form of cooperation with the Soviet Union than was the administration, Congress, and the Republicans in particular, did not follow this up with any enthusiasm for costly measures to combat communist influence. Anticommunism was to be strong, but cheap. It took time before Congress became willing to face the economic and military expenses in Western Europe which the administration favored. However, it is important to recognize that, with slight modifications, in the end Congress always followed the lead of the administration.

Expansion, Limitation, and Scandinavia

Most accounts of the early cold war period focus on Europe in general and Western Europe in particular. Very little, if anything, is written about the role of Scandinavia and the policies of the United States toward this part of Europe. Since Scandinavia was a peripheral part of Western

Europe, it was to be expected that the United States would take less interest in its affairs than in those of the main parts of Europe. But the fact that this was indeed so serves to illustrate the limitations in Washington's policies toward Western Europe.

In late 1944 and in 1945 several prominent policy makers in Washington occasionally worried about how susceptible the Scandinavian countries would be to Soviet influence in the postwar period. The Soviet liberation of parts of northern Norway and of the Danish island of Bornholm sharpened this concern. But even then Scandinavia was never near the center of interest in the American capital. As the postwar picture stabilized and the Red Army withdrew from Norway and Denmark, it became obvious that none of the three Scandinavian countries would fall under strong Soviet influence. This being so, the region largely disappeared from the view of top policy makers. In the years from 1945 to 1947 Scandinavian affairs were, with few exceptions, dealt with by the regional experts in the State Department. Almost all communications went only in one direction—from the local embassies to the State Department in Washington.

It was an obvious goal for the Truman administration, both from a strategic and from a political point of view, to prevent any of the Scandinavian countries from falling under Soviet domination. With this minimum goal secured, there was little reason to pay further attention to Scandinavia, since the administration attached only little economic importance to the region. True, the military showed an interest in obtaining bases in Norway and Denmark on grounds primarily related to the responsibilities the United States faced in occupied territories after the war. But after the State Department strongly argued that this would only open the door for similar Soviet demands, the matter was dropped without any request having been made to the two countries.

The limitations on Washington's interest in this part of Western Europe from 1945 through mid-1947 showed both in the political and in the economic field. On the political side the Truman administration had few complaints about the nature of the so-called bridge-building policies of the Scandinavians. Although they undoubtedly felt closer to the West than to the East, their overriding objective was to avoid having to take clear sides. In the UN they supported the Western Powers more often than not if disagreements arose with the Soviet Union. Yet, they sometimes expressed views different from those of the United States, and social democrats in all three countries frequently criticized American foreign as well as domestic policies. They felt much closer to Britain under the Labour party than to the United States and often analyzed the cold war confrontation in terms of a conflict between communism and capitalism, with socialism being in the middle.[15]

Few if any indications can be found that Washington took serious objection to Scandinavia's reluctance to come out clearly against the Soviet Union and to become more firmly associated with Britain and the United States. To some extent the Truman administration was even willing to make concessions in favor of the Soviet Union.

This was illustrated by the Spitsbergen question. Spitsbergen was a peripheral part of Scandinavia, just as Scandinavia was a peripheral part of Western Europe, so too much should not be made of Washington's policies in this area. Nevertheless, it is of importance that in 1945 and 1946 both the State Department and the Joint Chiefs were only mildly opposed to changes in the status of these islands. Washington preferred that no concessions be made in favor of the Soviet Union. It appears likely, however, that had the Soviets pressed this issue, Washington might have been willing to yield. Many policy makers saw little significance in the Spitsbergen question at all. Despite this, Spitsbergen was one of the very few Scandinavian questions in which high levels within the State Department and the military took any interest whatsoever.

Of main importance to the diplomats and the military were that the United States obtained base rights on Greenland and Iceland, and that the Red Army left the Norwegian mainland. Greenland and Iceland were of primary concern to Washington, and were often discussed in high-level meetings among representatives from the State, War, and Navy departments. With the Azores, the Americans saw these as the most important bases they had anywhere in the world. They were indispensable for communications between North America and Western Europe. The United States would have preferred to buy Greenland from Denmark and to obtain very long-term base rights in Iceland, but in the end had to settle for much less. Greenland and Iceland illustrated U.S. expansion on the outskirts of Scandinavia, Spitsbergen most clearly the limitations of this expansion.[16]

In the economic-political field, an important American objective was to promote freer trade among nations. This did not really conflict much with the long-term goals of Scandinavian social democrats since all three countries were much more dependent on foreign trade than was the United States. Yet there were short-term differences. Due primarily to the dislocations of the war, the Scandinavians needed a period of adjustment to international competition. Washington disliked the bilateral trade agreements which they concluded to control foreign trade in this short-term perspective. But since the differences between the United States and the three northern countries were not that significant, and since Scandinavia was of little economic importance to the United States, no major conflicts arose. Even the one billion kronor credit the Swedes extended to the Soviet Union met with only mild disfavor in Washington. What objections the Americans made were apparently related less to East-West considerations than to such distortions in the flow of trade which the credit might cause.

The Scandinavian states, and in particular Norway, established a comprehensive network of regulations to control their economies—regulations which gave the governments wide powers over the way in which private business operated. While little socialization took place, in a few cases the governments built new state-owned factories. But the controls imposed by the social democrats did not cause serious difficulties in relations with the United States. It was obvious that such policies were quite different from those pursued in the United States, and different from the natural sympathies of policy makers dealing with Scandinavia. On the other hand, as long as the overall orientation of the Scandinavian countries was acceptable and the governments in the region resulted from free elections, it was not the business of the United States to interfere in their domestic policies.

One example can be found of the United States trying to halt a measure of socialization, although it is not a very clear-cut one. Sweden planned to create a petroleum monopoly. U.S. petroleum interests with close contacts within the State Department strongly disliked these plans. Others within the department, however, argued that if the Swedes paid compensation to the firms involved and if business was conducted along commercial as opposed to political lines, Washington ought not to interfere. The result was that, again, American objections were presented in rather mild terms.

Indications can even be found that the Truman administration did see some advantages in having a labor-oriented government in power rather than a conservative one. An important point in this connection was the feeling that social democrats would often be the most effective in combating communist influence. To some extent this was seen to be the case in the Scandinavian countries. Occasionally fear could be noted that a conservative government would be more nationalistic than a social democratic one. This aspect, however, was much more evident in appraisals of the situations in Britain and France than in Scandinavia. Nevertheless, Norwegian Conservative leader Hambro was no favorite of the embassy in Oslo.[17]

In the countries where the Americans established most direct control, namely in the U.S. zone of Germany and in Japan, they pursued policies with few tinges of socialism. Where the United States was free to act it generally preferred slightly conservative policies. Yet the attitude to the British Labour government and to Scandinavian social democrats showed that Washington had few difficulties in cooperating with more radical governments when their foreign policy orientation was acceptable and they resulted from free elections.

In the course of 1947 the attitude to Scandinavia changed. The situation in the three countries came to be studied with more interest than in the preceding years. In connection with the implementation of the Marshall Plan and the UN General Assembly in the fall of 1947, Scandinavian matters became of occasional concern even to top policy makers in the State Department. No longer were the affairs of the region dealt with almost exclusively by the local embassies and the regional specialists in the department.

The sources of this increased interest were the further development of the American-Soviet conflict, and economic conditions in Western Europe. It had become evident that the United States would be involved in European affairs on a much closer basis than had been foreseen immediately after the war. After the Soviet expansion in Eastern Europe, interest was focused on border areas where Moscow had not gained control.

While in 1945–46 the United States had been satisfied to have Scandinavia remain outside the area of Soviet influence, Washington now came to step up its demands. In 1947 the State Department introduced new criteria for what constituted a government friendly to the United States. No longer was it sufficient to be skeptical of the Soviet Union. Now the most important thing was to come out in favor of the United States and the Western Powers.

A new accentuation could be noticed in the final stage of the Spitsbergen question in early 1947. Despite the State Department still doing little to encourage the Norwegian government to resist Soviet demands for the militarization of the islands, other policy makers wanted to adopt a firmer attitude. This was true of the Joint Chiefs of Staff and, in particular, Secretary of the Navy Forrestal and Secretary of War Patterson. Due to their unyielding stand, a Soviet-American deal over Greenland and Iceland on the one hand and Spitsbergen on the other was quite unlikely. Yet, it can well be argued that the remarkable thing was not that Washington's position on Spitsbergen changed, but how little it changed.

The Spitsbergen question did not lead to any breaks in the American attitude to the affairs of the Scandinavian mainland. At this time the bridge-building activities of the three northern countries were still acceptable. The development of the Marshall Plan further illustrated how objectives toward Scandinavia were only gradually stepped up. At first Washington was satisfied simply to have Norway, Sweden, and Denmark participate in the plan. That was no small point for countries which had been reluctant to take a clear stand with the West. But gradually the Truman administration came to insist that further goals be met. When the Europeans did not on their own work out desirable policies to correct the imbalances of their economies, the United States intervened more directly. The Americans came to press for measures of economic and political integration. The opposition encountered from Sweden and Norway came to sour relations between these two countries and the United States.

The strain on Scandinavian-American relations was increased by the voting behavior of all three northern states in the UN General Assembly in late 1947. By refusing to support the United States on some important issues, they were seen as destroying bridges to the West. This, however, did not improve standings with a Soviet Union that was also stepping up its demands for loyalty. The Scandinavians were failing to meet the tests of either side.

The expansionist side was growing ever stronger on the American side. Interest in Scandinavia was rising. Commitments, still primarily in the form of economic assistance through the Marshall Plan, were stepped up. The Marshall Plan also came to represent a great increase in American influence on the economic policies, foreign and domestic, of Scandinavia. Norway and Denmark in particular had to agree to ban exports of certain products to the Soviet Union and its allies in Eastern Europe. The economic systems of all three countries had to adjust more, although far from completely, to the liberal ideas prevailing in the United States and in part in continental Europe. Controls had to be scaled down, especially on the foreign trade side. Payments had to be liberalized and financial policies somewhat tightened. A climate was created that certainly did not encourage any further experimentation along socialist lines.

The United States was not satisfied with changes in the economic sphere. In fact, the overriding point was that the Scandinavians be willing to stand up and be counted on the side of the West in the struggle against the Soviet Union and communism. In late 1947 this was still measured by acceptance of an ever more encompassing Marshall Plan, and "correct" votes in the United Nations.

In 1948 loyalty to the West had to include cooperation in the military field as well. After the Truman administration had made up its mind in the spring of 1948 that the United States ought to become closely associated with the Western European defense effort, preferably in the form of membership in a North Atlantic security system, Washington came to take a strong interest in the scope and content of such an arrangement. It was evident that Washington wanted the Scandinavian countries, and in particular Norway and Denmark, to take part in this common defense effort. The so-called stepping stones in communications between North America and Western Europe were seen as of great strategic significance. In addition to Norway and Denmark (Greenland), these included Iceland, Portugal, and even Ireland. The administration insisted that the alliance include the stepping stones if the United States were to participate. This was most strongly expressed by Under Secretary Lovett on December 13 when he told the representatives of the Western Union countries and Canada that ". . . if the treaty were to appeal to American opinion, membership should not be confined to the seven countries now represented at the talks. From the point of view of the Western Atlantic powers, the desirability of an association limited to these seven governments would be materially less, if it existed at all."[18]

In various ways Washington tried to strengthen the Western orientation of the three Scandinavian countries.

The United States wanted to encourage the growing Western affiliation of Norway and Denmark by extending military assistance, although the U.S. military doubted that Denmark could really be defended. Sweden, on the other hand, was to be denied any significant military equipment until it modified its neutralist policies. Not only did Washington refuse to license assistance to Sweden, it also attempted to make the British follow similar policies. The administration pointed out that while there would probably not be enough supplies to fulfill the needs of a neutral Scandinavian defense arrangement, assistance could be obtained if the three countries entered into association with the Western Powers. Finally, indications can be found that to some limited extent the United States attempted to present its economic assistance in such a way as to encourage the Scandinavians to break with neutrality and join with the West.

On a few occasions in 1948–49 President Truman himself and the top policy-making establishment even outside the State Department became involved in Scandinavian affairs. This happened in March 1948 when it was feared that the Soviet Union might try to bring Norway into a pact on the Finnish model. This fear hastened America's association with the Western European defense effort. The President was also brought into discussions about the role of the Scandinavian countries within the Atlantic security system. The military leadership spent considerable time in analyzing the strategic importance of the region and in deciding on assistance to Norway and Denmark. The National Security Council drew up several papers aimed at inducing at least Norway and Denmark to become associated with the West. All these elements were pulled together in connection with the visit of Norwegian Foreign Minister Lange to Washington in February 1949. Then, for a few days, Truman, the top military leadership, and the State Department were all actively involved in discussions about Scandinavia's relationship with the Western Powers.

Thus, the 1945 to 1949 period witnessed an expansion of American commitments to and influence and interest in Scandinavia. Norway and Denmark came to work closely together with the United States in NATO. The United States maintained its base rights on Greenland. Through the Marshall Plan and the OEEC Americans exercised an unprecedented influence on economic developments and policies in all the Scandinavian countries. Contacts between the United States and Scandinavia expanded, and not only on the leadership level. Scholarly exchanges took on new dimensions, the trade unions became actively involved, and tourism developed further.[19]

As a result of all this, it was only natural that Scandinavian notions about the United States changed too. Instead of discussing international relations in terms of divisions between capitalism, socialism, and communism as had often been done by Scandinavian social democrats in the first two years after the war, the new dividing line was one between democracy led by the United States and dictatorship led by the Soviet Union. Obviously, this development went further in Norway and Denmark than in Sweden.

Yet, although the expansionist side was undoubtedly becoming stronger and stronger throughout the 1945 to 1949 period, important limitations could be found on U.S. commitments to and interest and influence in Sweden, Denmark, and Norway. Lack of interest may perhaps be illustrated by the fact that, also at the highest level, policy makers in Washington were not always well informed about Scandinavia. Just to mention some slightly humorous examples, Acheson in his testimony to the Senate Foreign Relations Committee on March 8, 1949, evidently thought that the Faroe Islands belonged to Norway.[20] (They belong to Denmark.) Almost equally prominent persons were even somewhat confused about the status of Greenland and Iceland. It was less than clear from some statements made by Vandenberg, Bohlen, and others that Greenland was under Denmark, not under Norway, and that Iceland at this time belonged to neither of them.[21]

Such matters aside, even in 1948–49 substantial limitations remained on America's role in Scandinavia. Although the region had certainly increased in importance as compared to the attention it received in the first years after the

war, in many contexts it was still seen as on the periphery of
Western Europe. Obviously events related to the major powers of Europe had to be of more concern than what took place
in Scandinavia. More interesting, Washington did not by any
means press consistently for solutions that would bring
about the closest possible integration of the three northern
countries into an Atlantic economic and military system.
America's limitations showed both in internal dicussions
about how Scandinavia was to be associated with the West,
and in the limited means used to bring about the desired
closer integration of that region with the rest of Western
Europe and with North America.

In 1948–49 Washington undoubtedly disliked neutrality
in general, and the Swedish version in particular. This was
most clearly illustrated by Marshall's memorandum of June
3, 1948, to President Truman, where the Secretary of State
argued that the Swedish policy of neutrality "has been of
more benefit to the Soviet Union than to the Western countries."[22] Disagreement arose, however, on the question of
how much neutrality had to be modified for the policies of
the Scandinavians to become acceptable to the Truman administration.

As to NATO, there were not only two alternatives on the
American side, those of either full membership, or a neutral
Scandinavian arrangement. Throughout the discussions of
1948–49 several important policy makers thought that ties
short of full membership in the Atlantic pact were not only
acceptable to the United States, but were even preferable to
the full membership of the three countries. The principal advocates of this position were George Kennan and Charles
Bohlen, and they had support from such a figure as John Foster Dulles. While there is reason to believe that the Secretaries of State in this period, George Marshall and to some
extent even Dean Acheson, both had some sympathy with
this view, neither expressed this sympathy in any decisive
manner.

Even those in the State Department and elsewhere who
argued that full membership was the preferable solution
were ready to accept looser forms of association on the part of

both Norway and Denmark and Sweden if for some reason their first choice could not be brought about. The concept of limited commitments, with Norway and Denmark taking on partial obligations in the Atlantic system and Sweden being still more loosely attached, was consented to not only by Robert Lovett, but also by John Hickerson. And they were the top policy makers within the State Department who took the strongest interest in Scandinavia's full membership. Even the military were apparently willing to accept such a fall-back position.

This study has not attempted to give a precise answer to the question of exactly how strong the Western orientation of a Scandinavian arrangement would have had to be if it were to become acceptable to the United States. A tentative answer would probably have to vary almost from month to month in 1948 and 1949. Basically, however, the question can not be dealt with in any satisfactory way. Washington never discussed in any detail what would constitute the minimum Western orientation. As long as the preferred maximum objective—the full participation of at least Norway and Denmark—could be achieved, there was little purpose in going into the exact makeup of various fallback positions. Furthermore, if the policy makers involved were really able to work out a joint minimum position that would quite likely mean that this then would be all the Americans could obtain.

The closest we can get to an answer is for the period of reappraisal in February 1949. It is possible, even likely, that at this time Washington could have accepted an arrangement where the delivery of arms from the United States and Britain was accompanied by some measure of joint planning between the military staffs of the three northern countries on the one side and representatives of the Atlantic alliance on the other. In addition, Greenland would have to be closely integrated with the defense of the Western Hemisphere. It may be that the Scandinavians could have reduced their ties with the West even further if they simply had presented the United States with a fait accompli. About this we can only speculate. It is also open to doubt whether Swedes and Norwegians would have been able to agree on any such minimum arrangement.

The Joint Chiefs and the military leadership accepted some important limitations as far as the status of Norway and Denmark within NATO was concerned. While pressing hard for bases on Greenland and Iceland, they did not really take any significant interest in similar rights in Denmark proper and in Norway. Naturally, strategic advantages could be found for having bases there as well. And at this time some of the military were apparently not adverse to establishing facilities even on Spitsbergen. But the important considerations from the American point of view were, first, to deny bases in Scandinavia to the Soviet Union and, second, to be able to use the territory of at least Norway and Denmark in time of war.

As long as these objectives could be met, the Joint Chiefs had few difficulties in accepting the insistence of Norwegian and Danish authorities that no foreign bases accompany their membership in the Atlantic alliance. It is interesting to note that the Joint Chiefs used as one of their arguments against bases in Norway that "The development of allied bases in Norway prior to outbreak of war would tend to precipitate a Soviet armed invasion of Norway."[23] This reasoning indicated that even the military were willing to show some consideration for Soviet sensitivity in this part of Scandinavia.

Considering the instruments at the disposal of the United States, the means actually used to strengthen the Western orientation of Norway, Sweden, and Denmark could be described as quite limited. Except for hints that supplies of raw materials going into the production of arms might be cut off, trade between the United States and Sweden was conducted in a normal way. As to arms, there was no absolute denial of assistance to Stockholm. The Swedes received some equipment on a commercial basis even in 1948–49 when their needs did not conflict with those of the prospective members of the Atlantic alliance. When the British almost nullified the effect of U.S. weapons restrictions toward Sweden, Washington did little more than express its disapproval, although admittedly this was done in rather harsh words.

State Department circles tried to bring political considerations related to the East-West conflict in as one aspect in the distribution of Marshall Plan money, particularly in the second quarter of 1948. Yet this could only be done marginally. In the main the amounts of assistance given the various countries were based on definable economic criteria.

And in the running of the plan, the United States used far from all the instruments it possessed to interpret the bilateral agreements in such a way that the Scandinavians would alter their economic policies according to Washington's desires. Not only did the Americans scale down their demands for European integration significantly, but even a more limited Scandinavian customs union was not really urged upon the three northern countries. Most important, the counterpart funds, which in theory represented a formidable weapon, were hardly exploited at all. In Norway these funds were used primarily for debt retirement, thereby giving the ECA little influence over the way in which the money was spent. Certainly the United States intervened in many different areas through the Marshall Plan, but on the whole this intervention was rather "imperfect."

To a large extent the American policy toward Scandinavia was determined by the bitterness of Soviet-American relations. With the cold war temperature increasing and America's involvement in European affairs growing, Washington stepped up its demands of loyalty from the Scandinavian countries.

In 1944-45 many in Washington thought that although the United States would develop firmer ties with Western Europe than it had in the past, these ties would still be relatively loose ones. It was quite possible that the United States would take its position somewhere between the Soviet Union and Britain, the two main antagonists. Naturally the United States would be much closer to the latter than to the former, but Washington would not be so closely aligned with the British that it could not act as an occasional mediator in international politics.[24] From the perspective of 1944-45 the need for ideological conformity and military alliances was small. In 1948–49, with the United States the leader of the "free world" in a bitter and still spiraling ideological, economic, and military struggle with Soviet Communism, the need was quite different.

The American Attitude and Scandinavian Foreign Policy

By placing my analysis of the policy toward Scandinavia in the years 1945–1949 within both the larger European context of Washington's policies and the historical debate on American diplomacy in this period, that analysis should be of some interest even for the study of U.S. foreign policy in general. That has at least been my aim.

Although the question has been alluded to repeatedly, it is really a separate matter to find out how much influence Washington had on Stockholm, Copenhagen, and Oslo. To answer this fully it would be necessary to probe rather deeply into the decision-making process in the Scandinavian capitals. This would go beyond the scope of this study. Yet, let me present a tentative summary as to the influence American policies had on the foreign policy choices of the three northern countries.

It is a natural tendency for historians to exaggerate the importance of the topic they study. The field of U.S. foreign policy is no exception. American historians writing about the policy of the United States toward a certain country too often assume that Washington's attitude represented the determining factor for the policies of that country.

This is illustrated by the few comments such different historians as Herbert Feis and Gabriel Kolko make about Scandinavia's choice between neutrality and NATO. Feis states that Acheson told Lange in February 1949 that unless Norway joined NATO, "the Americans could not promise military equipment. Thus, bluntly faced with a choice, the Norwegian Parliament had authorized Norwegian participation." The conclusion to be drawn from this is that Norway joined NATO because the United States could not guarantee delivery of military assistance if it chose to stay outside. Denmark then followed Norway.

The Kolkos support this interpretation. Although they are not as explicit as Feis on this point, they apparently agree that by withholding weapons from a neutral Scandinavian arrangement, the Americans brought Norway and Denmark into NATO. Thus, despite the title of their book *The Limits of Power,* the Kolkos, like many other American historians, often see the United States as determining the attitude of other countries to basic foreign policy questions.[25]

This was of course sometimes the case. However, I feel that in this period the influence of the United States on the foreign policy choices of the Scandinavian states, although certainly important, was not decisive.

It may well be that if the United States had indicated its willingness to provide a Scandinavian arrangement with military equipment even if it had no other ties with the West than the supply of weapons, that then the efforts to conclude a joint defense pact would have succeeded. In this sense the American policy was of great significance for the decisions made by the Scandinavian countries.

Yet, it is a fact that all through 1948 significant differences had existed in the attitudes of Norway on the one side and Sweden on the other, with Denmark often trying to take up some kind of mediating position. In the end Norway and Denmark chose NATO while Sweden remained outside. These different positions sprang primarily not from Washington's attitude to the three countries, but from historical, strategic, economic, and political differences among the Scandinavians. Regardless of the policies of the Western Powers, Norway and in part Denmark simply felt much closer to the West than did Sweden.

American political scientist Barbara Haskel has explained the splits among the Scandinavians by the theory that the three countries had different fallback positions. Her point is that even if they had a common first choice—a Scandinavian pact—they were also influenced by their second and third choices in their calculations of costs. The Danish preference order was Scandinavia, West, alone; Norway's Scandinavia, West, alone; Sweden's Scandinavia, alone, West.[26]

This to me is begging the question of why their fallback positions were different. To begin with, the three countries had gone through quite dissimilar experiences during World War II. Sweden had been able to continue its tradition of neutrality that went all the way back to the Napoleonic wars. To Swedish ears, the word neutrality had few negative connotations. It had served the country well, and there was little reason to change a successful policy. Denmark and Norway, on the other hand, had not been able to protect their neutrality. The German attack on the ninth of April 1940 had shattered that neutrality and forever created doubts about the possibility of remaining outside a Great Power confrontation.[27]

While both Denmark and Norway had been attacked by Nazi Germany, only the Norwegians had immediately taken up the struggle. In the course of the war Norway, unlike Denmark, became allied with the United States, the Soviet Union, and, most closely, with Great Britain. With Norway traditionally feeling close to Britain and with the Norwegian government being located in London during the war, strong bonds were created between the two countries.

Significant differences existed among the Scandinavian states even in the period from 1945 to 1947. Norway and Denmark came to take part in the occupation of Germany in close cooperation with the British—the Swedes naturally did no such thing. Norway and Denmark received most of their military equipment from Britain, while Sweden was more self-sufficient. Economically, Sweden had strengthened its position during the war. Denmark and in particular Norway had been considerably damaged and needed their resources for reconstruction purposes. It was much more important for Norwegians and Danes to obtain weapons at the lowest possible cost than it was for the Swedes. Sweden not only produced considerable military equipment itself, but was also able to pay for whatever it had to obtain from the West.

Then, the strategic positions of the three countries were different. The events in 1940 were seen to have proven that

Norway was more exposed than Sweden. In the interwar period Norwegians had felt themselves under the protection of the British Navy.[28] After the Germans had shattered their belief in the effectiveness of this protection, the natural conclusion was that if the danger of a Great Power conflict arose again, Norway could not sit back to see what happened. On the contrary, preparations had to be made in time of peace with those who would become Norway's allies, in order to ensure the country's defense. There was little doubt who those allies would be. They were the Western Powers in general and Britain in particular.[29]

Both from a Western and from a Soviet point of view the strategic importance of Norway was greater than that of Sweden. Norway bordered on the Soviet Union, Sweden did not. Norway was of considerable significance for communications across the Atlantic, Sweden was not.

Despite Denmark having an even larger trade with Britain than did Norway and Sweden, it could be argued that its Western ties were not of such unrivaled predominance as was the case for Norway. It constituted a part of the European continent in ways Norway did not. Denmark's geographic position meant that it was heavily dependent on what happened in Germany. This resulted in the Danes feeling very exposed as the temperature of the cold war increased. Yet, the German connection also implied that Denmark already received some protection, in the form of the Western forces of occupation. These forces would be involved in case of a Soviet attack in Germany. Since an isolated advance against Denmark was regarded as less likely than that country being brought into war as a result of developments in Germany, this quite likely meant that Western forces would be involved even in case of aggression against Denmark. The orientation toward the continent also helps explain Copenhagen's acceptance of measures of European integration from which Oslo and Stockholm held back. In a similar way Greenland was already protected through the American bases there.

Yet, the impression was widespread within the Danish government that the United States and Britain considered

Denmark's security problems nearly insoluble. If Germany could not be defended in case of a Soviet onslaught, and at least before 1950 this was thought to be so, then the same would definitely be true for Denmark. Perhaps the Swedes could intervene more rapidly in greater numbers than could the Americans and the British. Such considerations strengthened the conclusion that little additional security could be gained from membership in the Atlantic alliance. Norwegian analyses of the benefits to be derived from Atlantic membership were consistently much more optimistic.

At least one other important difference between the situations in Denmark and Norway should be noted. In Norway there was considerable pressure from the nonsocialists and from important elements within the Labor party in favor of Atlantic cooperation. This was generally not so in Denmark. The isolationist tradition had remained stronger in Denmark than in Norway, both in the Social Democratic movement and within at least one nonsocialist party, the Radicals.

Compared especially to Norway, Sweden had traditionally maintained relatively strong ties with the Baltic states in Eastern Europe. In 1948–49 this showed most clearly in the strength of the Finnish argument in that country as compared to Norway and Denmark. The Swedish government repeatedly stressed the point that Finland's situation should not be made worse than it was. If Sweden joined NATO, this might very well result in Moscow once more stepping up its pressure to bring Finland further into the Soviet sphere.

Thus, from 1947 through 1948 the dispositions of the Scandinavian countries were already different. Norway, feeling exposed, its tradition of neutrality shattered, and with strong underlying ties with the British, was anxious to do nothing which might cause a break with the Western Powers. The preferable solution was to have a Scandinavian arrangement where all three states also joined the Atlantic pact. However, if the United States and Britain would not support the Scandinavian effort, then Norway would have to choose the West.[30]

Sweden, much more confident of itself, its tradition of neutrality unbroken, and feeling less exposed, would not leave the key with the West in the manner of the Norwegians. No explicit ties with the West were desirable. Stockholm considered it had gone far when it agreed to defend weak Norway and Denmark. If the three countries simply went ahead and formed a Scandinavian arrangement, the Western Powers would have to take this fact into account. It would be in their interest to develop close relations with such a group since the West surely understood that it would never become involved in war on the side of the Soviet Union.

Denmark, exposed but having little extra security to gain from a Western orientation, modified its tradition of neutrality but with not quite the same strong orientation to the West as Norway, took a middle position. Anything Sweden and Norway would be able to agree on would be acceptable to Denmark. This disposition was strengthened by the truly Scandinavian beliefs of several prominent Danish politicians, in particular Prime Minister Hans Hedtoft. However, if Norway and Sweden failed to reach agreement, then Denmark would most likely choose to follow the course of the former.

Therefore, when Washington drew up its policies in 1948–49, these would not have the same impact in the three Scandinavian countries. Toward Sweden the powers of the United States were quite limited. Although Washington did achieve its objectives toward Norway and Denmark, this could not have been done without strong forces in these countries on their own desiring such a course. This was particularly true for Norway, which would then help set the course for Denmark.

Perhaps these final comments may give us some direction as to where we, and particularly non-American students of the cold war, might move in future research. Once and for all we should try to get away from the futile search for the guilty persons, states, or systems behind the East-West conflict. More important in this perspective, we should insist on the relevance of various local dimensions. Of course U.S. foreign policy was formulated in Washington in response to foreign and domestic pressures as felt by American policy makers. Still, we understand through comparison. To understand how and why other states pursued the policies they did will give added understanding of what characterized American attitudes. In addition, the impact of American policies can seldom be determined from Washington, but only through a study of the local scene. There were obviously limitations to the extent to which the United States could determine events in most other countries.

Notes

Short Titles and Abbreviations Used in the Notes

Acheson (Dean) Papers.
Harry S. Truman Library, Independence, Mo.

Allen (George V.) Papers.
Harry S. Truman Library, Independence, Mo.

Alsop (Joseph W. and Stewart) Papers.
Library of Congress, Washington, D.C.

Baruch (Bernhard M.) Papers.
Princeton University Library, Princeton, N.J.

Blaisdell (Thomas C.) Papers.
Harry S. Truman Library, Independence, Mo.

Bush (Vannevar) Papers.
Library of Congress, Washington, D.C.

Byrnes (James F.) Papers.
Robert Muldrow Cooper Library, Clemson University, Clemson, S.C.

Clayton (William L.) Papers.
Harry S. Truman Library, Independence, Mo.

Clifford (Clark M.) Papers.
Harry S. Truman Library, Independence, Mo.

Colbjörnsen (Ole) Papers.
Arbeiderbevegelsens Arkiv, Oslo, Norway.

Connally (Tom) Papers.	Library of Congress, Washington, D.C.
Connelly (Matthew J.) Papers.	Harry S. Truman Library, Independence, Mo.
Cox (Oscar) Papers.	Franklin D. Roosevelt Library, Hyde Park, N.Y.
Daniels (Jonathan) Papers.	Harry S. Truman Library, Independence, Mo.
Davies (Joseph E.) Papers.	Library of Congress, Washington, D.C.
Dulles (John Foster) Papers.	Princeton University Library, Princeton, N.J.
Elsey (George M.) Papers.	Harry S. Truman Library, Independence, Mo.
Feis (Herbert) Papers.	Library of Congress, Washington, D.C.
Forrestal (James V.) Papers.	Princeton University Library, Princeton, N.J.
FRUS, year.	Foreign Relations of the United States, Washington, D.C.
Garwood (Ellen Clayton) Papers.	Harry S. Truman Library, Independence, Mo.
Grew (Joseph C.) Papers.	Houghton Library, Harvard University, Cambridge, Mass.
Henderson (Leon) Papers.	Franklin D. Roosevelt Library, Hyde Park, N.Y.
Hopkins (Harry L.) Papers.	Franklin D. Roosevelt Library, Hyde Park, N.Y.
Hovde (Bryn) Papers.	Harry S. Truman Library, Independence, Mo.
Hull (Cordell) Papers.	Library of Congress, Washington, D.C.
Humphrey (Hubert H.) Papers.	Minnesota Historical Society, St. Paul, Minn.
Jahn (Gunnar) Papers.	University Library, Oslo, Norway.
Jones (Joseph M.) Papers.	Harry S. Truman Library, Independence, Mo.
Kennan (George F.) Papers.	Princeton University Library, Princeton, N.J.

Krock (Arthur) Papers.

Princeton University Library, Princeton, N.J.

Lane (Arthur Bliss) Papers.

Yale University Library, New Haven, Conn.

Langhelle (Nils) Papers.

Arbeiderbevegelsens Arkiv, Oslo, Norway.

Leahy (William D.) Papers.

Library of Congress, Washington, D.C.

Morgenthau (Henry, Jr.) Papers.

Franklin D. Roosevelt Library, Hyde Park, N.Y.

NA (National Archives, Department of State).

All decimal numbers on Sweden, Denmark, and Norway 1945–1949, including the Stockholm, Copenhagen, and Oslo post files in the Federal Records Center, Suitland; Decimal numbers on European Recovery Program and European Defense; Acheson files; Bohlen files; Clayton-Thorp reading files; Committee of Three files; Memoranda for the President files; Matthews-Hickerson files; Notter files; Policy Planning Staff files; Records of the Executive Secretariat; Records Relating to the Establishment of NATO, 1948–49; State-War-Navy Coordinating Committee files; Records of Economic Cooperation Administration, Norway.

———— Modern Military Branch

Combined Chiefs of Staff files; Joint Chiefs of Staff geographic files; ABC files; P & O files; National Security Council files; Office of Strategic Services files; Central Intelligence Agency files.

—— Treasury Department — National Advisory Council files.

Nordahl (Konrad) Papers. — Arbeiderbevegelsens Arkiv, Oslo, Norway.

Ording (Arne) Papers. — University Library, Oslo, Norway.

Patterson (Robert P.) Papers. — Library of Congress, Washington, D.C.

President's Advisory Commission on Universal Training. — Harry S. Truman Library, Independence, Mo.

President's Air Policy Commission. — Harry S. Truman Library, Independence, Mo.

President's Committee on Foreign Aid, Records, 1947–48. — Harry S. Truman Library, Independence, Mo.

President's Official File. — Harry S. Truman Library, Independence, Mo.

President's Secretary's File. — Harry S. Truman Library, Independence, Mo.

Price (Harry B.) Papers. — Harry S. Truman Library, Independence, Mo.

Roosevelt (Franklin D.) Papers. — Franklin D. Roosevelt Library, Hyde Park, N.Y.

Rosenman (Samuel I.) Papers. — Franklin D. Roosevelt Library, Hyde Park, N.Y.

Ross (Charles G.) Papers. — Harry S. Truman Library, Independence, Mo.

Smith (Harold D.) Papers. — Franklin D. Roosevelt Library, Hyde Park, N.Y.

Snyder (John W.) Papers. — Harry S. Truman Library, Independence, Mo.

Steinhardt (Laurence A.) Papers. — Library of Congress, Washington, D.C.

Stettinius (Edward R.) Papers. — University of Virginia Library, Charlottesville, Va.

Stimson (Henry L.) Papers. — Yale University Library, New Haven, Conn.

Tannenwald (Theodore, Jr.) Papers. — Harry S. Truman Library, Independence, Mo.

Taussig (Charles) Papers.

Thomas (Elbert H.) Papers.

Truman (Harry S.) Papers.

UD Papers

U.S. President's Soviet
Protocol Committee.

Wallace (Henry A.) Papers.

White (Harry Dexter) Papers.

Franklin D. Roosevelt Library,
Hyde Park, N.Y.

Harry S. Truman Library,
Independence, Mo.

Harry S. Truman Library,
Independence, Mo.

Norwegian Foreign Office files,
Oslo, Norway.

Franklin D. Roosevelt Library,
Hyde Park, N.Y.

Library of Congress,
Washington, D.C.

Princeton University Library,
Princeton, N.J.

Introduction

1. Franklin D. Scott, *Scandinavia* (Cambridge, Mass.: Harvard University Press, 1975).

2. Barbara G. Haskel, *The Scandinavian Option: Opportunities and Opportunity Costs in Postwar Scandinavian Foreign Policies* (Oslo: Universitetsforlaget, 1976).

3. Magne Skodvin, *Norden eller NATO? Utenriksdepartementet og alliansespørsmålet 1947–1949* (Scandinavia or NATO? The Foreign Office and the Question of Alliance 1947–1949) (Oslo: Universitetsforlaget, 1971); Knut Einar Eriksen, *DNA og NATO: Striden om norsk NATO-medlemskap innen regjeringspartiet 1948–49* (The Labor Party and NATO: The Struggle Within the Governing Party About Membership for Norway in NATO 1948–49) (Oslo: Gyldendal, 1972).

4. For Skodvin's most extensive treatment of the attitude of the United States, see his *Norden eller NATO?*, pp. 154–70 and 260–65. For some comments by Eriksen on the American attitude, see his *DNA og NATO*, pp. 228–32.

5. Nils Morten Udgaard, *Great Power Politics and Norwegian Foreign Policy: A Study of Norway's Foreign Relations November 1940–February 1948* (Oslo: Universitetsforlaget, 1973). For his treatment of the American attitude and the importance of the polar strategy, see pp. 50–54, 136–41, 250–51.

6. Krister Wahlbäck, "Norden och Blockuppdelningen" (Scandinavia and the Division of the Blocs 1948–49), *Internationella Studier* (International Studies) (1973), vol. B (Stockholm: The Swedish Institute of International Affairs). For his treatment of the policies of the Western Powers, see pp. 39–46, 58–68.

7. The most comprehensive study on the Danish side, despite its primary focus on the Soviet Union, is still Mary Dau's *Danmark og Sovjetunionen 1944–49* (Denmark and the Soviet Union 1944–49) (Copenhagen: Munksgaard, 1969). See also the articles by Nikolaj Petersen and Niels Amstrup in Niels Amstrup and Ib Faurby, eds., *Studier i dansk udenrigspolitik* (Studies in Danish Foreign Policy), (Århus: Politica, 1978), pp. 155–235; Jack W. Jensen and Sören H. Pedersen, *Dansk*

udenrigs-og sikkerhedspolitik 1945–49 (Danish Foreign and Security Policy 1945–49) (Copenhagen: Gyldendal, 1978); Eric Einhorn, *National Security and Domestic Politics in Post-War Denmark* (Odense: Odense University Press, 1975).

8. The two works which show most (but still very little) interest in Scandinavian affairs are Herbert Feis, *From Trust to Terror: The Onset of the Cold War, 1945–1950* (New York: Norton, 1970), pp. 231, 248, 250, 268, 298, 377, 381; and Joyce and Gabriel Kolko, *The Limits of Power: The World and United States Foreign Policy, 1945–1954* (New York: Harper & Row, 1972), pp. 164, 499–500.

1. American Historians and American Foreign Policy, 1945–1947

1. In the rapidly growing literature on the various interpretations of American foreign policy in the early cold war period at least the following should be mentioned: Charles S. Maier, "Revisionism and the Interpretation of Cold War Origins," *Perspectives in American History* (1970), 4:313–50; J. L. Richardson, "Cold-War Revisionism: A Critique," *World Politics* (1972), 24:579–613; Ole R. Holsti, "The Study of International Politics Makes Strange Bedfellows: Theories of the Radical Right and the Radical Left," *American Political Science Review* (1974), 68:217–42; Robert W. Tucker, *The Radical Left and American Foreign Policy* (Baltimore: Johns Hopkins University Press, 1971); Joseph M. Siracusa, *The New Left Diplomatic Histories and Historians: The American Revisionists* (Port Washington: Kennikat Press, 1973); Christopher Lasch, "The Cold War, Revisited and Re-visioned," *New York Times Magazine,* January 14, 1968, pp. 26–27 ff.

For two historiographic books in Scandinavian languages see Göran Rystad, ed., *Det Kalla Kriget. Atombomben* (The Cold War. The Atomic Bomb), (Lund-Malmö: Studentlitteratur, 1970); Helge Pharo, ed., *USA og den kalde krigen* (The United States and the Cold War) (Oslo: Gyldendal, 1972).

2. Geir Lundestad, *The American Non-Policy Towards Eastern Europe, 1943–1947: Universalism in an Area Not of Essential Interest to the United States* (Tromsø-Oslo-Bergen-New York: Universitetsforlaget-Humanities Press, 1975), pp. 17–29.

3. Of Feis's many books, those of greatest interest in this context are *Churchill, Roosevelt and Stalin: The War They Waged and the Peace They Sought* (Princeton, N.J.: Princeton University Press, 1967), *Between War and Peace: The Potsdam Conference* (Princeton, N.J.: Princeton University Press, 1960), *The Atomic Bomb and the End of World War II* (Princeton, N.J.: Princeton University Press, 1970), and *From Trust to Terror: The Onset of the Cold War, 1945–1950* (New York: Norton, 1970).

4. Arthur M. Schlesinger, Jr., "The Origins of the Cold War" (originally published in *Foreign Affairs,* October 1967, pp. 22–52), here quoted from his *The Crisis of Confidence: Ideas, Power and Violence in America Today* (New York: Bantam Books, 1969); Martin F. Herz, *Beginnings of the Cold War* (New York: McGraw-Hill, 1969); Gaddis Smith, *American Diplomacy During the Second World War 1941–1945* (New York: Wiley, 1965); Joseph M. Jones, *The Fifteen Weeks: An Inside Account of the Genesis of the Marshall Plan* (New York: Harcourt, Brace & World, 1955).

5. Robert A. Divine, *Roosevelt and World War II* (Baltimore: Penguin Books, 1970). See also his introduction to *Causes and Consequences of World War II* (Chicago: Quadrangle, 1969); and *Since 1945: Politics and Diplomacy in Recent American History* (New York: Wiley, 1975).

William Hardy McNeill, *America, Britain and Russia: Their Cooperation and Conflict* (New York-London: Oxford University Press, 1953).

6. Louis J. Halle, *The Cold War as History* (New York: Harper & Row, 1967).

7. William Appleman Williams, *American-Russian Relations, 1781–1947* (New York: Rinehart, 1952); Williams, *The Tragedy of American Diplomacy* (rev. ed., New York: Delta Books, 1962); Denna Frank Fleming, *The Cold War and Its Origins, 1917–1960,* 2 vols. (Garden City: Doubleday, 1961).

8. Gabriel Kolko, *The Politics of War: The World and United States Foreign Policy 1943–1945* (New York: Random House, 1968); Joyce and Gabriel Kolko, *The Limits of Power: The World and United States Foreign Policy, 1945–1954* (New York: Harper & Row, 1972).

Lloyd C. Gardner, *Economic Aspects of New Deal Diplomacy* (Boston: Beacon Press, 1964), and *Architects of Illusion: Men and Ideas in American Foreign Policy, 1941–1949* (Chicago: Quadrangle, 1970).

Walter LaFeber, *America, Russia and the Cold War, 1945–1966* (New York: Wiley, 1967).

Gar Alperovitz, *Atomic Diplomacy: Hiroshima and Potsdam* (London: Swecker & Warburg, 1965); see also his *Cold War Essays* (Garden City, N.Y.: Anchor Books, 1970).

David Horowitz, *From Yalta to Vietnam: American Foreign Policy in the Cold War* (Harmondsworth: Penguin Books, 1967); Horowitz, *Imperialism and Revolution* (Harmondsworth: Penguin Books, 1969).

9. Gaddis Smith, *Dean Acheson,* volume 16 in the series The American Secretaries of State and Their Diplomacy (New York: Cooper Square Publishers, 1972). There is a curious inconsistency in the book between the main portion and the revisionist-inspired conclusion.

10. Lisle A. Rose, *After Yalta: America and the Origins of the Cold War* (New York: Scribner, 1973); Rose, *Dubious Victory: The United States and the End of World War II* (Kent, Ohio: Kent State University Press, 1973). The emphasis might be said to be somewhat more revisionist in Rose's latest book *Roots of Tragedy: The United States and the Struggle for Asia, 1945–1953* (Westport: Greenwood, 1976); Lynn Etheridge Davis, *The Cold War Begins: Soviet American Conflict over Eastern Europe* (Princeton, N.J.: Princeton University Press, 1974); Robert James Maddox, *The New Left and the Origins of the Cold War* (Princeton, N.J.: Princeton University Press, 1973).

11. For an indication of how Bernstein's position has apparently changed from one considerably influenced by Alperovitz to one more like that of Sherwin's post-revisionism, compare his introduction to Bernstein, ed., *Politics and Policies of the Truman Administration* (Chicago: Quadrangle, 1972), pp. 15–60, with his "The Uneasy Alliance: Roosevelt, Churchill, and the Atomic Bomb, 1940–1945," *Western Political Quarterly* (1976) 2:202–31.

12. Alperovitz, *Cold War Essays,* pp. 93, 95–96, 103; Horowitz, *Imperialism and Revolution,* pp. 84–89, 95–96, 190–95. See also Lundestad, *The American Non-Policy,* p. 27 and p. 471, n.67.

13. John Lewis Gaddis, *The United States and the Origins of the Cold War, 1941–1947* (New York: Columbia University Press, 1972).

14. George C. Herring, Jr., *Aid to Russia 1941–1946: Strategy, Diplomacy, and the Origins of the Cold War* (New York: Columbia University Press, 1973); Martin J. Sherwin, *A World Destroyed: The Atomic Bomb and the Grand Alliance* (New York: Knopf, 1975); Daniel Yergin, *Shattered Peace: The Origins of the Cold War and the National Security State* (Boston: Houghton Mifflin, 1977).

15. Stephen E. Ambrose, *Rise to Globalism: American Foreign Policy Since 1938* (Baltimore, Md.: Penguin Books, 1971); Diane Shaver Clemens, *Yalta* (London-New York: Oxford University Press, 1970). The main part of Clemens' book is primarily a nonideological interpretation of the Yalta Conference. Then in the conclusion it takes a clearly revisionist tone, closely resembling the arguments of Alperovitz.

16. Richard M. Freeland, *The Truman Doctrine and the Origins of Mc-Carthyism: Foreign Policy, Domestic Politics and Internal Security 1946–48* (New York: Knopf, 1972); Thomas G. Paterson, *Soviet-American Confrontation: Postwar Reconstruction and the Origins of the Cold War* (Baltimore, Md.: Johns Hopkins University Press, 1973).

17. John Gimbel, *The Origins of the Marshall Plan* (Stanford, Calif.: Stanford University Press, 1976). See also his *The American Occupation of Germany: Politics and the Military, 1945–1949* (Stanford, Calif.: Stanford University Press, 1968).

18. Jones, *The Fifteen Weeks*, p. 8.

19. Halle, *The Cold War as History*, pp. 102, 121.

20. Feis, *From Trust to Terror*, p. vi.

21. For examples of McNeill's emphasis on how long it took for the United States to change its policies, see for instance *America, Britain, and Russia*, pp. 611–12, 614, 659–60.

22. *Ibid.*, p. 690.

23. Kolko and Kolko, *The Limits of Power*, p. 46. For their treatment of the Truman Doctrine and the Marshall Plan, see, for instance, *ibid.*, pp. 336, 339, 359–60, 376–77. The Kolkos seem to view the Marshall Plan as the culmination of policies which had dominated the State Department at least since Woodrow Wilson's administration. For this, see *ibid.*, pp. 376–77.

24. Alperovitz, *Atomic Diplomacy*, p. 13.

25. Gardner, *Architects of Illusion*, p. 313. For other indications of his view on the 1945–47 period, see *ibid.*, pp. 56–57, 75–76, 206–7, 302–9. For a slightly different emphasis, see Gardner's chapter on the postwar period in William Appleman Williams, ed., *From Colony to Empire: Essays in the History of American Foreign Relations* (New York: Wiley, 1972), pp. 338–41, 345–46, 351–52. For LaFeber's view, see LaFeber, *America, Russia, and the Cold War*, pp. 6, 52–53.

26. For a summary of how revisionists deal with the various levers used in U.S. foreign policy, see for instance Lundestad, *The American Non-Policy*, pp. 27–28.

27. Gaddis, *The United States and the Origins of the Cold War*, pp. 312–13, 316–18. For a slightly different—and more traditionalist—approach by Gaddis, see his "Was the Truman Doctrine a Real Turning Point?" in *Foreign Affairs*, January 1974, pp. 386–402, and *Russia, the Soviet Union, and the United States: An Interpretive History* (New York: Wiley, 1978), pp. 180–86.

28. Herring, *Aid to Russia*, passim, in particular pp. 200, 208–11, 223–26, 255–56, 282, 287–89, 291–93.

29. Sherwin, *A World Destroyed*, passim. A good summing up of Sherwin's position is found on pp. 198–200.

30. Daniel Yergin pays little attention to this question. His *Shattered Peace* has so many turning points in overall Soviet-American relations that the term becomes practically meaningless. See, for instance, pp. 105, 162, 170, 222, 225, 334.

31. Alperovitz, *Atomic Diplomacy*, p. 240. Alperovitz, however, is not consistent in his interpretation of why the bomb was used. For indications of his vacillation, see *ibid.*, pp. 13–14, 88–89, 104–6, 113–14, 239–40. For one of many rebuttals of the

theories of Alperovitz, see Thomas T. Hammond, "Atomic Diplomacy Revisited," *Orbis* (1976/76), 4:1403–28.

32. Alperovitz, *Atomic Diplomacy,* pp. 202–3; Lundestad, *The American Non-Policy,* pp. 231–42, 361–62.

33. See, for instance, Henry L. Stimson Diary, Yale University Library, June 6, July 17 through 23, September 4, 1945; Jonathan Daniels, *The Man of Independence* (London: Gollancz, 1951), p. 266; James F. Byrnes, *Speaking Frankly* (London: Heineman, 1947), p. 265; Harry S. Truman, *Year of Decisions* (New York: Signet Books, 1965), p. 104; Leo Szilard, "Reminiscences," *Perspectives in American History* (1968), 3:127–28; Diary of July 29, 1945, Davies Papers, Box 14.

34. Sherwin, *A World Destroyed,* pp. 100–5. For an earlier version of his argument, see "The Atomic Bomb and the Origins of the Cold War: U.S. Atomic Energy Policy and Diplomacy, 1941–45," *American Historical Review* (1973), 78:945–68. For an indication of how Sherwin's findings have changed the views of other historians, see the references to the works of Bernstein under note 11. See also Brian Loring Villa, "The Atomic Bomb and the Normandy Invasion," *Perspectives in American History* (1977–78), 11:463–502.

35. John Morton Blum, ed., *The Price of Vision: The Diary of Henry A. Wallace, 1942–1946* (Boston: Houghton Mifflin, 1973), p. 305; Memorandum of Conversation by Clayton, January 25, 1945, *FRUS, 1945,* 5:966; Crowley to Byrnes, October 4, 1955, Byrnes Papers, Folder 922, p. 2; Secretary's Staff Committee, Minutes of Meeting January 19, 1945, Stettinius Papers, Box 235, p. 2. See also Herring, *Aid to Russia,* pp. 169–71, and Lundestad, *American Non-Policy,* p. 286.

36. For an account of the atomic bomb as part of the mobilization strategy, see George H. Quester, *Nuclear Diplomacy: The First Twenty-Five Years* (New York: Dunellen, 1970), pp. 1–9, 32–39. For a more detailed recent account, see David Allan Rosenberg, "American Atomic Strategy and the Hydrogen Bomb Decision," *Journal of American History,* (1979), 66:63–87.

37. Memorandum of conversations between Truman and de Gaulle, August 22, 1945, *FRUS, 1945,* 4:710. For an even more explicit comment by Truman in 1949, see *The Journals of David E. Lilienthal,* vol. 2: *The Atomic Energy Years* (New York: Harper & Row, 1964), p. 464.

38. Memorandum of conversation by the Secretary of State, November 20, 1948, *FRUS, 1948,* 3:281.

39. Yergin, *Shattered Peace,* in particular pp, 17–41. See also Daniel F. Harrington," Kennan, Bohlen and the Riga Axioms." *Diplomatic History* (1978), 2:423–37.

40. *The Conferences at Cairo and Tehran, 1943,* pp. 845–46. For a good summary of American attitudes toward the Soviet Union during the war, see Gaddis, *The United States and the Origins of the Cold War,* pp. 32–62.

41. Harriman to Roosevelt, July 5, 1943, Hopkins Papers, Box 96; Harriman to Secretary of State, December 18 and 20, 1943, *FRUS, 1943,* 3:728–33; Harriman to Secretary of State, August 17, 1944, *ibid.,* p. 1389, note 11.

42. Harriman to Secretary of State, August 17, 1944, *FRUS, 1944,* 3:1389, note 11; Hull to Harriman, September 18, 1944, *FRUS, 1944,* 4:991; Memorandum by Bohlen, September 19, 1944, and Harriman to Secretary of State, September 20, 1944, *ibid.,* pp. 992–98.

Kennan to Harriman, September 19, 1944, Kennan Papers, Box 3; Memorandum by George Kennan, September 1944, *FRUS, 1944,* 4:902–14; Blum, ed., *The Price of Vision,* October 6, 1944; Averell Harriman, *America and Russia in a*

Changing World: A Half Century of Personal Observation (Garden City, N.Y.: Doubleday, 1971), p. 43.

43. Cordell Hull, *The Memoirs of Cordell Hull* (New York: Macmillan, 1948), 2:1460; Hull to Harriman, September 18, 1944, *FRUS, 1944,* 4:991; *The Conference at Quebec, 1944,* State Department Briefing papers on the Soviet Union and on Poland, undated, pp. 193–94; Joseph C. Grew, *Turbulent Era: A Diplomatic Record of Forty Years, 1904–1945* (London: Hammond, Hammond, 1953), pp. 1445–47. See also references under note 44.

44. For Forrestal and the Navy Department, see Vincent Davis, *Postwar Defense Policy and the US Navy, 1943–1946* (Chapel Hill: University of North Carolina Press, 1966), pp. 101–2; Walter Millis, ed., *The Forrestal Diaries* (New York: Viking, 1951), p. 14. There are few references to the Soviet danger in Forrestal's papers and diary before September 1944. Afterward they are numerous.

45. For a discussion of Roosevelt's attitude, see Lundestad, *The American Non-Policy,* pp. 199–200.

46. Accounts of the meetings in connection with Molotov's visit are found in Truman, *Year of Decisions,* pp. 93–95; Millis, *Forrestal Diaries,* pp. 49–50; William D. Leahy, *I Was There* (London: Gollancz, 1950), pp. 411–14; Minutes on meetings regarding the Polish question, *FRUS, 1945,* 5:237–40, 252–57.

47. A discussion of Byrnes's role in the negotiation of the peace treaties for the Axis satellites in Eastern Europe is found in Lundestad, *The American Non-Policy,* pp. 329–46.

48. For an account of the firing of Wallace in September 1946, see for instance Gaddis, *The United States and the Origins of the Cold War,* pp. 337–41. For Stimson's position, see Lundestad, *The American Non-Policy,* pp. 73–74. For an analysis of the attitudes of the military leadership, see Michael Sherry, *Preparing for the Next War: American Plans for Postwar Defense, 1941–45* (New Haven: Yale University Press, 1977), pp. 159–60, 213–19.

49. Gaddis, *The United States and the Origins of the Cold War,* pp. 357–61.

50. Hadley Cantril and Mildred Strunk, eds., *Public Opinion, 1935–1946* (Princeton, N.J.: Princeton University Press, 1951), pp. 370–71. For two studies of U.S. opinion on the Soviet Union, see Harold J. Sylvester, "American Public Reaction to Communist Expansion: From Yalta to NATO," Ph.D. dissertation, St. Louis University, 1972, in particular pp. 34–42, 52–65; Ralph B. Levering, *American Opinion and the Russian Alliance, 1939–1945* (Chapel Hill: University of North Carolina Press, 1976), in particular pp. 194–99.

51. For an account of this incident, see Harriman, *America and Russia,* pp. 42–43.

52. Francis Williams, ed., *A Prime Minister Remembers: The War and Post-War Memoirs of the R. Hon. Earl Attlee* (London: Heineman, 1961), pp. 162–63; Leahy Diary, February 10, March 3, 5, 1946; Gaddis, *The United States and the Origins of the Cold War,* pp. 307–9. George Curry, *James F. Byrnes,* vol. 14 in the series The American Secretaries of State and Their Diplomacy (New York: Cooper Square Publishers, 1965), pp. 202–4.

53. For a similar argument, see Walter LaFeber, "American Policy Makers, Public Opinion, and the Outbreak of the Cold War, 1945–50," in Yonosuke Nagai and Akira Iriye, eds., *The Origins of the Cold War in Asia* (New York: Columbia University Press, 1977), pp. 43–65. Both LaFeber's and my own arguments undoubtedly need to be considerably refined. Obviously, the impact of Congress and of public opinion varied somewhat from question to question. In some cases the fiscal conservatism of Congress would strain relations with the Soviet Union (as to loans

to the Soviet Union and the Eastern European countries), in others it would have the opposite effect (as to appropriations for the Marshall Plan and military assistance to Western Europe). This is not the place, however, to elaborate further on this. For an interesting article on the role of Congress, see John T. Rourke, "Congress and the Cold War," *World Affairs* (1976/77), 4:259–77.

54. For the 1945–1947 figures, see *The European Recovery Program: Basic Documents and Background Information* (Washington, D.C., 1947), pp. 30–32; U.S. Foreign Assistance Programs as of December 31, 1947, *FRUS, 1947*, 1:1026–27. It should be noted that the figures for assistance given through the Marshall Plan vary somewhat from publication to publication depending on exactly what is included in the various figures.

55. For an account of American economic assistance to Eastern Europe, see Lundestad, *The American Non-Policy*. A summary of this aspect is found on pp. 392–94. For the attitude toward Czechoslovakia, see *ibid.*, pp. 167–73.

56. Byrnes to Clayton, September 24, 1946, *FRUS, 1946*, 7:223.

57. Memo of State Department Meeting, October 28, 1946, *ibid.*, p. 255.

58. *Ibid.*, p. 255; Lundestad, *The American Non-Policy*, pp. 170–72; Gaddis, *The United States and the Origins of the Cold War*, pp. 336–37.

59. For an account of U.S. policies in Latin America after World War II, see for instance David Green, *The Containment of Latin America: A History of the Myths and Realities of the Good Neighbor Policy* (Chicago: Quadrangle, 1971). See also Green's "The Cold War Comes to Latin America," in Bernstein, ed., *Politics and Policies of the Truman Administration*, pp. 149–95. Two works by Thomas M. Campbell that deal with the debate in Washington in 1944–45 on the role of Latin America are *Masquerade Peace: America's UN Policy, 1944–1945* (Tallahassee: Florida State University Press, 1973), pp. 159–75, and "Nationalism in America's UN Policy, 1944–1945," *International Organization* (1973), 27:25–44.

60. Record of conversation Byrnes-Bevin, December 17, 1945, *FRUS, 1945*, 2:629.

61. Millis, *Forrestal Diaries*, pp. 44–45; Byrnes, *Speaking Frankly*, pp. 219–21. For a striking example of Truman's attitude in this case, see *The Public Papers of Harry S. Truman, 1946*, pp. 20–21.

62. *New York Times*, September 23, 1945, p. 3. See also Truman, *Year of Decisions*, p. 455.

63. See, for instance, Dean Acheson, *Present at the Creation: My Years in the State Department* (New York: Norton, 1969), pp. 426–28.

64. Apparently not much research has been done on postwar American-Philippine relations. For a summary of what has been done, see Peter W. Stanley, "The Forgotten Philippines, 1790–1946," in Ernest R. May and James C. Thomson, Jr., eds., *American-East Asian Relations: A Survey* (Cambridge, Mass.: Harvard University Press), pp. 291–316, in particular pp. 309–12.

65. See *FRUS, 1946*, 1:1110–96, in particular Memorandum Prepared for Secretary of Staff Committee, November 16, 1945, pp. 1123–28, and Memorandum by Joint Chiefs of Staff to State-War-Navy Coordinating Committee, June 5, 1946, pp. 1174–77.

66. Matthews to Hayter, January 19, 1944, *FRUS, 1944*, 1:20. For a discussion of areas of military responsibility, see Lundestad, *American Non-Policy*, pp. 75–88.

67. Lundestad, *The American Non-Policy*, pp. 81–88.

68. *Ibid.*, pp. 81–82. See also John C. Campbell, *The United States in World Affairs, 1945–1947* (New York: Harper, 1948), p. 54.

69. Gimbel, *Origins of the Marshall Plan*, pp. 122–26.

70. *The Conference of Berlin,* 1, nos. 223 and 224, pp. 253–64, especially pp. 259, 262–64, State Department Briefing Book papers.

71. This is succinctly brought out in Jim Peck's article "America and the Chinese Revolution, 1942–1946: An Interpretation," in May and Thomson, *American-East Asian Relations: A Survey,* pp. 319–55, in particular pp. 349–55.

72. The best account of U.S. policies toward China in this period is probably still Tang Tsou, *America's Failure in China, 1945–50* (Chicago: University of Chicago Press, 1963). See also Herbert Feis, *The China Tangle* (Princeton, N.J.: Princeton University Press, 1953); Ernest R. May, *The Truman Administration and China, 1945–1949* (Philadelphia: Lippincott, 1975).

73. Tang Tsou, *America's Failure in China,* pp. 466–79.

74. Kolko and Kolko, *The Limits of Power,* pp. 246–76, 534–62. Kolko's general harangues are most prominent in the conclusions of *The Limits of Power* and *The Politics of War.* For further comments on this aspect in relation to other revisionists, see Lundestad, *The American Non-Policy,* pp. 421–22. Kolko's argument that U.S. capitalists did not make a determined effort to save Chiang because they saw little difference between Nationalist and Communist policies will not do. For a rebuttal of this argument, see May, *The Truman Administration and China,* pp. 37–38, 106.

75. For a valuable anthology on the early phase of the cold war in Asia, see Nagai and Iriye, *The Origins of the Cold War in Asia.* For articles on Vietnam and Korea by George McT. Kahin and John Lewis Gaddis, see pp. 277–98, 338–61.

76. U.S. House, Committee on Foreign Relations, *Hearings on Assistance to Greece and Turkey,* 80th Congress, 1st Session, pp. 14–15; Jones, *The Fifteen Weeks,* pp. 193–94; Acheson, *Present at the Creation,* pp. 224–24.

77. For an account of U.S. policies toward Hungary at this time, see Lundestad, *The American Non-Policy,* pp. 135–46.

78. The paragraphs that follow represent the gist of the argument in my *The American Non-Policy.* See in particular pp. 98–104.

79. Truman, *Year of Decision,* pp. 560–63; Millis, *Forrestal Diaries,* pp. 102, 129; Department of State *Bulletin,* March 24, 1946, p. 482; Byrnes to Patterson, November 29, 1945, *FRUS, 1946,* 1:1128–29. The figures mentioned are taken from Oscar T. Barck, *A History of the United States Since 1945* (New York: Dell, Laurel edition, 1965), pp. 36–39. See also Quester, *Nuclear Diplomacy,* p. 294.

80. The quotation is from Ambrose, *Rise to Globalism,* p. 138. For similar comments, see Patterson to Byrnes, February 11, 1947, Byrnes Papers, Folder 673; Blum, *The Price of Vision,* September 18, 1946; Minutes of Meetings, January 3 and 10, 1947, President's Advisory Commission on Universal Training, Selected Records, 1946–1947, Box 2, Folder: Universal Military Training, and Testimony by Byrnes, pp. 193, 195, 197.

81. Thomas W. Wolfe, *Soviet Power and Europe, 1945–1970* (Baltimore, Md.: Johns Hopkins University Press, 1970), pp. 10–11. See also Adam B. Ulam, *The Rivals: America and Russia Since World War II* (New York: Viking, 1971); pp. 130–31; Quester, *Nuclear Diplomacy,* p. 294.

82. Gaddis, "Was the Truman Doctrine a Real Turning Point?" pp. 386–402.

83. Accounts about the development of the defense budget in the 1945–50 period are found in Edward A. Kolodziej, *The Uncommon Defense and Congress, 1945–1963* (Columbus: Ohio State University Press, 1966); Samuel P. Huntington, *The Common Defense: Strategic Programs in National Politics* (New York: Columbia University Press, 1961), pp. 33–47; Paul Y. Hammond, "Super Carriers and B-36 Bombers: Appropriations, Strategy and Politics," in Harold Stein, ed., *American Civil-Military Decisions: A Book of Case Studies* (Birmingham: University of Ala-

bama Press, 1963), pp. 465–567; Hans Günter Brauch, "Struktureller Wandel und Rüstungspolitik der USA (1940–1950). Zur Weltführungsrolle und Ihren Innenpolitischen Bedingungen," Ph.D. dissertation, University of Heidelberg, West Germany, 1976 (Ann Arbor: University Microfilms), pp. 635, 641, 658–63, 839, 1119, 1163–64, 1169–70.

84. For a further discussion of this, with particular relevance for American policies toward Eastern Europe, see Lundestad, *The American Non-Policy*, pp. 304–24.

85. U.S. Dept. of Commerce, Bureau of the Census, *Historical Statistics of the United States: Colonial Times to 1970* (Washington, D.C., 1975), pp. 884–87. These figures seem to be at odds with the graphic illustration of the development of U.S. foreign trade and investment in this century in Bruce M. Russett and Elizabeth C. Hanson, *Interest and Ideology: The Foreign Policy Beliefs of American Businessmen* (San Francisco: Freeman, 1975), p. 39. See also Nils Petter Gleditsch, *Norge i verdenssamfunnet* (Norway in the World Community) (Oslo: Pax, 1970), pp. 229–30.

86. *Historical Statistics of the United States*, pp. 870–72, Feis, *From Trust to Terror*, p. 228.

87. This aspect will be further discussed in chapter 6. For accounts of British foreign and defense policies in the postwar era, see Christopher Montague Woodhouse, *British Foreign Policy Since the Second World War* (London: Hutchinson, 1961); Christopher John Bartlett, *The Long Retreat: A Short History of British Defense Policy, 1945–70* (London: Macmillan, 1972). See also Williams, *A Prime Minister Remembers*, and *The Memoirs of Field-Marshal the Viscount Montgomery of Alamein* (London: Heineman, 1958).

2. American Policies Toward Scandinavia, 1945–1947

1. For further comments on this, see Geir Lundestad, *The American Non-Policy Towards Eastern Europe 1943–1947: Universalism in an Area Not of Essential Interest to the United States* (Tromsø-Oslo-Bergen-New York: Universitetsforlaget-Humanities Press, 1975), pp. 18–28.

2. Walter LaFeber, *America, Russia, and the Cold War, 1945–1966* (New York: Wiley, 1967), p. 6. In this respect Lloyd Gardner seems to differ somewhat from other revisionists. For this and the opposition of Williams to Gardner, see William Appleman Williams, ed., *From Colony to Empire: Essays in the History of American Foreign Relations* (New York: Wiley, 1972), p. 6.

3. Harry S. Truman, *Year of Decisions* (New York: Signet Books, 1955), pp. 106–12, 118, 125, 227–29, 264.

4. For a fuller discussion of these aspects, see Lundestad, *The American Non-Policy*, pp. 75–88.

5. *The Conference at Quebec, 1944,* Joint Chiefs of Staff to Secretary of State, September 12, 1944, enc. 1, pp. 399–401.

6. Beatrice Bishop Berle and Travis Beal Jacobs, eds., *Navigating the Rapids 1918–1971: From the Papers of Adolf A. Berle* (New York: Harcourt Brace Jovanovich, 1973), p. 462.

7. For accounts of the Soviet advance, see Nils Morten Udgaard, *Great Power Politics and Norwegian Foreign Policy: A Study of Norway's Foreign Relations November 1940–February 1948* (Oslo: Universitetsforlaget, 1973), pp. 62–67; Harald Sandvik, *Frigjøringen av Finnmark 1944–45* (The Liberation of Finnmark 1944–45) (Oslo: Gyldendal, 1975).

8. Memorandum of Conversation Berle/Morgenstierne, October 30, 1944, NA, State Dept. Papers, Matthews File, Box 17, Folder 5. For a most interesting account of Roosevelt's earlier ideas on free ports in northern Norway, see Olav Riste, "Free Ports in North Norway," *Journal of Contemporary History* (1970), 5:77–96.

9. Forrestal Diaries, February 7, 1945, pp. 170–79, in particular pp. 170–72, 176–77.

10. Minutes of meeting February 20, 1945, NA, Committee of Three files, p. 5.

11. For a fuller discussion of this, see Udgaard, *Great Power Politics and Norwegian Foreign Policy,* pp. 82–86; Letter from Lie to Eden, January 15, 1945, NA, Federal Records Center at Suitland, Maryland, Oslo Post File.

12. Stettinius to American Embassy London, January 20, 1945, NA, Federal Records Center at Suitland, Maryland, Oslo Post File; Prince Olaf's [sic] Mission and Norwegian Matters Generally, NA, 857.20/2-845, Division of European Affairs.

13. Occupation of Liberated Portion of Norway, February 25, 1945, NA, Modern Military Branch, ABC files, 384 Norway, Sec. I-A, CCS 785. For the more limited plan, see *ibid.,* Sec. I-B, CCS 785/4, April 17, 1945. See also Udgaard, *Great Power Politics and Norwegian Foreign Policy,* pp. 82–86.

14. For a fuller treatment of this, see Lundestad, *The American Non-Policy,* pp. 369–79; Vojtech Mastny, *Russia's Road to the Cold War: Diplomacy, Warfare, and the Politics of Communism, 1941–1945* (New York: Columbia University Press, 1979), pp. 272–79.

15. Truman, *Year of Decisions,* pp. 241–42; Stephen E. Ambrose, *The Supreme Commander: The War Years of General Dwight D. Eisenhower* (London: Cassell, 1971), pp. 652–53; Forrest C. Pogue, *The Supreme Command: United States Army in World War II: The European Theater of Operations* (Washington, D.C.: Dept. of the Army, 1954), p. 446; Alfred D. Chandler, Jr., ed., *The Papers of Dwight David Eisenhower: The War Years* (Baltimore, Md.: Johns Hopkins University Press, 1970), 4:2592–93, 2609–12, 2640–41, 2650–53.

16. Mary Dau, *Danmark og Sovjetunionen 1944–49* (Denmark and the Soviet Union 1944–49) (Copenhagen: Munksgaard, 1969), pp. 112–15; Mastny, *Russia's Road to the Cold War,* pp. 270, 273, 278–79.

17. *The Conference of Berlin, I,* British Plan for a Western European Bloc: The United States View, pp. 256–64.

18. Udgaard, *Great Power Politics and Norwegian Foreign Policy,* pp. 52–54, 158–65; F. S. V. Donnison, *Civil Affairs and Military Government: North-West Europe 1944–1946* (London: Her Majesty's Stationery Office, 1961), pp. 153–70.

19. President's Secretary's File, Box 186, Folders: Reports—Current Foreign Developments, Folder 1, May 11, 1945, p. 3.

20. *Ibid.,* Folder 2, June 7, 1945, p. 1. Norwegian authorities, however, had been notified of the arrival of the Soviet officers. For this, see Andrew Thorne, *General Thorne's rapport om frigjøringen i Norge* (General Thorne's Report on the Liberation of Norway) (Oslo: Forsvarsdepartementet, 1955), pp. 41–42.

21. Memorandum by the Division of Northern European Affairs, Political Summary—Norway, May 1945, NA, 857.00/6-845, p. 4; Pogue, *The Supreme Command,* pp. 509–11; Thorne, *General Thorne's rapport,* pp. 26, 41–42, 56.

22. Deane and Gammell to Antonov, June 16, 1945, U.S. Military Mission to Moscow, Cables and Messages October 1943–October 1945, NA, Modern Military Branch, RG 334, Records of Interservice Agencies; Deane to Tedder, July 3, 1945, and from SHAEF to Military Mission, Moscow, July 11, 1945, *ibid.,* Subject File October 1943–October 1945, Norway. See also Mastny, *Russia's Road to the Cold War,* pp. 288–89, for a slightly more dramatic interpretation.

23. The quotation is from Memorandum by Division of Northern European Affairs, Political Summary—Norway, May 1945, NA, 857.00/6-845, p. 4; Jorstad to Hickerson, September 19, 1945, UD Papers, Group 25.4/47, Folder 8, p. 1.

24. Dau, *Danmark og Sovjetunionen*, pp. 112–20; Ackerson to Secretary of State, March 12 and March 20, 1946, *FRUS, 1946*, 5: 392, 393–94. For the State Department's desire to be kept informed, see Byrnes to American Legation, Copenhagen, NA 759.61/3-1146.

25. Patterson to President, July 27, 1946, Clifford Papers, Box 15, attachment I, pp. 3–4.

26. There are no satisfactory accounts of Swedish and Danish policies at this time. For Norway, see Knut Einar Eriksen, "Norge i det vestlige samarbeid" (Norway in the Western Community), in Trond Bergh and Helge Pharo, eds., *Vekst og Velstand* (Growth and Prosperity) (Oslo: Universitetsforlaget, 1977), pp. 169–88. See also Udgaard, *Great Power Politics and Norwegian Foreign Policy*, and Magne Skodvin, *Norden eller NATO? Utenriksdepartementet og alliansespørsmålet 1947–49* (Scandinavia or NATO? The Foreign Office and the Question of Alliance 1947–1949) (Oslo: Universitetsforlaget, 1971), pp. 20–34.

27. William Hardy McNeill, *America, Britain, and Russia: Their Cooperation and Conflict* (London: Oxford University Press, 1953), p. 614. See also Lundestad, *The American Non-Policy*, pp. 18–20.

28. Lundestad, *The American Non-Policy*, pp. 20–26. For the extreme revisionist version, see Gabriel Kolko, *The Politics of War: The World and United States Foreign Policy, 1943–1945* (New York: Random House, 1968), pp. 170–71.

29. The numbers for embassy/legation personnel have been obtained from the *Foreign Service List*, published quarterly by the Department of State. Information on the Division of Northern European Affairs is available in the annual volumes of the *Official Register of the United States* and in the annual volumes of the Department of State's *Biographic Register*. Figures for the foreign service as a whole have been derived from Elmer Plischke, *Conduct of American Diplomacy* (Princeton, N.J.: Princeton University Press, 1961), p. 247, and directly by the author from Fredrick Aandahl, Office of the Historian, Department of State.

30. Policy and Information Statement, Norway, August 28, 1946, Byrnes Papers, pp. 11–12.

31. *Ibid.*, p. 2–3, 12.

32. Bay to Secretary of State, NA, 857.00/4-1147, p. 3. See also pp. 6–9.

33. Policy and Information Statement, Denmark, August 12, 1946, Byrnes Papers, pp. 1, 7–8.

34. *Ibid.*, Sweden, September 6, 1946, p. 10.

35. *Ibid.*, pp. 1–2, 8–11. The quotation is from p. 8. For a somewhat more critical attitude toward Sweden, see Ravndal to Secretary of State, NA, 758.00/7-946.

36. A discussion of this is found in Lundestad, *The American Non-Policy*, pp. 309–12.

37. Bevin to Secretary of State, January 14, 1946, *FRUS, 1946*, 5: 389. See also p. 390. For the answer from Byrnes to Bevin, see pp. 390–92.

38. Balfour to Acting Secretary of State, June 12, 1946, *ibid.*, pp. 394–97. For the answer from the State Department, see pp. 397–98. See also Dau, *Danmark og Sovjetunionen*, pp. 121–24.

39. Report by the Subcommittee on Rearmament to the State-War-Navy Coordinating Committee, March 21, 1946, *FRUS, 1946*, 1:1149, 1156.

40. *Ibid.*, pp. 1149–50, 1155–56.

41. For the quotation, see Trimble to Cumming, NA, 857.24/6-2046 CS/V, p. 2.

See also Trimble to Cumming and Hickerson, NA, 857.24/5-1546 CS/V; and Acheson to American Embassy, Oslo, NA, 857.24/7-1146.

42. American Embassy, Oslo, to Secretary of State, NA, 857.24/2-1847; Marshall to American Embassy, Oslo, NA, 857.24/10-1447; Shenefield to Cumming, NA, 857.24—FLC/11-547; American Embassy, Oslo, to Secretary of State, NA, 857.24/12-1947; Commander Heinrich U.S. Navy to Deputy Field Commissioner for Military Programs, Department of State, NA, 847.34/3-3148.

43. It is quite possible that the Danes received more matériel than this. For equipment sold to Norway and Denmark, see Department of State *Bulletin,* September 28, 1947, p. 657, and January 25, 1948, pp. 122–23. For the planes, see Hickerson to Acting Secretary of State, NA, 858.24/6-2746. See also Morgan to Hickerson, NA, 859.24/9-2947.

44. Hickerson to Acheson, NA, 858.24/3-1346.

45. Cumming to Hickerson, April 18, 1946, NA, 858.23/3-1346.

46. Acheson to American Legation, Stockholm, NA, 858.24/5-646; Memorandum of Conversation Morgan-de Aminoff, NA, 858.24/8-2046.

47. Legal Adviser to NOE, NA, 858.24/6-646.

48. Patterson to Secretary of State, NA, 858.248/7-2446.

49. Byrnes Papers, Policy and Information Statement, Sweden, p. 13; Hickerson to Acting Secretary, NA 858.24/6-2746; Meeting of Secretaries of State, War, and Navy, October 2, 1946, NA, State Dept. Papers, Committee of Three Box, 811.002/1-246, p. 4; Acheson to Legation, Stockholm, October 9, 1946, NA, 858.24/5-646; Memoranda of Conversation 1947–48, Acheson/H. Ericksson, January 15, 1947, NA, Hickerson File, Box 3.

50. Udgaard, *Great Power Politics and Norwegian Foreign Policy,* pp. 153–55; Policy and Information Statement, Sweden, Byrnes Papers, pp. 2–3.

51. For an easily available summary of financial assistance from the United States to various countries in the world, see U.S. Foreign Assistance Program as of December 31, 1947, *FRUS, 1947,* 1:1026–27.

52. *Ibid.,* p. 1027. For a fuller discussion of assistance to Eastern Europe, see Lundestad, *The American Non-Policy,* pp. 384–94.

53. Policy and Information Statement, Denmark, Byrnes Papers, pp. 2–3.

54. U.S. Foreign Assistance Program as of December 31, *FRUS, 1947,* 1:1027.

55. *Stortingsforhandlingene, 1945/46,* vol. 2a, St. prp. no. 91: Om opptagelse av kreditt i Export-Import Bank, pp. 1–2; *ibid.,* 7b, pp. 1879–80. See also Nils Aasheim, "Høyres holdning til utenrikspolitiske spørsmål 1945–49" (The Attitude of the Conservatives to Foreign Policy Questions 1945–49) (Dissertation, Oslo, 1972), pp. 23–28. *Stortingsforhandlingene 1947,* 2b, St. prp. no. 85; *ibid.,* 6a, Innst. S. no. 89, and 7a, pp. 1022–44.

56. Clayton to Smith, NA, 857.51/7-846. Clayton to Smith, 857.51/5-2946; From Acting Secretary of State to Bay, 857.51/10-1146.

57. Truman, *Year of Decisions,* p. 264.

58. Osborne to Dean Acheson, NA, 811.20257/1-2546. Osborne asked Acheson to consign the memorandum to the fire if the Under Secretary found the contents worthless. The reason for this was that the ambassador doubted "whether it would do any good to the Department (or me) to have it known in the wrong places that a representative of the Department had advocated "propaganda" and "spying" directed, in effect, at Soviet Russia."

59. Attachment, Acheson to McCormack, February 7, 1946, *ibid.;* Memo from

William L. Langer to Undersecretary [sic] of State, May 24, 1946, *ibid.;* Interview with Marselis C. Parsons, Jr. See also William Colby, *Honorable Men: My Life in the CIA* (New York: Simon & Schuster, 1978), pp. 81–102.

60. Osborne to Acheson, NA, 811.20257/1-2546, pp. 2–5.

61. Trimble to Cumming: Soviet Policy Towards Scandinavia, NA, 757d.61/7-1646. The quotations are from pp. 1 and 4.

62. Report by the Subcommittee on Rearmament to the State-War-Navy Coordinating Committee, March 21, 1946, *FRUS, 1946,* 1:1156. The report from the subcommittee was approved by the Coordinating Committee on March 21. For this, see *ibid.,* pp. 1145–46, n. 63.

63. Walter Millis, ed., *The Forrestal Diaries* (New York: Viking, 1951), p. 266.

64. Joyce and Gabriel Kolko, *The Limits of Power: The World and United States Foreign Policy, 1945–1954* (New York: Harper & Row, 1972), p. 164; Lloyd Gardner, *Architects of Illusion: Men and Ideas in American Foreign Policy 1941–1949* (Chicago: Quadrangle, 1970), p. 134.

65. Policy and Information Statement, Sweden, Byrnes Papers, pp. 8–10.

66. Tage Erlander, *1940–1949.* (Stockholm: Tiden, 1973), pp. 273–78; Ernst Wigforss, *Minnen* (Remembrances) *1932–1949* (Stockholm: Tiden, 1954), 3:326–35; Bertil Ohlin, *Memoarer* (Memoirs) *1940–1951* (Stockholm: Bonniers, 1975), pp. 60–65; Gunnar Hägglof, *Fredens Vägar* (The Roads of Peace), *1945–1950* (Stockholm: Norstedt, 1973), pp. 31–35. See also Thomas A. Bailey, *The Marshall Plan Summer: An Eyewitness Report on Europe and the Russians in 1947* (Stanford, Calif.: Stanford University Press, 1977), pp. 187–88.

67. Policy and Information Statement, Norway, Byrnes Papers, p. 15; Bay to Secretary of State, NA, 857.00/4-1147, pp. 7–8. The State Department let the Norwegians understand that it would "certainly be a very serious matter for a nation against which action had been taken by the United Nations [Spain] to put into effect retaliatory measures" against Norway. For this, see Memo of Conversation Acheson-Morgenstierne, February 20, 1947, NA, Hickerson File, Box 3; and Memo of Conversation Cumming-Morgenstierne, February 24, 1947, *ibid.* For the American attitude toward Spain in general, see Gaddis Smith, *Dean Acheson,* vol. 16 in series The American Secretaries of State and Their Diplomacy (New York: Cooper Square Publishers, 1972), pp. 367–71; Theodore J. Lowi, "Bases in Spain," in Harold Stein, ed., *American Civil-Military Decisions: A Book of Case Studies* (Birmingham: University of Alabama Press, 1963), pp. 669–72.

68. Minutes of Meeting of United States Delegation, January 26, 1946, *FRUS, 1946,* 1:172–73. For Vandenberg's attitude at the Paris Peace Conference, see Diary of Arne Ording, October 14, 1946, University Library, Oslo.

69. For an account by the Secretary General of how he was elected, see Trygve Lie, *Syv år for freden* (Oslo: Tiden, 1954), pp. 14–31; American version: *In the Cause of Peace* (New York: Macmillan, 1954).

70. Minutes of Meeting of U.S. Delegation, January 26, 1946, *FRUS, 1946,* 1:173–74, see also pp. 134–44, 152–53, 167–68, 172–82, 184; Udgaard, *Great Power Politics and Norwegian Foreign Policy,* pp. 170–71. For the tabulation of votes on the question of internationalization of the Danube, see *FRUS, 1946,* 3:785–86, 812, 835–36, 842, and 4:79–80, 100, 108, 933, 946.

71. Indications of the attitude of British diplomats in Oslo are found in the Ording diary, May 3, 18, and June 27, 1946. See also Lie, *Syv år for freden,* pp. 14–31, in particular pp. 23, 27, 30–31.

72. For a short account of the Norwegian forces in the British zone of Germany,

see Geir Lundestad, "Norske holdninger overfor Vest-Tyskland 1947–1951" (Norwegian Attitudes Toward West Germany 1947–1951), (Dissertation, Oslo, 1970), pp. 27–29, 91–95, 154–56.

73. For reflections in American sources of difficulties in Anglo-Norwegian and Anglo-Danish relations; see Nielsen to Secretary of State, NA, 741.57/7-1546; Gallman to Secretary of State, NA, 741.57/9-3046.

74. Osborne to Secretary of State, NA, 857.20/9-345.

75. For just one indication of the importance of the three base areas, see Base Rights in Greenland, Iceland and the Azores, November 25, 1947, NA, NSC 2/1, p. 1. For indications of the limited role the polar strategy played at this time, see Hans W. Weigert, "Iceland, Greenland and the United States," *Foreign Affairs,* October 1944, pp. 112–19; Perry McCoy Smith, *The Air Force Plans for Peace 1943–1945* (Baltimore, Md.: Johns Hopkins University Press, 1970), pp. 56–57, 75–83, 110–11.

76. *FRUS, 1945,* Harriman to Secretary of State, April 14, 1945, 5:215–17; Stettinius to Truman, April 15, 1945, enclosing messages from Churchill to Truman and Truman to Harriman, *ibid.,* pp. 218–21. The quotation is from p. 217.

77. To the Secretary, Subject: U.S. Military Bases in Countries Dealt with by Office of European Affairs, January 16, 1947, NA, Matthews File, Box 17, Folder: Lot #5. The quotation is from p. 1.

78. Requirements for U.S. Air Forces in Europe During Occupational Period, Enc. JCS 1332, NA, SWNCC Papers, SWNCC 134, May 23, 1945. The quotation is from p. 6. For the size of the planned bases, see pp. 11–12.

79. *Ibid.,* pp. 9–10.

80. Memorandum for Secretary of State from Matthews, June 2, 1945, *ibid.*

81. Meeting of June 26, 1945, NA, Minutes of Committee of Three; Diary, June 26–30, 1945, Stimson Papers.

82. Memorandum by Hickerson, September 19, 1945, Enc. Osborne to Secretary of State, August 30, 1945, NA, SWNCC Papers, SWNCC 134. For indications of unofficial contacts between American and Norwegian authorities, see the minutes of the Norwegian party Venstre as reported in Knut Einar Eriksen, *DNA og NATO: Striden om norsk NATO-medlemskap innen regjeringspartiet 1948–49* (The Labor Party and NATO: The Struggle Within the Governing Party About Membership for Norway in NATO 1948–49) (Oslo: Gyldendal, 1972), p. 268. The references in the minutes of Venstre are far from clear in their content, however.

83. Telegram from Eisenhower to War Department, September 26, 1945, NA, SWNCC Papers, SWNCC 134/3. For the earlier opinion of Eisenhower and General Spaatz, see Spaatz to Commanding General, Army Air Forces, *ibid.,* Enc. to SWNCC 134.

84. Memorandum for Secretary of State from A. D. Reid, NA, 859.20/10-2745; Memorandum for Secretary of State, NA, SWNCC 134/3; Memorandum by Joint Chiefs of Staff, February 26, 1946, NA, SWNCC Papers, SWNCC 134/8; Memorandum by Joint Chiefs of Staff, June 17, 1946, *ibid.,* 134/9.

85. The best account of the Norwegian-Soviet talks is found in Knut E. Eriksen, "Svalbard 1944–47—et brennpunkt i øst-vest-rivaliseringen" (Svalbard 1944–47—A Focal Point in East-West Rivalry), *Internasjonal Politikk* (International Politics) (1977), 1:109–37. See in particular pp. 109–18.

86. To Secretary, Subject: Russian Demands for Defense and Economic Privileges in Spitsbergen, January 3, 1947, NA, Matthews File, Box 2, pp. 1–3; Cumming to Secretary of State, NA, 757.619/2-2747, p. 1; Osborne to Secretary of State, July 5, 1945, *FRUS, 1945,* 5:91–92. See also pp. 92–94.

87. Memorandum by Joint Chiefs of Staff to State-War-Navy Coordinating Committee, July 23, 1945, *FRUS, 1945,* 5:96–97; see also pp. 92–94.

88. Memorandum by Hickerson, July 13, 1945, *FRUS, 1945,* 5:92–94. The quotation is from pp. 92–93. The wording was based on a memorandum from the Division of Northern European Affairs. For this, see the division's memo of July 9, 1945, entitled Soviet Interest in Bases: Spitsbergen and Bear Island, NA, SWNCC Papers, Box 27.

89. Soviet Demands with Respect to Bear Island and the Spitsbergen Archipelago, July 23, 1945, NA, Joint Chiefs of Staff—Geographic File, Folder: 092 Spitsbergen, JCS 1443/2; *ibid.,* JCS 1443/1, July 17, 1945, Appendix to Enc. "A"; *ibid.,* JCS 1443/2, July 23, 1945.

90. *Ibid.,* JCS 1443/1, July 17, 1945, Enc. "A."

91. Memorandum by Joint Chiefs of Staff to State-War-Navy Coordinating Committee, July 23, 1945, *FRUS, 1945,* 5:96–97; Memorandum by Hickerson, July 23, 1945, *FRUS, 1945,* 5:92–94.

92. Memorandum by Joint Chiefs of Staff to State-War-Navy Coordinating Committee, July 23, 1945, *ibid.,* pp. 96–97. This memorandum was approved by the SWNCC on July 26—see p. 96, n.46.

93. Memorandum by Dunn to Secretary of State, August 27, 1945, *ibid.,* 97–98.

94. Memo by Division of Northern European Affairs, July 9, 1945, Soviet Interest in Bases: Spitsbergen and Bear Island, NA, SWNCC Papers, Box 27, pp. 7–8.

95. Eriksen, "Svalbard 1944–47," pp. 115, 127–29, 130–34. For the Norwegian position in March–April 1945, see also Osborne to Secretary of State, July 26, 1945, NA, SWNCC Papers, Box 27. For later developments, see Cumming to Secretary of State, NA, 757.619/2-2747.

96. Acheson to American Embassy, Oslo, NA, 857.00/10-2146.

97. Benedikt Grøndal, *Iceland: From Neutrality to NATO Membership* (Oslo: Universitetsforlaget, 1971), pp. 35–40; Department of State *Bulletin,* May 5, 1946, p. 773 and September 29, 1946, pp. 583–84. Developments relating to the base in Iceland were discussed in numerous meetings between the Secretaries of State, War, and Navy. For this, see Meetings of April 2, 10, 17, June 20, 26, July 10, 17, August 21, September 25, and October 2, 1946, NA, Committee of Three Files, 811.002/1-246.

98. For a good summary of contacts between Denmark and the United States on this question, see Niels Amstrup, "Grønland i det amerikansk-danske forhold 1945–48" (Greenland in American-Danish Relations 1945-48), in Niels Amstrup and Ib Faurby, eds., *Studier i dansk udenrigspolitik* (Studies in Danish Foreign Policy) (Århus: Politica, 1978), pp. 155–98.

99. Memorandum by Matthews to Secretary of State, January 17, 1947, *FRUS, 1947,* 1:709. The memorandum handed to Foreign Minister Rasmussen by Byrnes in New York on December 14, 1946, is found in United States Interests in the North Atlantic, NA, Att. to 840.20/1-1747.

100. Secretary of State to Legation in Denmark, January 2, 1947, *FRUS, 1947,* 3:657–58.

101. Documentation with regard to the Jan Mayen question is found in *FRUS, 1945,* 5:100–9. See, in particular, Norwegian note to the United States of January 27, 1945, pp. 100–2, and the American reply of March 14, 1945, p. 102.

102. Memorandum by Hickerson, July 23, 1945, *FRUS, 1945,* 5:102–3.

103. Osborne to Secretary of State, November 20 and November 24, 1945, *ibid.,* 103, 104–5; Secretary of State to Osborne, November 27, 1945, *ibid.,* p. 106.

104. Memorandum by Dunn to Secretary of State, December 17, 1945, *ibid.*, pp. 107–8. For the announcement that the American personnel had left, see *Arbeiderbladet*, April 24, 1946, p. 1.

105. Memorandum by Hickerson, July 31, 1945, Subject: Views of British Joint Chiefs of Staff and British Foreign Office With Respect to Soviet Demands on Bear Island and Spitsbergen, NA, SWNCC Papers, Box 3, SWNCC 159/5. The British position is summarily referred to in *FRUS, 1947*, 3:1015 and 1:711. See also Memo of Conversation Cumming-Cecil, NA, 861.24 557 H/1-1547; Eriksen, "Svalbard 1944–47," pp. 124–27.

106. Soviet Demands with Respect to Bear Island and Spitsbergen Archipelago, January 15, 1947, NA, Modern Military Branch, CCS 092 Spitsbergen (7-13-45), Sec. 2, JCS 1443/12. The quotation is from pp. 1–2. See also Memorandum by Matthews to Secretary of State, January 17, 1947, *FRUS, 1947*, 1: Add. 711–12.

107. Patterson and Forrestal to Secretary of State, February 4, 1947, *FRUS, 1947*, 3:1012–13.

108. Marshall to Forrestal, February 18, 1947, *ibid.*, pp. 1013–14.

109. Bay to Secretary of State, January 11, 1947, *ibid.*, pp. 1006–8; Eriksen, "Svalbard 1944–47," pp. 133–34.

110. Udgaard, *Great Power Politics and Norwegian Foreign Policy*, pp. 55–56, 196–97; Amstrup, "Grönland i det amerikansk-danske forhold," pp. 164–65.

111. NA, Modern Military Branch, CCS 092 Spitsbergen, Sec. 2, JCS 1443/12, January 5, 1947, pp. 40–43 (the quotation is from p. 42); Intelligence File, CIA Report on Norway, September 1, 1947, President's Secretary's File, Box 255, pp. v-1. For the limited importance of the Arctic regions in 1944–45, see the references under note 75.

112. Strategic Guidance on the Arctic, NA, Modern Military Branch, CCS 381 Arctic Area (10-1-46), Sec. I, JSPC 815/6. Box 3, Folders Antarctic and Arctic Area also give several other examples of the interest of parts of the military in polar questions; Base Rights in Greenland, Iceland, and the Azores, November 25, 1947, *ibid.*, NSC Papers, NSC 2/1: pp. 1–2; articles by Ellsworth Huntingdon and Henry Arnold, President's Air Policy Commission, Box 24, Folders 1–4. See also *New York Times*, April 15, 1948, p. 16, May 5, 1948, p. 8, and May 20, 1948, p. 10; Bernhard Brodie's articles in *Bulletin of Atomic Scientists*, 1947, pp. 154, 209; Vincent Davis, *Postwar Defense Policy and the U.S. Navy, 1943–1946* (Chapel Hill: University of North Carolina Press, 1966), pp. 196, 211, 215–16; Vincent Davis, *The Admirals Lobby* (Chapel Hill: University of North Carolina Press, 1967), pp. 195–96; *Survival in the Air Age: A Report by the President's Air Policy Commission* (Washington, D.C., 1948), pp. 10–19; Daniel Yergin, *Shattered Peace. The Origins of the Cold War and the National Security State* (Boston: Houghton Mifflin, 1977), pp. 210–11.

113. See the references to the JCS papers in the preceding note; Digest of Public Discussion, September-December 1947, President's Air Policy Commission, Box 24, part 2, sec. 3: Guided Missiles.

114. Policy and Information Statement, Greenland, July 30, 1946, Byrnes Papers, pp. 1–2, 5–7; Cunningham to Morgan, NA, 711.58/8-947; Amstrup, "Grønland i det amerikansk-danske forhold," pp. 164–65.

115. Reports on Soviet activities on Spitsbergen are found in NA, State Department Papers, 861.24 557 H file. See for instance Huston to the Secretary of State, 861.24 557 H/5-1947. The quotation is from a memo by geographer Paul A. Siple to General Aurand, October 10, 1947, in NA, JCS-Geographic File, 1948–1950, Box 3, p. 2. For the attitude of the military, see the documents—most of them still classified—in NA, JCS-Geographic File, CCS 092 Spitsbergen, Sec. 3.

116. Memo of Conversation Lacy/Skaug, NA, 711.57/3-1047, p. 1.

117. Clayton to Huston, undated, President's Official File, Folder 123: Miscellaneous; Letter from the Office of Temporary Controls, April 7, 1947, *ibid.;* Memorandum for Steelman from Lovett, December 12, 1947, President's Secretary's File, Box 34, Folder 10, pp. 1–4.

118. Council of Foreign Ministers Meeting in Moscow, February 26, 1947, Dulles Papers.

119. Higgs to Secretary of State, NA, 858.00/5-2847. For the poll itself, see Dreyfus to Secretary of State, NA, 858.00/5-1447.

120. Millis, *Forrestal Diaries,* p. 266.

121. *Arbeiderbladet,* June 30, 1947, p. 1, July 1, p. 1; *Aftenposten,* June 30, 1947, Aftennummeret, p. 1; *Dagbladet,* July 1, 1947, p. 1; Udgaard, *Great Power Politics and Norwegian Foreign Policy,* pp. 202–4.

122. Millis, *Forrestal Diaries,* p. 184.

123. John Gimbel, *The Origins of the Marshall Plan* (Stanford, Calif.: Stanford University Press, 1976). See for instance pp. 4–5, 276–77.

124. For a discussion of this, see Geir Lundestad, "The Marshall Plan and Eastern Europe: What the Two Reveal About Each Other and American Foreign Policy in 1947," pp. 1–3, paper presented at the Conference "Marshall Plan und Europäische Linke," Essen, West Germany, July 7–11, 1977. See also Scott Jackson, "Prologue to the Marshall Plan: The Origins of the American Commitment for a European Recovery Program," *Journal of American History* (1979), 65:1043–68.

125. Memorandum by Kennan, May 16, 1947, *FRUS, 1947,* 3:220–23. The quotation is from p. 220. The May 23 memo by Kennan is found on pp. 223–30, and Clayton's on pp. 230–32.

126. For the April 21 report of the ad hoc committee of the State-War-Navy Coordinating Committee, see *FRUS, 1947,* 3:204–19. The quotation is from Memo to Reber from Eddy, NA, 840.50 Recovery/3-2047. The ad hoc committee prepared special studies of the following European countries: Italy, France, Austria, Hungary, Belgium and Luxembourg, the Netherlands, Portugal, Czechoslovakia, and Poland. For these reports, see Report of the Special Ad Hoc Committee of the SWNCC, April 21, 1947, NA, SWNCC Files, Series 360, Annex C to Appendix A.

127. Report of Ad Hoc Committee of SWNCC, *FRUS, 1947,* 3:206–7.

128. Memo by Kennan, May 16, 1947, *ibid.,* pp. 221–22; Report of Ad Hoc Committee of SWNCC, *ibid.,* p. 212.

129. Report by the Special Ad Hoc Committee to State-War-Navy Coordinating Committee, April 21, 1947, *FRUS, 1947,* 1:726–27, 730. The report did observe that it would be contrary to current U.S. policies to supply military assistance to Spain.

130. Memorandum by Joint Chiefs of Staff to State-War-Navy Coordinating Committee, May 12, 1947, *ibid.,* pp. 734–50.

131. Appendix: United States Assistance to Other Countries from Standpoint of National Security, Report by Joint Strategic Survey Committee, *ibid.,* pp. 741–42.

132. For a discussion of this, see Lundestad, *The American Non-Policy,* pp. 403–6.

133. Douglas to Secretary of State, July 4, 1947, *FRUS, 1947,* 3:311; Caffery to Secretary of State, July 8 and July 10, *ibid.,* pp. 315, 317.

134. Morgenstierne to Lange, July 9, 1947, UD Papers, 25 4/47, Folder 12; Bay to Secretary of State, NA, 840.50 Recovery /6-1947. See also Bay to Secretary of State, NA, 840.50 Recovery /7-547.

135. *Aftenposten,* June 30, 1947, Aftennummeret, p. 2; Bay to Secretary of State, NA, 840.50 Recovery/7-2847, p. 1.

136. Bay to Secretary of State, NA, 840.50 Recovery/7-1247; Bay to Secretary of State, *ibid.,* 7-1647; Huston to Secretary of State, *ibid.,* 7-2247.

137. Lundestad, *The American Non-Policy,* pp. 397–404. The quotation is from Balfour to Secretary of State, July 16, 1947, *FRUS, 1947,* 3:331.

3. Neutrality Rejected

1. Woolridge to Hickerson, Attached: Chiefs of Staff Committee-Joint Planning Staff, Scandinavian Defense, NA, 857 D. 20/10-747, p. 5.

2. *Ibid.,* p. 2.

3. Marvel to Secretary of State, NA, 757 D. 00/3-1347; Ackerson to Secretary of State, NA, 757 D. 00/4-1047; Marvel to Secretary of State, NA, 757 D. 00/4-2947; Marvel to Secretary of State, NA, 757 D. 00/5-2347.

4. Foreign Office Questions, NA, 857 D. 20/10-747, Annex: pp. 6–7, Memorandum for Joint Staff Planners, August 18, 1947, NA, Modern Military Branch, ABC 384 NW Europe (8-20-43), sec. 2. Enc.: Memo by C. R. Price, August 15, 1947.

5. Woolridge to Hickerson, NA, 857 D. 20/10-747. p. 1.

6. Hickerson to Woolridge, *ibid.*

7. Morgan to Hickerson, NA, FW 857 D. 20/10-747.

8. *Ibid.*

9. Thompson to Hickerson, *ibid.*

10. Intelligence File, CIA Report, Norway, September 1, 1947, President's Secretary's File, Box 355, p. vi–1. For a slightly more critical report made by the predecessor of the CIA, the OSS, see Analysis of Current Political and Economic Situation in Norway, July 25, 1947, NA, OSS Papers, Research and Analysis Branch, in particular pp. 11–12.

11. For Marshall's speech, see for instance *A Decade of American Foreign Policy: Basic Documents 1941–49* (Washington, D.C., 1950), pp. 1268–70. The quotation is from p. 1269.

12. Memorandum by Clayton, May 27, 1947, *FRUS,* 1947, 3:232.

13. Secretary of State to Clayton, July 10, 1947, *ibid.,* p. 323; Minutes of Meeting on Marshall Plan, August 22, 1947, *ibid.,* pp. 369–72.

14. Lovett to Marshall, August 24, 1947, *ibid.,* pp. 372–75. The quotation is from pp. 372–73. See also, To Marshall and Lovett from Clayton, August 31, 1947, *ibid.,* pp. 391–96; Marshall to Lovett, August 25, 1947, *ibid.,* p. 375, n. 5.

15. *Ibid.,* pp. 392–93.

16. Lovett to Diplomatic Representatives Accredited to Countries Participating in Paris Conference, September 7, 1947, *ibid.,* p. 413.

17. For an account of the negotiations in Paris from the Norwegian point of view, see Helge Pharo, "Bridgebuilding and Reconstruction: Norway Faces the Marshall Plan," *Scandinavian Journal of History* (1976), 1:125–53.

18. *Ibid.,* pp. 138–49. For an early summary of the Norwegian position, see Memorandum of Conversation by Huston with Lange, NA, 840.50 Recovery /7-2247.

19. Caffery to Secretary of State, July 20, 1947, *FRUS, 1947,* 3:334; Memo of Conversation by Chargé Huston, NA, 840.50 Recovery /7-2247, p. 2.

20. Caffery to Lovett, August 26, 1947, *FRUS, 1947,* 3:381; Memo by Raeder and Skaug, July 30, 1947, UD Papers, 44.2/26, 4; Memo by Raeder, September 8, 1947, *ibid.,* 44.2/26,5.

21. Memorandum by Kennan, September 4, 1947, *FRUS, 1947,* 3:398.

22. Pharo, "Bridgebuilding and Reconstruction," pp. 113–38; Clayton to Marshall and Lovett, August 31, 1947, *FRUS, 1947,* 3:395.

23. Secretary of State to Embassy in the United Kingdom, September 8, 1947, *FRUS, 1947,* 3:418–19.

24. Douglas to Secretary of State, September 9, 1947, *ibid.,* p. 420; Secretary of State to Embassy in London, September 11, 1947, *ibid.,* p. 424; Douglas to Secretary of State, September 17, 1947, *ibid.,* pp. 434–35.

25. Bay to Secretary of State, NA, 840.50 Recovery/9-1047; Bay to Secretary of State, NA, 840.50 Recovery /9-1147; Caffery to Lovett, September 17, 1947, *FRUS, 1947,* 3:434; Pharo, "Bridgebuilding and Reconstruction," pp. 147–48.

26. For Norway's attitude in this period, see *Stortingsforhandlingene, 1947,* 2b, St. meld. no. 34, pp. 11–12, 18; *ibid.,* 2b, St. meld. no. 36, pp. 21–23; *ibid.,* 7b, pp. 1671–75.

See also Kurt H. Jacobsen, "The Nordic Countries in the United Nations," Institute of Political Science, University of Oslo, pp. 88, 107 (mimeo); Nils Morten Udgaard, *Great Power Politics and Norwegian Foreign Policy: A Study of Norway's Foreign Relations November 1940–February 1948* (Oslo: Universitetsforlaget, 1973), pp. 170–76; Knut E. Eriksen, "Norge i det vestlige samarbeid" (Norway in the Western Community), in Trond Bergh and Helge Pharo, eds., *Vekst og Velstand: Norsk Politisk Historie 1945–1965* (Growth and Prosperity: The Political History of Norway 1945–1965) (Oslo: Universitetsforlaget, 1977), pp. 179–88.

For Norway's attitude on the German question, see Geir Lundestad, "Norske holdninger overfor Vest-Tyskland 1947–1951" (Norwegian Attitudes toward West Germany 1947–1951), dissertation, Oslo, 1970, in particular pp. 22–27.

27. *Stortingsforhandlingene, 1948,* volume 2b, St. meld. 47, pp. 22–24.

28. *Ibid.,* pp. 11–12, 20–21, 24–25.

29. Hickerson to NOE, October 28, 1947, NA, State Department Papers, Hickerson File, Box 3.

30. Morgenstierne to Norwegian Foreign Office, December 16, 1947, UD Papers, 25.4/47, Folder 13, pp. 1–3.

31. Hickerson to Armour, NA, 711.57/10-747, pp. 1–3.

32. *Ibid.*

33. Armour to Lovett, NA, 711.57/10-1047; Memo of Conversation Baldwin-Morgenstierne, December 9, 1947, NA, Hickerson File, Box 3, p. 4.

34. See references under note 33 above.

35. Bay to Secretary of State, October 9, 1947, NA, 857.00/10-947, p. 10. For the April report, see Bay to Secretary of State, NA, 857.00/4-1147.

36. Bay to Secretary of State, NA, 857.00/10-947, pp. 7–11. The quotation is from p. 11.

37. For Morgenstierne's attitude, see for instance Memo of Conversation Hickerson-Morgenstierne, December 9, 1947, NA, Hickerson File, Box 3, in particular pp. 3–4. For contacts between Haakon Lie and the embassy, see for instance Memo of Conversation with Haakon Lie, NA, 711.57/7-1747; Bay to Secretary of State, NA, 857 D. 00/9-1147.

38. Villard to Secretary of State, NA, 757.00/11-448. See also Huston to Secretary of State, NA, 757.00/10-2847.

39. Marvel to Secretary of State, July 22, 1947, *FRUS, 1947,* 3:674–75.

40. *Ibid.,* July 25, 1947, pp. 675–76, and November 15, 1947, p. 685.

41. Niels Amstrup, "Grønland i det amerikansk-danske forhold 1945–48" (Greenland in American-Danish Relations 1945–48), pp. 196–97 in Niels Amstrup

and Ib Faurby, eds., *Studier i dansk udenrigspolitik* (Studies in Danish Foreign Policy) (Århus, 1978).

42. United States Interest in North Atlantic, Att.: Copy of Memorandum handed by Byrnes to Rasmussen, December 14, 1946, NA, 840.20/1-1747, p. 4. See also Memorandum by Matthews to Secretary of State, January 17, 1947, *FRUS, 1947,* 1:709.

43. Marshall to Embassy in Denmark, May 27, 1947, *FRUS, 1947,* 3:662–63.

44. *Ibid.,* p. 660, n. 2; Marvel to Secretary of State, July 14, 1947, *ibid.,* pp. 673–74.

45. See for instance Memorandum by Hickerson to Secretary of State, June 16, 1947, *FRUS, 1947,* 3:668–69.

46. Memorandum by Hickerson to Secretary of State, October 10, 1947, *ibid.,* pp. 677–78; Amstrup, "Grønland i det amerikansk-danske forhold,' " pp. 187–94.

47. Interview with H. Freeman Matthews, June 7, 1973, Harry S. Truman Library, Oral History Collection, pp. 15–16; letter from Hickerson, personal communication, October 27, 1978.

48. *New York Times,* June 10, 1947, p. 1; *ibid.,* May 12, 1947, p. 1 and May 13, p. 8.

49. Ravndal to Peurifoy, January 6, 1949, President's Secretary's File, Box 35, Folder 15. It is a point of some interest in this connection that the American ambassador to Sweden was higher paid than those to Norway, Denmark, and Finland. Those three were in turn better paid than the ambassador to Iceland. For this, see Acheson to Truman, Classification of Positions of Chiefs of Mission, November 29, 1946, *ibid.,* Box 34, Folder 6.

50. To Hulley From Ness, NA, 858.51/12-3147.

51. *Ibid.* See also Lovett to Embassy in Stockholm, NA, 858.51/1-2248.

52. Lovett to Embassy in Stockholm, NA, 858.51/12-3147; Records of the National Advisory Council, Meeting No. 85, January 29, 1948, NA, Treasury Dept. Papers, p. 2, and Staff Meeting No. 108, January 27, 1948, p. 2.

53. Estimate of Probable Developments in the World Political Situation up to 1957, by Joint Strategic Plans Committee, December 11, 1947, in Thomas H. Etzold and John Lewis Gaddis, eds., *Containment: Documents on American Foreign Policy and Strategy, 1945–1950* (New York: Columbia University Press, 1978), p. 293.

54. For a discussion of Soviet policies in Eastern Europe, see Lundestad, *The American Non-Policy Towards Eastern Europe 1943–1947: Universalism in an Area Not of Essential Interest to the United States* (Oslo-New York: Universitetsforlaget-Humanities Press, 1975), pp. 435–65. The account of U.S. policies is based on the same book, in particular pp. 192–224 (Poland), 225–47 (Rumania), and 257–78 (Bulgaria).

55. Gabriel Kolko, *The Politics of War: The World and United States Foreign Policy, 1943–1945* (New York: Random House, 1968), pp. 128, 170–71, 410–11.

56. Arthur M. Schlesinger, Jr., "The Origins of the Cold War," in his *The Crisis of Confidence: Ideas, Power, and Violence in America Today* (New York: Bantam Books, 1969), p. 94; Herbert Feis, *From Trust to Terror: The Onset of the Cold War, 1945–1950* (New York: Norton, 1970), pp. 291–95. See also Norman A. Graebner, *Cold War Diplomacy 1945–1960* (New York: Van Nostrand, 1962), pp. 45–46.

57. Lundestad, *The American Non-Policy,* pp. 159–82.

58. Joyce and Gabriel Kolko, *The Limits of Power: The World and United States Foreign Policy, 1945–1954* (New York: Harper & Row, 1972), p. 164; Lloyd Gardner, *Architects of Illusion: Men and Ideas in American Foreign Policy 1941–1949* (Chicago: Quadrangle, 1970), p. 134.

59. For the Soviet attitude, see for instance Eriksen, "Norge i det vestlige samarbeid," pp. 182–92; Udgaard, *Great Power Politics and Norwegian Foreign Policy*, pp. 202–5.

60. Lundestad, *The American Non-Policy*, pp. 56–59. For a short review of American-Spanish relations, see Theodore J. Lowi, "Bases in Spain," in Harold Stein, ed., *American Civil-Military Decisions* (Birmingham: University of Alabama Press, 1963), pp. 669–72.

61. Memo from Lovett to President, September 8, 1947, President's Secretary's File, Confidential, Box 159, Folder: Secretary of State—Foreign Countries.

62. Memo from Truman to Lovett, *ibid.*, Box 188, Folder: Switzerland.

63. For a short account of the American attitude toward Finland, see Lundestad, *The American Non-Policy*, pp. 285–96, 309–12.

64. Memo to Secretary of State from Matthews, July 15, 1947, NA, Matthews File –Lot 54 D 394, Box 2; pp. 3–4.

4. Socialism and Scandinavian Social Democrats

1. Joyce and Gabriel Kolko, *The Limits of Power: The World and United States Foreign Policy, 1945–1954* (New York: Harper & Row, 1972), p. 2.

2. Kolko and Kolko, *The Limits of Power*, pp. 456–57, see also pp. 443–44. The overall view of Gabriel Kolko is perhaps most clearly expressed in the introduction to his *The Politics of War: The World and United States Foreign Policy, 1943–1945* (New York: Random House, 1968), pp. 3–9.

3. The quotation is from Kolko and Kolko, *The Limits of Power*, p. 65. For their attitude to the SFIO, see *ibid.*, p. 153.

4. Thomas G. Paterson, *Soviet-American Confrontation: Postwar Reconstruction and the Origins of the Cold War* (Baltimore, Md., Johns Hopkins University Press, 1973), pp. 105, 170, 260–67. The quotation is from p. 170.

5. Walter LaFeber, *America, Russia, and the Cold War, 1945–1966* (New York: Wiley, 1968), pp. 8–11; Lloyd C. Gardner, *Architects of Illusion: Men and Ideas in American Foreign Policy 1941–1949* (Chicago: Quadrangle, 1970), pp. 120–22.

6. Herbert Feis, *From Trust to Terror: The Onset of the Cold War, 1945–1950* (New York: Norton, 1970), pp. 229–31. For his appraisal of the loan to France, see pp. 231–32; William Hardy McNeill, *America, Britain, and Russia: Their Cooperation and Conflict 1941–1946* (London: Oxford University Press), pp. 610–12, 682–88.

7. John Lewis Gaddis, *The United States and the Origins of the Cold War, 1941–1947* (New York: Columbia University Press, 1972), pp. 11–13, 50, 63, 133–34, 138, 151, 175.

8. Department of State *Bulletin*, December 9, 1945, pp. 923–24; Geir Lundestad, *The American Non-Policy Towards Eastern Europe, 1943–1947* (Oslo-New York: Universitetsforlaget-Humanities Press, 1975), pp. 64–66.

9. For some expressions of this belief on the part of President Truman, see *Public Papers of Harry S. Truman, 1946* (Washington, D.C., 1962), p. 168; *ibid., 1947*, pp. 169–70.

10. For the text of the agreement with Britain, see *A Decade of American Foreign Policy: Basic Documents, 1941–49* (Washington, D.C., 1950), pp. 735–44. For the agreement with France, see pp. 728–35.

11. For indications of the skepticism of some prominent policy makers about socialization and other measures of the Labour party in Britain as reflected in the

Forrestal Diaries, see Walter Millis, ed., *The Forrestal Diaries* (New York: Viking, 1951), pp. 302, 303, 311, 328.

12. Richard J. Barnet, *Roots of War: The Men and Institutions Behind U.S. Foreign Policy* (Baltimore, Md.: Penguin Books, 1973), pp. 179–82.

13. See, for instance, the diaries of James Forrestal, Princeton University Library (unpublished version), September 29, 1948.

14. LaFeber, *America, Russia, and the Cold War*, p. 9.

15. William L. Clayton—1946, Clayton to Baruch, December 16, 1946, Baruch Papers, Box 68. It should be noted that Lloyd Gardner quotes this passage in full. For this, see Gardner, *Architects of Illusion*, p. 125.

16. This line of reasoning is clearly brought out in, for instance, a speech delivered by George Marshall in January 1948 on foreign aid and reconstruction. For this, see Department of State *Bulletin*, January 25, 1948, p. 111.

17. Department of State Policy Statement, June 11, 1948, *FRUS, 1948,* 3:1092–93. See also Hugh Dalton, *High Tide and After: Memoirs 1945–1960* (London: Mullex, 1962), pp. 135–40, 248–56, 308–10.

18. Meeting of National Advisory Council, April 25, 1946, *FRUS, 1946,* 5:432. See also *ibid.,* pp. 441, 445; and Jean Monnet, *Memoirs* (London: Collins, 1978), pp. 228–29, 249–56.

19. The socialization issue is dealt with in John Gimbel, *The American Occupation of Germany: Politics and the Military, 1945–1949* (Stanford, Calif.: Stanford University Press, 1968), pp. 117–20, 126–28, 155–58, 170–71.

20. Memorandum of Conversation Marshall-Clayton, June 20, 1947, *FRUS, 1947,* 2:929.

21. For the American policy toward internal issues in Austria, see Fritz Weber, "Die Österreichische Sozialdemokratie zu Beginn des Kalten Krieges," paper submitted at the Conference "Marshall-Plan und Europäische Linke," Essen, West Germany, July 7–11, 1977, pp. 10–11, 15, 17–18.

22. For the American skepticism of de Gaulle in 1947, see Lovett to Embassy in France, October 25, 1947, *FRUS, 1947,* 3:790–91; Caffery to the Secretary of State, October 29, 1947, *ibid.,* pp. 793–95. For a representative analysis in 1948, see Policy Statement of Department of State, September 20, 1948, *FRUS, 1948,* 3:653–54.

23. For a discussion of the relative merits of a Labour government versus a Conservative one, see Paper Prepared in U.S. Embassy in United Kingdom, August 18, 1949, *FRUS, 1949,* 4:814–15. For an earlier and even more positive evaluation of Labour's policies, see Winant to Secretary of State, January 11, 1946, *FRUS, 1945,* 6:200–4.

24. There is no indication of an active American policy to throw the communists out of the government in France in that part of the State Department papers published in *FRUS, 1947,* vol. 3. But many Americans were relieved once they were out. For this, see, for instance, Caffery to Secretary of State, May 12, 1947, *FRUS, 1947,* 3:709; Memorandum from Matthews to Lovett, July 11, 1947, *ibid.,* p. 721; MacArthur to Wallner, October 10, 1947, *ibid.,* p. 76. For a similar conclusion, see Wilfried Loth, "Das Ausscheiden der französischen Kommunisten aus der Regierung 1947," in *Vierteljahrshefte für die Zeitgeschichte* (1978), 26:9–65, in particular pp. 56–58. Despite our similar conclusions, I have reservations about Loth's use of some American sources.

25. Secretary of State to Embassy in Italy, May 1, 1947, *FRUS, 1947,* 3:889; Dunn to Secretary of State, May 3, 1947, *ibid.,* pp. 889–92. See also pp. 893–94, 897–902, 911–13.

Memo of Conversation Marshall/Tarchiani, May 16, 1947, *ibid.*, pp. 905–6; Secretary of State to Embassy in Italy, May 20, 1947, *ibid.*, pp. 909–10.

26. Secretary of State to Embassy in Italy, June 6, 1947, *FRUS, 1947,* 3:919; Editorial Note, *ibid.*, p. 965; Dunn to Secretary of State, December 17, 1947, *FRUS, 1948,* 3:753. For the attitude of American labor to these questions, see Ronald Radosh, *American Labor and United States Foreign Policy* (New York: Random House, 1969), pp. 304–47.

27. Lundestad, *The American Non-Policy,* pp. 324–28.

28. *FRUS, 1946,* 1:1387; Policy and Information Statement on Sweden, September 6, 1946, Byrnes Papers, pp. 2–3, and Denmark, August 12, 1946, pp. 2–3; *Stortingsforhandlingene, 1945/46,* 2, St. prp. no. 6, Appendix I, pp. 19, 65, 99–100, 120, and 8a, pp. 106–8, 121.

29. Wilcox to Secretary of State, December 27, 1946, *FRUS, 1946,* 1:1362; Dennison to Carter, December 13, 1947, *FRUS, 1948,* 1 (2):809, 813.

30. The question of periods of transition in bilateral trade is best brought out in the Policy and Information statements on the three Scandinavian countries, found in the Byrnes Papers. See the statement on Sweden, September 6, 1946, pp. 3, 8–10; Denmark, August 12, 1946, pp. 2–3; Norway, August 28, 1946, pp. 3–4.

31. Policy and Information Statement on Sweden, September 6, 1946, Byrnes Papers, pp. 8–10. For a request by Minister of Commerce Myrdal that the United States send a top-ranking economic expert to Sweden to whom he could explain Swedish policies, see Clayton to Hawkins, NA, 858.50/9-466.

32. Sweden—General 1946–49, From Schmidt to Overby, March 31, 1947, Snyder Papers, Box 12, pp. 2–3.

33. *Ibid.;* and Department of State *Bulletin,* July 6, 1947, pp. 42–45.

34. Bay to Secretary of State, NA, 840.50 Recovery /2-448, pp. 1–4. Conover to Secretary of State, NA, 840.50 Recovery /1-349, p. 4.

35. *Aftenposten,* September 22, 1948, p. 1; Bay to Secretary of State, NA, 840.50 Recovery /7-2847, Enc., pp. 1–2; *New York Times,* December 12, 1947, p. 55. For a short account of Bay's business background, see Henry Serrano Villard, *Affairs At State* (New York: Crowell, 1965), p. 177.

36. Policy Statement of Department of State, August 15, 1949, *FRUS, 1949,* 4:779.

37. Acheson to American Embassy, Oslo, NA, 857.51/3-1347, p. 1. The understanding was included in Article 1 of the final American-Norwegian agreement. No further comment was made on this by government spokesmen, despite the fact that the point had not been included in the preliminary agreement of 1946. For this, see *Stortingsforhandlingene, 1945/46,* 2, St. prp. no. 91; *ibid.,* 7b, pp. 1858–80; *ibid.,* 1947, 2a, St. prp. no. 85; *ibid.,* 6, Innst S. no. 89; *ibid.,* 7a, pp. 1022–1044. The point was, however, briefly mentioned in the presentation of the agreement in *Arbeiderbladet,* April 14, 1947, p. 1. More remarkable than the government's playing down of this understanding was the lack of attention paid to it by the opposition, in particular the communists.

38. Clayton to Baruch, December 16, 1946, Baruch Papers, Box 28, File: William L. Clayton—1946. For a more general discussion of this, see Lundestad, *The American Non-Policy,* pp. 54–56, 58–59, 64–66.

39. Brown to Wilcox: United States Attitude toward Other Countries' Nationalization of Their Industries, NA, FW 858.6363/10-1645; Brown to Wilcox, January 8, 1946, *ibid.* See also Austin T. Foster of Socony-Vacuum Oil Company to John A. Loftus, Chief, Petroleum Division, October 23, 1945, NA, State Department Papers, unnumbered; Johnson to Secretary of State, NA, 858.6363/10-645.

40. Acheson to Legation in Stockholm, March 27, 1946, NA 858.6363/10-645. See also Acheson to Legation in Stockholm, March 11, 1947, NA, 858.6363/2-2547.

41. Leif Lewin, *Planhushållningsdebatten* (The Debate on a Planned Economy) (Stockholm: Almqvist och Wiksell, 1967), pp. 263–347, in particular pp. 324–26. For a summing up of the American position, see Policy and Information Statement on Sweden, September 6, 1946, Byrnes Papers, pp. 3–4.

42. Loftus to Michler of Standard Oil, NA, 857.6363/1-1146. See also enclosures to same, paraphrases of messages from the embassy in Oslo, dated December 29, 1945, and January 5, 1946.

43. Osborne to Secretary of State, NA, 857.00/8-2145.

44. NA, State Department Papers, Research and Analysis Branch, no. 3685, p. 6. See also Policy and Information Statement on Norway, Byrnes Papers, pp. 11–12.

45. Osborne to Secretary of State, NA, 857.00/6-2545, Enclosure, pp. 2–7.

46. *Ibid.,* p. 2; Osborne to Secretary of State, NA, 857.00/7-2645.

47. Osborne to Secretary of State, NA, 857.00/7-2645.

48. NA, Davis to Secretary of State, 859.00/8-2745. For reports on later unity talks in Norway, see NA, 857.00/5-2347, CS/A; Huston to Secretary of State, 857.00/5-2947; Policy and Information Statement on Norway, August 28, 1946, Byrnes Papers, p. 13.

49. Osborne to Secretary of State, NA, 857.00/10-945; Osborne to Secretary of State, NA, 857.00/11-745; Osborne to Secretary of State, NA, 857.00/10-945; Policy and Information Statement on Norway, August 28, 1946, Byrnes Papers, p. 13. For the 1949 report, see Analysis of Norwegian Parliamentary Election, October 25, 1949, NA, OSS File, Research and Analysis Branch, Report no. 5083, p. 9.

50. Report dated October 16, 1945, NA, OSS File, Record Group 226, XL 24465; Report dated October 26, 1945, *ibid.,* XL 28146; Report dated March 14, 1946) *ibid.,* XL 48074. Evaluations made by Ellingsen's superiors are attached to these reports. Ellingsen must have left the embassy shortly after March 1946 since he is not found in the *Foreign Service List* of July 1946.

51. Analysis of the Current Political and Economic Situation in Norway, July 25, 1947, NA, OSS File, Research and Analysis Branch, Report no. 4443, pp. 5–6; Bay to Secretary of State, NA, 857.00/4-1147, pp. 4–5; Marvel to Secretary of State, NA, 859.00/8-2847, pp. 7–8; Higgs to Secretary of State, NA, 858.00/8-1447, in particular pp. 5–6.

52. Policy and Information Statement on Norway, August 28, 1946, Byrnes Papers, p. 1.

53. *Ibid.,* p. 3.

54. Bay to Secretary of State, NA, 857.00/4-1147, pp. 4, 12; Bay to Secretary of State NA, 857.00/10-947, pp. 2–5. The quotation is from p. 3.

55. NA, State Department Papers, Research and Analysis Branch, no. 3689, A, July 11, 1946, p. 3; Ravndal to Secretary of State, NA, 711.58/4-1046, pp. 3–4.

56. Davis to Secretary of State, NA, 859.00/10-2345, in particular p. 16.

57. Marvel to Secretary of State, November 15, 1947, *FRUS, 1947,* 3:685. See also Marvel to Secretary of State, NA, 859.00/8-2847, pp. 7–8.

58. Memorandum Prepared in Office of Special Political Affairs, August 1, 1947, *FRUS, 1947,* 1:106. See also Policy and Information Statement on Sweden, Byrnes Papers, September 6, 1946.

59. Policy Statement of Department of State on Sweden, August 15, 1949, *FRUS, 1949,* 4:776; National Security Council Report on Position of United States with Respect to Scandinavia, September 3, 1948, NA, National Security Council files, Modern Military Branch, NSC 28/1, p. 3.

60. Policy Statement of Department of State on Sweden, August 15, 1949, *FRUS, 1949*, 4:778.

61. The Lex Thagaard is discussed in Trond Bergh's article "Norsk økonomisk politikk 1945-65" (Norwegian Economic Policy 1945-65) in Trond Bergh and Helge Pharo, eds., *Vekst og Velstand: Norsk Politisk Historie 1945-1965* (Growth and Prosperity: Norwegian Political History 1945-1965) (Oslo: Universitetsforlaget, 1977), in particular pp. 30-33, 51-58.

62. Memo by W. C. Trimble, NA, 857.00/6-845, p. 5.

63. Bay to Secretary of State, NA, 857.00/10-947, pp. 3, 17.

64. *Ibid.*, p. 4.

65. Reports by Central Intelligence Agency and Central Intelligence Group, Norway, September 1, 1947, President's Secretary's File, Box 14—Intelligence Reports, pp. 1, ii–8—ii–9; Opposition to ECA in Participating Countries, Central Intelligence Agency, February 10, 1949, Declassified Documents Reference System, 1945-49 (75) 2B, ORE 68-48, pp. 3-4.

66. R. Harris Smith, *OSS: The Secret History of America's First Central Intelligence Agency* (Berkeley, Calif.: University of California Press, 1972), in particular pp. 361-83.

5. The Marshall Plan and Norway: A Case Study

1. Joyce and Gabriel Kolko, *The Limits of Power: The World and United States Foreign Policy, 1945-54* (New York: Harper & Row, 1972), pp. 428-29, 450-52.

2. Walter LaFeber, *America, Russia, and the Cold War, 1945-1966* (New York: Wiley, 1967), p. 51.

3. Herbert Feis, *From Trust to Terror: The Onset of the Cold War, 1945-1950* (New York: Norton, 1970), p. 252, n.15; Robert H. Ferrell, *George C. Marshall*, vol. 15 in the series The American Secretaries of State and Their Diplomacy (New York: Cooper Square Publishers, 1966), pp. 99-134.

4. Hadley Arkes, *Bureaucracy, the Marshall Plan, and the National Interest* (Princeton, N.J.: Princeton University Press, 1972); Harry Bayard Price, *The Marshall Plan and Its Meaning* (Ithaca: Cornell University Press, 1955).

5. Arkes, *Bureaucracy*, pp. 273-300 (chapter 13 is called "The Imperfect Interventionist"); and pp. 138-52, 156-58, 164-71, 275-76, 279-85, 301-2, 325-26.

6. *Ibid.*, pp. 195-97, 202-10, 263-72.

7. Price, *The Marshall Plan and Its Meaning*, pp. 315-16.

8. For Kennan's memo to Acheson, May 23, 1947, see *FRUS, 1947*, 3:225. For Marshall's speech, see *A Decade of American Foreign Policy. Basic Documents, 1941-49* (Washington, D.C., 1950), p. 1269. For an attack by Acheson on the Soviet Union for pursuing "policies diametrically opposed to the very premises of international accord and recovery," see *New York Times*, June 16, 1947, p. 1. For indications of a similar line of reasoning by President Truman, see Harry S. Truman, *Year of Decisions* (New York: Signet Books, 1955), pp. 263-64; and *Years of Trial and Hope* (New York: Signet Books, 1956), pp. 134-37, 268-70.

9. Dunn to Secretary of State, March 20, 1948, *FRUS, 1948*, 3:857. See also Dunn to Secretary of State, March 1, 1948, *ibid.*, p. 835; Marshall to Embassy in Great Britain, March 10, 1948, *ibid.*, pp. 847-48; Dunn to Secretary of State, March 16, 1948, *ibid.*, p. 852 and pp. 853-54. For State Department support for measures against the communists in France, see Memo of Conversation Marshall-Queuille, November 18, 1948, *ibid.*, pp. 679-81.

10. For a discussion of this from the Norwegian point of view, see Øivind Stenersen, "Venstrekreftene i norsk politikk 1945–65" (The Left in Norwegian Politics 1945–65), in Trond Bergh and Helge Pharo, eds., *Vekst og Velstand: Norsk Politisk Historie 1945–1965* (Growth and Prosperity: Norwegian Political History 1945–1965) (Oslo: Universitetsforlaget, 1977), pp. 346–51.

11. Conover to Secretary of State, Subject: Visit of ECA Labor Advisers to Norway, NA, 840.50 Recovery /7-2748, p. 4.

12. Bay to Secretary of State, NA, 840.50 Recovery /1-2948, pp. 4–5.

13. Bay to Secretary of State, NA, 840.50 Recovery /2-248; Bay to Secretary of State, NA, 840.50 Recovery /1-2748; Bay to Secretary of State, NA, 840.50 Recovery /1-2948.

14. Bay to Secretary of State, NA, 840.50 Recovery /2-448. For a Norwegian dissertation on the attitude of the Labor party to the Marshall Plan, see Terje Emblem, "Arbeiderpartiet og Norges tilslutning til Marshallplanen" (The Labor Party and Norway's Acceptance of the Marshall Plan) (University of Bergen, 1977), in particular pp. 22–27, 32–37, 59–61, 61–66. Mimeo.

15. Bay to Secretary of State, NA, 840.50 Recovery /1-2948, pp. 4–5; the quotation is from T. B. Olson to Secretary of State, NA 840.50 Recovery /2-548.

16. The Carey mission will be further analyzed in chapter 7. For Bay's change of attitude about a visit from Carey, see in particular Personal for Armour from Bay, NA, 840.50 Recovery /2-2148.

17. Bay to Secretary of State, NA, 840.50 Recovery /4-248, pp. 4–5; Publicity in Norway Concerning Operations of Economic Cooperation Administration, NA, 840.50 Recovery /7-848, Enc. no. 1, p. 1.

18. For a somewhat broader treatment of this, see Geir Lundestad, *The American Non-Policy Towards Eastern Europe 1943–47* (Oslo-New York: Universitetsforlaget-Humanities Press, 1975), pp. 406–7.

19. *Ibid.*, p. 406; Gunnar Adler-Karlsson, *Vestblokkens økonomiske krigføring 1947–1967* (The Economic Warfare of the West 1947–1967) (Oslo: Pax, 1970), pp. 29–52, in particular pp. 40–41; Memorandum on Current Economic Developments, November 22, 1948, *FRUS, 1948*, 4:585.

20. Memorandum on Current Economic Developments, November 22, 1948, *FRUS, 1948*, 4:587; Lovett to Embassy in France, June 1, 1949, *FRUS, 1949*, 5:123; Policy Paper Approved by Foreign Assistance Correlation Committee, July 1, 1949, *ibid.*, pp. 131–32; Policy Statement on Norway, September 15, 1950, *FRUS, 1950*, 3:1537.

21. Memorandum on Current Economic Developments, *FRUS, 1948*, 4:587; Policy Statement of Department of State, August 15, 1949, *FRUS, 1949*, 4:778; Adler-Karlsson, *Vestblokkens økonomiske krigføring*, pp. 74–76; Policy Paper Approved by Foreign Assistance Correlation Committee, July 1, 1949, *FRUS, 1949*, 5:131–132.

22. Lovett to Embassy in Sweden, NA, 840.50 Recovery /1-749, p. 1; Foster to Lovett, NA, 840.50 Recovery /12-3048; Matthews to Secretary of State, NA, 840.50 Recovery /1-749.

23. Adler-Karlsson, *Vestblokkens økonomiske krigføring*, pp. 74–76; Some Loopholes in U.S. Export Control Program, May 31, 1949, Declassified Documents Reference System, 1978, CIA Intelligence Memorandum No. 174; Policy Paper Approved by Foreign Assistance Correlation Committee, July 1, 1949, *FRUS, 1949*, 5:131–132. See also Harriman to Hoffman, October 15, 1949, *ibid.*, p. 150, n. 1. For a description of what Sweden exported to the Soviet Union and Eastern Europe, see Matthews to Secretary of State, NA, 840.50 Recovery /12-1649.

24. United Nations, *Economic Bulletin for Europe,* 3(2):49–64; Acheson to Embassy in France, November 2, 1949, *FRUS, 1949,* 4:350–51; Adler-Karlsson, *Vestblokkens økonomiske krigføring,* pp. 39–44.

25. Recommendations of National Association of Manufacturers on Principles, Conditions, and Administration of Economic Aid to Europe (undated), Clifford Papers, Folder: Economic Cooperation Administration, point E.1.

26. Norway—Country Study, Economic Cooperation Administration, Washington, D.C., 1949, Hovde Papers, Box 5, Folder: Norway #1, p. 41.

27. Bay to Secretary of State, NA, 840.50 Recovery /10-1347, pp. 1–2; Baldwin to Secretary of State: Norwegian Steel Mill Project, NA, 857.6511/11-148.

28. Interview with former Minister of Finance (and Commerce) Erik Brofoss, July 31, 1974, and with the present Director of the Norwegian Central Bank, Knut Getz-Wold, October 20, 1973. The latter had close contact with the ECA mission in Oslo during the period of the Marshall Plan. For the report by the director of the works, Ulf Styren, see Marshallplanen—OEEC, January–November 1948, letters from Ulf Styren to Colbjørnsen, dated January 8 and 9, 1948, Colbjørnsen Papers, Box 7.

29. Perkins to Fulbright, NA, 857.6511/9-2849; Policy Statement on Norway, September 15, 1950, *FRUS, 1950,* 3:1536.

30. Acheson to Embassy in London, NA, 840.20/3-2349, p. 2; Bay to Secretary of State, NA, 840.20/6-2149, sec. 1, pp. 6–7.

31. *Stortingsforhandlingene, 1951,* 2a, St. prp. no. 123; *ibid.,* 7b, pp. 2267–85; *ibid., 1953,* 2b, St. meld. no. 7. See also interviews referred to in note 28.

32. Morgenstierne to Norwegian Foreign Office, October 13, 1948, UD Papers, Record Group 44.2/26, Folder 13. For this point in the Economic Cooperation Act of 1948, see *A Decade of American Foreign Policy, 1941 40* (Washington, D.C., 1950), p. 1312.

33. Answer delivered by Morgenstierne to State Department, October 11, 1948, UD Papers, Record Group 44.2/26, Folder 13. For a more general account of private versus state trading, see Arkes, *Bureaucracy,* pp. 325–26.

34. Knut Einar Eriksen, "Norge i det vestlige samarbeid" (Norway in the Western Community), in *Vekst og Velstand,* pp. 191–92; Interview with Jens Boyesen, Price Papers, Box 1; Interview with Erik Brofoss, *ibid.,* pp. 5–7.

35. See, for instance, Diverse Notater (Miscellaneous), Brofoss on June 14(?), 1949, Langhelle Papers, Box 11.

36. Caffery to Secretary of State, March 20, 1948, *FRUS, 1948,* 3:395–98.

37. Caffery to Secretary of State, March 23, 1948, *ibid.,* pp. 401–13 and March 28, 1948, pp. 404–8.

38. Lovett to Embassy in France, April 8, 1948, *FRUS, 1948,* 3:414–17.

39. For the Economic Cooperation Act of 1948, see *A Decade of American Foreign Policy, 1941–49,* pp. 1299–1321.

40. For the Norwegian-American agreement, see *Stortingsforhandlingene, 1948,* vol. 2a, St. prp. no. 107. As to the negotiations on the bilateral agreements, see pp. 1–2.

41. *Ibid.,* pp. 7–8, point III, c. The corresponding article in the Economic Cooperation Act is found in *A Decade of American Foreign Policy, 1941–49,* p. 1315, art. 115b, 2.

42. Annex, Interpretative notes, point 2, *Stortingsforhandlingene, 1948,* St. prp. no. 107, p. 18. For Brofoss's dislike of this article, see *Stortingsforhandlingene, 1948,* 7b, p. 1901. See also Conover to Secretary of State, Enc. no. 1, NA, 840.50 Recovery /7-1548.

43. Staley to ECA, Washington, December 6, 1948, Records of Economic Cooperation Administration, Box 2, Folder 2; *Stortingsforhandlingene, 1948,* 7b, p. 1901. For an analysis of the policy of the Norwegian government in this period, see Trond Bergh, "Norsk økonomisk politikk 1945–65" (Norwegian Economic Policy 1945–65), in *Vekst og Velstand,* pp. 33–35. In a study on the Netherlands it has been suggested that the Dutch government had to agree to a reduction in government subsidies. For this, see Herman Langeveld, "Die Niederländische Gewerkschaftsbewegung unter der Marshall-Plan" (The Dutch Trade Union Movement under the Marshall Plan), paper submitted to the conference "Marshall-Plan und Europäische Linke" (The Marshall Plan and the European Left), Essen, West Germany, July 7–11, 1977, pp. 18–19.

In Norway no reduction in subsidies took place before in 1950. However, this reduction was followed by new increases in 1951–52. For this, see *Norges økonomi etter krigen* (The Norwegian Post-War Economy), (Oslo: Statistisk Sentralbyrå, 1965), pp. 385–87. Most likely no general policy existed against consumer subsidies. Instead, the cuts in the Dutch budget probably reflected the desire to see a balanced budget.

44. Franklin D. Scott, *Scandinavia* (Cambridge, Mass.: Harvard University Press, 1975), pp. 253–54; William Jansen, "Devalueringen i 1949" (The Devaluation of 1949) (Dissertation, Trondheim, 1975), pp. 63–65.

45. Hoffman to Harriman, March 17, 1949, *FRUS, 1949,* 4:377–80. See also Hoffman to Katz, August 3, 1949, *ibid.,* p. 413.

46. Hoffman to Harriman, March 17, 1949, *ibid.,* p. 379; Webb to Embassy in United Kingdom, May 28, 1949, *ibid.,* p. 398.

47. Position Paper on Pound-Dollar Problems by Policy Planning Staff, September 3, 1949, *ibid.,* pp. 827–29. For the communiqué after the American-British-Canadian meeting of September 7–12, leading to the British devaluation, see *ibid.,* pp. 833–39, in particular p. 834. See also Dean Acheson, *Present at the Creation: My Years in the State Department* (New York: Norton, 1969), pp. 322–25.

48. Norway, ECA Country Study, p. 32; European Recovery Program, Statement by A. E. Staley, Jr., Snyder Papers, Box 12, p. 15.

49. *Stortingsforhandlingene, 1948,* vol. 2a, St. prp. no. 107, p. 8, article II, 1d.

50. For Washington's attitude to Franco-Italian cooperation, see Policy Statement of Department of State, September 20, 1948, *FRUS, 1948,* 3:656; and Memo of Conversation Marshall-Queuille, November 18, 1948, p. 681. For discussions about a Scandinavian customs union in the fall of 1947, see Helge Pharo, "Bridgebuilding and Reconstruction: Norway Faces the Marshall Plan," *Scandinavian Journal of History* (1976), 1:145.

51. Bay to Secretary of State, NA, 840.50 Recovery /2-648. For a somewhat less categorical attitude on the part of Minister of Commerce Brofoss, see Baldwin to Secretary of State, *ibid.,* 857.50/10-1848, pp. 1–2.

52. European Recovery Program, Statement by A. E. Staley, Jr., Snyder Papers, Box 12, pp. 16–17.

53. Trip File, Europe, July 2–24, 1949, Memo for President, undated, Snyder Papers, Box 33, pp. 2–3. For a discussion of how the Norwegian government expected to be protected by the British, see Pharo, "Bridgebuilding and Reconstruction," pp. 139–40.

54. *Stortingsforhandlingene, 1950,* 2a, St. prp. no. 8; *ibid.,* 7b, p. 2316.

55. Editorial Note, *FRUS, 1949,* 4:397. See also Foster to Hoffman, April 29, 1949, *ibid.,* p. 386; Ernst H. Van der Beugel, *From Marshall Aid to Atlantic Part-*

nership: European Integration as a Concern of American Foreign Policy (Amsterdam: Elsevier, 1966), pp. 188–203.

56. *Stortingsforhandlingene, 1950,* 2b, St. meld. no. 21, pp. 7–10.

57. Hysen to Gross, December 9, 1949, Records of Economic Cooperation Administration, ACC 56-A-21, Box 4, Folder 10; Brofoss to Nordnes, January 23, 1950, *ibid.;* Harriman to Marshall, Perkins, and Hoffman, December 1, 1949, NA, 840.50 Recovery /12-149; Acheson to Harriman, NA, 840.50 Recovery /12-549. See also *Norges økonomi etter krigen,* pp. 384–85; *Stortingsforhandlingene, 1950,* 2b, St. meld. no. 21, pp. 7–10; *ibid., 1951,* 2b, St. meld. no. 11, pp. 14–15; Halvard M. Lange, "European Union: False Hopes and Realities," *Foreign Affairs* (1950), 28:441–50.

58. Arkes, *Bureaucracy,* pp. 164–71, 195–97, 202–10, 263–72.

59. Arkes, *Bureaucracy,* pp. 166–70, 268–70; For Klemmer from Saugstad, NA, 840.50 Recovery /7-2748; Bay to Secretary of State, NA, 840.50 Recovery /7-2048. For an interesting remark by Clayton on the influence of the shipping lobby, see Memorandum by Clayton, May 31, 1947, *FRUS, 1947,* 3:231.

60. *Stortingsforhandlingene, 1948,* St. prp. no. 107, pp. 11–12 (for the corresponding article in the Economic Cooperation Act of 1948, see *A Decade of American Foreign Policy, 1941–49,* p. 1315, point 5); *Stortingsforhandlingene, 1948,* St. prp. no. 107, pp. 3, 21–22.

61. European Recovery Program, Statement by A. E. Staley, Jr., Snyder Papers, Box 12, p. 16; Colbjørnsen to Foreign Office, September 23, 1948, UD Papers, Record Group 44 .2/26, Folder 12. After 1950 Norway delivered magnesium to the United States under Article V of the bilateral agreement. For this, see *Stortingsforhandlingene, 1951,* 7b, p. 2272.

62. Baldwin to Secretary of State, NA, 857.6359/11-248; Baldwin to Secretary of State, NA, 857.50/10-1848, pp. 4–5; Villard to Secretary of State, NA, 840.50 Recovery /11-149; Conover to Secretary of State, NA, 840.50 Recovery /7-1548, p. 2; *Stortingsforhandlingene, 1948,* 7b, pp. 1875–81, 1901. In the end the sale of molybdenum to the Soviet Union was stopped, although apparently not for East-West political reasons. For this, see Policy Statement on Norway, September 15, 1950, *FRUS, 1950,* 3:1537.

63. For an account of how the counterpart funds worked, see Arkes, *Bureaucracy,* pp. 156–58, 285–300. For this part of the Norwegian-American agreement, see *Stortingsforhandlingene, 1948,* St. prp. no. 107, pp. 9–11, article IV.

64. Staley to Brofoss, November 3, 1948, Records of Economic Cooperation Administration, ACC 56-A-21, Box 2, Folder 2; To National Advisory Council from NAC Staff Committee, December 3, 1948, Subject: Use of Counterpart Funds in Norway, *ibid.;* Hoffman to Harriman, October 30, 1948; *ibid.;* National Advisory Council, Document 88, December 31, 1948, *ibid.;* Staley to ECA, Washington, November 16 and December 6, 1948, *ibid.;* Staley to Harriman, October 13, 1948, *ibid.*

65. Bourneuf to Gross, October 17, 1949, Records of Economic Cooperation Administration, ACC 56-A-21, Box 2, Folder 4; Meeting with Brofoss, October 25, 1949, *ibid.;* Conference with Brofoss, December 16, 1949, *ibid.;* Gross to Pozzy, July 11, 1950, *ibid.;* Harriman to ECA, Oslo, October 12, 1949, *ibid.,* Folder 2. For the discussion in 1952, see Gross to Secretary of State, March 20, 1952, *ibid.,* Box 2, Folder 7; Wiggins to Woodbridge, February 29, 1952, *ibid.;* From National Advisory Council Staff Committee to National Advisory Council, March 29, 1952, *ibid.;* Gross to Mutual Security Administration, Washington, July 1, 1952, *ibid.*

66. *Stortingsforhandlingene, 1952,* 2a, St. prp. no. 40; *1952,* St. prp. no. 123;

ibid., 1953, St. prp. no. 132; *ibid., 1950,* 2a, St. prp. no. 92; *ibid., 1952,* 7a, pp. 1471–75.

67. Arkes, *Bureaucracy,* pp. 292–93.

68. *Ibid.,* pp. 293–94; Price, *The Marshall Plan and Its Meaning,* pp. 315–16.

69. Arkes, *Bureaucracy,* p. 293; and Foster to ECA Mission in France, December 6, 1949, *FRUS, 1949,* 4:684.

70. Memorandum of Conversation Marshall-Queuille, November 18, 1948, *FRUS, 1948,* 3:681.

71. See, for instance, Memorandum of Conversation Marshall-Queuille, *FRUS, 1948,* 3:681; Bruce to Hoffman, April 4, 1949, *FRUS, 1949,* 4:637–38; Hoffman to ECA Mission in France, April 6, 1949, *ibid.,* pp. 638–39; Reed to Hoffman, May 23, 1949, *ibid.,* pp. 643–45; Webb to Embassy in France, October 4, 1949, *ibid.,* pp. 667–68.

72. Bingham to Hoffman, October 22, 1949, *FRUS, 1949,* 4:671–72. See also Bingham to Hoffman, November 21, 1949, *ibid.,* pp. 678–80; Foster to ECA Mission in France, December 6, 1949, *ibid.,* pp. 682–86.

73. Webb to Embassy in France, October 4, 1949, *FRUS, 1949,* 5:667–68; Foster to ECA Mission in France, December 6, 1949, *ibid.,* pp. 683–84.

74. Country Study on Norway, Economic Cooperation Administration, February 1949, pp. 4–5. For a similar analysis by the State Department, see Policy Statement on Norway, September 15, 1950, *FRUS, 1950,* 3:1533–36.

75. Country Study on Norway, Economic Cooperation Administration, February 1949, pp. 4–5, 14–15, 34, 49; Statement by A. E. Staley, Jr., Snyder Papers, Box 12, Folder: European Recovery Program, pp. 14, 17; interview with Bay, *Aftenposten,* September 22, 1948, p. 1.

76. Mission Comments on Norwegian Investment Program, July 14, 1950, Records of Economic Cooperation Administration, ACC 56-A-21, Box 5, Folder 8, pp. 1–5; Country Study on Norway, Economic Cooperation Administration, February 1949, pp. 47–48, 59–60; Policy Statement on Norway, September 15, 1950, *FRUS, 1950,* 3:1535–36.

77. Conversation with Brofoss, February 21, 1950, Records of Economic Cooperation Administration, ACC 56-A-21, Box 2, Folder 5; Country Study on Norway, Economic Cooperation Administration, February 1949, pp. 47–48, 59–60. For efforts to increase tourism in Norway, see *Stortingsforhandlingene, 1950,* 2a, St. prp. no. 10. For an account of the Norwegian system of control and regulation, see *Norges økonomi etter krigen,* pp. 363–96. For Staley's defense of Norwegian price controls and subsidies, see Staley to ECA, Washington, December 6, 1948, Records of the Economic Cooperation Administration, ACC 56-A-21, Box 2, Folder 2.

78. See Geir Lundestad, "Hovedtendenser i norsk politikk 1945–65" (Main Trends in Norwegian Politics 1945–65), in *Vekst og Velstand,* pp. 485–86. Interview with Knut Getz-Wold, Truman Library, Oral History Collection on the Marshall Plan, pp. 9–10.

79. *Stortingsforhandlingene, 1948,* 7b, pp. 1951–81, in particular pp. 1980–81; Lundestad, "Hovedtendenser i norsk politikk 1945–65," pp. 485–86.

80. See for instance Conover to Secretary of State, NA, 840.50 Recovery /1-349, pp. 1–3.

81. Interview with Shaw Livermore, Truman Library, Oral History Collection, p. 37. See also Interview with Harriman, Price Papers, Box 1, p. 3; Statement by A. E. Staley, Jr., Snyder Papers, Box 12, Folder: European Recovery Program, p. 11, also pp. 12, 18–21. For a quite favorable account of Norwegian economic policies by a former member both of the ECA mission in Oslo and later in Paris, see Alice

Bourneuf, *Norway: The Planned Revival* (Cambridge, Mass.: Harvard University Press, 1958), particularly pp. 198–212. See also Interview with Alice Bourneuf, Price Papers, Box 1, pp. 1–2; Interview with Arne Skaug, *ibid.*, pp. 1–2.

82. Statement by A. E. Staley, Jr., Snyder Papers, Box 12, Folder: European Recovery Program, p. 13; Country Study on Norway, Economic Cooperation Administration, February 1949, p. 14.

83. Statement by A. E. Staley, Jr., Snyder Papers, Box 12, Folder: European Recovery Program, pp. 18–21. For an important letter from Staley to Paul Hoffman, see Bay to Secretary of State, NA, 840.50 Recovery /3-1549, Enc. (1). For Bay's attitude, see Bay to Secretary of State, NA, 840.50 Recovery /3-1549. For a discussion of the way the 1949–50 distribution was decided within the OEEC, see Van der Beugel, *From Marshall Aid to Atlantic Partnership*, pp. 157–66.

84. Bay to Secretary of State, NA, 840.50 Recovery /4-248, p. 4. Bay to Secretary of State, NA, 840.50 Recovery /7-2048; Baldwin to Secretary of State, NA, 840.50 Recovery /7-3048; Baldwin to Secretary of State, NA, 840.50 Recovery /8-648.

85. Interview with Brofoss, Price Papers, Box 1, p. 8; Interview with Knut Getz-Wold, October 29, 1973; Labouisse to Radius, NA 840.50 Recovery /2-349.

86. Baldwin to Secretary of State, NA, 840.50 Recovery /6-248; State Department to Embassy in Oslo, NA, 840.50 Recovery /1-449.

87. Bay to Secretary of State, NA, 840.50 Recovery /8-349; Villard to Secretary of State, NA, 840.50 Recovery /11-1749; Acheson to Embassy in Oslo, 840.50 Recovery /11-1749.

88. See, for instance, The Diary of Arne Ording, University Library of Oslo, December 12, 1949. See also Conover to Secretary of State, NA, 840.50 Recovery /7-2748.

89. Brofoss to Foreign Office, June 16, 1949, UD Papers, Papers from Department of Commerce, Box B 1, CEA Special Mission to Norway.

90. For statistics on Norwegian-American trade, see *Norges økonomi etter krigen*, p. 204. Detailed figures for Scandinavian trade with the United States have been obtained from the Norwegian Central Bureau of Statistics.

91. Arkes, *Bureaucracy*, pp. 291–92. For the figures for the 1945–1947 period, see United States Foreign Assistance Program as of December 31, 1947, *FRUS, 1947*, 1:1026–27.

92. This conclusion to a considerable extent follows that reached by Ernst H. Van der Beugel in his *From Marshall Aid to Atlantic Partnership*, passim, in particular pp. 166–72, 215–25.

93. For a discussion of this point with regard to U.S. policies in Eastern Europe, see Lundestad, *The American Non-Policy*, pp. 320–24.

94. Memorandum by Secretary of State to President on United States Credit and Investment Policy, August 20, 1948, *FRUS, 1948*, 1(2): 952–58. The quotation is from p. 955.

95. For a comparison with Eastern Europe, see Lundestad, *The American Non-Policy*, pp. 324–28.

96. For short accounts of the policies of the Truman administration toward Yugoslavia after Tito's break with the Soviet Union, see Gaddis Smith, *Dean Acheson*, pp. 363–67, in vol. 16 of the series The American Secretaries of State and Their Diplomacy (New York: Cooper Square Publishers, 1972); Lorraine M. Lees, "The American Decision to Assist Tito, 1948–1949," *Diplomatic History* (1978), 2(4): 407–22.

6. The Origins of NATO

1. Herbert Feis, *From Trust to Terror: The Onset of the Cold War, 1945–1950* (New York: Norton, 1970), pp. 381, 383.
2. *Ibid.,* p. 308.
3. Louis J. Halle, *The Cold War As History* (New York: Harper & Row, 1967), pp. 180–84. The quotation is from p. 180.
4. Joyce and Gabriel Kolko, *The Limits of Power: The World and United States Foreign Policy, 1945–1954* (New York: Harper & Row, 1972), p. 715.
5. *Ibid.,* p. 499.
6. William Appleman Williams, *The Tragedy of American Diplomacy* (New York: Delta Books, 1962), p. 273.
7. Walter LaFeber, *America, Russia, and the Cold War, 1945–1966* (New York: Wiley, 1968), p. 78. See also pp. 64–65, 67–68. For the views of Gardner, Fleming, and Horowitz, see the Lloyd C. Gardner essay on the postwar period in William A. Williams, ed., *From Colony to Empire: Essays in the History of American Foreign Relations* (New York: Wiley, 1972), pp. 359–64, especially pp. 359–60. Also Gardner, *Architects of Illusion: Men and Ideas in American Foreign Policy* (Chicago: Quadrangle, 1970), p. 231; D. F. Fleming, *The Cold War and Its Origins, 1917–1960* (London: Allen and Unwin, 1961), 1:514–15; David Horowitz, *From Yalta to Vietnam* (Harmondsworth: Pelican Books, 1969), pp. 262–64.
8. Stephen E. Ambrose, *Rise to Globalism: American Foreign Policy Since 1938* (Baltimore: Penguin Books, 1971), p. 177. See also, pp. 165–66, 169–71, 173–74, 180–82.
9. For an account of the events leading up to the Dunkirk treaty, see Duff Cooper, *Old Men Forget* (London: Rupert Hart-Davis, 1953), pp. 359–73.
10. For the Bevin-Marshall talks, see Memorandum by the British Foreign Office, undated, *FRUS, 1947,* 3:818–19; British Memorandum of Conversation, undated, *ibid.,* 2:815–29. The quotation is from p. 815.
11. Gallman to Secretary of State, December 22, 1947, *FRUS, 1948,* 3:102, in particular n. 7, p. 2. See also Daniel Yergin, *Shattered Peace: The Origins of the Cold War and the National Security State* (Boston: Houghton Mifflin, 1977), pp. 362–64.
12. For Spaak's attitude, see, for instance, Hickerson to Secretary of State and, attached to this, Millard to Secretary of State, January 17, 1948, NA, 840.20/1-1948.
13. Hickerson to Secretary of State, NA, 840.20/1-948. Another memorandum from Hickerson of the same date is printed in *FRUS, 1948,* 3:6–7. See also interview with Achilles in the Oral History Collection of the Harry S. Truman Library, pp. 8–18.
14. Memorandum from Hickerson to Secretary of State, January 19, 1948, *FRUS, 1948,* 3:6–7.
15. Memorandum by Kennan to Secretary of State, January 20, 1948, *FRUS, 1948,* 3:7–8. For Kennan's own account of his attitude, see his *Memoirs 1925–1950* (Boston: Atlantic-Little, Brown, 1967), pp. 397–406.
16. For an account of the differences between Clayton and Kennan over the Marshall Plan, see my "The Marshall Plan and Eastern Europe: What the Two Reveal About Each Other and American Foreign Policy in 1947," paper presented at the conference "Marshall-Plan und Europäische Linke," Essen, West Germany, July 7–11, 1977, parts 2 and 3.

17. Secretary of State to Inverchapel, January 20, 1948, *FRUS, 1948*, 3:8–9.

18. Memorandum of Conversation by Hickerson, January 21, 1948, *ibid.*, pp. 9–12. The quotation is from p. 11. According to Hickerson, this "inconsistency" was approved by Marshall to satisfy somewhat divergent attitudes within the State Department—my Interview with Hickerson, August 18, 1978; Theodore C. Achilles, "US Role in Negotiations that Led to Atlantic Alliance," *NATO Review* (1979), 4:12.

19. Inverchapel to Lovett, January 27, 1948, *FRUS, 1948*, 3:14–16; The quotation is from p. 14. See also Memorandum of Conversation by Lovett, pp. 12–14.

20. Lovett to Inverchapel, February 2, 1948. *FRUS, 1948*, 3:17–18.

21. Inverchapel to Lovett, February 6, 1948, *ibid.*, pp. 19–20.

22. Memorandum of Conversation by Hickerson, February 7, 1948, *FRUS, 1948*, 3:21–23; The quotation is from p. 22.

23. Secretary of State to Embassy in Belgium, March 3, 1948, *FRUS, 1948*, 3:35; Memorandum by Hickerson, March 8, 1948, *ibid.*, pp. 40–42; Secretary of State to Embassy in Italy, March 11, 1948, *ibid.*, pp. 45–46; Secretary of State to Embassy in France, February 24, 1948, *FRUS, 1948*, 4:735–36.

24. Caffery to Secretary of State, NA, 840.20/3-448. A paraphrase of the message from Bidault to Marshall is found in Editorial Note, *FRUS, 1948*, 3:38. See also Paul-Henri Spaak, *The Continuing Battle: Memoirs of a European 1936–1966* (London: Weidenfeld, 1971), pp. 143–51.

25. Memo by Hickerson, *FRUS, 1948*, 3:40–42.

26. Walter Millis, ed., *The Forrestal Diaries* (New York: Viking, 1951), pp. 387–88; and Memorandum for the Secretary, Subject: The March "Crisis," dated December 23, 1948, Forrestal Papers. It is interesting to note that there are few references to the Clay telegram in the papers of the State Department and hardly any at all in the papers published in *FRUS, 1948*, 3.

For a collection of Clay's messages which reveals how isolated the one of March 5 stands in his reports from Germany, see Jean Edward Smith, ed., *The Papers of General Lucius D. Clay. Germany 1945–1949*, 2 vols (Bloomington: Indiana University Press, 1974). In December 1948 Clay himself objected to the way in which the March 5 report was read out of context with others—see *Papers of General Lucius D. Clay*, 2:961-62. For this argument as presented by his biographer, see Jean Edward Smith, "From Compromise to Confrontation: US Foreign Policy from Byrnes to Marshall." Paper presented at the conference "Marshall-Plan und Europäische Linke," Essen, West Germany, July 7–11, 1977, pp. 29–31.

27. Secretary of State to Embassy in Italy, March 11, 1948, *FRUS, 1948*, 3:45–46.

28. Secretary of State to Inverchapel, March 12, 1948, *FRUS, 1948*, 3:48. The British had to ask for a little time for further study before their representatives could leave for the talks in Washington. For this, see Inverchapel to Secretary of State, March 14, 1948, *FRUS, 1948*, 3:52.

29. The reports from Helsinki, Warsaw, and Moscow are most extensively dealt with in Magne Skodvin, *Norden eller NATO? Utenriksdepartementet og alliansespørsmålet 1947–1949* (Scandinavia or NATO? The Foreign Office and the Question of Alliance 1947–1949) (Oslo: Universitetsforlaget, 1971), pp. 93–96.

30. Skodvin, *Norden eller NATO?* pp. 96–103. See also Bay to Secretary of State, March 11, 1948, *FRUS, 1948*, 3:44–45; and British Embassy to Department of State, March 11, 1948, p. 46. For Bay's reports on his conversation with Lange, see Bay to Secretary of State, NA 857.20/3-948; and Bay to Secretary of State, March 11, 1948, *FRUS, 1948*, 3:44–45.

31. British Embassy to Department of State, March 11, 1948, *FRUS, 1948*,

3:46–47. In his book *The Challenge of Scandinavia: Norway, Sweden, Denmark, and Finland in Our Time* (London: R. Hale, 1956), pp. 15–16, William Shirer suggests that the United States, in information to the Norwegian government, exaggerated the Soviet threat to Norway for its own purposes. There seems to be no evidence to substantiate such a view.

32. Secretary of State to Inverchapel, March 12, 1948, *FRUS, 1948,* 3:48; Inverchapel to Secretary of State, March 14, 1948, *ibid.,* p. 52; Secretary of State to Embassy in France, March 12, 1948, *ibid.,* p. 50; and British Embassy to Department of State, March 11, 1948, *ibid.,* pp. 47–48.

33. The only reports in the *New York Times* in March 1948 about the alleged threat to Norway were denials by two Norwegian politicians that Norway had received any Soviet request for a defense pact. For these, see *New York Times,* March 15, 1948, p. 4 and March 25, 1948, p. 3.

34. For Truman's speech to Congress, see, for instance, Department of State *Bulletin,* March 28, 1948, pp. 418—20. The quotation is from p. 419.

35. The only one who deals with this problem, however briefly, is Herbert Feis. And even he just summarizes information from the Forrestal Diaries. For this, see Feis, *From Trust to Terror,* p. 298.

36. The Right Honourable Lester B. Pearson, *Memoirs 1948–1957: The International Years* (London: Gollancz, 1974), pp. 39, 41–42, 48; Escott Reid, *Time of Fear and Hope: The Making of the North Atlantic Treaty 1947–1949* (Toronto: McClelland and Stewart, 1977), pp. 19–21, 42–43, 50, 70.

37. For the complete message from Marshall to Forrestal, see Marshall to Forrestal, NA, 840.20/2-1148. For the part published in the Forrestal Diaries, see Millis, *Forrestal Diaries,* p. 392. See also Achilles, "US Role in Negotiations," p. 12.

38. Minutes of First Meeting of United States-United Kingdom-Canada Security Conversations, March 22, 1948, *FRUS, 1948,* 3:61.

39. For Dunn's reports on the situation in Italy, see *FRUS, 1948,* 3, particularly pp. 845–47, 850–52, 858–70, 877–78. For Kennan's view, see Kennan to Secretary of State, March 15, 1948, pp. 848–49. For Hickerson's comments, see p. 849, n. 1.

40. See, for instance, Caffery to Secretary of State, March 2, 1948, *FRUS, 1948,* 3:34–35 and Millard to Secretary of State, March 10, 1948, *ibid.,* p. 42.

41. Department of State *Bulletin,* March 28, 1948, p. 419.

42. Joint Message from Bidault and Bevin to Secretary of State, March 17, 1948, *FRUS, 1948,* 3:55–56.

43. Minutes of First Meeting of US-UK-Canada Security Conversations, March 22, 1948, *FRUS, 1948,* 3:60–61. For Canada's role, see Reid, *Time of Fear and Hope,* pp. 10, 30–44.

44. Memorandum by George H. Butler, March 19, 1948, *FRUS, 1948,* 3:58–59. (see also NA, Minutes of the Policy Planning Staff, Meetings on March 16, March 17 [two meetings], March 19); Minutes of First Meeting of US-UK-Canada Security Conversations, March 22, 1948, *FRUS, 1948,* 3:60–61.

45. Memorandum by George Butler, March 19, 1948, *ibid.,* p. 59.

46. Minutes of First Meeting of US-UK-Canada Security Conversations, March 22, 1948, *FRUS, 1948,* 3:60–61; Minutes of Second Meeting of Security Conversations, March 23, 1948, *ibid.,* pp. 64–65; and Report by Policy Planning Staff, March 23, 1948, *ibid.,* pp. 62–63. It should be noted that Kennan did not participate in the writing of this report. For this, see Kennan, *Memoirs: 1925–50,* p. 404.

47. Minutes of Second Meeting of Security Conversations, March 23, 1948, *FRUS, 1948,* 3:64; Minutes of Sixth Meeting of Security Conversations, April 1,

1948, Enclosure-Final Draft, *ibid.,* pp. 73–74. See also Minutes of Second Meeting of Security Conversations, March 23, 1948, *ibid.,* p. 64.

48. Minutes of Second Meeting of Security Conversations, March 23, 1948, *FRUS, 1948,* 3:64–65; Minutes of Third Meeting of Security Conversations, March 24, 1948, *ibid.,* pp. 66–67; and Final Draft, undated, *ibid.,* pp. 73–74.

49. For the list of the participants at the first meeting, see Minutes of First Meeting of Security Conversations, March 22, 1948, *FRUS, 1948,* 3:59. The participants were (with minor exceptions, mostly due to absence), the same throughout the series of meetings.

50. For a good account of Hickerson's ideas and the relationship between Hickerson and Achilles, see the interview with Achilles in the Oral History Collection of the Harry S. Truman Library, pp. 8–27; and Interview with Hickerson, August 18, 1978.

51. There are no good sources as to the view held by Ambassador Douglas. For what indications we have of the position he held in the security talks, see the minutes of these meetings in *FRUS, 1948,* 3:59–60, 69–70, 70–71. For Butler's position, see Memorandum by George H. Butler, March 19, 1948, *FRUS, 1948,* 3:58–59; Report by Policy Planning Staff Concerning Western Union and Related Problems, March 23, 1948, *ibid.,* pp. 61–64. See also NA, Minutes of the Policy Planning Staff, March 16, March 17, and March 19, 1948.

52. For their lack of strong opinions even in military matters, see Minutes of Fourth Meeting of Security Conversations, March 29, 1948, *FRUS, 1948,* 3:69.

53. Reid, *Time of Fear and Hope,* pp. 48, 62–63, 68; Minutes of Sixth Meeting of Security Conversations, April 1, 1948, *FRUS, 1948,* 3:71–72. Marshall was chairman of the U.S. delegation to the Ninth International Conference of American States in Bogotá, Colombia, which opened on March 30 and lasted until May 2. The Secretary returned to Washington on April 24. For this, see *FRUS, 1948,* 3:68, n. 1 and 103, n. 3. In a letter to the author dated October 27, 1978, Hickerson has denied that he did not consult with his superiors.

54. Final Draft, undated, *FRUS, 1948,* 3:72–75.

55. Report Prepared by Policy Planning Staff Concerning Western Union and Related Problems, March 23, 1948, *ibid.,* pp. 61–64. For Marshall's transmittal, see ibid., p. 61, n. 1. Kennan had not participated in the drafting of this PPS report.

56. Lovett to Secretary of State, April 20, 1948, *FRUS, 1948,* 3:96–97. The conclusion about the information received by Marshall is based on this source as well as on an examination of all the other telegrams sent to the Secretary of State while he was in Bogotá. The telegrams not found in *FRUS* can be located in NA, State Department papers, 710.J-series.

57. Marshall to Lovett, April 23, 1948, *FRUS, 1948,* 3:103.

58. Position of the United States with Respect to Support for Western Union and Other Related Free Countries, April 13, 1948, *ibid.,* pp. 85–88, NSC 9. For NSC 9/1, see NA, Files of the National Security Council, Modern Military Branch, NSC 9/1, April 23, 1948. The fact that NSC 9/1 generally followed NSC 9 can be taken as an indication that the essential features of the latter had been supported by the NSC. See also Minutes-1948, Butler to Lovett, April 15, NA, Papers of Policy Planning Staff, Box 32; Lovett to Marshall, April 20, 1948, *FRUS, 1948,* 3:96; Kenneth W. Condit, "The History of the Joint Chiefs of Staff: The Joint Chiefs of Staff and National Policy, vol. 2, 1947–1949," NA, Modern Military Branch, 1976, pp. 359–66, mimeo; Millis, *Forrestal Diaries,* pp. 422–25.

59. Foreign Policy—Western Union, Memo from Elsey, dated May 5, 1948, Elsey Papers, Box 66; Memo of April 30, 1948, *ibid.* These two memos have been

read out of context with other sources, thus leading to exaggerated conclusions about the President's lack of influence, in Martin Ivan Elzy's "The Origins of American Military Policy, 1945–1950," Ph.D. dissertation, University of Miami, 1975, pp. 234ff.

60. Lovett to Marshall, April 20, 1948, *FRUS, 1948,* 3:96. Foreign Policy— Western Union, Note of April 13, 1948, Western Union Chronology, Elsey Papers, Box 66.

61. For NSC 9 of April 13, see *FRUS, 1948,* 3:85–88. For NSC 9/1 of April 23, 1948, see NA, Files of the National Security Council.

62. For NSC 9/2 of May 11, 1948, see NA, Files of the National Security Council. The quotation is from p. 3.

63. Kennan to Secretary of State, March 15, 1948, *FRUS, 1948,* 3:848–49. See also Eduard Mark, "The Question of Containment: A Reply to John Lewis Gaddis," *Foreign Affairs* (1978), 56:430–40. It seems, however, that in disputing Gaddis's analysis of Kennan's containment policy, Mark goes too far in blurring the differences which undoubtedly existed between Kennan and many other policy makers in Washington. Nevertheless, Kennan's attitude in mid-March is most interesting and certainly at variance with what Kennan himself—and Gaddis—have written about it. For Kennan's position as stated by himself, see his *Memoirs: 1925–50,* pp. 400–4; for Gaddis's analysis, see his "Containment: A Reassessment," *Foreign Affairs* (1977), 55:873–88.

64. Kennan, *Memoirs: 1925–50,* pp. 406–7.

65. Kennan to Souers, April 23, 1948, *FRUS, 1948,* 3:100–3; Kennan to Lovett, April 29, *ibid.,* pp. 108–9. For an indication of the strength of Kennan and Bohlen, see Memorandum from Achilles to Hickerson, May 19, 1948, *ibid.,* pp. 127–28.

66. Kennan to Lovett, May 7, *ibid.,* pp. 116–18.

67. See for instance Memo of Conversation by Lovett, April 27, 1948, *FRUS, 1948,* 3:104–8. The participants in the meeting were Marshall, Lovett, Vandenberg, and Dulles. See also Millis, *Forrestal Diaries,* pp. 434–35; Condit, "History of the Joint Chiefs," pp. 362–63.

68. For indications of uncertainty as to how Congress would react to proposals for American involvement in a military regional arrangement, see for instance the talks between Vandenberg and representatives of the State Department as reported in *FRUS, 1948,* 3:92–96 and 104–8.

69. For the importance of this factor, see for instance Kennan to Lovett, May 7, 1948, *FRUS, 1948,* 3:118; NA, Files of the National Security Council, NSC 9/2, p. 3; Reid, *Time of Fear and Hope,* pp. 87–88.

70. Reid, *Time of Fear and Hope,* pp. 49–51; Lovett to Marshall, NA, 710.J/4-848.

71. For NSC 9/3 of June 28, see *FRUS, 1948,* 3:140–41.

72. For the most important of these talks as far as the role of the United States was concerned, see Minutes of Fifth Meeting of Washington Exploratory Talks on Security, July 9, 1948, *FRUS, 1948,* 3:169–82; Memorandum of Conversation by Lovett, August 20, *ibid.,* pp. 214–21; Sixth Meeting of Exploratory Talks, September 3, pp. 228–32. For Reid's most interesting account, see his *Time of Fear and Hope,* pp. 113–25.

73. Reid, *Time of Fear and Hope,* pp. 62, 68, 103–6; Millis, *Forrestal Diaries,* pp. 422–23; Interview with Hickerson, August 18, 1978.

74. Kennan to Marshall and Lovett, May 24, 1948, *FRUS, 1948,* 3:129–30; Minutes of Fifth Meeting of Exploratory Talks, July 9, 1948, *ibid.,* pp. 169–82; Reid, *Time of Fear and Hope,* pp. 109–11.

75. For Lovett's presentation of the mood of Congress to the participants in the

Washington exploratory talks, see Minutes of First Meeting of Washington Exploratory Talks on Security, July 6, 1948, *FRUS, 1948,* 3:149–50. For the Vandenberg Resolution, see *ibid.,* pp. 135–36.

76. For an indication of differences that remained, see, for instance, Memo of Conversation by Lovett, August 20, 1948, *FRUS, 1948,* 3:214–21.

77. Caffery to Secretary of State, March 2, 1948, *FRUS, 1948,* 3:34–35.

78. For indications of this, see Douglas to Secretary of State, February 26, 1948, *FRUS, 1948,* 3:32–33; Memo by Hickerson to Secretary of State, *ibid.,* pp. 40–42; Memo by Secretary of State to President Truman, March 12, 1948, *ibid.,* pp. 49–50; Reid, *Time of Fear and Hope,* pp. 13–24. For an analysis of the threat of Soviet expansion before 1948, see Lundestad, *The American Non-Policy,* pp. 66–73.

79. Minutes of Second Meeting of United States-United Kingdom-Canada Security Conversations, March 23, 1948, *FRUS, 1948,* 3:64.

80. Memorandum by Participants in Washington Exploratory Talks, September 9, 1948, *ibid.,* p. 238. See also Reid, *Time of Fear and Hope,* pp. 126–33.

81. Minutes of Tenth Meeting of Washington Exploratory Talks, December 22, 1948, *FRUS, 1948,* 3:328–29, 331–32; and Report of International Working Group to Ambassadors' Committee, December 24, 1948, Annex C, (V) Greece and Turkey, *ibid.,* p. 342.

82. Achilles to Bonbright, NA, 840.20/1-1749; Report of International Working Group to Ambassadors' Committee, December 24, 1948, *FRUS, 1948,* 3:339–42; Reid, *Time of Fear and Hope,* pp. 200–11.

83. Achilles to Bonbright, NA, 840.20/1-1749; Minutes of Eleventh Meeting of Washington Exploratory Talks on Security, January 14, 1949, *FRUS, 1949,* 4:27–34. For a detailed presentation of the attitude of the JCS, see NA, Policy Planning Staff Papers, Memorandum for the Secretary of Defense from the JCS, January 5, 1949, pp. 1–5.

84. Memorandum by Participants in Washington Security Talks, September 9, 1948, *FRUS,* 1948, 3:242; Condit, "History of the Joint Chiefs," pp. 365–66; Gaddis Smith, *Dean Acheson,* vol. 16 in the series The American Secretaries of State and Their Diplomacy (New York: Cooper Square Publishers, 1972), pp. 367–71; Theodore J. Lowi, "Bases in Spain," in Harold Stein, ed., *American Civil-Military Decisions: A Book of Case Studies* (Birmingham, Ala.: University of Alabama Press, 1963), pp. 669–70.

85. Memorandum by Participants in Washington Security Talks, September 9, 1948, *FRUS,* 1948, 3:242. The best account of the decision to rearm West Germany is still Laurence W. Martin's "The American Decision to Rearm Germany," in Stein, *American Civil-Military Decisions,* pp. 643–60. See also Condit, "History of the Joint Chiefs," pp. 365–66.

86. Smith, *Dean Acheson,* pp. 108–137; Tang Tsou, *America's Failure in China 1941–50* (Chicago: University of Chicago Press), pp. 494–551.

87. For a study of some of the changes brought about by the Korean War, see John Lewis Gaddis, "Was The Truman Doctrine a Real Turning Point?" *Foreign Affairs* (1974), 52:386–402.

7. Scandinavia: Neutralism or Western Orientation?

1. For Bevin's speech, see *Parliamentary Debates,* House of Commons, 1947–48, 5th series, volume 446, columns 383–403. The quotation is from column 397.

2. Inverchapel to Secretary of State, January 13, 1948, Enc.: Summary of a Memorandum Representing Mr. Bevin's Views on the Formation of a Western Union, *FRUS, 1948,* 3:5; Douglas in London to Secretary of State, February 26, 1948, *ibid.,* p. 33; Prebensen to Norwegian Foreign Office, January 27, 1948, UD Papers, Record Group 25.2/62; Prebensen to Foreign Office, January 23, 1948, *ibid.*

3. Memorandum by Kennan to Secretary of State, January 20, 1948, *FRUS, 1948,* 3:7.

4. For Achilles, see NA, Thoughts on Western European Security, signed by T. C. Achilles, State Department Papers, 840.00/1-2048. For Dulles's position, see Council of Foreign Relations Report on Marshall Plan, February 1948, Discussion Meeting Report, Supplement of 1971, Box 9 of 15, Correspondence 1948–50, pp. 2–4.

5. Memorandum by Hickerson, March 8, 1948, *FRUS, 1948,* 3:42.

6. Matthews to Secretary of State, NA, 758.00/2-448; Matthews to Secretary of State, 758.00/2-648. For a general and brief account of Swedish foreign policy after the Second World War, see Nils Andrén and Åke Landquist, *Svensk utrikespolitik efter 1945* (Swedish Foreign Policy After 1945) (Stockholm: Almquist och Wiksell, 1965). For the reaction to Bevin's speech, see *ibid.,* pp. 40–41, 97–100.

7. Danish Foreign Office, *Dansk Sikkerhedspolitik, 1948–1966. I, Fremstilling* (Danish Security Policy 1948–1966. I, Account) (Copenhagen, 1968), pp. 22–23.

8. Morgenstierne to Lange, February 17, 1948, UD Papers, Record Group 25.4/47. For an account of the resolution and its background, see Knut Einar Eriksen, *DNA og NATO: Striden om norsk NATO-medlemskap innen regjeringspartiet 1948–49* (The Labor Party and NATO: The Struggle Within the Governing Party About Membership for Norway in NATO 1948–49) (Oslo: Gyldendal, 1972), pp. 33–43.

9. For the reaction of the three countries to Bevin's speech, see Eriksen, *DNA og NATO,* pp. 33, 39–41; Magne Skodvin, *Norden eller NATO? Utenriksdepartementet og alliansespørsmålet 1947–1949* (Scandinavia or NATO? The Foreign Office and the Question of Alliance 1947–1949) (Oslo: Universitetsforlaget, 1971), pp. 73–89. See also Bay to Secretary of State, February 6, 1948, *FRUS, 1948,* 3:20–21.

10. Bay to Secretary of State, NA, 840.50 Recovery /2-1348.

11. For reports in January–February 1948 on the Swedish attitude to the European Recovery Program, see Matthews to Secretary of State, NA 840.50 Recovery /1-548; Marshall to Embassy in Stockholm, January 15, 1948, NA, 840.50 Recovery /1-548; Matthews to Secretary of State, NA, 840.50 Recovery /1-1548; Matthews to Secretary of State, NA, 840.50 Recovery /2-348; Caffery to Secretary of State, NA, 840.50 Recovery /2-2448.

12. Matthews to Secretary of State, February 16, 1948, *FRUS, 1948,* 3:23–24. For this alleged special feature in Sweden's national character, see Matthews to Secretary of State, NA, 758.00/3-348; and Matthews to Secretary of State, 741.57D/7-1248.

13. Matthews to Secretary of State, NA, 758.00/3-348.

14. Bay to Secretary of State, February 19, 1948, *FRUS, 1948,* 3:24–26.

15. Bay to Secretary of State, February 25, 1948, *ibid.,* pp. 30–32. For a similar report from Trimble in Iceland, see Trimble to Secretary of State, NA, 840.50 Recovery /3-348.

16. For an account of the Gerhardsen speech and its background, see Øivind Stenersen, "Venstrekreftene i norsk politikk 1945–65" (The Left in Norwegian Politics 1945–65) in Trond Bergh and Helge Pharo, eds., *Vekst og velstand: Norsk poli-*

tisk historie 1945–1965 (Growth and Prosperity: Norwegian Political History 1945–1965). (Oslo: Universitetsforlaget, 1977), pp. 346–51.

17. See, for instance, Hickerson's comments to Morgenstierne as reported in UD Papers, Record Group 25.4/47, Morgenstierne to Lange, February 26, 1948.

18. Morgenstierne to Lange, February 17, 1948 and February 26, 1948, UD Papers, Record Group 25.4/47.

19. Morgenstierne to Lange, March 3, 1948 and February 24, 1948, *ibid.*

20. Matthews to Lovett, NA, 711.58/2-1748. See also Lovett to Matthews, February 21, 1948, NA, 711.58/2-1748; for Matthews' letter to Hickerson, see Matthews to Hickerson, March 16, 1948, NA, 711.58/3-2348.

21. Marshall to Embassy in Stockholm, January 31, 1948, NA, 758.00/1-2748 (for Matthews's conversation with Vougt, see Matthews to Secretary of State, 758.00/1-2748); Matthews to Lovett, NA, 711.58/3-2348. Lovett's letter to Matthews of March 5 is missing from the files. See also Lovett to Matthews, March 27, 1948, NA, 711.58/3-2348; and Matthews to Lovett, NA, 711.58/4-848.

22. Matthews to Lovett, NA, 711.58/3-2348, in particular pp. 1–2; Matthews to Hickerson, March 16, 1948, *ibid.* The quotation is from p. 2.

23. Bay to Armour, NA, 840.50 Recovery /2-648. See also Bay to Armour, NA, 840.50 Recovery /2-2148; Bay to Armour, NA, 840.50 Recovery /2-2748; Armour to Bay, March 24, 1948, NA, 840.50 Recovery /2-2748.

24. Armour to Bay, February 26, 1948, NA, 840.50 Recovery /2-648. See also Armour to Bay, March 24, 1948, NA, 840.50 Recovery /2-2748.

25. Armour to Symington, Sullivan, and Royall, all dated February 25, 1948, NA, 857.20/2-1948.

26. Inverchapel to Secretary of State, March 14, 1948, *FRUS, 1948,* 3:52; Minutes of Second Meeting of United States-United Kingdom-Canada Security Conversations, March 23, 1948, *ibid.,* pp. 64–66; Minutes of Sixth Meeting, April 1, 1948, Enc.: Final Draft, *ibid.,* p. 73.

27. Secretary of State to Embassy in Oslo, March 12, 1948, *FRUS, 1948,* 3:51–52.

28. Bay to Secretary of State, NA, 857.20/3-1348; Bay to Secretary of State, March 11, 1948, *FRUS, 1948,* 3:44–45.

29. Bay to Secretary of State, NA, 857.20/3-948; Memo of Conversation Hickerson-Morgenstierne, NA, 840.20/3-1748.

30. Marvel to Secretary of State, March 12, 1948, *FRUS, 1948,* 3:51; Memo of Conversation Rogers-Åström, NA, 840.20/3-3148; Lovett to Marshall, NA, 710.J/4-548, p. 3.

31. The quotation is from a Summary of Remarks by Hugh S. Cumming, Jr., before the Policy Planning Staff, May 4, 1948, NA, State Department Papers, Federal Records Center, Suitland Maryland, Stockholm Post Files, p. 3. For some typical reports from Matthews, see Matthews to Secretary of State, February 16, 1948, *FRUS, 1948,* 3:23–24; Matthews to Secretary of State, April 21, 1948, *ibid.,* 97–98; and Memo of Conversation Matthews-Grafström, May 5, 1948, *ibid.,* pp. 112–14.

32. Memorandum by Secretary of State to President Truman, June 3, 1948, *FRUS, 1948,* 3:134. The memorandum had apparently been drafted by Hickerson and Hulley. For this, see notations on the memo as found in Marshall to Truman, NA, 758.00/6-348.

33. For a clear-cut example of this attitude on the part of Secretary of State Marshall, see Memo of Conversation Marshall-Undén, October 14, 1948, *FRUS, 1948,* 3:264–66.

34. For an account of the American policy toward Finland in the first years after the war, see Lundestad, *The American Non-Policy Towards Eastern Europe 1943–1947* (Oslo-New York: Universitetsforlaget-Humanities Press, 1975), pp. 290–96. See also Raimo Väyrynen, "Finland's Role in Western Policy since the Second World War," in *Cooperation and Conflict* (1977), 2:87–108. For the relevant chapters on Finland in *FRUS*, see *FRUS, 1948,* 4:759–88 and *FRUS, 1949,* 5:434–50, and for a summing up of the American attitude in late 1949, see Department of State Policy Statement, December 1, 1949, *FRUS, 1949,* 5:443–50.

35. Matthews to Secretary of State, February 16, 1948, *FRUS, 1948,* 3:23–24; Matthews to Secretary of State, April 21, 1948, *ibid.,* pp. 97–98; and Memo of Conversation Matthews-Grafström, May 5, 1948, *ibid.,* pp. 112–14. For Marshall's attitude, see Memo of Conversation Marshall-Undén, October 14, 1948, *ibid.,* pp. 264–66.

36. The quotation is from Thorp to Embassy in Copenhagen, NA, 711.59/2-1748. See also Marvel to Secretary of State, NA, 859.24/3-1248; Marvel to Secretary of State, March 24, 1948, *FRUS, 1948,* 3:67–68; *Dansk Sikkerhedspolitik,* pp. 23–25; and Memo of Conversation H. F. Cunningham-Bang-Jensen, NA, 759.61/3-448.

37. Marvel to Secretary of State, March 24, 1948, *FRUS, 1948,* 3:67–68; CIA to Secretary of State, NA, 757 D.00/2-1048; CIA to Secretary of State, 757 D.00/3-2348.

38. See, for instance, Marvel to Secretary of State, NA, 840.00/4-3048; Memo of Conversation Marshall/Lange, October 6, 1948, *FRUS, 1948,* 3:260.

39. For the role of the reciprocity idea in the American-British-Canadian talks in March, see *FRUS, 1948,* 3:73–74, Final Draft, undated. For Vandenberg's attitude, see Memo of Conversation Lovett/Vandenberg, April 18, 1948, *ibid.,* pp. 92–96; Memo of Conversation Marshall/Lovett/Vandenberg/Dulles, April 27, 1948, *ibid.,* pp. 104–8. See also Escott Reid, *Time of Fear and Hope: The Making of the North Atlantic Treaty 1947–1949* (Toronto: McClelland and Stewart, 1977), pp. 102–3.

40. Marvel to Secretary of State, NA, 840.00/4-3048.

41. Personal for Matthews from Hickerson, NA, 857.20/3-2548.

42. Bay to Secretary of State, April 9, 1948, *FRUS, 1948,* 3:80–81.

43. Bay to Secretary of State, NA, 757.00/4-2348, p. 3.

44. Bay to Secretary of State, May 18, 1948, *FRUS, 1948,* 3:126–27. For accounts of Undén's initiative, see Skodvin, *Norden eller NATO?* pp. 123–37; Eriksen, *DNA og NATO,* pp. 124–27.

45. For the early phase of the Scandinavian talks, see Skodvin, *Norden eller NATO?* pp. 137–46, 170–82; Eriksen, *DNA og NATO,* pp. 124–27.

46. Bay to Secretary of State, May 18, 1948, *FRUS, 1948,* 3:126–27; Huston to Secretary of State, June 1, 1948, NA, 757D.00/6-148.

47. Bay to Secretary of State, July 7, 1948, *FRUS, 1948,* 3:160–63. See also Bay to Secretary of State, May 18, 1948, *ibid.,* pp. 126–27; Bay to Secretary of State, NA, 857D.00/9-748.

48. For the situation within the government and the parliamentary group of the Labor Party, see Eriksen, *DNA og NATO,* pp. 110–18, 128–40; for Gerhardsen's position at this time, see Skodvin, *Norden eller NATO?* pp. 137–46; Eriksen, *DNA og NATO,* pp. 114–18. For Matthews's report, see Matthews to Secretary of State, NA, 757.58/5-1348. See also Bay to Secretary of State, May 18, 1948, *FRUS, 1948,* 3:126–127; Bay to Secretary of State, NA, 857.00/5-1548.

49. Bay to Secretary of State, May 18, 1948, *FRUS, 1948,* 3:127.

50. Bay to Secretary of State, NA, 857.00/5-1548; Memo of Conversation Rogers-Morgenstierne, NA, 757.58/6-348.

51. Richard M. Freeland, *The Truman Doctrine and the Origins of Mc-Carthyism: Foreign Policy, Domestic Politics, and Internal Security 1946-1948* (New York: Knopf, 1975), pp. 176–78; Skodvin, *Norden eller NATO?*, pp. 226–27.

52. For an account of the role of the OEEC, see Hadley Arkes, *Bureaucracy, the Marshall Plan, and the National Interest* (Princeton, N.J.: Princeton University Press, 1972), pp. 132–52.

53. For the American reaction to Dutch policies in Indonesia in relation to the European Recovery Program, see Dirk Stikker, *Men of Responsibility* (New York: Harper & Row, 1966), pp. 114–19, 131–32, 139, 145–46, 285–86. See also Arkes, *Bureaucracy*, p. 326; Memo of Conversation Acheson-Stikker, NA, 840.50, Recovery /3-3149.

54. Arkes, *Bureaucracy,* pp. 147–48.

55. Bay to Secretary of State, NA, 840.50 Recovery /2-1148 (quotation from p. 4); for Bay's attitude, see, for instance, Bay to Secretary of State, NA, 840.50 Recovery /4-2248; Bay to Secretary of State, May 8, 1948, *FRUS, 1948*, 3:437–38. For Matthews's attitude, see, for instance, Matthews to Secretary of State, NA, 758.00/3-348.

56. Morgenstierne to Lange, February 13, 1948, UD Papers, Record Group 44.2/26. See also Morgenstierne to Foreign Office, January 24, 1948, *ibid.*

57. NA, Treasury Department Records, Record Group 56, NAC Minutes, Meeting of January 22, 1948, pp. 5-7; Staff Meeting of January 2, p. 2 and January 9, *ibid.*, p. 4.

58. See the references under note 56. See also Memo of Conversation Lovett-Morgenstierne, February 4, 1948, Clayton-Thorp File, Harry S. Truman Library, Box 15.

59. Secretary of State to Embassy in Oslo, NA, 840.50 Recovery /3-2248 (see also Secretary of State to Certain Diplomatic Offices in Europe, March 17, 1948, *FRUS, 1948*, 3:394–95); Marshall to Embassy in Oslo, NA, 840.50 Recovery /5-848.

60. Records of the Economic Cooperation Administration, ACC 56-A-21, Box 2, Folder 2, National Advisory Council Staff, Document no. 228, May 25, 1948, pp. 3–4; Bay to Secretary of State, NA, 840.50 Recovery /4-748; Bay to Secretary of State, NA, 840.50 Recovery /4-1548; Marshall-planen-OEEC, Folder: January–November 1948, PM from Norwegian Embassy to State Department, April 28, 1948, Colbjørnsen Papers, Box 7; Norwegian Embassy in Washington to Foreign Office, March 16, 1948, April 19, 1948, and April 20, 1948, UD Papers, Record Group 44.2/26; *ibid.*, Foreign Office to Embassy in Washington, April 16, 1948.

61. Staff meeting of April 13, 1948, NA, Treasury Department Records, Record Group 56, NAC Minutes, pp. 2–3.

62. Hulley to Labouisse, NA, 840.50 Recovery /3-548. For Hulley's recommendation about Iceland, see Hulley to Labouisse, NA, 840.50 Recovery /3-448.

63. Staff meeting of April 15, NA, Treasury Department Records, Record Group 56, Minutes of the NAC, pp. 4–5.

64. Lovett to Embassy in Oslo, NA, 840.50 Recovery /4-1948. See also Current Economic Developments, May 3, 1948, *FRUS, 1948*, 3:433–35.

65. Lovett to Embassy in Oslo, NA, 840.50 Recovery /4-1948.

66. Bay to Secretary of State, May 8, 1948, *FRUS, 1948*, 3:437–38. See also Bay to Secretary of State, NA, 840.50 Recovery /4-2248; Bay to Secretary of State, NA, 840.50 Recovery /4-2948, pp. 1–2.

67. Marshall to Embassy in Oslo, NA, 840.50 Recovery /5-1848. See also Embassy in Washington to Foreign Office, April 20, 1948, UD Papers, Record Group 44.2/26.

68. Letter from Lynch to Snyder, dated February 10, 1949, Snyder Papers, Box 12, Folder: European Recovery Program 9/27/48–2/11/49, Attachments, table II.

69. Arkes, *Bureaucracy*, p. 292.

70. Robert Ferrell, *George C. Marshall,* vol. 15 in the series The American Secretaries of State and Their Diplomacy (New York: Cooper Square Publishers, 1966), pp. 132–33; Freeland, *The Truman Doctrine,* pp. 177–78.

71. Morgenstierne to Gerhardsen and Brofoss, June 12, 1948, UD Papers, Record Group 44.2/26; *ibid.,* Letter from Nygaard, August 5, 1948; Diary of Gunnar Jahn, University Library, Oslo, May 12, 1948, January 24, 1949; Diary of Arne Ording, University Library, Oslo, January 9 and January 28, 1949; Memo from Bryn, May 12, 1948, Langhelle Papers, Box 1.

72. Eriksen, *DNA og NATO,* pp. 67–68, 228–32.

73. Matthews to Secretary of State, April 21, 1948, *FRUS, 1948,* 3:97–98.

74. Matthews to Secretary of State, NA, 758.00/6-148; Matthews to Secretary of State, April 21, 1948, *FRUS, 1948,* 3:97–98.

75. Memo from Hickerson to Lovett, June 18, 1948, *FRUS, 1948,* 1(pt. 2): 714.

76. Report by National Security Council, Position of United States with Respect to Scandinavia, September 3, 1948, *FRUS, 1948,* NSC 28/1, 3:233. The report was approved by the President on September 4—see p. 232, n. 1.

77. Matthews to Hickerson, no. 442, and to Secretary of State, no. 441, NA, 758.00/4-848. For Hickerson's answer, see Hickerson to Matthews, April 15, 1948, NA, 758.00/4-848.

78. Matthews to Secretary of State, April 21, 1948, *FRUS, 1948,* 3:97–98; Matthews to Secretary of State, NA, 758.00/5-1348; Matthews to Secretary of State, NA, 758.00/6-148.

79. Hulley to Hickerson, NA, 858.24/4-649, Subject: Status of Certain Swedish Arms Matters.

80. Matthews to Secretary of State, July 26, 1948, NA, Federal Records Center, Suitland, Maryland, Oslo Post Files; *ibid.,* Matthews to Secretary of State, August 5, 1948. For the quotation, see Memo from Hickerson to Lovett, September 21, 1948, *FRUS, 1948,* 3:253–54, in particular n. 4, p. 254.

81. Aide-Mémoire from State Department to British Embassy in Washington, NA, 711.58/9-2148.

82. Anderson to Gruenther, September 23, 1948, NA, Modern Military Branch, CCS 381 (8-14-47), Sec. 2; Memorandum for the Records by Lalor, September 22, 1948, *ibid.;* Lovett to Embassy in Sweden, October 22, 1948, *FRUS, 1948,* 3:259.

83. Memo for the files by Thompson, NA, 711.58/8-1748; Matthews to Secretary of State, NA, 840.00/9-2148. See also Lovett to Embassy, Stockholm, NA, 840.00/8-1248; Matthews to Secretary of State, NA, 840.00/8-1248.

84. Rogers to Thompson, NA, 858.00/7-2348.

85. Aide-Mémoire from Norwegian Embassy, NA, 857.20/4-1648. For additional requests see Aide-Mémoire from Norwegian Embassy, NA, 857.20/5-1848; Aide-Mémoire from Norwegian Embassy, NA, 857.20/6-1748; Hickerson to Lovett, April 21, 1948, NA, 857.20/4-1648; Lovett to Forrestal, April 26, 1948, NA, 857.20/4-1648.

86. Memorandum for file by Rogers, NA, 857.20/5-348. See also Memo of Conversation Draper-Bryn, NA, 857.20/4-2648; Memo from Bryn, May 12, 1948, Langhelle Papers, Box 1.

87. Memorandum for Secretary of Defense from William D. Leahy on behalf of Joint Chiefs of Staff, June 10, 1948, Subject: Request by Norwegian Defense Minister for Information on United States Assistance in Case of War, NA, Modern Mili-

tary Branch, p. 1; Request by Norwegian Defense Minister for Information on United States Assistance in Case of War, May 21, 1948, Enc. Forrestal to Marshall, June 14, 1948, *ibid.,* CCS 381 (8-14-47), Sec. 1, JCS 1846/2.

88. Memo from Leahy to Secretary of Defense, June 10, 1948, NA, Modern Military Branch, p. 1.

89. Marshall to Embassy in London, NA, 857.20/7-2048 (see also Marshall to Embassy in Oslo, NA, 857.20/6-2148); Hickerson to Secretary of State, NA, 857.20/6-1448; Position of United States with Respect to Scandinavia, September 10, 1948, Enc.: Memorandum for Wedemeyer, September 1, 1948, NA, Modern Military Branch, CCS 381, Sec. 1, JCS 1929/2; NA, Modern Military Branch, CCS 381, Sec. 1, JCS 1846/2, May 21, 1948, Enc. "C," pp. 20–21.

90. Marshall to Embassy in London, NA, 857.20/7-2048; Douglas to Secretary of State, NA, 857.20/8-1846.

91. Bay to Secretary of State, NA, 857.20/8-2048. For Matthews's support of Bay's telegram, see Matthews to Secretary of State, August 24, 1948, NA, Federal Records Center, Suitland, Maryland, Oslo Post Files.

92. Marshall to Embassy in Oslo, August 27, 1948, NA, 857.20/8-2048; Aide-Mémoire from State Department to Norwegian Embassy, Washington, August 27, 1948, NA, 857.20/6-1748; Hickerson to Nitze, 857.20/9-1048.

93. Lovett to Forrestal, December 20, 1948, NA, 857.20/7-2048. See also Marshall to Forrestal, September 15, 1948, 857.20/7-2048.

94. Memorandum for file from Division of Northern European Affairs, NA, 859.24/4-1349; Memo of Conversation Hickerson-Kauffmann, NA, 840.00/9-1648; Memo of Conversation Gross/Hickerson-Rasmussen/Kauffmann, NA, 840.20/3-1449.

95. Draper to Secretary of State, NA, 859.24/5-2248

96. Wedemeyer to Hickerson, NA, 859.24/6-2148. See also Hulley to Hickerson, NA, 859.24/5-2548; Hickerson to Marvel, NA, 859.24/6-248.

97. Lovett to Forrestal, NA, 859.24/4-1648; Lovett to Embassy in Copenhagen, NA, 859.24/3-1248; Hickerson to Secretary of State, NA, 859.24/7-248; Memo of Conversation Hulley–Bang-Jensen, NA, 859.24/8-2448. But see NA, 859.24/4-1349 for an indication that the State Department refrained from invoking overriding political considerations.

98. Marshall to Embassy in Copenhagen, NA, 859.24/8-648; Cumming to Secretary of State, NA, 858.243/4-1149.

99. For NSC 28/1, see *FRUS, 1948,* 3:233, in particular footnote. See also Memo of Conversation Hulley–Bang-Jensen, NA, 859.24/8-2448; Marshall to Nygaard, August 27, 1948, NA, 857.20/6-1748; Symington to Secretary of State, NA, 857.20/10-1248.

100. Current Position of the U.S. Respecting Base Negotiations with Denmark and Norway, November 17, 1948, NA, Modern Military Branch, NSC 32/1: pp. 1–2.

101. Memo of Conversation Lovett-van Kleffens, August 21, 1948, *FRUS, 1948,* 1(pt. 1):111–13; and Marshall to Embassy in Oslo, September 2, 1948, *ibid.,* pp. 120–21.

102. Marshall to Embassy in Oslo, September 2, 1948, *ibid.,* pp. 120–21. See also Bay to Secretary of State, September 8, 1948, *ibid.,* pp. 235–36; Marshall to Jessup, September 10, 1948, *ibid.,* pp. 132–33. For further developments leading up to the election of Norway to a seat on the Security Council, see pp. 138, 143–44, 150–51, 161–62.

103. *Stortingsforhandlingene, 1949,* 2b, St. meld. no. 32, pp. 22–23, 27–28, 32–33.

104. Position of the United States with Respect to Scandinavia, September 3,

1948, *FRUS, 1948*, 3:233. For the attitude of the JCS, see Position of the United States with Respect to Scandinavia, August 27, 1948, Draft Memorandum for Secretary of Defense, NA, Modern Military Branch, CCS 381, Sec. 1, JCS 1929/1.

105. Memo by Gullion to Secretary of State, March 9, 1948, *FRUS, 1948*, 1(pt. 2): 699; Matthews to Secretary of State, NA, 840.50 Recovery /1-749; Lovett to Embassy in Stockholm, January 14, 1949, 840.50 Recovery /1-749.

106. Hickerson to Lovett, June 18, 1948, *FRUS, 1948*, 1(pt. 2):714.

107. Lovett to Matthews, July 2, 1948, *ibid.*, pp. 712–14 and 716.

108. Lovett to Matthews, July 2, 1948, *FRUS, 1948*, 1(pt. 2):716–19.

109. Matthews to Lovett, July 15, 1948, *FRUS, 1948*, 1(pt. 2):728–32. The quotation is from p. 730.

110. *Ibid.*, p. 730. For Lovett's comment, see Lovett to Matthews, July 2, 1948, *ibid.*, pp. 718–19.

111. Marshall to Embassy in Stockholm, August 30, 1948, *FRUS, 1948*, 1(pt. 2):748–49. See also Lovett to Matthews, July 2, 1948, *ibid.*, p. 717; Position of the United States with Respect to Scandinavia, September 3, 1948, NSC 28/1, *ibid., 1948*, 3:323–33.

112. A Report to President by Special Committee of National Security Council on Atomic Energy Policy, March 2, 1949, *FRUS, 1949*, 1:457. See also pp. 449–50.

8. Scandinavia and a Western Military Arrangement in 1948

1. For an account of the Lange-Bevin talks, see Magne Skodvin, *Norden eller NATO? Utenriksdepartementet og alliansespørsmålet 1947–1949* (Scandinavia or NATO? The Foreign Office and the Question of Alliance 1947–1949) (Oslo: Universitetsforlaget, 1971), pp. 103–6. Also, interview by author with Lange, September 9, 1971.

2. For accounts of British-Norwegian cooperation in this period, see Skodvin, *Norden eller NATO?*, pp. 25–34; Knut Einar Eriksen, "Norge i det vestlige samarbeid" (Norway in the Western Community), in Trond Bergh and Helge Pharo, eds., *Vekst og Velstand: Norsk politisk historie 1945–1965* (Growth and Prosperity: Norwegian Political History 1945–1965) (Oslo: Universitetsforlaget, 1977); Nils Morten Udgaard, *Great Power Politics and Norwegian Foreign Policy: A Study of Norway's Foreign Relations November 1940–February 1948* (Oslo: Universitetsforlaget, 1973), pp. 158–76.

3. Herbert Feis, *From Trust to Terror: The Onset of The Cold War, 1945–1950* (New York: Norton, 1970), p. 377.

4. Joyce and Gabriel Kolko, *The Limits of Power: The World and United States Foreign Policy, 1945–1954* (New York: Harper & Row, 1972), p. 500.

5. Skodvin, *Norden eller NATO?* pp. 154–70, 260–65; Knut Einar Eriksen, *DNA og NATO: Striden om norsk NATO-medlemskap innen regjeringspartiet 1948–49* (The Labor Party and NATO: The Struggle Within the Governing Party About Membership for Norway in NATO 1948–49) (Oslo: Gyldendal, 1972), pp. 228–32. For Skodvin's emphasis on the Arctic regions, see for instance *Norden eller NATO?*, pp. 228, 330.

6. Krister Wahlbäck, "Norden och Blockuppdelningen 1948–49" (Scandinavia and the Division of the Blocs 1948–49), *Internationella Studier* (International Studies), vol. B, 1973, Stockholm, pp. 58–62 in particular.

7. *Ibid.*, p. 42.

8. Krister Wahlbäck, "USA i Skandinavien 1948–1949" (The USA in Scan-

dinavia 1948–1949), 1, *Internationella Studier* (1976), 5:197–98; and Eriksen, "Norge i det vestlige samarbeid," pp. 210–14.

9. Draft presented at PPS meeting, March 16, 1948, NA, State Department Papers, Files of Policy Planning Staff, p. 4. See also *ibid.*, Minutes of and drafts presented at meetings on March 17 (two meetings), and March 19.

10. Report Prepared by Policy Planning Staff Concerning Western Union and Related Problems, March 23, 1948, *FRUS, 1948,* 3:62.

11. Final Draft, undated, *FRUS, 1948,* 3:73. See also minutes from the meetings, pp. 61, 62, 64–65, 66, 69.

12. Washington Exploratory Talks on Security, Memorandum of Meeting, July 28, 1948, NA, 840.20/2-349: Problem Summaries, p. 1. See also Editorial Note, *FRUS, 1948,* 3:204–5.

13. Annex B-Hickerson Draft, NA, 840.00/8-3148. See also Memorandum by Kennan to Lovett, August 31, 1948, *FRUS, 1948,* 3:225. The following paragraphs are based on the same sources.

14. Memo from Hickerson to Kennan, November 26, 1948, NA, 840.20/11-2648; Washington Exploratory Talks on Security, Memorandum of Meeting, July 28, 1948, 840.20/2-349: Problem Summaries. For the question about consultation in case of aggression, see Annex B—Hickerson Draft, 840.00/8-3148.

15. For Kennan's position, see Memorandum by Kennan, November 24, 1948, *FRUS, 1948,* 3:283–89, in particular pp. 286–87. For Hickerson's attitude to this memorandum, see Hickerson to Kennan, November 26, 1948, NA, 840.20/11-2648.

16. For Achilles' attitude, an interesting source is the long interview with him in the Oral History Collection of the Truman Library, in particular pp. 8–30, 58–62. See also Achilles to Bonbright, NA, 840.20/1-1749; Hickerson to Kennan, 840.20/11-2648. For Achilles' comment on the "one-man Hickerson treaty," see Interview with Achilles, Oral History Collection, Truman Library, p. 38. In addition to the role of Hickerson, Achilles placed emphasis on the importance of Vandenberg, Lovett, and himself. For this, see pp. 122–25.

17. Interview with Hulley, Oral History Collection, Truman Library, pp. 17–19.

18. Hulley to Hickerson, NA, 857D.20/6-1048, p. 2.

19. Bohlen participated in the UN General Assembly in Paris from September 19 to December 14, 1948. Interview with Achilles, Oral History Collection, Truman Library, pp. 32–36. See also Charles E. Bohlen, *Witness to History 1929–1969* (New York: Norton, 1973) pp. 267–68; Escott Reid, *Time of Fear and Hope: The Making of the North Atlantic Treaty 1947–1949* (Toronto: McClelland and Stewart, 1977), p. 112.

20. For Lovett's position, see the minutes of the Washington exploratory talks in *FRUS, 1948,* 3:165, 169, 179–81, 217–18, 244. The quotation is from p. 217.

21. Memorandum by Participants in Washington Security Talks, July 6 to September 9, Submitted to Respective Governments for Study and Comment, September 9, 1948, *FRUS, 1948,* 3:244.

22. Minutes of Fifth Meeting of Washington Exploratory Talks, July 9, 1948, *FRUS, 1948,* 3:179; Memorandum of Conversation by Lovett, August 20, 1948, *ibid.*, p. 218.

23. Memorandum of Conversation Marshall, Lovett-Vandenberg, Dulles, April 27, 1948, *FRUS, 1948,* 3:105.

24. *Ibid.*

25. Memorandum from Bohlen to Secretary of State, NA, 840.20/2-1049. Morgenstierne also reported, on the basis of a conversation with the senator, that

Vandenberg wanted Norway in the alliance. For this, see Morgenstierne to Lange, December 31, 1948, UD Papers, Record Group 25.2/72, No. 001552.

26. Memorandum for the Secretary of Defense, Subject: Request by Norwegian Defense Minister for Information on United States Assistance in the Case of War, June 10, 1948, NA, Modern Military Branch, Record Group, 330, Secretary of Defense Office, Administrative Secretary, Correspondence Control Section, Numerical File, September 1947–June 1950.

27. *Ibid.*, p. 1; NA, Modern Military Branch, CCS 381 (8/14/47), Sec. 1, JCS 1846/2, Enc. "C," pp. 19–20.

28. Position of the United States with Respect to Scandinavia, August 26, 1948, NA, National Security Council Files, Modern Military Branch, NSC 28; Position of the United States with Respect to Scandinavia, September 3, 1948, *ibid.*, NSC 28/1. The conclusions of NSC 28/1 are found in *FRUS, 1948*, 3:232–34.

29. Memorandum by Participants in Washington Security Talks, September 9, 1948, *FRUS, 1948*, 3:241.

30. Minutes of meetings of the United States-United Kingdom-Canada Security Conversations, *FRUS, 1948*, 3:60, 64–65, 73–74. For emphasis on the importance of Norway and Denmark in the July–August talks, see *FRUS, 1948*, 3:164, 175, and in particular p. 217.

31. Memorandum by Participants in Washington Security Talks, September 9, 1948, *FRUS, 1948*, 3:241–42.

32. The Military Implications to United States of a Scandinavian Pact, December 15, 1948, NA, Modern Military Branch, CCS 381 (8-14-47), Sec. 2, JCS 1929/4, pp. 17, 20; and Position of the United States with Respect to Scandinavia, September 2, 1948, NA, National Security Council Files, Modern Military Branch, NSC 28/1, pp. 1–6. See also *Survival in the Air Age: A Report by the President's Air Policy Commission* (Washington, D.C., 1948), pp. 10–19; and George H. Quester, *Nuclear Diplomacy: The First Twenty-Five Years* (New York: Dunellen, 1970), pp. 32–33.

33. For the quotation, see Position of the United States with Respect to Scandinavia, NA, National Security Council Files, Modern Military Branch, NSC 28/1, p. 1. See also Forrestal to Secretary of State, February 10, 1949, *FRUS, 1949*, 4:96, 99–101.

34. Military Implications to United States of a Scandinavian Pact, December 15, 1948, NA, Modern Military Branch, CCS 381 (8-14-47), Sec. 2, JCS 1929/4, pp. 17, 20–25.

35. *Ibid.*, pp. 20–23; Forrestal to Secretary of State, February 10, 1949, *FRUS, 1949*, 4:98–99.

36. Memorandum of Conversation Acheson-Lange, NA 840.20/2-1149, p. 13. See also Memo of Conversation Hickerson-Morgenstierne, December 31, 1948, *FRUS, 1948*, 3:348–51; and Skodvin, *Norden eller NATO?*, pp. 205, 208, 228, 324–25.

37. Minutes of meetings held in Washington, *FRUS, 1948*, 3:169–82, 214–21, 226–28, 241, 244. See also Position of United States with Respect to Scandinavia, NA, National Security Council Files, Modern Military Branch, NSC 28/1, pp. 1–2.

38. British Embassy to Department of State, March 11, 1948, *FRUS, 1948*, 3:46–48; Secretary of State to Acting Secretary, September 30, 1948, pp. 256–57; Policy and Information Statement on Norway, August 28, 1946, Byrnes Papers, p. 1. See also Diary of Arne Ording, Oslo University Library, April 12, 1948 and February 17, 1949.

39. Position of United States with Respect to Scandinavia, September 3, 1948,

NA, National Security Council Files, Modern Military Branch, NSC 28/1, pp. 1–2. See also Courses of Action in Event Soviets Attempt to Close Baltic, September 26, 1950, NA, Modern Military Branch, CCS 800.221 Baltic Sea (9-13-50), JCS 2160/1.

40. For a discussion of Danish-American relations over Greenland, see the section on bases and the polar regions in chapter 2 of this study. See also Forrestal to Secretary of State, February 10, 1949, *FRUS, 1949,* 4:98.

41. For the importance of oil shale and kolm deposits, see Position of the United States with Respect to Scandinavia, NA, National Security Council Files, Modern Military Branch, NSC 28/1, pp. 1–2. For the importance of the Norwegian merchant marine, see Minutes of Twelfth Meeting of Washington Exploratory Talks, February 8, 1949, *FRUS, 1949,* 4:79; Memo of Conversation Marshall-Lange, UD Papers, Record Group 25.2/72, Nr. 031504.

42. For various expressions of the view that zones of neutrality represented a threat to peace, see Memo by Hickerson, March 8, 1948, *FRUS, 1948,* 3:40; Memo from British Embassy to Secretary of State, *ibid.,* pp. 46–48; Minutes of Fourth Meeting of US-UK-Canada Conversations, March 29, 1948, *ibid.,* pp. 69–70; Position of United States with Respect to Support for Western Union and Other Related Free Countries, April 13, 1948, *ibid.,* pp. 86–88; Matthews to Secretary of State, April 21, 1948, *ibid.,* pp. 97–98; Matthews to Secretary of State, May 5, 1948, *ibid.,* pp. 112–14; Memorandum by Marshall to President Truman, June 3, 1948, *ibid.,* p. 134; Memorandum of Conversation Marshall-Undén, October 14, 1948, *ibid.,* pp. 264–66.

43. For expressions of this attitude, see Memorandum by Marshall to President Truman, June 3, 1948, *FRUS, 1948,* 3:134; Memorandum of Conversation Marshall-Undén, October 14, 1948, pp. 264–66. For a more general discussion of the American attitude to Finland, see Lundestad *The American Non-Policy Towards Eastern Europe 1943–1947* (Oslo-New York: Universitetsforlaget-Humanities Press, 1975), pp. 290–96, 309–11.

44. Papers Relating to North Atlantic Pact, International Working Group, January 13, 1949, NA, 840.20/4-2149, pp. 1–2.

45. *Ibid.,* p. 2.

46. For an account of the history of the Long Telegram, see George F. Kennan, *Memoirs: 1925–1950* (Boston: Atlantic-Little, Brown, 1967), pp. 271–97. The quotation is from p. 294.

47. The best analysis of the climate in Washington at this time is probably found in Daniel Yergin, *Shattered Peace: The Origins of the Cold War and the National Security State* (Boston: Houghton Mifflin, 1977), pp. 163–92, in particular pp. 168–71.

48. Memorandum by Kennan, November 24, 1948, *FRUS, 1948,* 3:284–85; Memorandum by Kennan to Secretary of State, January 20, 1948, *ibid.,* pp. 7–8. For an interesting discussion about Kennan's views, see John Lewis Gaddis, "Containment: A Reassessment," *Foreign Affairs* (1977), 55:873–88; Eduard Mark, "The Question of Containment: A Reply to John Lewis Gaddis," *Foreign Affairs* (1978), 56:430–31.

49. Memo by Kennan, November 24, 1948, *FRUS, 1948,* 3:285–88; Kennan, *Memoirs: 1925–1950,* pp. 406–13. The quotation is from *FRUS, 1948,* 3:287. See also Kennan, *Memoirs: 1925–50,* pp. 418–27, 442–46; Gaddis, "Containment: A Reassessment," *Foreign Affairs* (1977), 55:881–84.

50. Kennan, *Memoirs: 1925–50,* p. 412; Memo from Kennan to Lovett, August 31, 1948, *FRUS, 1948,* 3:225; Memo by Kennan, November 24, 1948, *ibid.,* pp. 285–87.

51. Annex A—Kennan Draft, NA, 840.00/8-3148. See also Memo from Kennan to Lovett, August 31, 1948, *FRUS, 1948,* 3:225.

52. Memorandum of Thirteenth Meeting of Washington Exploratory Talks, September 2, 1948, *FRUS, 1948,* 3:227.

53. Minutes of Fourth Meeting of Washington Exploratory Talks, July 8, 1948, *ibid.,* p. 165.

54. Annex A—Kennan Draft, NA, 840.00/8-3148.

55. Papers Relating to North Atlantic Pact, Washington Exploratory Talks on Security, September 9, 1948, NA, 840.20/4-2149, p. 3.

56. For indications of this, see Bohlen, *Witness to History,* p. 267; Minutes of Ninth Meeting of Washington Exploratory Talks, August 9, 1948, *FRUS, 1948,* 3:210-11; Reid, *Time of Fear and Hope,* p. 107.

57. John Foster Dulles, *War or Peace* (New York: Macmillan, 1950), p. 97. For similar statements by Dulles in March 1949, see *New York Times,* March 11, 1949, p. 8 and March 21, 1949, p. 5.

58. For expressions of the attitude of Dulles, see Memo of Conversation Marshall/Lovett/Vandenberg/Dulles, April 27, 1948, *FRUS, 1948,* 3:104-8; Dulles to Secretary of State, November 26, 1948, p. 295. For Scandinavian reports on his attitude, see Danish Foreign Office, *Dansk Sikkerhedspolitik, 1948-1966* (Danish Security Policy, 1948-1966) (Copenhagen, 1968) 2:76. From Morgenstierne to Lange, approx. February 15, 1949, UD Papers, Record Group 25.2/72, no. C21/49.

59. For an example of the State Department trying to stem the influence of Lippmann's idea of Scandinavia as a neutral belt, see Lovett to American Embassy, Reykjavik, NA, 840.20/1-1149. See also *Dansk Sikkerhedspolitik, 1948-1966,* 2:76; Morgenstierne to Lange, January 11, 1949, UD Papers, Record Group 25.3/72, No. 01695/48. For Kennan's reflections on Lippmann's criticism of his X-article, see Kennan, *Memoirs: 1925-50,* pp. 359-67.

60. Minutes of Fourth Meeting of Washington Exploratory Talks, *FRUS, 1948,* 3:164-65, 166; Memo of Conversation Bohlen-Berard, August 6, 1948, *ibid.,* pp. 206-8. See also Minutes of Twelfth Meeting of Washington Exploratory Talks, February 8, 1949, *FRUS, 1949,* 4:76-77, 83. For reports on the French attitude in the files of the Norwegian Foreign Office, see Memo of Conversation Schuman-Lange, November 13, 1948, UD Papers, Record Group 25.2/72, no. 037431; Report from Embassy in Paris, January 24, 1949, no. 02597; Report from Embassy in Paris, February 9, 1948, no. 04674; Memo of Conversation Undén-Lange, November 20, 1948, no. 037040, pp. 4, 8. See also Reid, *Time of Fear and Hope,* pp. 196, 200-11.

61. Memorandum of meeting, September 9, 1948, NA, 840.20/4-2149, Papers Relating to North Atlantic Pact, Washington Exploratory Talks on Security, p. 2. For the Belgian attitude, see also Kirk to Secretary of State, November 20, and November 29, 1948, *FRUS, 1948,* 3:279, 298-99.

62. Minutes of Fourth Meeting of Washington Exploratory Talks, July 8, 1948, *FRUS, 1948,* pp. 163-64, 166, 167.

63. For this argument on the part of the Swedes, see for instance Memo of Conversation Marshall-Undén, October 14, 1948, *FRUS, 1948,* 3:264-66.

64. Kennan, *Memoirs: 1925-50,* p. 412. See also Minutes of Fourth Meeting of Washington Exploratory Talks, July 8, 1948, *FRUS, 1948,* 3:162; and Memorandum by Kennan, November 24, 1948, *ibid.,* pp. 285-88.

65. Memo of Conversation Marshall-Undén, October 14, 1948, *FRUS, 1948,* 3:264-66; Smith to Secretary of State, NA, 757D.00/12-1848. See also Hickerson to Bedell Smith, NA, 711.57D/9-1748; Memo of Conversation Hickerson-Boheman,

NA, 758.00/11-548, p. 2. Letter to the author from Hickerson, dated October 17, 1978.

66. NSC 28/1, Position of United States with Respect to Scandinavia, September 3, 1948, *FRUS, 1948*, 3:233.

67. For various versions of these arguments, see Matthews to Hickerson, NA, 840.20/11-1948, p. 2; Memo of Conversation Thompson-Boheman, NA, 840.20/12-2248; Matthews to Secretary of State, NA, 758.00/12-648; Memo of Conversation Hickerson-Boheman, NA, 758.00/11-548; Smith to Secretary of State, NA, 757D.00/12-1848.

68. For a discussion of the prehistory of the Marshall Plan, see my "The Marshall Plan and Eastern Europe," paper presented at the conference on "Marshall-Plan und Europäische Linke," Essen, West Germany, July 7–11, 1977, pp. 1–10. See also Bohlen, *Witness to History*, pp. 261–64; Joseph Marion Jones, *The Fifteen Weeks: An Inside Account of the Genesis of the Marshall Plan* (New York: Harcourt, Brace & World, 1955), pp. 214–56.

69. Marshall to Lovett, NA, 758.00/10-2048; Memo of Conversation Hickerson-Boheman, NA, 758.00/10-1248. See also Hickerson to Carter, NA, 711.58/10-2348; Carter to Hickerson, November 2, 1948, NA, 711.58/10-2348.

70. Marshall to Lovett, April 23, 1948, *FRUS, 1948*, 3:103. For Marshall's reaction to the Truman Doctrine, see Bohlen, *Witness to History*, pp. 261–62; Yergin, *Shattered Peace*, pp. 282–83. For Marshall's reaction to Truman's speech of March 17, 1948, see Yergin, *Shattered Peace*, p. 353.

71. For the American memo of conversation, see Secretary of State to Acting Secretary of State, September 30, 1948, *FRUS, 1948*, 3:256–57. For the more comprehensive Norwegian memo of conversation, see Memo of Conversation Lange Marshall, September 29, 1948, UD Papers, Record Group 25.2/72, no. 031054. For the statement on the southwest coast, see p. 5.

72. Memo of Conversation Hickerson-Morgenstierne, UD Papers, Record Group 25.2/72, no. 030697, From Embassy in Washington to Norwegian Foreign Office; Memo of Conversation Hickerson-Morgenstierne, NA, 840.00/9-2948.

73. Lovett to Secretary of State, October 1, 1948, *FRUS, 1948*, 3:258–59.

74. Memo of Conversation Marshall-Rasmussen, NA, 740.00119 Council/10-548, pp. 2–3.

75. Memo of Conversation Marshall-Bevin, NA, 840.00/10-448, p. 3.

76. Memo of Conversation Marshall-Lange, October 6, 1948, *FRUS,* 1948, 3:260. See also Skodvin, *Norden eller NATO?*, pp. 187–88, based on Memo of Conversation Lange-Marshall, September 29, 1948, UD Papers, Record Group, 25.2/72, no. 031054.

77. For Lovett's recommendation, see Lovett to Secretary of State, October 1, 1948, *FRUS, 1948*, 3:258; for the Norwegian interpretation of Marshall's answer, see Skodvin, *Norden eller NATO?*, p. 188.

78. Memo of Conversation Lovett-Morgenstierne, October 7, 1948, NA, 840.20/10-748; Memo of Conversation Hickerson-Morgenstierne, NA, 840.00/9-2948. The U.S. embassy in Oslo advised that Lange be given discretion to inform the Swedes when and if he wanted to do so. The argument was that "Lange would use information to best advantage only if necessary and that he is in position to determine whether use information would facilitate attainment objectives desired by Norway and US." For this, see Baldwin to Secretary of State, NA, 857.D.20/10-148.

79. Memo of Conversation Marshall-Lange, November 20, 1948, *FRUS, 1948*, 3:279–80; Skodvin, *Norden eller NATO?*, pp. 198–99.

80. Memorandum by Kennan, November 24, 1948, *FRUS, 1948,* 3:286–87.

81. Hickerson to Kennan, NA, 840.20/11-2648; Memorandum for Secretary from Bohlen, NA, 840.20/2-1049.

82. *FRUS, 1948,* 3:284, n. 2. See also Humelsine to Secretary of State, NA, 840.20/2-1049.

83. Memo of Conversation Marshall, Lovett, Vandenberg, Dulles, April 27, 1948, *FRUS, 1948,* 3:107; Minutes of Fifth Meeting of Washington Exploratory Talks, July 9, 1948, *ibid.,* p. 179.

84. Hickerson to Kennan, NA, 840.20/11-2648. See also references under note 82. In January 1949 Lovett apparently again became more skeptical about Italy's role. For this, see Minutes of Eleventh Meeting of Washington Exploratory Talks, January 14, 1949, *FRUS, 1949,* 4:31. See also Reid, *Time of Fear and Hope,* pp. 200–1, 204–5.

85. Robert H. Ferrell, *George C. Marshall,* vol. 15 in the series The American Secretaries of State and Their Diplomacy (New York: Cooper Square Publishers, 1966), p. 259. See also interview with Achilles, Oral History Collection, Truman Library, pp. 122–25.

86. Memorandum by Kennan to Under Secretary of State (Lovett), August 31, 1948, *FRUS, 1948,* 3:225.

87. Position of United States With Respect to Support for Western Union and Other Related Free Countries, April 13, 1948, NA, National Security Council Files, NSC 9: pp. 2–3.

88. *Ibid.,* pp. 3–4.

89. Position of United States With Respect to Support for Western Union and Other Related Free Countries, April 23, 1948, NA, NSC 9/1: pp. 2–5.

90. Position of United States With Respect to Support for Western Union and Other Related Free Countries, May 11, 1948, NA, NSC 9/2, p. 3.

91. *Ibid.,* p. 2.

92. Position of United States With Respect to Support for Western Union and Other Related Free Countries, June 28, 1948, NA, NSC 9/3: p. 2. This document is also found in *FRUS, 1948,* 3:140–43. For Truman's approval, see *ibid.,* p. 140, n. 2.

93. Washington Security Talks, NA, 840.20/7-2248. For an almost identical document, see Territorial Scope of a North Atlantic Security Arrangement and its Relationship to Security of Other Nations, NA, 840.20/7-948. See also *FRUS, 1948,* 3:182, 209–10.

94. Territorial Scope of a North Atlantic Security Arrangement and its Relationship to Security of Other Nations, NA, 840.20/7-2248, p. 1.

95. *Ibid.,* pp. 1–2.

96. *Ibid.,* p. 2.

97. *Ibid.,* pp. 2–3.

98. *Ibid.,* p. 3. See also Kenneth W. Condit, "The History of the Joint Chiefs of Staff: The Joint Chiefs of Staff and National Policy, 1947–1949" NA, Modern Military Branch, 1976), 2:365–66. Mimeo.

99. Position of United States with Respect to Scandinavia, August 26, 1948, NA, National Security Council Files, NSC 28, pp. 6–7; Position of United States with Respect to Scandinavia, September 3, 1948, *ibid.,* NSC 28/1, pp. 6–7. The conclusions of NSC 28/1 are found in *FRUS, 1948,* 3:232–34.

100. To Hickerson from Achilles, NA, 840.20/5-1948; To Secretary of State from Embassy in Stockholm, June 10, 1948, *FRUS, 1948,* 3:135; Memo of Conversa-

tion Hickerson-Morgenstierne, NA, 840.00/9-2949, p. 2; Memo of Conversation Lovett-Kauffmann, NA; 711.59/9-2049 CS/N, p. 2.

101. For the September 9 memo, see Memorandum by Participants in Washington Security Talks, July 6 to September 9, Submitted to Respective Governments for Study and Comment, September 9, 1948, *FRUS, 1948,* 3:237–48, in particular pp. 240–42. The quotation is from p. 241.

102. *Ibid.,* p. 241. For the July wording, see Territorial Scope of a North Atlantic Security Arrangement and its Relationship to Security of Other Nations, NA, 840.20/7-948, p. 2.

103. Papers Relating to North Atlantic Pact, Washington Exploratory Talks on Security, Memorandum of Meeting, September 9, 1948, NA, 840.20/4-2149, p. 2.

104. *Ibid.,* p. 3.

105. Memorandum by Participants in Washington Security Talks, September 9, 1948, *FRUS, 1948,* 3:240. See also Papers Relating to North Atlantic Pact, Washington Exploratory Talks on Security, Memorandum of Meeting, September 9, 1948, NA, 840.20/4-2149, pp. 2–3.

106. Territorial Scope of a North Atlantic Security Arrangement and its Relationship to Security of Other Nations, NA, 840.20/7-948. p. 3. See also Memorandum by Participants in Washington Security Talks, September 9, 1948, *FRUS, 1948,* 3:240–42.

107. In the State Department Papers in the National Archives there are two papers, both unsigned, entitled Territorial Scope of a North Atlantic Security Arrangement and its Relationship to the Security of Other Nations. They have the same decimal number, 840.20/9-248. It is possible that one has been written by Kennan and the other by Hickerson, since they have some resemblance to the drafts Kennan and Hickerson submitted to Lovett on August 31. For those, see Annex A—Kennan Draft and Annex B—Hickerson Draft, NA, 840.00/8-3148. The possible "Hickerson" draft of the Territorial Scope paper does not contain the statement about nonrepresentation on the agencies responsible for military decisions.

108. Acting Secretary of State to Embassy in France (for Bohlen from Hickerson), November 9, 1948, *FRUS, 1948,* 3:271.

109. Acting Secretary of State to Embassy in Denmark, November 17, 1948, *ibid.,* pp. 271–72.

110. Prebensen to Lange, UD Papers, Record Group 25.2/72, no. 032305; Prebensen to Lange, *ibid.,* no. 32304. Hankey, Chief of the Northern Department within the Foreign Office, had developed the plan. On the British side, it had been agreed to at least by the Chiefs of Staff.

111. For the Norwegian reaction to the Hankey plan, see Message to Embassy in London from Lange, October 19, 1948, UD Papers, Record Group 25.2/72; Lange to Prebensen, October 20, 1948, *ibid.* For Hankey's reaction to the Norwegian response, see Prebensen to Lange, *ibid.,* no. 033820; From Embassy in London to Foreign Office in Oslo, January 2, 1949, *ibid.,* no. 2/1949. See also Knut E. Eriksen, "NATO, Norden og 'den utro tjener' Halvard Lange" (NATO, Scandinavia and "the Unfaithful Servant" Halvard Lange), *Internasjonal Politikk* (International Politics) (1977), 2:274–76. Eriksen plays down somewhat the Norwegian domestic arguments for rejecting the Hankey plan.

112. Hickerson to Hoyer-Millar, NA, 840.20/11-1548. The following paragraphs are also based on this source. See also Lovett to Embassy in Sweden, November 17, 1948, *FRUS, 1948,* 3:272–73; Lovett to Embassy in France, November 9, 1948, *ibid.,* p. 271.

113. Marvel to Secretary of State, NA, 840.20/11-1948. For Matthews's views, see Matthews to Hickerson, NA, 840.20/11-1948. See also *FRUS, 1948,* 3:273, n.3. For the attitude of the embassy in Oslo, see Villard to Secretary of State, NA, 840.20/11-2748; Villard to Secretary of State, NA, 840.20/11-3048.

114. Matthews to Hickerson, NA, 840.20/11-1948, p. 4.

115. Marvel to Secretary of State, NA, 840.20/11-2248; Marvel to Secretary of State, NA, 840.20/11-2648; Villard to Secretary of State, NA, 840.20/11-3048. See also From Embassy in London to Norwegian Foreign Office, January 2, 1949, UD Papers, Record Group 25.2/72, no. 2/1949.

116. Memo of Conversation Hickerson–Hoyer-Millar, NA, 840.20/12-948, enc.

117. Kennan, *Memoirs: 1925–50,* pp. 413–14.

118. Military Implications to United States of a Scandinavian Pact, December 15, 1948, approved by the JCS on January 28, 1949, NA, Modern Military Branch, CCS 381 (8-14-47), Sec. 2, JCS 1929/4; See also Forrestal to Secretary of State, February 10, 1949, *FRUS, 1949,* 4:95–101, enc. For an earlier and more indirect expression of the views of the Joint Chiefs of Staff, see Memorandum by Joint Chiefs of Staff to Forrestal, November 24, 1948, *FRUS, 1948,* 3:289–93.

119. Memorandum for Secretary from Bohlen, NA, 840.20/2-1049.

120. Minutes of Ninth Meeting of Washington Exploratory Talks on Security, December 13, 1948, *FRUS, 1948,* 3:316; Canadian Commentary on Washington Paper of September 9, 1948, dated December 6, 1948, NATO Research Files, Lot 57 D 271, Box 14, pp. 4–5.

121. Minutes of Ninth Meeting of Washington Exploratory Talks, *FRUS, 1948,* 3:318, 320. For earlier strong expressions of the American position on the stepping-stone countries, see Minutes of Fourth Meeting of Exploratory Talks, July 8, 1948, *ibid.,* p. 165; Memorandum of Conversation by Lovett, August 20, 1948, *ibid.,* p. 217; Memorandum by Participants in Washington Security Talks, September 9, 1948, *ibid.,* p. 244.

122. Verbatim Records of Washington Exploratory Talks on Security 1948–49, Meeting of December 13, 1948, NA, Record Group 353, pp. 15–16. The minutes found in *FRUS* are not verbatim and some points have been entirely left out in these minutes.

123. *Ibid.,* pp. 17–18; Ninth Meeting of Washington Talks, December 13, 1948, *FRUS, 1948,* 3:318–19.

124. Minutes of Tenth Meeting of Washington Exploratory Talks, December 22, 1948, *FRUS, 1948,* 3:327–28,331. The Belgian ambassador's statements on that occasion should be compared with those of February 8, 1949, as reported in Minutes of Twelfth Meeting of Washington Exploratory Talks, *FRUS, 1949,* 4:81–84.

125. Minutes of Tenth Meeting of Washington Exploratory Talks, December 22, 1948, *FRUS, 1948,* 3:332.

126. Meeting of December 22, 1948, NA, Record Group 353, Verbatim Records of Washington Exploratory Talks on Security 1948–49. pp. 16–17. See also Minutes of Meeting, December 22, 1948, *FRUS, 1948,* 3:332.

127. December 24 Draft Treaty, Annex C—Italy, *FRUS, 1948,* 3:339–42; Reid, *Time of Fear and Hope,* pp. 202–6.

128. December 24 Draft Treaty, Annex D—Procedure for Negotiations and Approaches to Other Governments, *FRUS, 1948,* 3:343.

129. *Ibid.*

9. Climax: The United States, Scandinavian Cooperation, and NATO

1. Memo of Conversation Hickerson-Morgenstierne, December 29, 1948, *FRUS, 1948,* 3:344–45.

2. Aide-Mémoire from Norwegian Foreign Office, December 29, 1948, *FRUS, 1948,* 3:345–46; Memo of Conversation Hickerson/Morgenstierne, December 31, 1948, *ibid.,* pp. 348–51. For Morgenstierne's report on this conversation, see Morgenstierne to Lange, UD Papers, Record Group 25.2/72, no. 001551.

3. Memo of Conversation Hickerson-Morgenstierne, December 31, 1948, *FRUS, 1948,* 3:349; Lovett to American Embassy in Oslo, NA, State Department Papers, 840.20/1-349, pp. 2–3; Memo of Conversation Hickerson-Bang-Jensen, January 3, 1949, *FRUS, 1949,* 4:2; Morgenstierne to Lange, December 31, 1948, UD Papers, Record Group 25.2/72, no. 001551, p. 4. See also Magne Skodvin, *Norden eller NATO? Utenriksdepartementet og alliansespørsmålet 1947–1949* (Scandinavia or NATO? The Foreign Office and the Question of Alliance 1947–1949) (Oslo: Universitetsforlaget, 1971), pp. 220–21.

4. For accounts of the Karlstad meeting, see Skodvin, *Norden eller NATO?,* pp. 235–44; Knut Einar Eriksen, *DNA og NATO: Striden om norsk NATO-medlemskap innen regjeringspartiet 1948–49* (The Labor Party and NATO: The Struggle Within the Governing Party About Membership for Norway in NATO 1948–49) (Oslo: Gyldendal, 1972), pp. 150–51; Krister Wahlbäck, "Norden och Blockuppdelningen 1948–49" (Scandinavia and the Division of the Blocs), *Internationella Studier* (International Studies) (1973), vol. B, pp. 46–51.

5. For Bay's reaction, see Bay to Secretary of State, NA, 840.20/1-1249. For some interesting comments by Morgenstierne, see Memo of Conversation Hickerson-Morgenstierne, *FRUS, 1949,* 4:24–25.

6. Matthews to Acting Secretary of State, January 14, 1949, *FRUS, 1949,* 4:25-26; Kohler to Secretary of State, NA, 840.20/1-1549. See also *FRUS, 1949,* 4:26, n. 2.

7. Marvel to Acting Secretary of State, January 12, 1949, *FRUS, 1949,* 4:20-22. For Marvel's more hesitant first reaction, see Marvel to Acting Secretary of State, January 10, 1949, *ibid.,* p. 17. For a slightly comical exchange between ambassadors Marvel and Matthews based on their different reactions to the policies of the Scandinavian countries, see Marvel to Secretary of State, NA, 840.20/1-2649; Matthews for Marvel, NA, 840.20/1-2849; Marvel for Matthews, NA, 840.20/1-2949; Matthews for Marvel, NA, 857.D/20/1-3149.

8. Bay to Secretary of State, NA, 840.20/1-1249. See also Memo of Conversation Hickerson-Morgenstierne, January 13, 1949, *FRUS, 1949,* 4:24-25.

9. Lovett to Embassy in Norway, January 14, 1949, *FRUS, 1949,* 4:27.

10. Lovett to Secretary of State, October 1, 1948, *FRUS, 1948,* 3:258.

11. Bay to Secretary of State, NA, 840.20/1-1249.

12. Marvel to Acting Secretary of State, January, 12, 1949, *FRUS, 1949,* 4:20-22, in particular p. 22; Papers Relating to North Atlantic Pact, International Working Group, January 13, 1949, NA, 840.20/4-2149, pp. 1–2.

13. Skodvin, *Norden eller NATO?,* pp. 258–59, 263–64; Eriksen, *DNA og NATO,* pp. 148-52, 156-59; Krister Wahlbäck, "USA i Skandinavien 1948-49" (The U.S.A. in Scandinavia 1948–49), *Internationella Studier* (1976), 5:197-98. In his study "Norden och Blockuppdelningen," even Wahlbäck presents the more traditional version of the American attitude in 1949—see, for instance, p. 53.

14. My earlier analysis of the American attitude is found in "USA, skandinavisk forsvarsforbund og Halvard Lange: En revurdering" (The U.S.A., a Scandinavian Defense Pact and Halvard Lange: A Reappraisal), *Internasjonal Politikk* (1977), 1:139–173. For the debate provoked by this article, see the contributions by Knut Einar Eriksen, Grethe Vernø, and myself in *Internasjonal Politikk* (1977), 2:261–329. See also Knut Einar Eriksen, "Norge i det vestlige samarbeid" (Norway in the Western Community), in Trond Bergh and Helge Pharo, eds., *Vekst og Velstand: Norsk Politisk Historie 1945–1965* (Growth and Prosperity: Norwegian Political History 1945–1965) (Oslo: Universitetsforlaget, 1977), pp. 210–14. For an earlier study on my part, see "USA's politikk overfor Norge 1945–1948: Truman-administrasjonens holdning til brobygging og sosialdemokrati" (The Policy of the United States Toward Norway 1945–1948: The Attitude of the Truman administration to Bridge Building and Social Democracy), Institutt for Samfunnsvitenskap, University of Tromsø, Stensilserie B (6), 1976. Mimeo.

15. Minutes of Twelfth Meeting of Washington Exploratory Talks on Security, February 8, 1949, *FRUS, 1949*, 4:82; Memo of Conversation Acheson-Boheman, February 9, 1949, *ibid.*, pp. 89–90.

16. Forrestal to Secretary of State, February 10, 1949, *FRUS, 1949*, 4:95–97, in particular p. 96; Acheson to Forrestal, NA, 840.20/2-949. Apparently Acheson was not at this time aware of the conclusions presented by the JCS in NSC 28/2 of February 3, 1949. For this, see Note Attached to Acheson's Letter to Forrestal, NA, Modern Military Branch, CCS 381 (8-14-47), Sec. 2, JCS 1929/4.

17. Princeton Seminars July 15–16, 1953, Acheson Papers, Box 64, p. 246. For a somewhat different emphasis on the problems of his first days in office, see Dean Acheson, *Present at the Creation: My Years in the State Department* (New York: Norton, 1969), pp. 254–55, 276–77.

18. For Acheson's style, see for instance George F. Kennan, *Memoirs: 1925–50* (Boston: Atlantic-Little, Brown, 1967), pp. 426–27. See also Gaddis Smith, *Dean Acheson*, vol. 16 in the series The American Secretaries of State and Their Diplomacy (New York: Cooper Square Publishers, 1972), pp. 391–413.

19. Memorandum to Secretary of State by Carter, February 14, 1949, Acheson Papers, Box: Memos of Conversation 1949, Folder: January-February 1949.

20. Memos CEB-1949, To Secretary of State from Bohlen, February 8, 1949, NA, State Department Papers, Record Group 59, Records of Charles E. Bohlen, Box 5; Memorandum for Secretary from Bohlen, NA 840.20/2-1049. For Kennan's November study, see Memorandum by Kennan, November 24, 1948, *FRUS, 1948*, 3:283–89.

21. Memorandum for Secretary from Bohlen, NA, 840.20/2-1049. For Bohlen's analysis of Soviet intentions, see for instance Memorandum for Secretary from Bohlen, Subject: Warburg's Letter Regarding Atlantic Pact, NA, 840.20/2-849.

22. Memorandum for Secretary from Bohlen, NA, 840.20/2-1049; Memorandum for Secretary from Bohlen, NA, 840.20/2-1449. For some evidence as to Tom Connally's role, see his *My Name is Tom Connally* (New York: Crowell, 1954), pp. 327–40.

23. Forrestal to Secretary of State, February 10, 1949, Enc. 1, Memorandum for Secretary of Defense from Joint Chiefs of Staff, *FRUS, 1949*, 4:96–97.

24. See for instance To Hickerson and Reber from Butler, NA, 840.20/7-2748; Papers Relating to North Atlantic Pact, International Working Group, January 13, 1949, NA, 840.20/4-2149, p. 2; Escott Reid, *Time of Fear and Hope: The Making of the North Atlantic Treaty 1947–1949* (Toronto: McClelland and Stewart, 1977), pp. 197–98.

25. Papers Relating to North Atlantic Pact, International Working Group, February 1, 1949, NA, 840.20/2-2149, p. 2. See also Marvel to Secretary of State, January 25, 1949, *FRUS, 1949,* 4:46; Marvel to Secretary of State, January 26, 1949, *ibid.,* p. 47; Memo of Conversation Acheson-Kauffmann, February 9, 1949, *ibid.,* p. 88.

26. Minutes of Twelfth Meeting of Washington Exploratory Talks on Security, February 8, 1949, *FRUS, 1949,* 4:82.

27. Despite this, the ambassador wanted to make even more certain about the outcome by intervening against Swedish pressure on Norway. For some of Morgenstierne's efforts in this direction, see Memo of Conversation Rogers-Morgenstierne, NA, 857 D.20/12-948; Memo of Conversation Rogers-Sivert A. Nielsen, NA, 840.20/12-1348; Memo of Conversation Hickerson-Morgenstierne, NA, 840.20/12-2348. For an interesting indication of how strongly Morgenstierne felt on the question of Norwegian membership in NATO, see his letter to Lithgow Osborne, former ambassador to Norway, dated March 25, 1949. Osborne apparently had considerable sympathy for a Scandinavian pact. Morgenstierne's letter is found in Morgenstierne to Osborne, NA, 757 D.00/3-2549. Hickerson received a copy of the letter which he then forwarded to Bohlen and Ernest A. Gross, legal adviser of the Department of State and coordinator for foreign assistance programs.

28. For the quotation, see Memorandum to Secretary of State from Raynor, NA, 840.21/11-2048. See also Villard to Secretary of State, NA, 840.20/12-848; Memo of Conversation Marshall-Bevin, NA, 840.20/10-448, pp. 2–3. For reports by Bay on the attitude of Lange, see Bay to Secretary of State, May 18, 1948, July 7, 1948, September 8, 1948, *FRUS, 1948,* 3:126–27, 160–63, 235–36. Lange had also told Marshall on September 29, 1948, that Norway would never accept a Scandinavian arrangement without sufficient ties with the West. For this, see Memo of Conversation Lange/Marshall, UD Papers, Record Group 25.2/72, no. 031054, pp. 1–4; Secretary of State to Acting Secretary, September 30, 1948, *FRUS, 1948,* 3:256–57.

29. Bay to Secretary of State, NA, 840.20/1-2749, no. 49; Bay to Secretary of State, 840.20/1-2749, no. 40, p. 2; Bay to Secretary of State, 840.20/1-2449. The most comprehensive report is found in Bay to Secretary of State, Subject: Opposition to Norwegian Participation in Atlantic Pact, 840.20/2-149. For a clearly different emphasis on the importance of the opposition, see Bay to Secretary of State, NA, 840.20/1-1249, p. 2.

30. Bay to Secretary of State, NA, 840.20/2-149. The quotations are from pp. 1, 8–9.

31. Acheson to American Embassy in Oslo, NA, 840.20/2-149. The report had been written by Lewis E. Gleeck and only signed by Bay.

32. Bay to Secretary of State, NA, 840.20/3-149; Acheson to American Embassy in Oslo, NA, 840.20/3-149.

33. Hickerson to Secretary of State, NA, 840.20/2-549. See also Bay to Secretary of State, NA, 840.20/2-549, no. 90; Bay to Secretary of State, NA, 840.20/2-549, no. 93.

34. Memo of Conversation Acheson-Lange, February 7, 1949, *FRUS, 1949,* 4:66–68; Memo of Conversation Bohlen-Lange, February 8, 1949, *ibid.,* pp. 69–73.

35. Forrestal to Secretary of State, February 10, 1949, *FRUS, 1949,* 4:95. For the answer from the Joint Chiefs, see Memorandum for Secretary of Defense, *ibid.,* pp. 95–97.

36. Memorandum by D(ean) A(cheson), item 3, NA, 840.20/2-1049.

37. *Ibid.* See also Memo to Secretary of State from Bohlen and Hickerson, NA, 840.20/2-1149, pp. 1–3, 5–6.

38. Memo to Secretary of State from Bohlen and Hickerson, NA, 840.20/2-1149, p. 1.

39. Memorandum for Secretary of Defense from Joint Chiefs of Staff, February 10, 1949, *FRUS, 1949,* 4:95–97.

40. Minutes of Twelfth Meeting of Washington Exploratory Talks, February 8, 1949, *FRUS, 1949,* 4:78–80.

41. For the attitude of Bonnet and the other representatives in the Washington exploratory talks in the meeting of February 8, 1949, see *FRUS, 1949,* 4:73–88, in particular pp. 76–77, 81–84, 87–88.

42. Memo of Conversation Acheson-Boheman, February 9, 1949, *FRUS, 1949,* 4:89–90.

43. To Hickerson from Rogers, NA, 840.20/2-749. In my interview with Sivert Nielsen on December 8, 1976, he argued that some of the phrases used by Rogers in the memo to Hickerson did not reflect quite accurately what he had said. Although this may be true, it does not change much as far as the basic realities of the conversation are concerned. Rogers's memo was treated in the utmost confidence within the State Department. Only three "personal" copies were made, a very low number. This is made clear by a notation on the memo. No report on the meeting is found in the files of the Norwegian Foreign Office.

44. For the analyses of the Scandinavian ambassadors in Washington, see Memo of meeting in Oslo, January 29, 4 P.M. UD Papers, Record Group 38.3/3, pp. 2–8.

45. Interview with Hickerson, August 18, 1978; and Interview with Sivert Nielsen, December 8, 1976. See also Grethe Vernö, "Norge og A-pakten 1948-49" (Norway and the Atlantic Alliance 1948-49), *Internasjonal Politikk* (1977), 2:315.

46. To Hickerson from Rogers, NA, 840.20/2-749; Interview with Sivert Nielsen, December 8, 1976.

47. Memo of Conversation Achilles-Nielsen, NA, 840.20/2-949; Interview with Nielsen, December 8, 1976 (again, nothing about this meeting can be found in the Norwegian Foreign Office files); *New York Times,* February 8, 1949, pp. 1, 24 (editorial), February 9, p. 1, February 11, p. 7, February 12, p. 1, and February 13, p. 1.

48. Memo of Conversation Achilles-Nielsen, NA, 840.20/2-949.

49. Memo of Conversation Acheson-Lange, February 7, 1949, *FRUS, 1949,* 4:66–68. For Acheson's impression of Lange, see Acheson, *Present at the Creation,* p. 278.

50. For the communications between the Soviet Union and Norway, see Editorial Note, *FRUS, 1949,* 4:53; Bay to Secretary of State, February 10, 1949, *ibid.,* pp. 91–93; Bay to Secretary of State, February 10, 1949, *ibid.,* pp. 93–94. See also Memo of Conversation Bohlen-Lange, February 8, 1949, *ibid.,* pp. 72–73; Bay to Secretary of State, March 3, 1949, *ibid.,* pp. 145–46.

51. Minutes of Twelfth Meeting of Washington Exploratory Talks, February 8, 1949, *FRUS, 1949,* 4:84; Memo to Secretary of State from Bohlen-Hickerson, NA, 840.20/2-1149, p. 1.

52. Minutes of Twelfth Meeting of Washington Exploratory Talks on Security, February 8, 1949, *FRUS, 1949,* 4:84. See also Butrick to Secretary of State, February 8, 1949, *ibid.,* p. 68; Butrick to Secretary of State, January 12, 1949, *ibid.,* p. 22.

53. Skodvin, *Norden eller NATO?,* passim (for a summary of his view, see pp. 314–17); Eriksen, *DNA og NATO,* pp. 228–32.

54. Wahlbäck, "USA i Skandinavien 1948–1949," pp. 195–98. For Wahlbäck's earlier position, see "Norden och Blockuppdelningen," pp. 62–68.

55. Memo of Conversation Acheson-Lange, pp. 10–11, NA, 840.20/2-1149.

56. For Dulles's position, see From Morgenstierne to Lange, about February 15, 1949, UD Papers, Record Group 25.2/72, C 21/49. For the Vandenberg Resolution, see *FRUS, 1948*, 3:135–36. For the September 9 memo, see *ibid.*, pp. 237–48, in particular pp. 240–42.

57. Memorandum by Norstad to Secretary of State, December 13, 1947, *FRUS, 1948*, 3:749–50; Memorandum by Reber to Acting Secretary of State, December 16, 1947, *ibid.*, pp. 750–51; Secretary of State to Embassy in Italy, January 12, 1948, *ibid.*, pp. 756–57; Report by State-Army-Navy-Air Force Coordinating Subcommittee, January 16, 1948, *ibid.*, pp. 757–62. For reports in February-April 1948 to and from the Embassy in Rome, and internal studies in Washington on the Italian scene with relevance to the question of delivery of arms, see *ibid.*, pp. 764–90, in particular pp. 765–69, NSC 1/2, Position of United States With Respect to Italy, February 10, 1948; Truman to Secretary of Defense, March 10, 1948, *ibid.*, p. 781.

The legal reasons that limited the ability of the United States to supply the necessary equipment to Norway and Denmark had to do with (a) requirements that proceeds of surplus sales revert to the Treasury and not to the Service departments, and (b) requirements that combatant vessels must either be demilitarized, or specific Congressional authorization received for their transfer. For this, see Marshall to American Embassy in London, NA, 857.20/7-2048.

58. See for instance Lovett to Embassy in France, November 22, 1948, *FRUS, 1948*, 3:282.

59. From Morgenstierne to Foreign Office, October 1, 1948, UD Papers, Record Group 25.2/72, no. 030697. Hickerson's own memo of conversation was rather more general on this point. For this, see Memo of Conversation Hickerson-Morgenstierne, NA, 840.00/0-2948.

60. Lovett to Embassy in Norway, September 22, 1948, *FRUS, 1948*, 3:255–56. This point was apparently not included in the information given Norwegian and Danish representatives in Washington on September 23. For this, see nos. 030793 and 030794, Nygaard to Lange, September 24, 1948, UD Papers, Record Group 25.2/72; Memo of Conversation Hickerson-Nygaard, NA, 840.20/9-2348.

61. Lovett to Embassy in Sweden, November 22, 1948, *FRUS, 1948*, 3:281–82. See also To Bohlen from Hickerson, Subject: Review of Discussions with Scandinavian Countries on North Atlantic Pact, February 21, 1949, NA, 840.20/2-2149, pp. 3–4; Memo of Conversation Marshall-Lange, November 20, 1948, *FRUS, 1948*, 3:280; Lovett to Embassy in France, November 22, 1948, *ibid.*, p. 282.

62. According to Bech-Friis of the Swedish Foreign Office, Matthews delivered a paper stating that "any Scandinavian defense arrangement based on neutrality *would be* incompatible with the intent of the Vandenberg resolution and *would of course* disqualify the signatories from getting any American aid, at least until the requirements of the members of a collective arrangement (*The North Atlantic Pact*, *Matthews explained*) would be fully met" (italics mine). For this, see Letter to Norwegian Foreign Office from Swedish Foreign Office, December 11, 1948, UD Papers, Record Group 38.3/3. This version is accepted by Skodvin as the official American position—see Skodvin, *Norden eller NATO?*, pp. 315–16.

63. Lovett to Embassy in France, November 22, 1948, *FRUS, 1948*, 3:282. See also Dulles to Secretary of State, November 26, 1948, *ibid.*, p. 295; Memo by Lange, November 26, 1948, UD Papers, Record Group 25.2/72, no. 037433.

64. Memo of Conversation Marshall-Lange, November 20, 1948, *FRUS, 1948*,

3:280. For the Norwegian memo of this conversation, see UD Papers, Record Group 25.2/72, no. 037042.

65. Bay to Secretary of State, September 8, 1948, *FRUS, 1948*, 3:235–36. For attempts by Morgenstierne to encourage the Americans to come out against the Swedish position, see Memo of Conversation Rogers-Sivert Nielsen, NA, 857D.20/12-948; Memo of Conversation Hickerson-Morgenstierne, NA, 840.20/12-2348. For a similar attempt by Arne Gunneng—the contact man between the Norwegian Foreign Office and Defense Department—see Matthews to Secretary of State, November 18, 1948, *FRUS, 1948*, 3:277–78. Even King Haakon apparently encouraged the Americans in the same direction. For this, see Bay to Secretary of State, NA, 840.20/1-2749, no. 47.

66. Matthews to Secretary of State, NA, 840.20/12-348; Lovett to American Embassy in Stockholm, 840.20/12-348; Memo of Conversation Hickerson-Boheman, 840.20/12-748, pp. 1–2. See also the oral statement by Boheman attached to this source, pp. 2–3.

67. Memo of Conversation Hickerson-Boheman, NA, 840.20/12-748, p. 2, and attached oral statement by Boheman, p. 3.

68. Lovett to Embassy in Norway, January 14, 1949. *FRUS, 1949*, 4:27. For the conversation with Morgenstierne, see Report from Embassy in Washington, February 14, 1949, UD Papers, Record Group 25.2/72, no. 01421. For the conversation with Boheman, see Memo of Conversation Hickerson-Boheman, NA, 857D.20/1-1449. See also Note by R. B. S. on conversation with Bay, UD Papers, Record Group 25.2/72.

69. From Morgenstierne to Lange, UD Papers, Record Group 25.2/72, no. 01784.

70. Memo of Conversation Hickerson-Morgenstierne, January 13, 1949, *FRUS, 1949*, 4:24–25; From Morgenstierne to Lange, January 17, 1949, UD Papers, Record Group 25.2/72, no. 02374, pp. 2–3; From Embassy in Washington to Foreign Office, February 27, 1949, *ibid.*, no. 7070. For the impressions of Ambassador Kauffmann, see Danish Foreign Office, *Dansk Sikkerhedspolitik 1948–1966* (Danish Security Policy 1948–1966), 2 (Copenhagen, 1968), pp. 74–80 (February 14, 1949), 96–102 (February 22).

71. Memorandum for Secretary of Defense from Joint Chiefs of Staff, February 10, 1949, *FRUS, 1949*, 4:96; Memo of Conversation Bohlen-Lange, February 8, 1949, *ibid.*, p. 71.

72. *Ibid.*, p. 71. See also Skodvin, *Norden eller NATO?*, pp. 302–3, 316–18.

73. For indications in American sources of how important the supply question was for the Norwegians, see the many reports from the embassy in Oslo and memos of conversation with Lange, in particular as found in *FRUS, 1948*, 3:80–81, 126–27, 134–35, 160–63, 163–69, 179, 210–11, 217, 223–24, 232–34, 235–36, 250–52, 253–56, 256–60, 271–72, 272–73, 279–82, 295–96, 304. See also Skodvin, *Norden eller NATO?*, pp. 176–78, 225–27, 237–38, 242–43, 249–51, 260–69, 314–24.

74. Papers Relating to North Atlantic Pact, International Working Group, January 13, 1949, NA, 840.20/4-2149, pp. 1–2; Military Attaché in Oslo to State Department, NA, 840.20/1-2149.

75. For Bay's opinion, see for instance his cables as found in *FRUS, 1948*, 3:160–63, 235–36. For the British appraisal, see Douglas to Secretary of State, December 8, 1948, NA, Federal Records Center, Suitland, Maryland, Oslo Post Files.

76. Papers Relating to North Atlantic Pact, International Working Group, February 1, 1949, NA, 840.20/4-2149, p. 2.

77. NSC 28/1, Position of United States With Respect to Scandinavia, September 3, 1948, *FRUS, 1948,* 3:232–33.

78. Aide-Mémoire from State Department to British Embassy in Washington, NA, 711.58/9-2148, p. 4.

79. Record of Conversation Bevin-Lange, February 14, 1949, UD Papers, Record Group 25.2/72, no. 3890, pp. 3–11; Memo of Conversation Achilles-Sivert Nielsen, NA, 840.20/2-1549. See also Acheson, *Present at the Creation,* pp. 280–82; Douglas to Secretary of State, NA, 840.20/2-1449; Hickerson to Secretary of State, with telegram from British Foreign Office on Conversation Between Bevin and Lange, NA, 857.20/2-1749; Report from Embassy in Washington, February 16, 1949, UD Papers, Record Group 25.2/72, no. 05446.

80. Unsigned message to Secretary of State, NA, 840.20/2-1449. In this source fear was expressed by Minister of Commerce Brofoss that the Soviet Union might suddenly occupy Finnmark or Svalbard. Even Lange would not entirely exclude this. For his attitude, see Record of Conversation Bevin-Lange, February 14, 1949, UD Papers, Record Group 25.2/72, no. 3890, p. 10. See also *Dansk Sikkerhedspolitik 1948–1966,* 2:103.

81. Western Union, Scandinavia and North Atlantic Pact, undated, NA, Records of Charles E. Bohlen, Box 8, Record of Conversation Bevin-Lange, February 14, 1949, UD Papers, Record Group 25.2/72, no. 3890, p. 9; From Embassy in London to Foreign Office in Oslo, March 5, 1949, *ibid.,* no. 7511. Bohlen apparently thought in similar ways at this time—see Memorandum from Bohlen to Secretary of State, NA, 840.20/2-149, pp. 1–2.

82. For the discussion within the Labor party, see Eriksen, *DNA og NATO,* pp. 164–66.

83. Bay to Secretary of State, NA, 757.00/2-2149. For an account of the conference, see Eriksen, *DNA og NATO,* pp. 198–219.

84. Memo of Conversation Hickerson-Morgenstierne NA, 840.20/2-2349; Memo to Acheson from Hickerson, NA, 840.20/2-2449. For the minutes of the thirteenth meeting of the Washington exploratory talks, see NA, 840.20/2-2549. See also Secretary of State to Embassy in France, February 25, 1949, *FRUS, 1949,* 4:122–24.

85. Secretary of State to Embassy in France, February 25, 1949, *FRUS, 1949,* 4:123. See also Reid, *Time of Fear and Hope,* pp. 206–8.

86. Secretary of State to Embassy in France, February 25, 1949, *FRUS, 1949,* 4:122–24. See also minutes of Thirteenth meeting of the Washington exploratory talks in NA, 840.20/2-2549; Minutes of Twelfth Meeting of Washington exploratory talks, February 8, 1949, *FRUS, 1949,* 4:73–88, in particular pp. 82–84.

87. Secretary of State to Embassy in France, February 25, 1949, *FRUS, 1949,* 4:123–24. See also December 24 Draft Treaty, Annex C—Italy, *FRUS, 1948,* 3:339–42.

88. Memorandum of Conversation by Secretary of State, Meeting with President, February 28, 1949, *FRUS, 1949,* 4:125. Memo by Dean Acheson on conversation with Senators Connally, George, and Vandenberg, NA, 840.20/2-2849. However, a few days later Vandenberg felt a mistake had been made "in regard to the Scandinavians." For this, see NA, Record Group 59, Office of Executive Secretariat, Box 1, Memorandum of Conversation, March 2, 1949.

89. Minutes of Fourteenth Meeting of Washington Exploratory Talks, March 1, 1949, *FRUS, 1949,* 4:126–35, in particular pp. 128–29, 134. For the meeting with Morgenstierne, see Memo of Conversation Acheson-Morgenstierne, March 1, 1949, *ibid.,* pp. 135–36; Memorandum of Discussion with President by Acheson, March 2,

1949, *ibid.*, pp. 141–45; Memorandum of Conversation, March 2, 1949, NA, Record Group 59, Office of the Executive Secretariat, Box 1; Achilles to Bonbright, NA, 840.20/1-1749; and Reid, *Time of Fear and Hope*, pp. 207–11.

90. Minutes of Fourteenth Meeting of Washington Exploratory Talks, March 1, 1949, *FRUS, 1949*, 4:133–35; Memo of Conversation Acheson/Morgenstierne, March 1, 1949, *ibid.*, pp. 135–36; Memorandum by Secretary of State on Discussion with President, March 2, 1949, *ibid.*, pp. 141–45; Minutes of Secretary's Staff Conference, February 28, NA, Record Group 59, Office of Executive Secretariat, Box 1, Item 4.

91. Minutes of Fourteenth Meeting of Washington Exploratory Talks, March 1, 1949, *FRUS, 1949*, 4:131–32; Papers Relating to North Atlantic Pact, Drafting of Treaty, Article 6, NA, 840.20/4-2149, pp. 20–22. See also Achilles to Bonbright, NA, 840.20/1-1749; Kenneth W. Condit, "The History of the Joint Chiefs of Staff: The Joint Chiefs of Staff and National Policy, vol. 2, 1947–1949," Mimeo. (NA, Modern Military Branch, 1976), pp. 376–80; Reid, *Time of Fear and Hope*, pp. 213–18.

92. Marvel to Secretary of State, March 2, 1949, *FRUS, 1949*, 4:139–40. See also *Dansk Sikkerhedspolitik 1948–1966*, 1:31–41 and 2:92; Hickerson to Secretary of State, NA, 840.20/3-949; Acheson, *Present at the Creation*, p. 279. The State Department had told Lange in mid-February that it had no objection to the Norwegians giving the Danes full information about the talks in Washington. For this, see Acheson to American Embassy in Oslo, NA, 840.20/2-1649.

93. Acheson, *Present at the Creation*, pp. 278–79.

94. Memo of Conversation Bohlen-Rasmussen, March 12, 1949, *FRUS, 1949*, 4:200–1; Memo of Conversation Acheson-Rasmussen, March 15, 1949, *ibid.*, pp. 210–13. See also Hickerson to Secretary of State, NA, 840.20/3-949.

95. For Benediktsson's talks in Washington, see the memos of conversation found in *FRUS, 1949*, 4:202–3, 203–6, 225–29, 236–37.

96. Memo of Conversation Hickerson-Benediktsson, March 15, 1949, *FRUS, 1949*, 4:225–29; Memo of Conversation Acheson-Benediktsson, March 17, 1949, *ibid.*, pp. 236–37; Secretary of State to Legation in Iceland, March 26, 1949, *ibid.*, p. 248; Policy Statement of Department of State, Iceland, August 23, 1949, *ibid.*, pp. 693–702. For a short account of the foreign policy of Iceland in the first postwar years, see Benedikt Grøndal, *Iceland: From Neutrality to NATO Membership* (Oslo: Universitetsforlaget, 1971), pp. 35–47.

97. *Dansk Sikkerhedspolitik*, 1:39–41. For the signatories to the North Atlantic Treaty, see *FRUS, 1949*, 4:284–85.

98. For an indication of the State Department's appraisal, see Papers Relating to North Atlantic Pact, International Working Group, January 13, 1949, NA, 840.20/4-2149, pp. 1–2.

99. Matthews to Secretary of State, NA, 840.20/1-2849. For a similar opinion expressed earlier in January, see Matthews to Acting Secretary of State, January 4, 1949, *FRUS, 1949*, 4:5. See also Matthews to Secretary of State, January 17, 1949, *ibid.*, p. 37.

100. Matthews to Secretary of State, NA, 840.20/2-2849.

101. *Ibid.*, p. 1; Matthews to Secretary of State, NA, 840.20/7-2549; Acheson Papers, Box 64, Folder: Princeton Seminars July 15–16, 1953, pp. 368–69.

102. Hulley to Hickerson, NA, 858.24/4-649; Webb to Symington, NA, 858.24/4-2549; Rogers to Hickerson, NA, 858.24/3-1149; Alexander to Webb, 858.24/9-749. For the skepticism of the JCS regarding even the rather strict guidelines for export of weapons to Sweden found in NSC 28, see Webb to Forrestal, NA, 858.20/12-3148 CS/N; Hickerson to Webb, March 1, 1949, FW 858.24/12-3148.

103. Cumming to Secretary of State, NA, 840.20/4-2149; Acheson to American Embassy in Oslo, NA, 840.20/4-2149.

104. Memo of Conversation Rogers-Nielsen, NA, 711.58/4-149; Memo of Conversation Rogers-Klaveness, NA, 711.58/4-449. For Bay's attitude, see Bay to Secretary of State, NA, 840.20/8-349 and 840.20/6-2449. See also Memo of Conversation Rogers-Colonel Sæbø, NA, 840.20/5-1349. The Norwegians even agreed to lease a radar station to Sweden. For this, see From Norwegian Foreign Office to Swedish Embassy in Oslo, January 29, 1949, UD Papers, Record Group 38.3/3, no. 372/49, and Note from Hauge, May 14, 1949, no. 650.

105. Matthews to Thompson, NA, 840.20/8-849.

106. Achilles to Matthews, NA, 840.20/8-849.

107. Rogers to Hickerson, NA, 711.58/3-3049, in particular pp. 5–6; Rogers to Hulley, 858.24/5-1149. For Rogers's 1948 position, see Rogers to Thompson, NA, 858.00/7-2348.

108. Policy Statement of Department of State, Sweden, August 15, 1949, FRUS, 1949, 773–75. The statement had probably been written largely by Charles Rogers and then cleared with Matthews, Hulley, and Thompson, among others. Their different views—particularly between Rogers and Matthews—may help explain its vagueness on many points. For this, see Green to Bell, June 22, 1949, and Bell to Thompson, June 23, 1949, NA, 711.58/10-2449.

109. Brief of a Joint Outline Emergency War Plan (OFFTACLE), JSPC 877/59, as quoted in Thomas H. Etzold and John Lewis Gaddis, eds., Containment: Documents on American Policy and Strategy, 1945–1950 (New York: Columbia University Press, 1978), pp. 325–26. For a more favorable opinion about Sweden, see Bell to Hickerson, NA, 858.20/6-1748.

110. Secretary of State to Embassy in Sweden, February 16, 1950, FRUS, 1950, 3:19–20. For Matthews's attitude, see his telegrams to the Secretary of State, dated February 7 and February 21, 1950, pp. 15–17, 22–25.

111. Ibid., Secretary of State to Embassy in Sweden, February 16, 1950, p. 19.

10. Conclusion: Expansion with Limitations

1. For a very short but stimulating discussion of the nature of American foreign policy in the period before World War II, see Robert W. Tucker, The Radical Left and American Foreign Policy (Baltimore, Md.: Johns Hopkins University Press, 1971), pp. 21–36.

2. For figures on U.S. investments abroad and exports and imports, see U.S. Dept. of Commerce, Bureau of the Census, Historical Statistics of the United States: Colonial Times to 1970 (Washington, D.C., 1975), pp. 869–71, 884–85.

3. Ibid., pp. 869–71, 873–75, 887, 903–7.

4. For a brief discussion of this, see John Lewis Gaddis, "Containment: A Reassessment," Foreign Affairs (1977), 55:878–81.

5. Points which have been documented in some detail in previous chapters will generally not be documented again in the conclusion.

6. The GNP of the United States increased in constant 1958 prices from $227.2 billion in 1940 to $355.2 billion in 1945. It has also been estimated that the wartime deaths of the U.S. military amounted to approximately 292,000. There were few civilian casualties. The Soviet Union on the other hand lost approximately 10 percent of its population through deaths indirectly or directly attributable to the war. In 1945 the Soviet Union produced only half the steel it had in 1941. For the Soviet

figures, see Adam B. Ulam, *The Rivals: America and Russia Since World War II* (New York: Viking, 1971), p. 6; for U.S. production figures, see *Historical Statistics of the United States,* p. 228.

7. For a discussion of Soviet policies in Eastern Europe, see Lundestad, *The American Non-Policy Towards Eastern Europe 1943–1947,* (Oslo-New York: Universitetsforlaget-Humanities Press, 1975), pp. 435–65.

8. For further discussion of the concept of Soviet and American spheres, see Daniel Yergin, *Shattered Peace: The Origins of the Cold War and the National Security State* (Boston: Houghton Mifflin, 1977), pp. 395–410, in particular pp. 396–97.

9. For some comments on these two revisionist assumptions in relation to Eastern Europe, see Lundestad, *The American Non-Policy,* passim, in particular pp. 422–24.

10. Thomas Wolfe, *Soviet Power and Europe* (Baltimore, Md.: Johns Hopkins University Press, 1970), pp. 10–11; Ulam, *The Rivals,* p. 8; Yergin, *Shattered Peace,* pp. 209–13, 242–43, 270–71, 380.

11. For figures on the American defense budgets and the shares going to the various services, see Hans Günter Brauch, "Struktureller Wandel und Rüstungspolitik der USA (1940–1950)," Ph.D. dissertation, University of Heidelberg, West Germany, 1976 (Ann Arbor: University Microfilms International, 1976), pp. 244–45, 641. See also Yergin, *Shattered Peace,* pp. 208–9, 339–43, 387–88.

12. This is further discussed in chapter 6 of the present study.

13. The point that it was always seen as safer to go on the worst assumption is brought out in Yergin, *Shattered Peace,* passim. See, for instance, pp. 12–14.

14. For the American policy toward Czechoslovakia, see Lundestad, *The American Non-Policy,* pp. 167–82.

15. This is best analyzed on the Norwegian side. For this, see Knut Einar Eriksen, "Norge i det vestlige samarbeid" (Norway in the Western Community), in Trond Bergh and Helge Pharo, eds., *Vekst og Velstand: Norsk politisk historie 1945–1965* (Growth and Prosperity: Norwegian Political History 1945–1965) (Oslo: Universitetsforlaget, 1977), pp. 179–202. For Denmark, see Danish Foreign Office, *Dansk Sikkerhedspolitik 1948–1966* (Danish Security Policy 1948–1966) (Copenhagen, 1968), 1:21–23. For Sweden, see Krister Wahlbäck, "Norden och Blockuppdelningen 1948–49" (Scandinavia and the Division of the Blocs 1948–49), *Internationella Studier* (International Studies) (Stockholm, 1973).

16. This is also discussed in the section on Bases and the Polar Regions in chapter 2 of the present study.

17. For the American attitude to the British and Scandinavian social democrats, see chapter 4 in the present study. For one indication of dissatisfaction with Hambro, see Osborne to Secretary of State, NA, 857.00/6-2545, pp. 2–3.

18. Minutes of Ninth Meeting of Washington Exploratory Talks on Security, December 13, 1948, *FRUS, 1948,* 3:318.

19. For increased cultural contacts between the United States and Norway, as one example, see Sigmund Skard, *The United States in Norwegian History* (Westport, Conn.: Greenwood Press, 1976), pp. 176–92. For a most frank conversation between representatives of the American and the Norwegian labor movements, see Conover to Secretary of State, Subject: Visit of ECA Labor Advisers to Norway, NA, 840.50 Recovery /7-2748.

20. *The Vandenberg Resolution and the North Atlantic Treaty,* Hearings held in Executive Session before Committee on Foreign Relations, U.S. Senate, 80th Cong., 2d Sess., Washington, D.C., 1976, p. 162.

21. Memorandum for Secretary from Bohlen, NA, 840.20/2-1049; Papers Relat-

ing to North Atlantic Pact, International Working Group, January 13, 1949, NA, 840.20/4-2149, p. 2.

22. Memorandum from Secretary of State to Truman, June 3, 1948, *FRUS, 1948*, 3:134.

23. Request by Norwegian Defense Minister for Information on United States Assistance in Case of War, May 21, 1948, NA, Modern Military Branch, CCS 381 (8-14-47), Sec. 1, JCS 1846/2, Enc. "C," pp. 19–21. See also Current Position of U.S. Respecting Base Negotiations with Denmark and Norway, NA, National Security Council files, Modern Military Branch, NSC 32/1; Forrestal to Secretary of State, February 10, 1949, *FRUS, 1949*, 4:95–101.

24. For a most interesting source on the American role as seen by the State Department and the military in 1944–45, see *The Conference of Berlin*, Briefing Book Paper, State Department Recommendations, July 7, 1945, 1:253–64.

25. Herbert Feis, *From Trust to Terror: The Onset of the Cold War, 1945–1950* (New York: Norton, 1970), p. 381; Joyce and Gabriel Kolko, *The Limits of Power: The World and United States Foreign Policy, 1945–1954* (New York: Harper & Row, 1972), p. 500.

26. Barbara G. Haskel, *The Scandinavian Option: Opportunities and Opportunity Costs in Postwar Scandinavian Foreign Policies* (Oslo: Universitetsforlaget, 1976), pp. 82–87. See also pp. 49–60.

27. Eriksen, "Norge i det vestlige samarbeid," pp. 208–9; Magne Skodvin, *Norden eller NATO? Utenriksdepartementet og alliansespørsmålet 1947–1949* (Scandinavia or NATO? The Foreign Office and the Question of Alliance 1947–1949) (Oslo: Universitetsforlaget, 1971), pp. 25–34.

28. For a stimulating presentation of this point of view, see Olav Riste, "Alliansepolitikk og brubygging" (Politics of Alliance and Bridge Building), *Historisk Tidsskrift* ([Norwegian] Historical Journal), 1973, pp. 262–63.

29. Skodvin, *Norden eller NATO?*, pp. 28–31, 33–34.

30. For an example of this attitude, see Memo of Conversation Acheson/Lange, February 7, 1949, *FRUS, 1949*, 4:67.

Index